ST/ESA/SER.A/236

Department of Economic and Social Affairs
Population Division

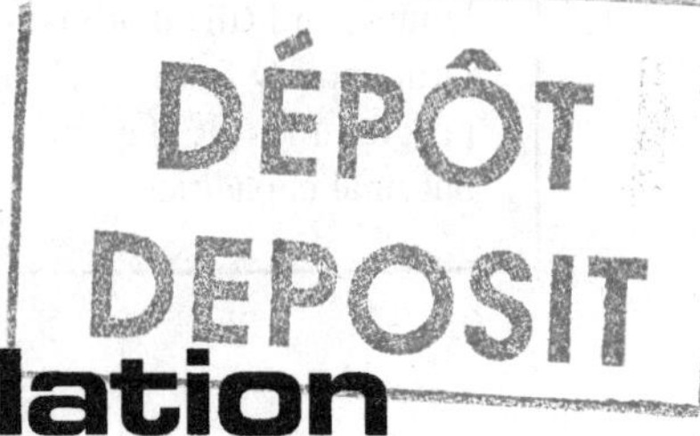

World Population to 2300

United Nations
New York, 2004

The Department of Economic and Social Affairs of the United Nations Secretariat is a vital interface between global policies in the economic, social and environmental spheres and national action. The Department works in three main interlinked areas: (i) it compiles, generates and analyses a wide range of economic, social and environmental data and information on which States Members of the United Nations draw to review common problems and to take stock of policy options; (ii) it facilitates the negotiations of Member States in many intergovernmental bodies on joint courses of action to address ongoing or emerging global challenges; and (iii) it advises interested Governments on the ways and means of translating policy frameworks developed in United Nations conferences and summits into programmes at the country level and, through technical assistance, helps build national capacities.

NOTE

The designations employed and the presentation of the material in this publication do not imply the expression of any opinion on the part of the Secretariat of the United Nations concerning the legal status of any country, territory, city or area or of its authorities, or concerning the delimitation of its frontiers or boundaries.

The designations "more developed regions" and "less developed regions" are intended for statistical convenience and do not necessarily express a judgement about the stage reached by a particular country or area in the development process.

The term "country" as used in the text of this publication also refers, as appropriate, to territories or areas.

The present report has been reproduced without formal editing.

ST/ESA/SER.A/236

UNITED NATIONS PUBLICATION
Sales No. E.04.XIII.11

ISBN 92-1-151401-0

Printed in United Nations, New York

PREFACE

Every two years the United Nations Department of Economic and Social Affairs' Population Division prepares the official United Nations estimates and projections of world, regional and national population size and growth, and demographic indicators. The results from the most recent set of estimates and projections were published in *World Population Prospects: The 2002 Revision*, a three-volume set issued over the period 2003-2004. The estimates and projections in the *2002 Revision* cover the period 1950-2050.

The United Nations also prepares supplementary world population projections covering a much longer period, referred to as long-range projections. The United Nations previously published long-range projections on six occasions, each being consistent with the population projections of the following revisions of the *World Population Prospects*: 1968, 1978, 1980, 1990, 1996 and 1998. These publications presented long-range projections for the world and its major areas, and since the 1990 set of projections, the long-range time horizon was until 2150.

The Population Division has adopted two major innovations for this new set of long-range population projections based on the *2002 Revision*. For the first time, the long-range projections are made at the national level, that is, for each of the 228 units constituting the world. In addition, the time horizon for the projections is extended to 2300, so as to allow for the eventual stabilization of the population in at least one scenario. In order to address the technical and substantive challenges posed by the preparation of long-range projections at the national level, the Population Division convened two meetings of the Technical Working Group on Long-Range Population Projections at United Nations Headquarters in New York. The purpose of the meetings was to discuss the assumptions, methodology and preliminary results of the national population projections to 2300.

This volume presents the results of the long-range projections, *World Population to 2300*, and includes a detailed analysis. A series of essays on the issue of long-range projections have also been incorporated in this report, enriching the debate on this important topic. Experts from outside the United Nations, many of whom took part in the technical working group meetings, authored these essays.

The United Nations Population Division is grateful to the National Institute on Aging of the United States of America (NIA) whose grant help support this study. Acknowledgement is also due to Rodolfo A. Bulatao, who assisted the Population Division in the preparation of this report. The Population Division extends its appreciation to all the experts for their suggestions and contributions to the preparation of the long-range projections.

This publication, as well as other population information, may also be accessed on the Population Division world wide web site at www.unpopulation.org. For further information about the long-range projections, please contact the office of Mr. Joseph Chamie, Director, Population Division, United Nations, New York, NY 10017, USA, tel: 212-963-3179 and fax: 212-963-2147.

CONTENTS

No. *Page*

PART TWO. ESSAYS

TABLES

No. *Page*

No. *Page*

FIGURES

ANNEX TABLES

Explanatory notes

Tables presented in this volume make use of the following symbols:

Two dots (..) indicate that data are not available or are not separately reported.
An em dash (—) indicates that the amount is nil or negligible.
A hyphen (-) indicates that the item is not applicable.
A minus sign (-) before a figure indicates a decrease.
A full stop (.) is used to indicate decimals.
Years given start on 1 July.
Use of a hyphen (-) between years, for example, 1995-2000, signifies the full period involved, from 1 July of the first year to 1 July of the second year.

Numbers and percentages in tables do not necessarily add to totals because of rounding.

Countries and areas are grouped geographically into six major areas: Africa; Asia; Europe; Latin America and the Caribbean; Northern America; and Oceania. These major areas are further divided into 21 geographical regions. In addition, for statistical convenience, the regions are classified as belonging to either of two categories: more developed or less developed. The less developed regions include all the regions of Africa, Asia (excluding Japan), and Latin America and the Caribbean, as well as Melanesia, Micronesia and Polynesia. The more developed regions comprise Australia/New Zealand, Europe, Northern America and Japan.

PART ONE. REPORT

EXECUTIVE SUMMARY

Long-range population projections are reported to 2300, covering twice as long a period as ever covered in previous United Nations projections. These projections are not done by major area and for selected large countries (China and India), as was the previous practice, but for all countries of the world, providing greater detail.

In these projections, world population peaks at 9.22 billion in 2075. Population therefore grows slightly beyond the level of 8.92 billion projected for 2050 in the *2002 Revision,* on which these projections are based. However, after reaching its maximum, world population declines slightly and then resumes increasing, slowly, to reach a level of 8.97 billion by 2300, not much different from the projected 2050 figure.

This pattern of rise, decline, and rise again results from assumptions about future trends in vital rates: that, country by country, fertility will fall below replacement level—though in some cases not for decades—and eventually return to replacement; and that, country by country, life expectancy will eventually follow a path of uninterrupted but slowing increase. With alternative assumptions about fertility, long-range trends could be quite different. With long-range total fertility 0.3 children above replacement, projected world population in 2300 is four times as large as the main projection; with total fertility 0.2 children below replacement, world population in 2300 is one-quarter of the main projection.

Regions and countries will follow similar demographic paths in the long run, given similar assumptions for different countries about long-range vital rate trends. However, because initial assumptions differ, and because this gives rise to slight variations in trends, countries and regions will not be exactly alike, even by 2300. In fact, what are today considered more developed and less developed regions will still be demographically distinguishable, with regard, for instance, to life expectancies and proportions at advanced ages. In addition, regions and countries will go through critical stages of growth—zero growth, subreplacement fertility, a return to positive growth—at different points in the future, giving rise to a global demographic map with areas that shrink and stretch at different times in the next three centuries.

Europe and Africa will be particularly out of phase. Europe will hit its low point in growth in 2050, Africa not till 80 years later, after all other major areas. From 2000 to 2100, Europe's share of world population is cut in half, 12.0 to 5.9 per cent, while Africa's almost doubles, from 13.1 to 24.9 per cent. While shares of world population for major areas will rise and fall over the following two centuries, the distribution by 2300 will resemble that in 2100.

Smaller regions within continents exhibit divergent patterns. For instance:

- Three African regions—Eastern Africa, Middle Africa, and Western Africa—will grow unusually fast in comparison to every other region through 2100, even though total fertility will be close to replacement by 2050.
- Southern Africa is seeing a decline in life expectancy to a lower level than anywhere else, but life expectancy will rebound, rise quite rapidly, and overtake other African regions.
- Asian regions will grow fastest to the west, slowest to the east, but in every case with growth rates, at least up to 2100, below Eastern, Middle and Western Africa. By 2100, Asia, instead of being four-and-a half times as populous as Africa, will be only 2.2 times as populous.
- Latin America and the Caribbean is the most homogenous major area, with most of its regions following relatively parallel fertility and life expectancy paths.
- Northern America is unusual as the only region that will not experience negative growth, mainly due to projected migration up to 2050. (No migration is incorporated in projections beyond that date.)
- Europe, like Asia, will experience higher growth to the west, lower growth to the east. East-

ern Europe stands out with low life expectancy, and even in the long run does not catch up with other regions.

Growth patterns depend on assumptions about vital rates. Total fertility is assumed to decline, at a varying pace dictated by country circumstances, to a below-replacement level of 1.85 children per woman. Countries already at this level or below, and other countries when they reach it, eventually return to replacement over a period of a century and stay at replacement indefinitely. All countries are projected to have reached replacement fertility by 2175, but past fertility trends continue to affect population trends for another 50 years.

Life expectancy is assumed to rise continuously, with no upper limit, though at a slowing pace dictated by recent country trends. By 2100, life expectancy is expected to vary across countries from 66 to 97 years, and by 2300 from 87 to 106 years. Rising life expectancy will produce small but continuing population growth by the end of the projections ranging from 0.03 to 0.07 per cent annually.

Growth patterns affect the balance between population and land. Density, in people per square kilometer of land, will continue to be especially variable in Oceania, where by 2100 it will range from 504 persons per sq. km. in Micronesia to 3.6 persons per sq. km. in Australia/New Zealand. Some large countries in South-central Asia will also be unusually dense by 2100, with India having 491 persons per sq. km., Pakistan 530 persons per sq. km., and Bangladesh 1,997 persons per sq. km.

These populations pressing on the land will be old by current standards. Where the world median age in 2000 is 26 years, by 2100 it will be 44 years, and by 2300, 48 years. Before they reach the point where those over 40 are half the population, countries go through a period labelled here the demographic window, when the proportion of children and youth under 15 years falls below 30 per cent and the proportion of people 65 years and older is still below 15 per cent. For a 30-40 year period, the proportion of the population in between, of working age, is particularly prominent in the population. Europe entered the demographic window before 1950 and is now leaving it and entering a third age when older people are particularly prominent in the age distribution. Much of Africa will not enter the demographic window until 2045 or later.

Beyond the demographic window, population ageing becomes a predominant demographic feature. Between 2100 and 2300, the proportion of world population 65 years and older will increase by one-third (from 24 to 32 per cent); the proportion 80 years and older will double (from 8.5 to 17 per cent); and the proportion 100 years and older will increase nine times (from 0.2 to 1.8 per cent). Assuming that the retirement age worldwide in 2000 is 65 years, people retire on average only two weeks short of their life expectancy. Assuming that retirement age stays unchanged, by 2300 people will retire 31 years short of their life expectancy.

INTRODUCTION

Projections recently issued by the United Nations suggest that world population by 2050 could reach 8.9 billion, but in alternative scenarios could be as high as 10.6 billion or as low as 7.4 billion. What will population trends be like beyond 2050? No one really knows. Any demographic projections, if they go 100, 200, or 300 years into the future, are little more than guesses. Societies change considerably over hundreds of years—as one can readily see if one looks back at where the world was in 1900, or 1800, or 1700. Demographic behaviour over such long time spans, like behaviour in many spheres of life, is largely unpredictable.

Nevertheless, this report presents projections of world population, and even of the populations of individual countries, over the next 300 years. Given the inherent impossibility of such an exercise, these projections have a special character. They are not forecasts. They do not say that population is expected to reach the projected levels. Rather, they are extrapolations of current trends. They give what paths population would follow if, and only if, historical trends and trends previously forecast up to 2050 continue. Of course one cannot expect these trends to continue as is, and certainly not country by country. But the implications of current trends are important and often can only be seen by looking far enough into the future.

These projections are presented, therefore, as a means of drawing out the long-range implications of shorter-run trends that are known or somewhat predictable. Constructing long-range projections such as these is a little like predicting the outcome of a basketball game after the first five minutes. No one can do that reliably. Why should it even be attempted? Probably for the same reason that a coach might call a timeout after five minutes: because the trends may look unfavourable and team play may require adjustment if the game is to be on. Similarly, to see if current population trends require adjustment, their implications are worked out over a long period. This should not be taken to imply that these trends are actually expected to continue. To some extent, the reverse is true. The projected long-range path for population is reported partly to facilitate thinking about how to prepare for it, but also to encourage action to modify this path, to make it more favourable, if that is possible, for collective welfare.

These long-range projections are based on and extend the recent United Nations projections, designated the *2002 Revision* (United Nations, 2003b, 2003c, 2004). Long-range projections have been reported before, the most recent having been based on the *1998 Revision* (United Nations, 2000a). Unlike earlier long-range projections, these projections go further, not just to 2150 but to 2300. These projections also are constructed not by major area but by country, providing a more detailed picture of long-range prospects.

This report

- reviews briefly some findings from the *2002 Revision* and the procedures used
- discusses the methodology used to extend population trends up to 2300
- describes the projected population growth or decline, beginning with the world as a whole and proceeding to major areas, regions, and countries that stand out
- discusses consequences of growth patterns, focusing on population density and changing age structures
- concludes with a brief reference to consequences of population change and the limitations of this work
- presents a series of essays produced by a group of experts.

An annex contains detailed tables, giving age structures and vital rates over time.

I. PROJECTIONS TO 2050

Projections to 2050, together with historical population estimates back to 1950, constitute the *2002 Revision* of the official United Nations population projections, the eighteenth and latest such revision. Reviewing these projections provides hints about what to expect in long-range projections and poses questions for them. Some results from the 50-year projections in the *2002 Revision* are illustrated; more results and analyses are available in other publications (United Nations, 2003b, 2003c, 2004).

A. WORLD POPULATION

World population is projected to grow from 6.1 billion in 2000 to 8.9 billion in 2050, increasing therefore by 47 per cent. The average annual population growth rate over this half-century will be 0.77 per cent, substantially lower than the 1.76 per cent average growth rate from 1950 to 2000. In addition, growth is projected to slow the further the projections go. For 2000-2005, the annual growth rate is estimated at 1.22 per cent; by 2045-2050, it will be only 0.33 per cent.

Although growth rates will fall, the annual increase in world population will remain large: 57 million a year on average between 2000 and 2050. This is smaller than the 71 million people added annually between 1950 and 2000 but still substantial. It means that, on average each year for 50 years, world population will expand by about as many people as now live in Italy. The increase, over 50 years, will be more than twice the current population of China, or more than twice the current population of all more developed regions combined. Although population growth will eventually subside, and a variety of countries will see little or no population growth, for the world as a whole the next 50 years can hardly be characterized as demographically tranquil.

How good are these figures? The estimate for the 2000 population, based on a greater number of well-executed national censuses than ever before, may well be more accurate than most estimates of current world population that have been made in the past. Projected figures for the near term (say up to around 2010) benefit from the accuracy of base data and are unlikely to be off by much. Projected figures for 2050, in contrast, are much less certain. To hedge its bets, the *2002 Revision* includes alternative projection scenarios, particularly high-growth and low-growth scenarios, according to which world population would reach 10.6 billion or 7.4 billion by 2050 (figure 1). Between the high and low scenarios, average annual growth rates for 2000-2050 range from 1.12 to 0.40 per cent, and annual increments range from 91.3 to 26.8 million.

B. MAJOR AREAS

Much of the demographic change up to 2050 will take place in the less developed regions. Collectively, these regions will grow 58 per cent over 50 years, as opposed to 2 per cent for more developed regions. Less developed regions will account for 99 per cent of the expected increment to world population in this period. Nevertheless, population growth in the less developed regions is expected to slow down in the future. The current annual growth rate of 1.6 per cent (for 1995-2000) will be halved in a little over 25 years and will be roughly halved again by mid-century. This will be due to falling fertility. Current total fertility of 3.11 children per woman (about double the rate in more developed regions) will fall to 2.04 by mid-century—just below replacement level but still above the current rate in more developed regions.

Among the less developed regions, demographic prospects vary. Africa, Asia, and Latin America and the Caribbean are considered less developed; Oceania, which has a relatively small population, is mixed, while Northern America and Europe are considered more developed.[2] Population growth in Asia looks impressively large, at 1.5 billion over 50 years. However, Asia's share of world population actually dips slightly, from 61 per cent in 2000 to 59 per cent in 2050. Growth will be much faster in Africa, which will add 1.0 billion and rise from 13 to 20 per cent of world population.

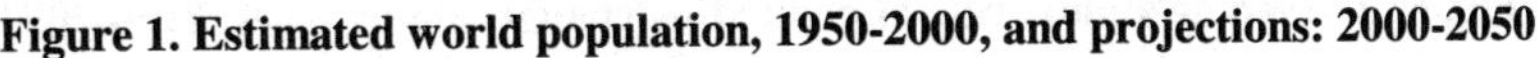

Figure 1. Estimated world population, 1950-2000, and projections: 2000-2050

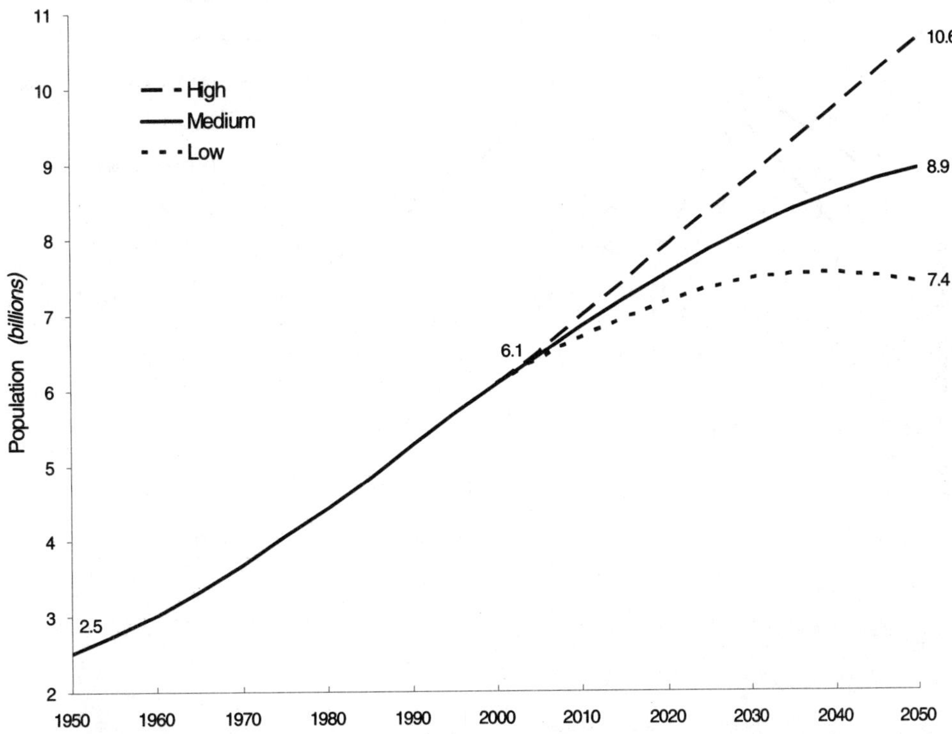

Average annual rates of population change show that Africa has experienced considerably faster growth than any other major area, for most of the 1950-2000 period (figure 2). Growth rates reached a higher peak in Africa (2.86 per cent) than anywhere else—in the early 1980s, at least 15 years after growth had begun to decline in every other major area. The projection for Africa, consequently, shows growth declining belatedly, though nevertheless following a downward path similar to that in other major areas. Europe is at the other end of the spectrum, with growth rates having just turned negative and continuing to fall up to 2050.

Though growth rates are at different levels, their decline is projected to be similar across major areas. The more developed regions show slightly slower decline in growth rates than the less developed regions, mainly because of international migration. If net migration were set to zero, the lines would be more nearly parallel. International migration is particularly important for Northern America (i.e., the United States and Canada), accounting for 0.5 percentage points of the growth rate for 2000-2050. For Europe, migration boosts the growth rate by 0.1-0.2 points, and for Oceania by around 0.25 points. (For Australia alone, migration adds about twice that to the growth rate.)

Growth rate declines are parallel (international migration aside) largely because assumptions about fertility change are similar. Figure 3 shows the substantial gap that currently exists—but is projected to narrow—between total fertility in Africa and total fertility in every other major area. A gap in fertility levels also exists between the other major areas of the world, but by 2050 levels are expected to converge in a narrow band between 1.84 and 1.92 children per woman. Europe will take the longest to enter this band, and will do so through rising fertility, in contrast to falling fertility in other major areas.

Mortality exerts some additional influence on the growth rate. Across major areas, its effect on growth largely counteracts that of fertility, since where fertility is higher, mortality also tends to be higher. Over time, life expectancy is expected to rise fairly smoothly.

Figure 2. Average annual rate of population change, major areas: 1950-2050

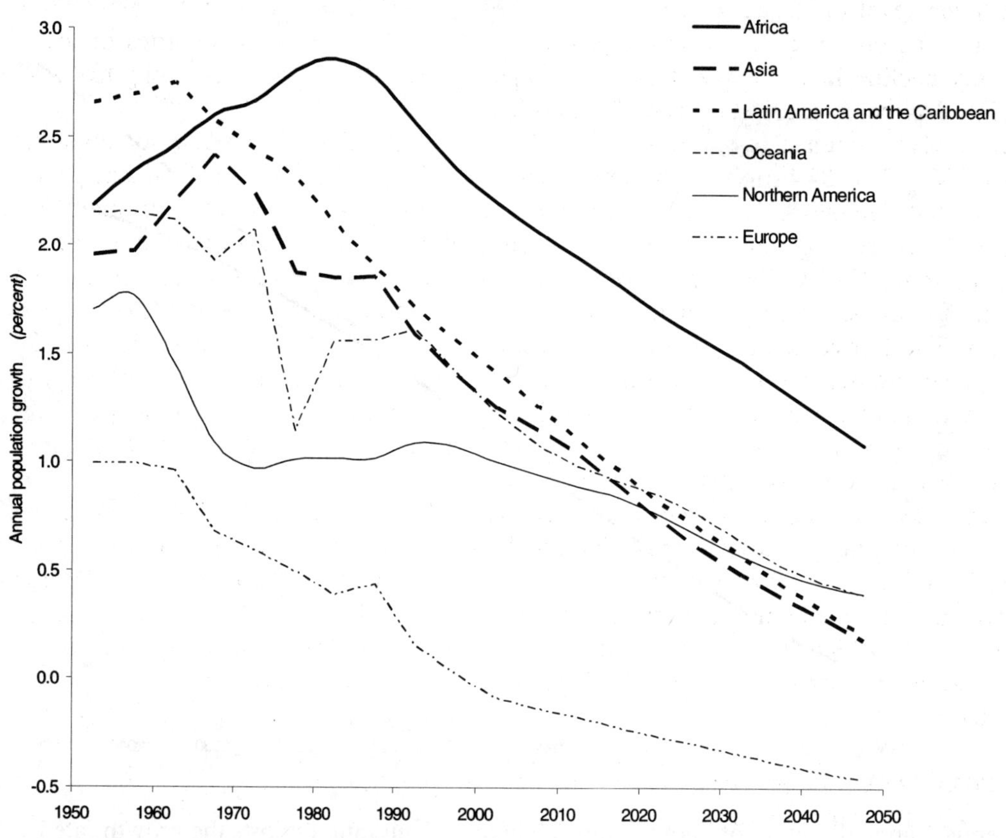

Figure 3. Total fertility, major areas: 1950-2050

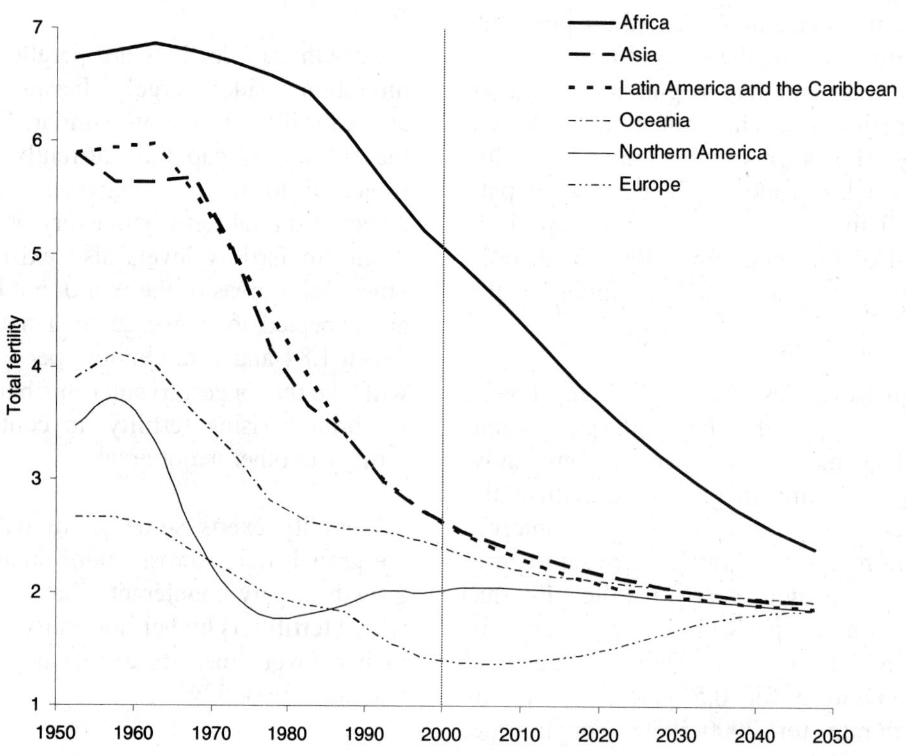

Africa again stands out, not only because of the much lower level of life expectancy but also because it is the only major area where projections show any decline in life expectancy for any period. The decline, in the first decade of the projections, involves countries severely affected by HIV/AIDS—37 of 54 in this major area. Though the projected decline looks small—only about a year for the entire major area—it leaves projected life expectancy in Africa even further behind other major areas, all projected to make steady progress. The Africa decline also appears to follow a preceding decline of over a year in life expectancy (beginning about the mid-1980s). However, it is important to note that these previous declines were not directly measured. Data on mortality and life expectancy are notoriously incomplete for developing countries, and particularly for sub-Saharan Africa. Mortality parameters may therefore be estimated with the same models used for projection, which is a particular problem for AIDS mortality. More is said about this uncertainty later.

By 2045-2050, life expectancy in Africa is projected to be 11 years shorter than in the next lowest case. The other major areas will be bunched, though not too tightly, between 76 and 82 years of life expectancy, with Asia and Latin America and the Caribbean behind the more developed regions.

C. Assumptions

The *2002 Revision* obtains the various scenarios through country by country projections constructed for successive five-year periods,[1] in which estimates of future fertility are manipulated. Within the *2002 Revision*, fertility at the world level was projected to decline from 2.8 children per woman in 1995-2000 to about 2 children in 20045-2050 (figure 4). Over the long run, total fertility is projected to settle at 1.85 children per woman in each country—in between the current rate for Northern America (which is just below replacement level) and the rate for Europe (which is currently well below). This figure is somewhat arbitrary; a higher figure would be necessary if population were to stabilize, but demographers do not agree about whether stabilization is inevitable. A lower figure is also possible, given that total fertility for 1995-2000 is between 1.1 and 1.2 in such countries or areas as Spain, the Czech Republic, and Hong Kong SAR.

Because of uncertainty about this long-range level, the high scenario has total fertility levels gradually diverging, eventually reaching a level 0.5 points higher than that in the medium scenario (2.35 vs. 1.85). The low scenario has total fertility settling at 0.5 points below that in the medium scenario, for an eventual level of 1.35, well below replacement. The spread of 0.5 children above or below the medium variant was reached by 2050 at the latest, but not the ultimate levels.

Fertility in developed countries, which is already relatively close to the long-range levels, is assumed to reach them (whether medium, high, or low) by the period 2045-2050, proceeding along a smooth path that takes recent trends into account. This allows for some cases where fertility initially moves away from these levels (e.g., dropping even further below them) for five or ten years. Fertility in developing countries also moves toward these levels, but since in some cases it is still well above them, it does not necessarily reach them by 2050. In developing countries with high fertility, the pace of total fertility decline is determined by models that relate decline in one period to the level previously reached. These models assume relatively slow decline from the highest fertility levels, faster decline (of as much as 0.12 points a year) once total fertility has fallen to 4-5, and slowing decline below that. (Details on the models are contained in United Nations, 2004.)

Mortality is projected by assuming that life expectancy rises according to one of three schedules, reflecting fast, medium, or slow improvements in existing mortality data for the specific country (United Nations, 2004). Each schedule provides for slower gains at higher levels. In the medium schedule, for instance, the annual gain in life expectancy is 0.4 years for males and 0.5 years for females from an initial combined life expectancy level of 60 years (typical of less developed regions). But the gain shrinks to 0.1 years for males and 0.2 years for females from an initial life expectancy level of 75 years (typical of more devel-

Figure 4. World total fertility and life expectancy at birth: 1995-2050

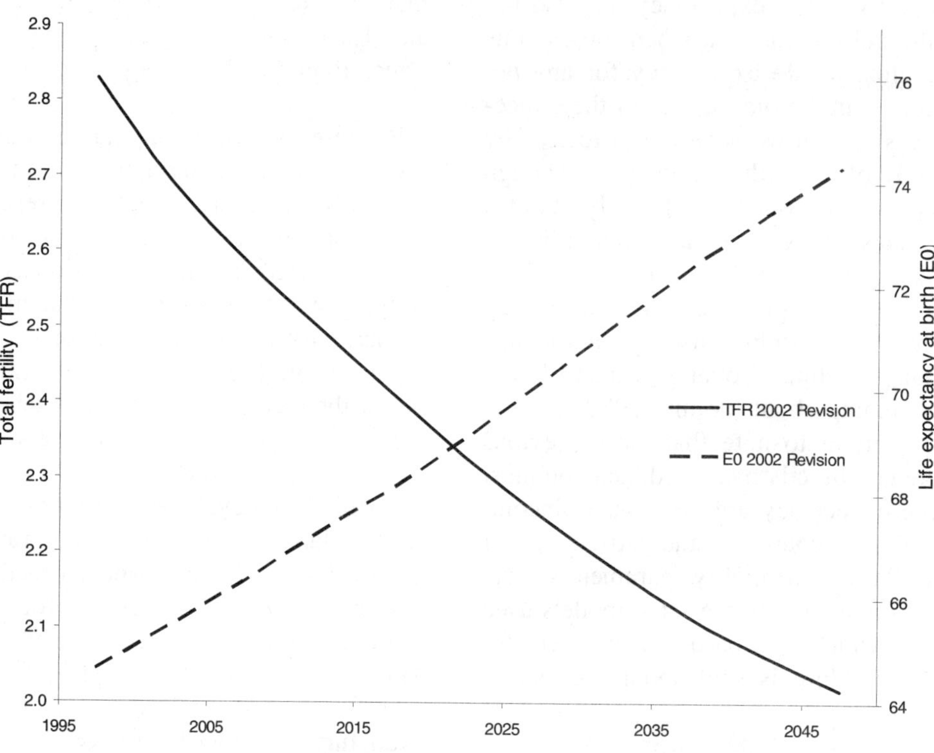

oped regions). Depending on their mortality experience, countries may stay on the chosen schedule of life expectancy improvement until 2050 or move to the medium schedule by 2025. (The latter was the typical practice in the *2002 Revision.*)

However, the impact of the HIV/AIDS epidemic is explicitly accounted for in 53 "highly" affected countries, that is, countries with an HIV/AIDS prevalence level of at least 1.9 per cent or with an important number of HIV/AIDS cases due to their large population. In these cases, non-AIDS mortality is projected to decline using similar models as for other countries—but in most cases with slower improvements. AIDS mortality is then added to these no-AIDS country scenarios. AIDS mortality is derived using a model developed by the UNAIDS Reference Group on Estimates, Modeling, and Projections (see United Nations, 2003a), which is fitted to historical estimates of HIV prevalence (also from UNAIDS) to estimate country-specific parameters for the epidemic. These parameters are used in projection, allowing HIV prevalence and subsequent AIDS deaths to follow an initial upward path and eventually reach a peak. The further assumption is added that HIV transmission gradually declines beginning in 2010. The result is a slower rise in life expectancy in these countries in comparison to others, or an actual decline. Overall, at the world level, life expectancy at birth within the *2002 Revision* was projected to increase from 64.6 years in 1995-2000 to 74.3 years in 2045-2050 (figure 4).

Assumptions are also made about international migration, based on past migration estimates and on public policy toward migrants. Migration assumptions are specified country by country—not following any standard model—and often assume little change in migration except where current patterns reflect unusual events unlikely to be repeated, such as the return of refugees to a specific country. Thus the United States, which receives the largest number of immigrants, is estimated as having 6.3 million net migrants in 1995-2000 and is projected to have only slightly fewer—5.5 million—in 2045-2050. China and Mexico lose the largest net number of net migrants in 1995-2000 and also in 2045-2050. Migration figures are adjusted where necessary to ensure a balance between immigrants and emigrants across countries. Migration assumptions have minimal effect on world projections but do affect country and regional results. Sudden large migrations have in fact, in the past, been a major source of error in projections (National Research Council, 2000).

Besides the medium, high, and low scenarios, a few other scenarios are provided in the *2002 Revision,* not as likely possibilities for the future but to facilitate analysis of the effects of various assumptions. Separate scenarios are provided with (a) country total fertility held constant at 1995-2000 levels, (b) fertility set for the entire projection period at exactly replacement level, (c) life expectancy by sex held constant at 1995-2000 levels, (d) AIDS eliminated from country projections for severely affected countries, or (e) all international migration eliminated.

D. LONG-RANGE POSSIBILITIES

These results for 50-year projections are only a small part of the results recently reported by the United Nations (2003b, 2003c, 2004). Among other things covered in considerable detail are smaller regions, individual countries, age structures, and the effect of HIV/AIDS. These results should foreshadow what one finds when projections are extended to 300 years. One can expect world population growth to level off—but when, and at what level, and will population eventually decline? One might expect the vital rates underlying the projections to follow parallel trajectories and eventually converge across regions. How long will this take, given the assumptions made in 50-year projections? How widely will countries diverge in the meantime, and how will their relative demographic positions change? Like regions, will individual countries also all converge, or will some differences persist? One should expect all populations to age—but how much, and how large can the oldest groups in the population become?

To provide answers to such questions, similar assumptions are needed to those that underlie the 50-year projections but also extend the methodology in consistent ways. These extensions are detailed next.

II. PROJECTIONS AFTER 2050: LONG-RANGE GROWTH AND DECLINE

A. SCENARIOS

To extend the projections to 2300, additional assumptions about the period after 2050 are needed. If fertility levels were projected to continue indefinitely at 1.85 children per woman, as the 50-year projections assume, long-range population decline would be inevitable. Instead, fertility is projected to stay below replacement level continuously for no more than 100 years per country over the period from 1950 forward, and to return to replacement after 100 years, or by the year 2175, whichever comes first. Replacement level, given the low mortality rates expected in the next century, would be around 2.05 children per woman. With this assumption, countries that now have below-replacement fertility return to replacement earlier than countries with fertility well above replacement, which first progress downward to a level of 1.85 in accordance with the models used for 50-year projections, and then take 100 years to return to replacement level.

To provide high and low alternatives to this main, medium scenario, the high and low scenarios in the 50-year projections are extended. The high scenario in the 50-year projections assumes that total fertility stays 0.5 children above the level in the medium scenario. Beyond 2050, this gap is initially narrowed to 0.25 children and then increased to approximately 0.3 children once fertility in the medium scenario returns to replacement. The long-range gap is approximate because fertility in the high scenario is fixed, eventually, at 2.35 children whereas replacement-level fertility in the medium scenario varies slightly across countries. The low scenario in the 50-year projections assumes that total fertility stays 0.5 children below the level in the medium scenario. This gap then narrows to 0.25 children after 2050, and narrows further, once replacement level is reached in the medium scenario, to approximately 0.2 children. Long-range fertility in the low scenario is fixed at 1.85. With these assumptions, fertility levels in the high and low scenarios are somewhat asymmetric around the medium scenario, with the high scenario diverging more. The asymmetric gaps between the ultimate replacement fertility level for the medium variant, on one hand, and the high and low variants on the other hand are caused by initially assuming a replacement fertility level of, approximately, 2.1 children per women and then adding or subtracting 0.25 children to this level to calculate the high and low variant, respectively. In the actual projection process, however, replacement fertility was calculated exactly as a net reproduction rate of one. This implies fluctuation of the true replacement fertility level about the approximate level of 2.1 children per women, and hence the asymmetry.

Besides these three scenarios, two other scenarios were developed for analytical purposes. The medium scenario, in the long run, assumes replacement fertility, or a net reproduction rate of 1. This does not assure zero population growth because mortality continues to decline at older ages, past reproductive age. One can however force zero growth, with births exactly equal to deaths. This requirement, imposed 50 years after a country returns to replacement fertility in the medium scenario, gives an alternative, zero-growth scenario.

A fifth scenario is added by simply extending the constant-fertility scenario in the *2002 Revision,* therefore holding total fertility indefinitely at its level in 1995-2000. This scenario produces an unrealistic, and almost unimaginable world population of 134 trillion by 2300.

Mortality assumptions are similar across all these scenarios, essentially involving an extrapolation of mortality patterns projected in the *2002 Revision.* Following an approach developed by Lee and Carter (1992), the matrix of projected age-specific mortality rates for both sexes combined in 2000-2050 is decomposed (after taking logs) into additive components representing the mean pattern for mortality by age, the product of the level of mortality (k) at a given time and the relative speed of change at each age, and a residual. An ARIMA time-series model is fitted for k and used in extrapolating trends beyond 2050 for males and females separately. No limit is set on life expectancy, and life tables are extended for projection purposes (following the Kannisto logistic function, Thatcher, Kannisto, Vaupel 1998) up to age 130.

Reasonable assumptions about long-range international migration are difficult to make. Essentially as a default, zero net international migration per country is assumed beyond 2050.

The methodology represents substantial departures from the previous United Nations long-range projections, which were based on the *1998 Revision* (United Nations, 2000). As already noted, the 50-year projections in the *2002 Revision* made important changes to previous methodology, which carry over to the long-range projections. More radical changes are also made.

Projections are run by country, as is implied in the assumptions described, rather than by major area, which was the standard practice in past long-range projections. This change leads to substantial differences in the way vital rate trends are specified. Specific countries will be considered, focusing, as has been the practice in shorter projections, mainly on the 192 countries or areas with current populations of at least 100,000. Projections were also made for 36 smaller countries and areas, to be included in aggregates, but specific country results will not be detailed.

The scenarios produced are a different, simplified set relative to the previous long-range projections. Although some comparisons will be drawn with earlier long-range projections, identifying the specific methodological reasons for changes in results is not possible.

These long-range projections are also extended to 2300 rather than stopping at 2150, which was the previous practice. This is meant to provide a longer perspective, to allow assumed demographic trends to entirely work themselves out. How long a projection is really necessary for this purpose depends on how far into the future vital rates are allowed to change. Since the current methodology allows life expectancy to rise indefinitely, projections could in fact be extended indefinitely.

One can, however, get some idea of how long a projection is needed to see the full effects of some other assumptions. Populations grow for four reasons: fertility is above replacement, mortality is falling, net international migration is positive, or the age structure favours growth. The age structure effect, for example, might involve having proportionally more people below, say, age 80, who are at lower risk of dying than older people.

Of these four effects on growth, net migration is eliminated by assuming it is zero after 2050. The effect of fertility should be eliminated once fertility reaches replacement, i.e., when net reproduction settles at 1. Results from the medium scenario indicate that all 192 countries will have reached this point by 2175 (figure 5). The mortality effect will never be eliminated under the assumption of continuously rising life expectancy. This should continue to affect the age structure too, but one can eliminate effects on the age structure from changing fertility. The zero-growth scenario accomplishes by forcing births to equal deaths beginning 50 years after replacement fertility is reached in a given country. Under this scenario, projected population growth is essentially zero in every one of 192 countries beginning in 2225. (It is always smaller than 0.002 per cent, in the absolute, for every country, but may not be exactly zero because of rounding errors in the calculations for small countries.)

Beyond 2150, therefore, number of births makes no direct contribution to population growth, and population change beyond that point—and in earlier periods too in some but not all countries—can be interpreted as due to mortality change or the age structure. Then, since most age structure effects disappear by 2225, population change beyond that point must stem mainly from continuously rising life expectancies.

Consideration of these vital rate assumptions suggests that the first half of these projections should be the more interesting part—the part where country vital rates vary more, rather than following similar trends. For the first 50 year of the projections, international migration is allowed

Figure 5. Maximum and minimum country values in each period for net reproduction rate and average annual rate of population change: 2050-2300

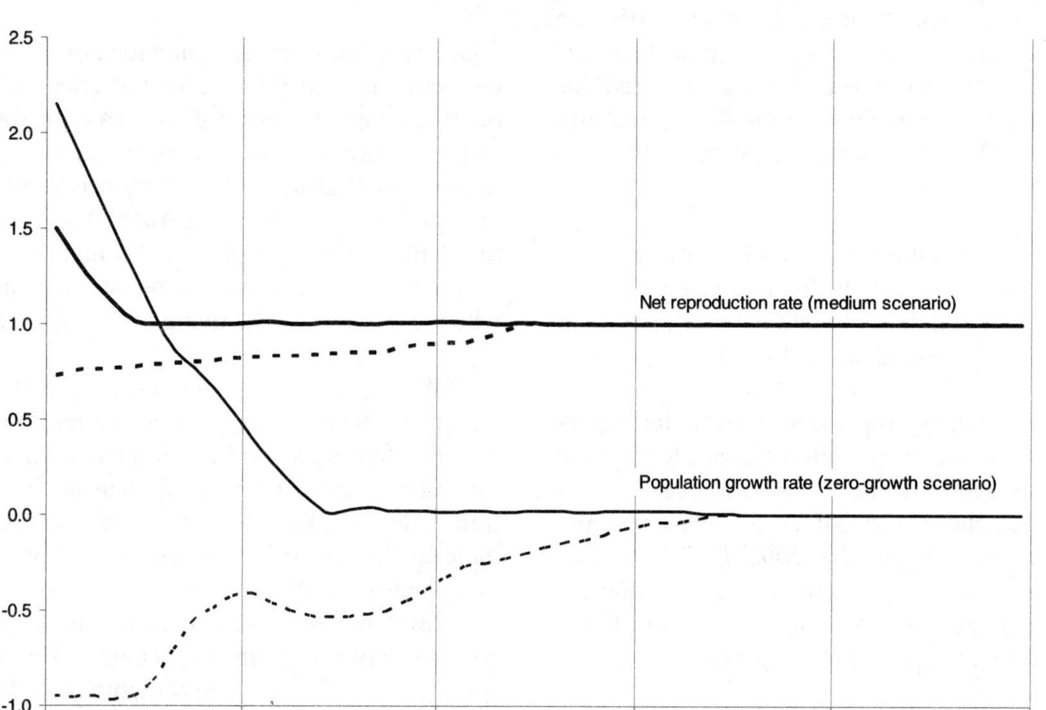

to vary. For the first 75 years, some countries will have fertility above replacement. For the first 100 years, some countries will not experience negative population growth. Therefore, the first century of the projections should hold the most interest, before countries are forced to follow uniform trends. Nevertheless, the variation in demographic trends over this century or so has effects that linger, requiring some attention to the longer run.

B. World population

Under the assumptions made in the medium scenario projection, world population will not vary greatly after reaching 8.92 billion in 2050 (figure 6). In another 25 years, by 2075, it is projected to peak at 9.22 billion, only 3.4 per cent above the 2050 estimate. It will then dip slightly to 8.43 billion by 2175 and rise gradually to 8.97 billion, very close to the initial 2050 figure, by 2300. Therefore, world population growth beyond 2050, at least for the following 250 years, is expected to be minimal.

The high and low scenarios are considerably different (table 1). Population will not level off in either case. In the high scenario, it will go from 10.63 billion in 2050 to 36.44 billion in 2300. In only the half century from 2050 to 2100, world population will grow by a third, by 3.39 billion. In the low scenario, over the same span, world population will be cut by one-fourth, and over the entire period to 2300, by two-thirds, from 7.41 billion in 2050 to 2.31 billion in 2300. Changes in world population over 50-year periods (figure 7) reinforce the impression that substantial long-range growth or decline is within the realm of possibility, though not necessarily the most likely future path for population.

The growth rates that produce differences among scenarios are shown in figure 8. In the medium projection, growth stays close to 0 per cent, falling below zero till around 2175 and then rising slightly above it. Growth rates in the high and low scenarios differ by about half a percentage point from the medium scenario in opposite directions. The differences are close to being symmetrical

Figure 6. Estimated world population: 1950-2000, and projections: 2000-2300

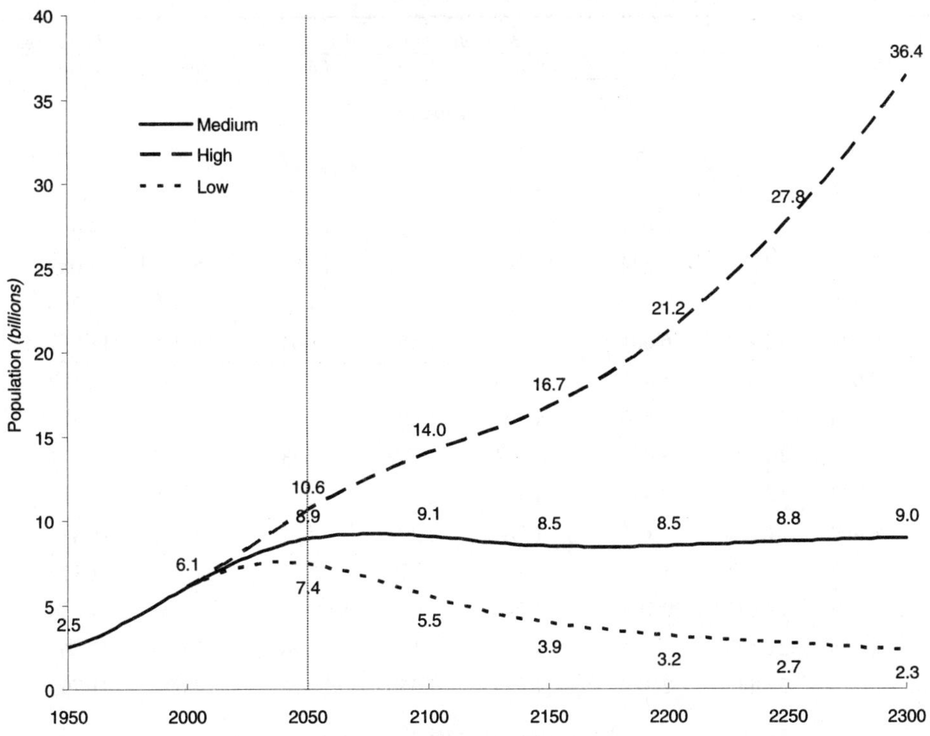

Figure 7. Change in world population over 50-year periods, estimates and three scenarios: 1950-2300

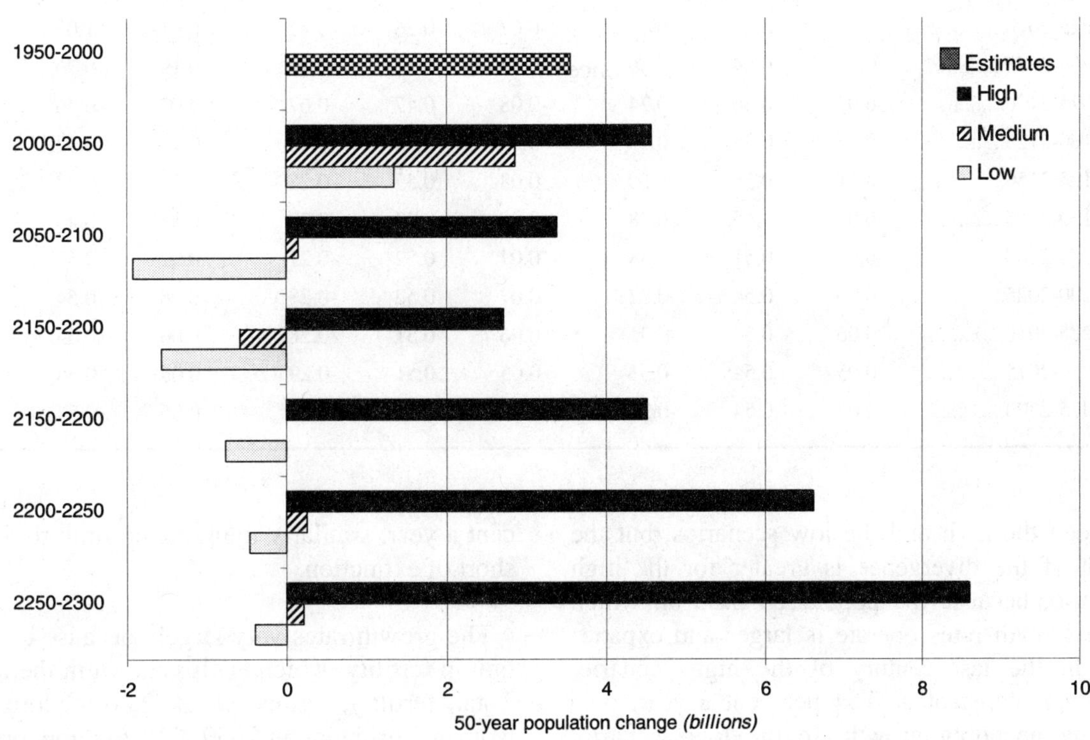

TABLE 1. POPULATION AND AVERAGE ANNUAL RATE OF CHANGE OF THE WORLD AND DEVELOPMENT GROUPS, ESTIMATES AND THREE SCENARIOS: 1950-2300

Year or period	*World*			*More developed regions*			*Less developed regions*		
	Medium	*High*	*Low*	*Medium*	*High*	*Low*	*Medium*	*High*	*Low*
				Population (millions)					
1950......................	2 519	—	—	813	—	—	1 706	—	—
1975......................	4 068	—	—	1 047	—	—	3 021	—	—
2000......................	6 071	6 071	6 071	1 194	1 194	1 194	4 877	4 877	4 877
2025......................	7 851	8 365	7 334	1 241	1 282	1 199	6 610	7 082	6 135
2050......................	8 919	10 633	7 409	1 220	1 370	1 084	7 699	9 263	6 325
2075......................	9 221	12 494	6 601	1 153	1 467	904	8 068	11 027	5 696
2100......................	9 064	14 018	5 491	1 131	1 651	766	7 933	12 367	4 726
2125......................	8 734	15 296	4 556	1 137	1 885	679	7 597	13 411	3 877
2150......................	8 494	16 722	3 921	1 161	2 152	633	7 333	14 571	3 288
2175......................	8 434	18 696	3 481	1 185	2 454	593	7 249	16 242	2 889
2200......................	8 499	21 236	3 165	1 207	2 795	554	7 291	18 441	2 612
2225......................	8 622	24 301	2 920	1 228	3 179	517	7 395	21 122	2 403
2250......................	8 752	27 842	2 704	1 246	3 612	482	7 506	24 230	2 223
2275......................	8 868	31 868	2 501	1 263	4 100	448	7 605	27 768	2 053
2300......................	8 972	36 444	2 310	1 278	4 650	416	7 694	31 793	1 894
				Average annual rate of change (per cent)					
1950-1975............	1.92	—	—	1.01	—	—	2.29	—	—
1975-2000............	1.60	—	—	0.52	—	—	1.92	—	—
2000-2025............	1.03	1.28	0.76	0.16	0.29	0.02	1.22	1.49	0.92
2025-2050............	0.51	0.96	0.04	-0.07	0.26	-0.41	0.61	1.07	0.12
2050-2075............	0.13	0.64	-0.46	-0.23	0.27	-0.72	0.19	0.70	-0.42
2075-2100............	-0.07	0.46	-0.74	-0.08	0.47	-0.67	-0.07	0.46	-0.75
2100-2125............	-0.15	0.35	-0.75	0.02	0.53	-0.48	-0.17	0.32	-0.79
2125-2150............	-0.11	0.36	-0.60	0.08	0.53	-0.28	-0.14	0.33	-0.66
2150-2175............	-0.03	0.45	-0.48	0.08	0.53	-0.27	-0.05	0.43	-0.52
2175-2200............	0.03	0.51	-0.38	0.07	0.52	-0.27	0.02	0.51	-0.40
2200-2025............	0.06	0.54	-0.32	0.07	0.52	-0.28	0.06	0.54	-0.33
2225-2050............	0.06	0.54	-0.31	0.06	0.51	-0.28	0.06	0.55	-0.31
2050-2075............	0.05	0.54	-0.31	0.05	0.51	-0.29	0.05	0.55	-0.32
2075-2300............	0.05	0.54	-0.32	0.05	0.50	-0.29	0.05	0.54	-0.32

between the high and the low scenarios, but the effect of the divergence is greater for the high scenario, because the population base on which these growth rates operate is larger and expanding. In the last century of the high scenario, growth is constant at 0.54 per cent a year, portending unending growth. In the low scenario, decline is essentially constant at around -0.32 per cent a year, similarly implying no limit to decline short of extinction.

The growth rates vary largely because of variation in fertility, which is also shown in the figure. Total fertility, projected at 2.00 children per woman worldwide in 2050, falls to a low point of 1.87 around 2075 (in the medium projection).

Figure 8. Average annual rate of change of the world population and total fertility, estimates and three scenarios: 1950-2300

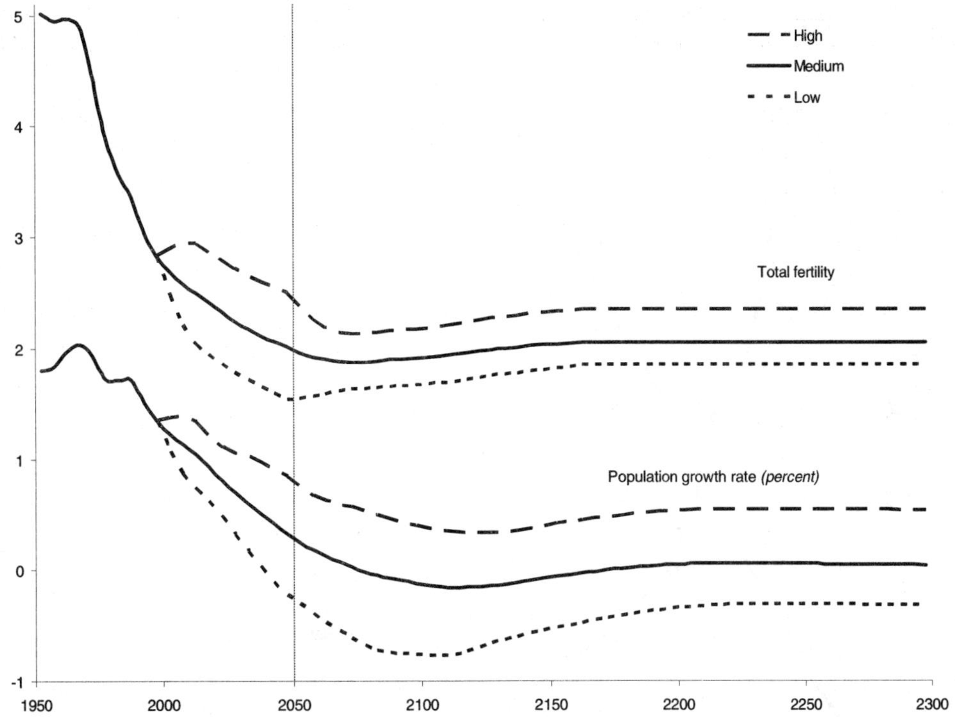

Forty years later, world population growth reaches its low point of -0.15 per cent. Population growth takes somewhat longer after fertility bottoms out to reach its minimum in the high and low scenarios, but the sequence is similar.

A comparison with the previous long-range projection indicates the importance of fertility assumptions. That projection was based on the *1998 Revision* and took population up to 2150. World population growth up to 2050 in the *2002 Revision* is strikingly similar to growth in the *1998 Revision,* as noted earlier. However, the long-range projections beyond 2050 are quite different, with that based on the *1998 Revision* showing steady growth (figure 9). The reason is fairly straightforward: fertility was assumed, in the earlier long-range projections, to stay only briefly below replacement, returning essentially to replacement a decade beyond 2050 rather than, as in the current projection, staying clearly below for a century after 2050. Many countries in developing regions, in the earlier projection, never fall below replacement fertility, but in the current projection they do. The assumption, therefore, that fertility will fall to low levels for a fairly long period, not just in more developed but also in less developed regions, is a distinctive characteristic of the current long-range projections.

Mortality levels play a role in long-range population growth, helping account for the temporary decline and being responsible for change once fertility has settled at replacement. The role of mortality, however, is not evident from trends in life expectancy. World life expectancy is projected to grow along a smooth path but at a slowing pace. It is expected to reach 74.8 years in 2050—after having risen about 20 years in 1950-2000 and rising further about 10 years in 2000-2050. Gains beyond 2050 diminish: for 2050-2100, 8 years, and then for subsequent 50-year periods 5, 4, 3, and finally 2 years for 2250-2300. By the time rising life expectancy becomes the dominant and indeed the sole influence on growth—in 2225—it will be at 92.8 years and rising slowly, leading to an annual population growth rate over the next half century of only 0.06 per cent.

There is no indication from these trends that mortality change could produce fluctuations in

Figure 9. Comparison of world population and net reproduction rate with previous long-range projections, estimates and medium scenario: 1950-2150

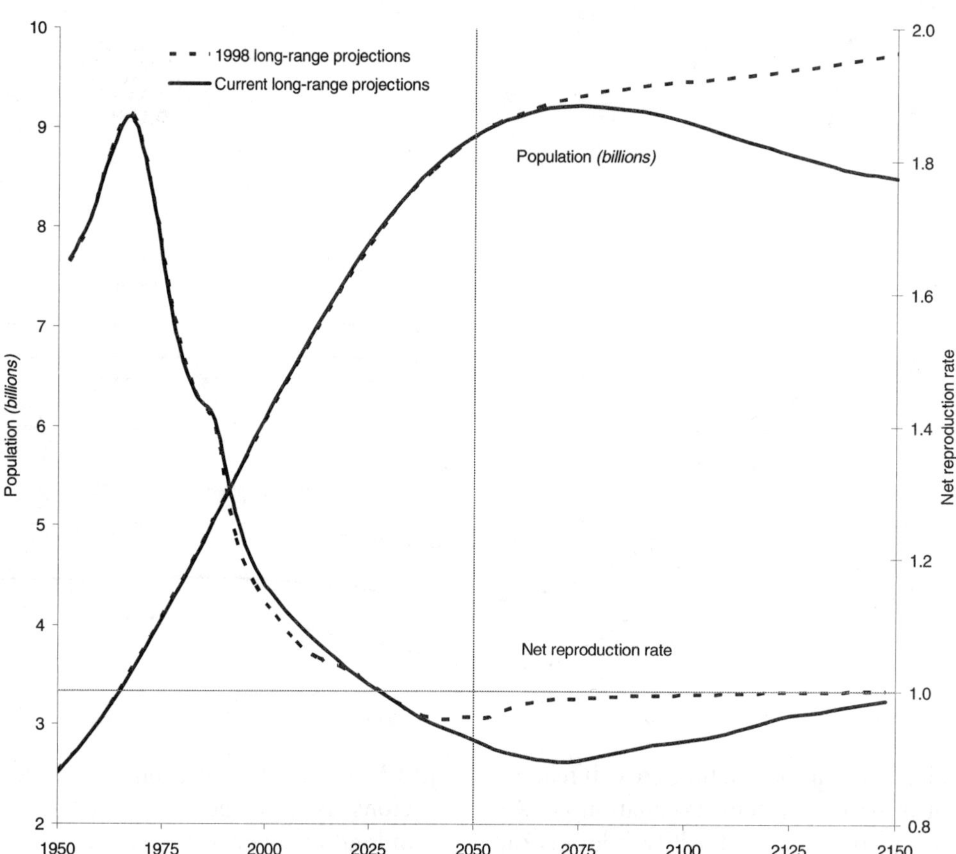

growth. Nevertheless, the crude death rate does in fact fluctuate. As births fall and populations age, the crude death rate rises, intersecting with the crude birth rate in 2075 and not falling below it again until 2170 (figure 10). Within this period, at least, the rise in the crude death rate is more substantial than the fall in the crude birth rate. Should the crude death rate instead stay at its 2050 level, no population decline would occur. Mortality change therefore does make an important contribution to growth trends.

The medium scenario implies that the still substantial population growth expected up to 2050 will not continue. If vital rates follow expected trends, world population will level off (though it may still continue to grow fairly slowly) close to the 2050 level. However, small, consistent deviations in vital rates from expected paths could have quite substantial effects. Population could instead (in the high scenario) be double its 2050 size about a century later, or (in the low scenario) be only half as large in 75 years. Is the projected range for future world population too wide? For many planning purposes it probably is, though not many people are in the business of planning centuries in advance. This range of possibilities may in fact be a reasonable reflection of the uncertainty that attends population projections of several centuries. A crude way to demonstrate this is to extrapolate the confidence intervals estimated for the *1998 Revision.* Doing this would set an upper limit of 37 billion by 2300, essentially the same as the high scenario. (An extrapolation for the lower limit, however, would give negative figures.)

Some patterns visible in the world projection reappear again and again in regional and country projections. Fluctuation in population growth, particularly a long period of decline and an eventual return to positive but minimal growth, are typical

Figure 10. Crude birth and death rate and rate of natural increase for the world, estimates and medium scenario: 1950-2300

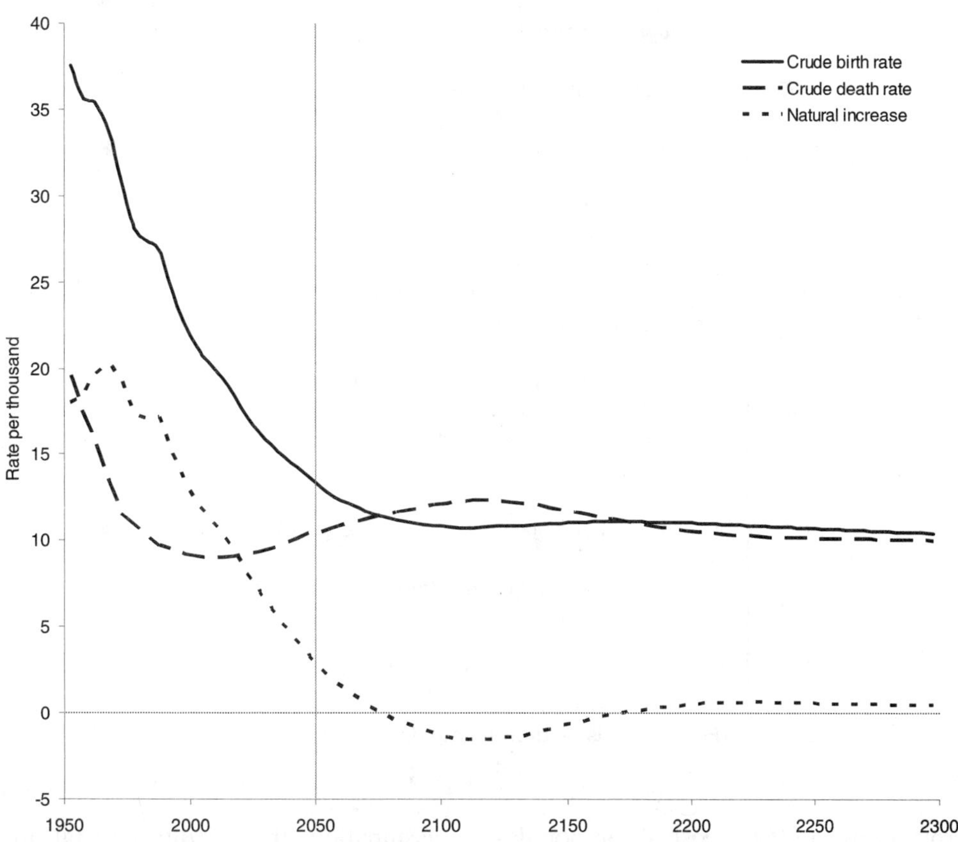

for most countries. That fluctuations eventuate in little change in the long run, such that population in 2300 is not much different from population in 2050, is also common. That fertility first declines below replacement and then recovers to replacement level, and that population growth follows, with turning points about half a century later, is also a general pattern. The steady rise in life expectancy, which paradoxically produces an initial rise in the crude death rate, also appears in many cases. That high and low scenarios provide a wide range around the medium scenario is the usual pattern.

These patterns recur in projections within various regions and countries. Some things do vary, however: specific levels of demographic parameters, as well as the timing of events. Regions and countries differ in how far fertility and growth fall, how high the crude death rate rises, and when exactly these events are projected to happen.

Figure 11 shows the projected time line of demographic milestones for world population. Similar events occur in most countries, but along different time lines. The similarity of patterns might seem to imply that rates of change for regions and countries should eventually converge. Whether this is in fact the case needs to be determined.

C. More developed and less developed regions

At present and in projections through 2050, more developed and less developed regions are strikingly different in demographic terms. Whether these regions will still be properly distinguished in the following centuries may be unlikely but is ultimately impossible to tell. One can however ask—regardless of what happens to economic, social, and political distinctions—whether these regions will remain demographically distinctive.

Figure 11. Significant world demographic events between 2000 and 2300

Year	*Demographic event*	*Population (billions)*
2005	Crude death rate starts rise (from 9.0 per 1000)	6.45
2025	Fertility falls to replacement (and keeps fallling)	7.85
2075	Crude death and birth rates intersect (at 11.4); population reaches maximum	9.22
2105	Crude birth rate falls to minimum (at 10.7)	9.00
2115	Crude death rate reaches maximum (at 12.3); growth rate at miminum (-.15% in 2105-2120)	8.86
2155	Fertility rises to replacement (and stays there)	8.47
2175	Crude death and birth rates intersect again (at 11.1)	8.43
2225	Fertility effects on growth have disappeared	8.62

In the projections to 2050, most of the population growth is in currently less developed regions rather than in currently more developed regions. From 2050 to 2300, in contrast, less developed regions are projected to decline marginally in size, from 7.70 to 7.69 billion, whereas more developed regions actually increase, from 1.22 to 1.28 billion (figure 12). Initially, the population growth rate for less developed regions will fall while the rate in more developed regions rises, the two crossing over around 2090. Then the trends will reverse until the growth rates converge permanently around 2210 (figure 13). High and low scenarios show similar patterns. The projected range between high and low projected populations is proportionally similar between more developed and less developed regions—though for less developed regions, with their substantially larger population, the difference between high and low absolute numbers is much greater.

The eventually similar growth between more developed and less developed regions is produced by similar long-range assumptions, especially the assumptions that fertility will fall in all countries below replacement (in the medium scenario) and rebound to replacement after a period largely similar across countries of a century or so. Starting their fertility declines later, less developed regions will reach low fertility levels after more developed regions but also stay at these levels until a later date. Figure 14 shows that total fertility for the two groups crosses over around 2055 and eventually converges, just like the growth rates, with the cross-over and the convergence preceding similar points in the growth rates by roughly 50 years.

The fact that growth converges for more developed and less developed regions is not surprising given the assumptions, and in a way less interesting than the time required for this convergence. In more developed regions, the crude death rate begins rising around 1970 and reaches its peak around 2045 (figure 15). It intersects with the crude birth rate in the course of this rise around 2010, starting a period of negative natural increase, and intersects again on a downward path

Figure 12. Total population, more developed and less developed regions, estimates and medium scenario: 1950-2300

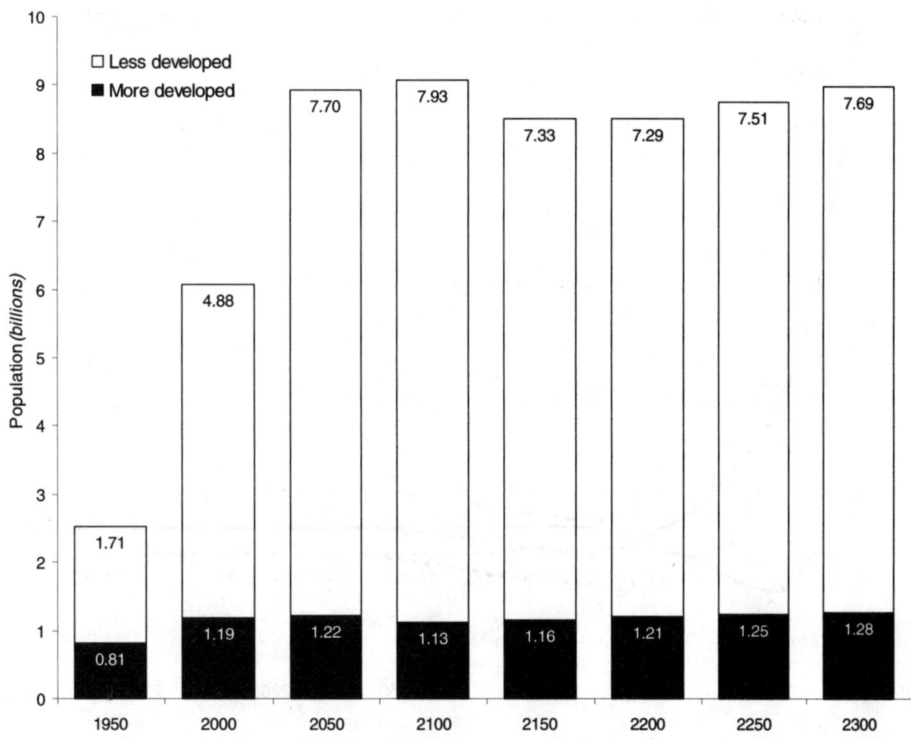

Figure 13. Average annual rate of change of the population of more developed and less developed regions, estimates and three scenarios: 1950-2300

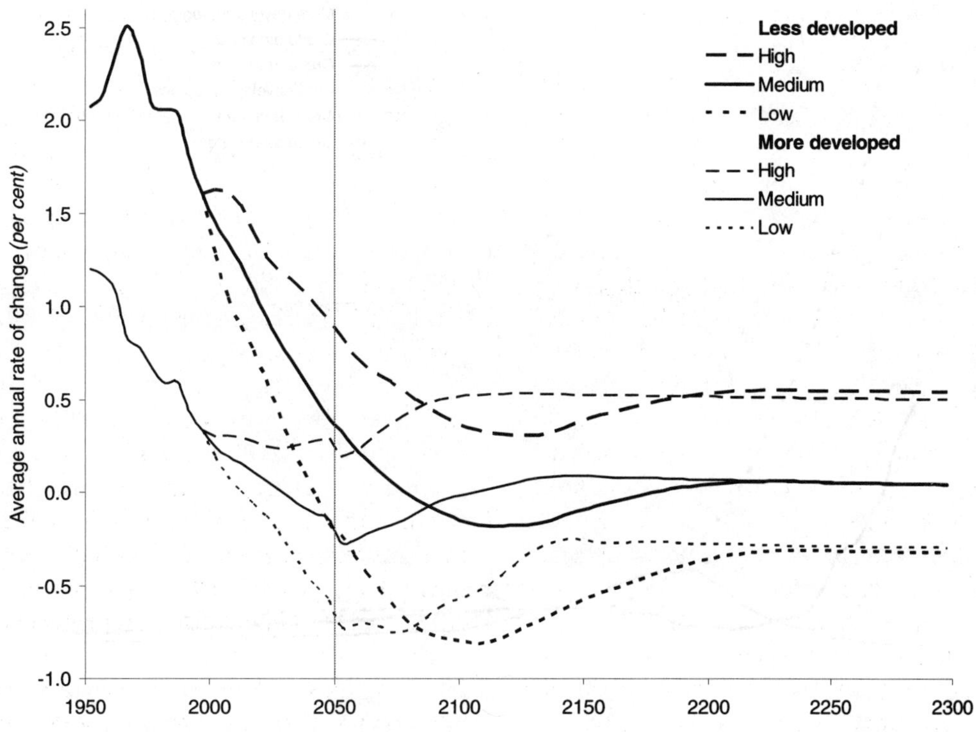

Figure 14. Total fertility, more developed and less developed regions, estimates and three scenarios: 1950-2300

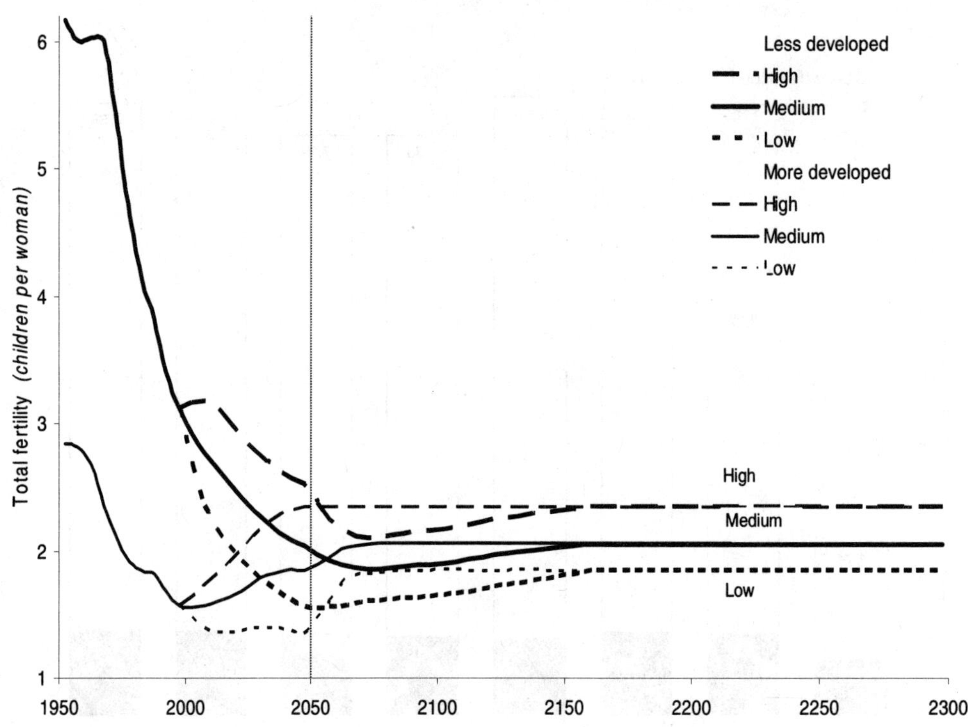

Figure 15. Crude birth and death rate, more developed and less developed regions, estimates and medium scenario: 1950-2300

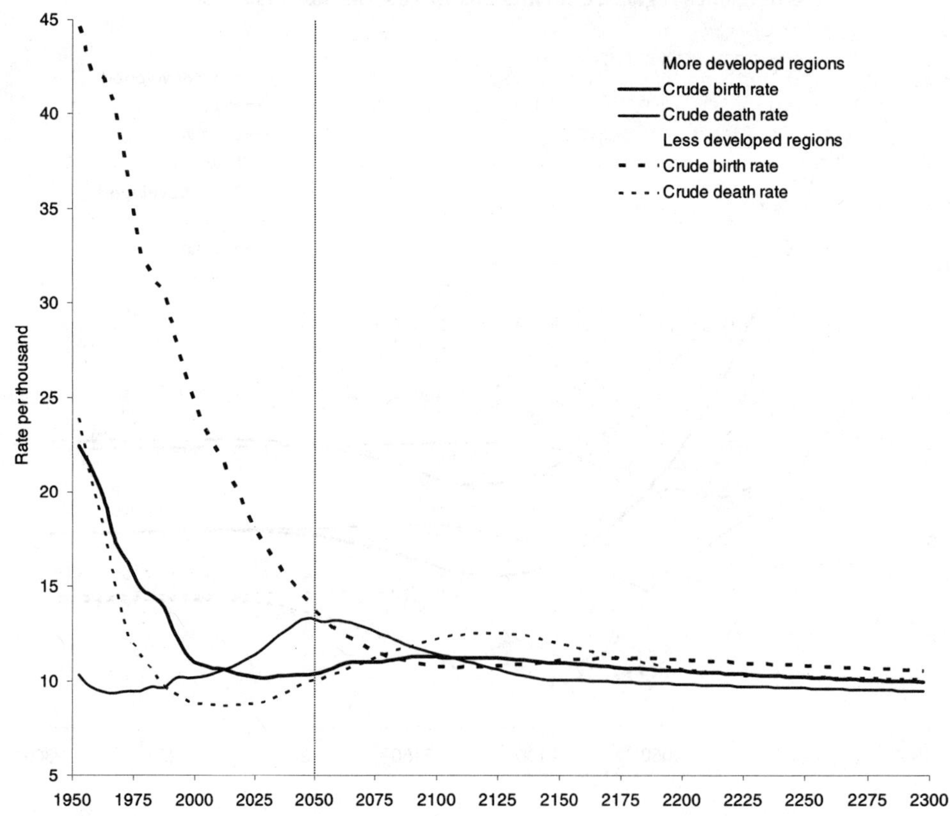

around 2105, ending the period. In less developed regions, the crude death rate does not begin rising until 2015 and peaks in 2120, intersecting the crude birth rate in 2080 and 2175. For less developed regions in comparison to more developed regions, these turning points come anywhere from 45 to 75 years later and at somewhat different levels of the vital rates. To take a somewhat different comparison, it takes more than 50 years from today (till about 2055) for total fertility in more developed and less developed regions to intersect, and then a century beyond that (till 2160) for total fertility to intersect again. Growth rates will take about 50 years longer, in each case, to intersect. The consequences of the late start for less developed regions in the demographic transition stretch out into the future. In the aggregate, despite parallel long-range assumptions, less developed regions do not catch up demographically with more developed regions for over 200 years from today. Based on crude rates, in fact, less developed regions never seem to fully catch up (figure 15).

In looking at life expectancies, this impression is reinforced (figure 16). Less developed regions made substantially faster gains in life expectancy than more developed regions in 1950-2000 and are projected to continue to make faster gains in 2000-2050, though by 2050 they will still be behind, with life expectancies of 71.5 years for males and 75.8 years for females (versus 79.0 and 84.9 in more developed regions). Beyond 2050, gains will be slighter and become almost equal. By 2300, life expectancies will reach 94.8 and 96.3 years for males and females, respectively, in less developed regions, still short of levels of 99.7 and 102.7 in more developed regions. Well before that, by around 2200, the gains in less developed regions will fall marginally below those in more developed regions, and the difference in gains, though very small, will increase over time. Less developed regions, therefore, when projected based on their demographic history, are likely to retain some distinctions, however small, from more developed regions.

Figure 16. Male and female life expectancy at birth, more developed and less developed regions: 1950-2300

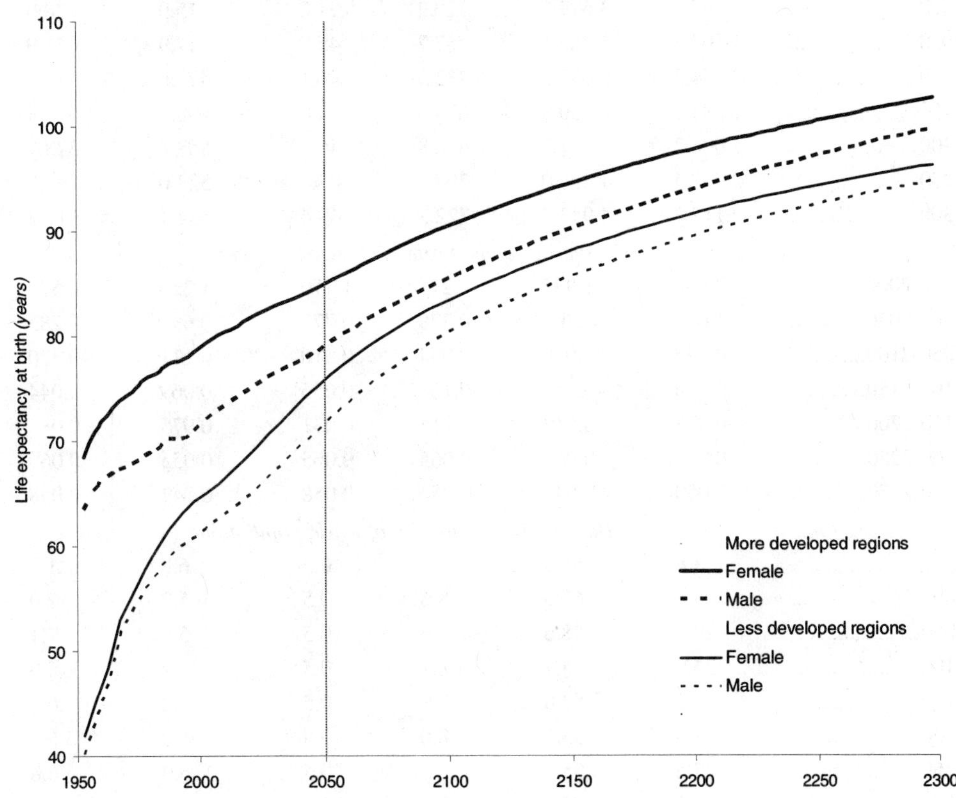

D. Major areas

Among major areas (table 2), the *2002 Revision* shows Africa and Europe at opposite ends of the spectrum, with the highest and lowest projected growth rates to 2050. Differences in growth across major areas eventually resolve themselves. African growth slows from 2050 to 2100, and over the following two centuries, Africa's share of world population will actually shrink slightly while Europe's share will grow slightly (figure 17).

Growth rates for the six major areas show the same pattern already seen for the world as a whole: an initial decline toward zero growth, the decline starting in the twentieth century; then about a century of subzero growth, meaning population decline; and an eventual return to positive growth but at a very low rate, generally close to 0.05 per cent annually (figure 18). The notable exception to this pattern is Northern America, whose growth rate does decline and recover but never falls below zero. As noted above, growth in Northern America is supported throughout the first half of the twenty-first century by substantial net immigration. Another major area of relatively high net immigration, Oceania, does experience negative growth, but for 65 years rather than a century.

The major areas differ in how low growth falls and in the timing of the decline. Growth falls to a lower level than anywhere else in Europe (-0.53 per cent annually). For Latin America and the Caribbean, Africa, and Asia, the lowest point is only half as low. Oceania has a shallow decline

TABLE 2. POPULATION, AVERAGE ANNUAL RATE OF CHANGE, AND DISTRIBUTION OF WORLD POPULATION, BY MAJOR AREA, ESTIMATES AND MEDIUM SCENARIO: 1950-2300

Year or period	*Africa*	*Asia*	*Latin America and the Caribbean*	*Oceania*	*Northern America*	*Europe*
			Population (millions)			
1950	221.2	1 398.5	167.1	12.8	171.6	547.4
2000	795.7	3 679.7	520.2	31.0	315.9	728.0
2050	1 803.3	5 222.1	767.7	45.8	447.9	631.9
2100	2 254.3	5 019.2	732.5	46.1	473.6	538.4
2150	2 083.1	4 650.8	675.0	44.8	490.1	550.4
2200	2 008.2	4 681.7	680.8	45.5	508.8	573.7
2250	2 060.4	4 824.0	703.5	47.0	523.0	593.8
2300	2 112.7	4 943.2	722.7	48.4	534.1	611.3
			Average annual rate of change (per cent)			
1950-2000	2.560	1.935	2.271	1.770	1.220	0.570
2000-2050	1.636	0.700	0.778	0.778	0.698	-0.283
2050-2100	0.446	-0.079	-0.094	0.010	0.111	-0.320
2100-2150	-0.158	-0.152	-0.164	-0.056	0.069	0.044
2150-2200	-0.073	0.013	0.017	0.031	0.075	0.083
2200-2250	0.051	0.060	0.065	0.065	0.055	0.069
2250-2300	0.050	0.049	0.054	0.058	0.042	0.058
			Percentage distribution of world population			
1950	8.8	55.5	6.6	0.5	6.8	21.7
2000	13.1	60.6	8.6	0.5	5.2	12.0
2050	20.2	58.6	8.6	0.5	5.0	7.1
2100	24.9	55.4	8.1	0.5	5.2	5.9
2150	24.5	54.8	7.9	0.5	5.8	6.5
2200	23.6	55.1	8.0	0.5	6.0	6.8
2250	23.5	55.1	8.0	0.5	6.0	6.8
2300	23.5	55.1	8.1	0.5	6.0	6.8

Figure 17. Population in major areas, estimates and medium scenario: 1950-2300

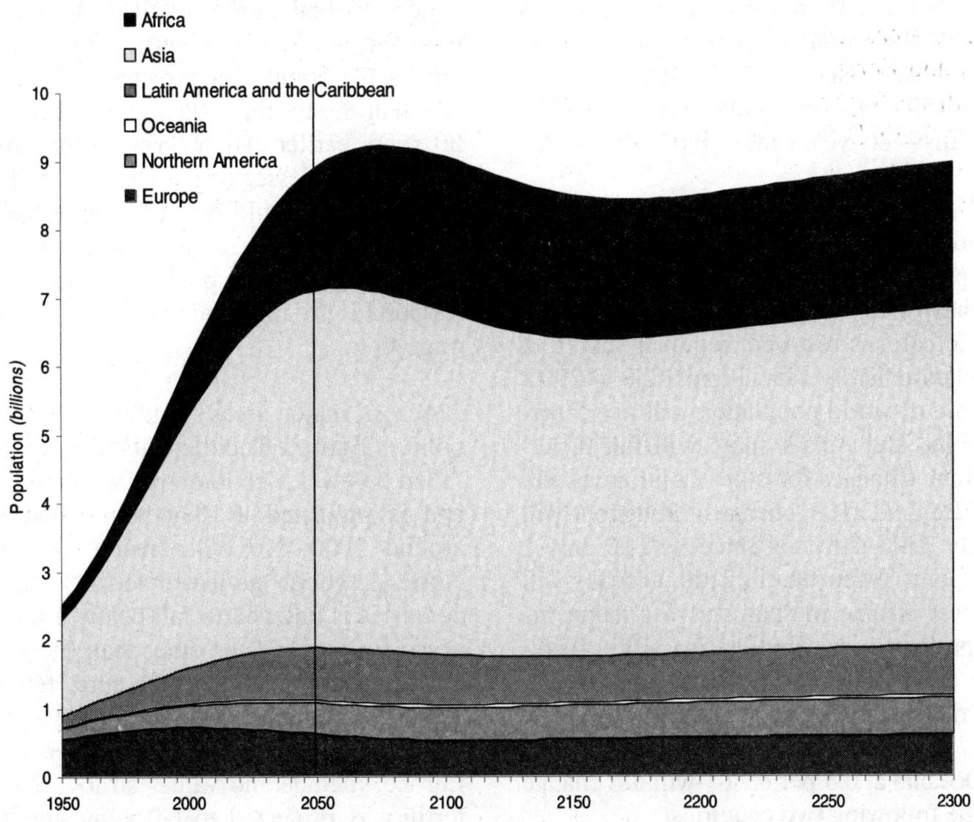

Figure 18. Average annual rate of change of the population of major areas, estimates and medium scenario: 1950-2300

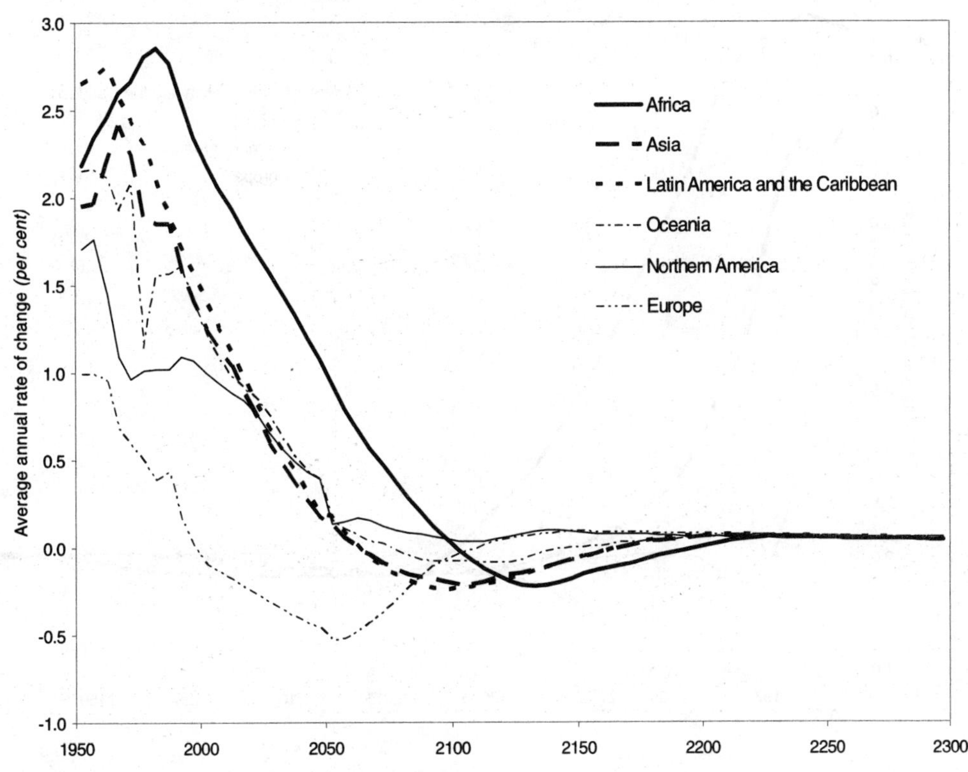

to -0.09 per cent, and Northern American growth does not go below 0.03 per cent. Europe reaches its low point first, around 2050. Latin America and the Caribbean, Northern America, and Asia follow about 50 years later, followed by Oceania and eventually—80 years after Europe—by Africa.

Because of this staggered pattern of growth and decline, population distribution across major areas appears to have small waves and troughs, but once demographic calm is restored, regional shares of world population hardly vary. From 2050 to 2100, Africa's share of world population will rise 5 percentage points, and Asia's share will fall 3 percentage points. Changes for other major areas will be smaller. Beyond 2100, changes throughout will be small. By 2300, Africa's share will be only 1 percentage point lower than in 2100, and this will be the biggest change in shares across major areas. The projected distribution in 2100, therefore—Asia at 55 per cent, Africa at 25 per cent, Latin America and the Caribbean at 9 per cent, Europe at 7 per cent, Northern America at 5 per cent, and Oceania at 0.5 per cent—will not change greatly in the following two centuries.

Convergence in fertility underlies this convergence in population growth. Curves representing total fertility trends (figure 19) in fact resemble curves for population growth, with the qualification that the turning points in fertility come about 50 years earlier. The curves for Northern America, and to a lesser extent Oceania, indicate lower fertility than would typically support the population growth rates shown earlier for 1950-2050 because, as has been pointed out, growth has been supported, in these major areas, by substantial migration.

Across major areas, fertility falls to its lowest point in Europe. Total fertility is estimated to have fallen below 1.5 children per woman around 1995 and is projected to stay below that level until around 2020. No other major area will come close. Although projected fertility for individual countries is allowed to fall below 1.85, it will not do so for major areas other than Europe. Fertility in Northern America, to be sure, fell to 1.78 in 1975-1980, but the projection beyond 2000 for this major area, and for all other ones except Europe, includes no values so low. Nevertheless, fertility is projected to be below replacement in

Figure 19. Total fertility, major areas, estimates and medium scenario: 1950-2175

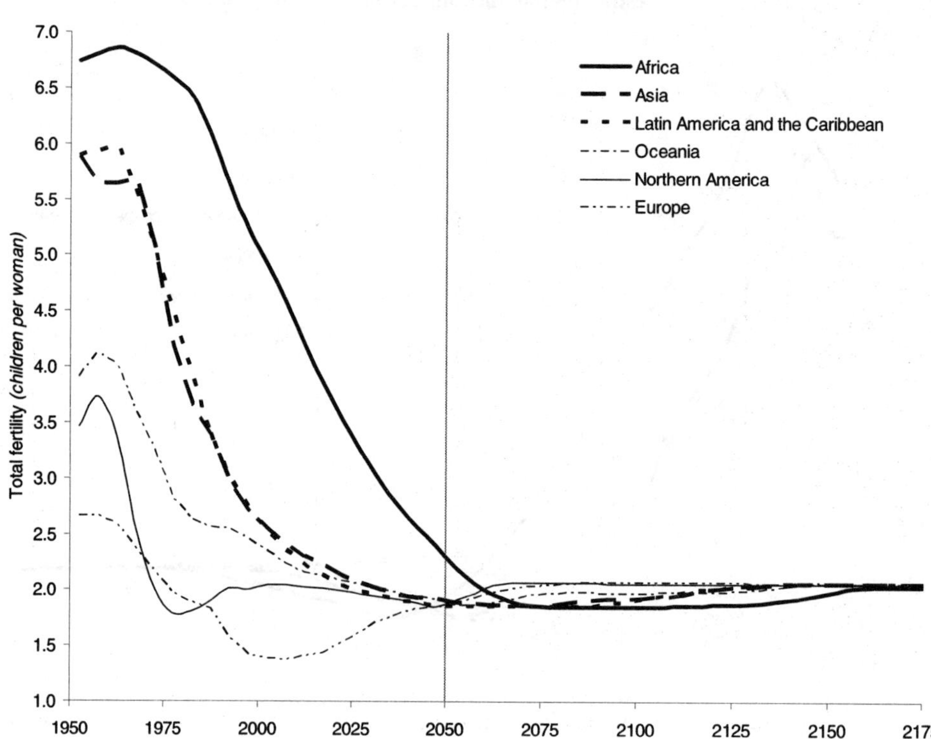

each major area for a century or a little more (figure 20). This below-replacement period varies. It comes early for Europe (1975-2085), latest for Africa (2050-2160). After this period is over, particularly after 2175, fertility flat-lines not only in each major area but also in each country (figure 5), therefore ceasing to be of much interest.

The crude birth rate generally tracks total fertility, falling below the crude death rate in most cases at the point where growth turns negative. This cross-over point is due, as has already been noted for the world and the more developed and less developed regions, not only to falling fertility but also to the rising crude death rate (figure 21). The crude death rate rises most from its minimum to its subsequent maximum, by 6.3 points per thousand, in Latin America and the Caribbean. It rises least, by only 2.6 points, in Northern America, partly accounting for the fact that this major area does not experience negative growth. Particularly notable among other regional contrasts is the way Europe and Africa appear to be out of phase, with Europe hitting its maximum crude death rate shortly after 2050 about when Africa hits its minimum, and the rates crossing over, about 50 years later, headed in opposite directions.

Though crude death rates appear to be out of phase, life expectancies are expected to rise roughly in parallel, but at different levels. As shown in the review of the *2002 Revision,* life expectancy is projected to be substantially shorter in Africa than in other major area. By 2050, it is projected at 65.8, at least 11 years shorter than in every other major area. Extending the projections suggests that Africa will close the gap substantially, especially over the following century, but not eliminate it. Figure 22 compares life expectancy in each major area to life expectancy in Latin America and the Caribbean, which is chosen as the standard because it is intermediate among the major areas. Africa gains, relative to Latin America and the Caribbean, up to 2210, though the gains in the latter decades of that period are quite small, but then life expectancies begin to diverge very slowly. By 2300, life expectancy in Africa is projected at 92.9 years, 5.1 years shorter than in Latin America and the Caribbean and 3.6 years shorter than in Asia. The main reason

Figure 20. Periods when net reproduction rate is below 1, major areas, estimates and medium scenario: 1950-2200

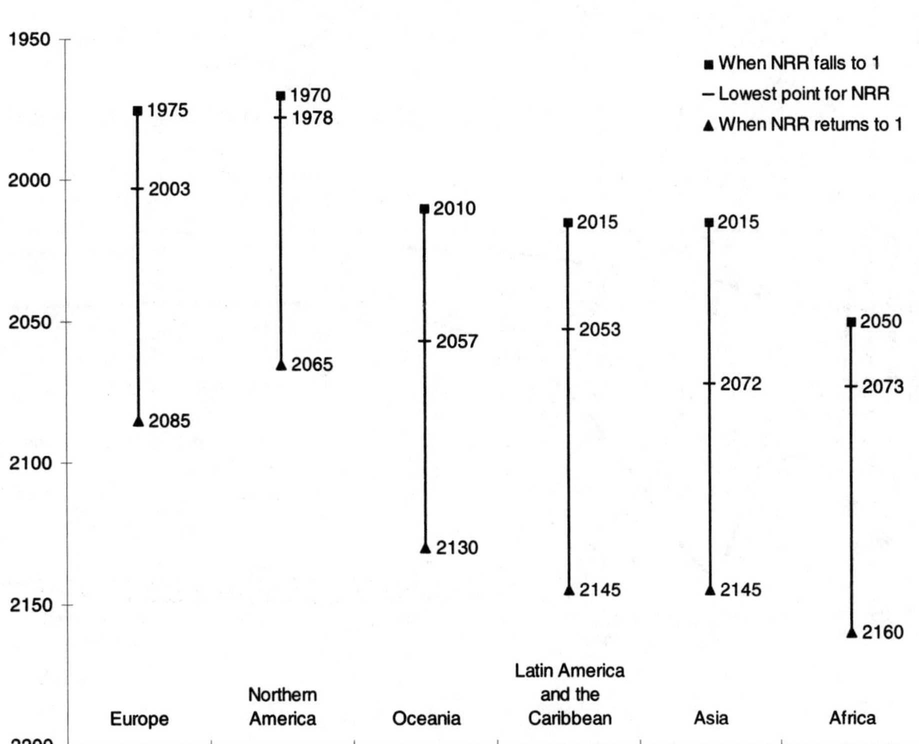

Figure 21. Crude death rate and points of intersection with crude birth rate, major areas, estimates and medium scenario: 1950-2300

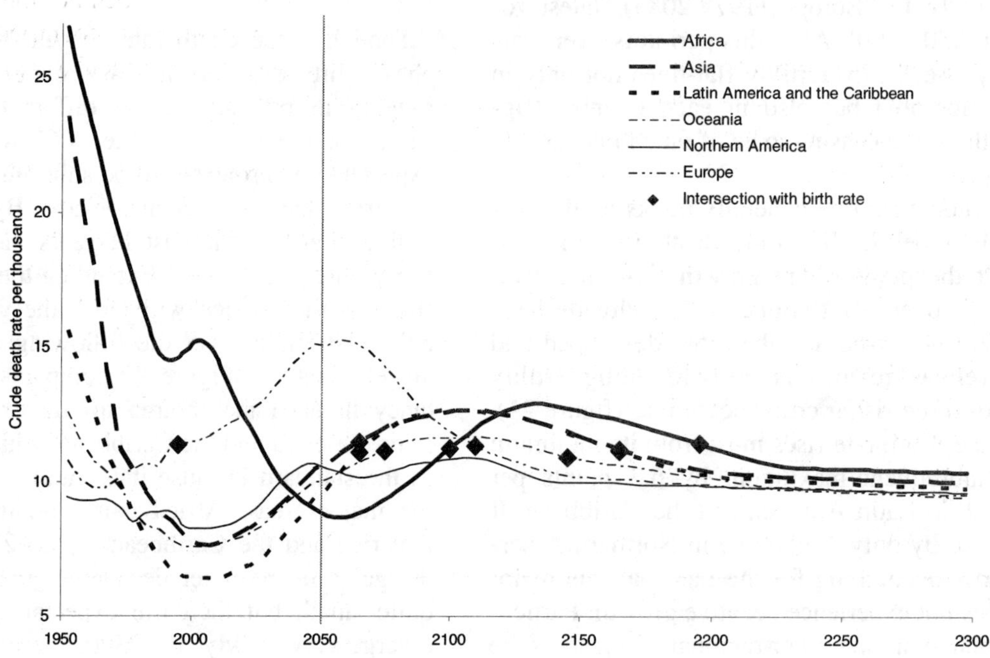

Figure 22. Difference between life expectancy at birth in each major area and in Latin America and the Caribbean: 1950-2300

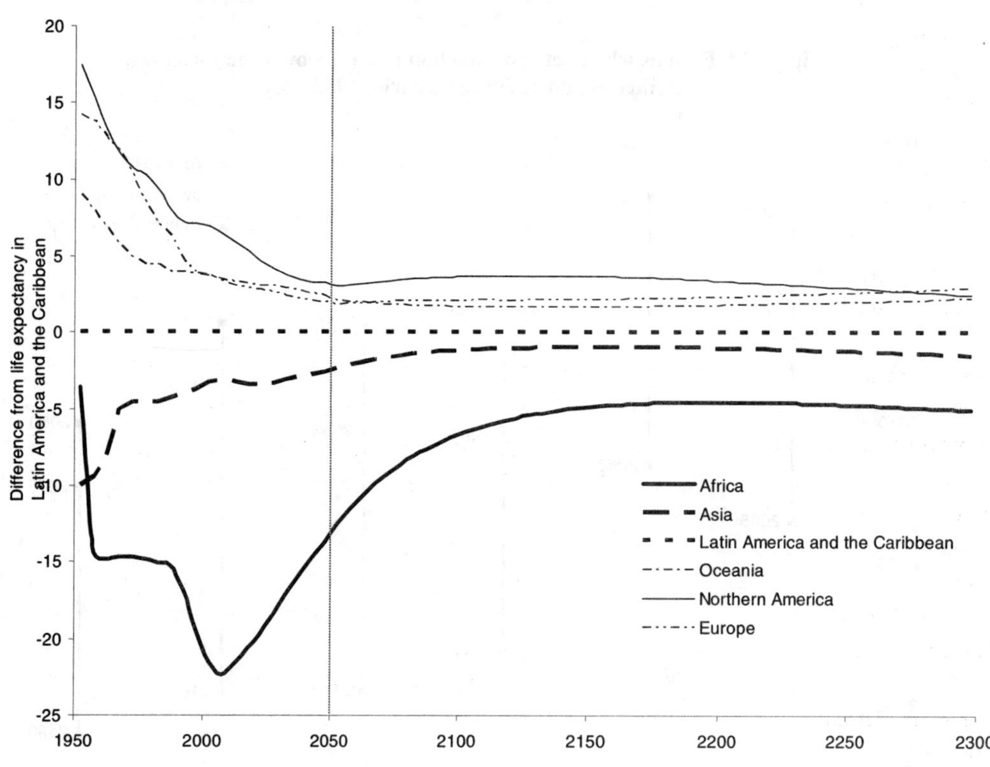

behind this is differential growth of countries in Africa, which changes the weights that go into calculating the average for the whole continent.

The very slow divergence of life expectancies in the long run, after almost two centuries, does not apply only to Africa but to all major areas, with the singular exception of Northern America. This divergence is consistent with the divergence between more developed and less developed regions. Why does this happen? Many factors are playing into this, but the most important is that the mortality was projected independently for each country. The diffusion of knowledge and technology, which could narrow the gaps between countries, was not factored into the projection methodology. Such an implicit assumption of independent trends does not affect short-term projections, but it seems to affect long-range projections like this one. Another factor behind the divergent trends can be attributed to countries changing their relative weight in a particular region, already mentioned above.

The following sections turn to the regions of the major areas to clarify such issues, as well to determine whether regional patterns apply to all parts of a major area, and possibly develop further insights into the causes of these patterns. Since the earlier summary of the *2002 Revision* did not go below the level of major areas, these sections touch on relevant aspects of the 50-year projections in describing the 300-year projections (tables 3 and 4).

TABLE 3. POPULATION BY MAJOR AREA AND REGION, ESTIMATES AND MEDIUM SCENARIO: 1950-2300
(millions)

Major area and region	*1950*	*2000*	*2050*	*2100*	*2150*	*2200*	*2250*	*2300*
Africa	221.2	795.7	1 803.3	2 254.3	2 083.1	2 008.2	2 060.4	2 112.7
Southern Africa	15.6	50.4	46.6	45.2	44.8	46.8	48.7	50.1
Eastern Africa	65.6	252.5	614.5	808.8	754.3	724.8	742.9	761.4
Middle Africa	26.3	93.0	266.3	354.7	320.4	304.2	312.3	321.1
Western Africa	60.4	226.1	569.9	735.5	681.3	651.5	666.7	683.2
Northern Africa	53.3	173.6	306.0	310.2	282.3	281.0	289.7	296.9
Asia	1 398.5	3 679.7	5 222.1	5 019.2	4 650.8	4 681.7	4 824.0	4 943.2
Western Asia	50.9	192.2	400.8	472.7	438.7	426.8	436.3	445.7
India	357.6	1 016.9	1 531.4	1 458.4	1 308.2	1 304.5	1 342.3	1 371.7
Other South-central Asia	140.9	469.1	932.5	1 010.3	903.3	880.4	902.8	922.9
South-eastern Asia	178.1	520.4	767.2	734.7	689.4	700.7	721.8	738.9
China	554.8	1 275.2	1 395.2	1 181.5	1 149.1	1 200.7	1 246.7	1 285.2
Other Eastern Asia	116.2	205.9	194.9	161.6	162.2	168.5	174.0	178.8
Latin America and the Caribbean	167.1	520.2	767.7	732.5	675.0	680.8	703.5	722.7
Brazil	54.0	171.8	233.1	212.4	202.2	208.8	216.3	222.6
Other South America	59.0	175.5	277.0	273.8	247.6	246.4	254.6	261.8
Caribbean	17.0	37.7	45.8	42.1	38.3	38.4	39.7	40.9
Central America	37.1	135.2	211.8	204.2	186.8	187.2	192.8	197.4
Oceania	12.8	31.0	45.8	46.1	44.8	45.5	47.0	48.4
Polynesia	0.2	0.6	0.9	1.0	0.9	0.9	0.9	1.0
Micronesia	0.2	0.5	0.9	0.9	0.9	0.9	0.9	1.0
Melanesia	2.3	7.0	14.0	15.4	13.8	13.3	13.7	14.0
Australia/New Zealand	10.1	22.9	30.1	28.8	29.2	30.4	31.4	32.4
Northern America	171.6	315.9	447.9	473.6	490.1	508.8	523.0	534.1
Europe	547.4	728.0	631.9	538.4	550.4	573.7	593.8	611.3
Eastern Europe	220.2	304.5	221.7	173.9	178.5	185.9	191.8	196.6
Southern Europe	109.0	145.8	125.6	98.5	98.5	102.6	106.3	109.6
Western Europe	140.9	183.5	184.5	170.6	175.4	183.3	190.3	196.6
Northern Europe	77.3	94.1	100.1	95.5	98.0	102.0	105.5	108.5

TABLE 4. AVERAGE ANNUAL RATE OF CHANGE FOR 50-YEAR PERIODS, BY MAJOR AREA AND REGION, ESTIMATES AND MEDIUM SCENARIO: 1950-2300
(per cent)

Major area and region	*1950-2000*	*2000-2050*	*2050-2100*	*2100-2150*	*2150-2200*	*2200-2250*	*2250-2300*
Africa	2.56	1.64	0.45	-0.16	-0.07	0.05	0.05
Southern Africa	2.34	-0.16	-0.06	-0.02	0.09	0.08	0.05
Eastern Africa	2.70	1.78	0.55	-0.14	-0.08	0.05	0.05
Middle Africa	2.52	2.10	0.57	-0.20	-0.10	0.05	0.06
Western Africa	2.64	1.85	0.51	-0.15	-0.09	0.05	0.05
Northern Africa	2.36	1.13	0.03	-0.19	-0.01	0.06	0.05
Asia	1.93	0.70	-0.08	-0.15	0.01	0.06	0.05
Western Asia	2.66	1.47	0.33	-0.15	-0.05	0.04	0.04
India	2.09	0.82	-0.10	-0.22	-0.01	0.06	0.04
Other South-central Asia	2.40	1.37	0.16	-0.22	-0.05	0.05	0.04
South-eastern Asia	2.14	0.78	-0.09	-0.13	0.03	0.06	0.05
China	1.66	0.18	-0.33	-0.06	0.09	0.08	0.06
Other Eastern Asia	1.14	-0.11	-0.37	0.01	0.08	0.06	0.05
Latin America and the Caribbean	2.27	0.78	-0.09	-0.16	0.02	0.07	0.05
Brazil	2.32	0.61	-0.19	-0.10	0.06	0.07	0.06
Other South America	2.18	0.91	-0.02	-0.20	-0.01	0.07	0.06
Caribbean	1.59	0.39	-0.17	-0.19	0.00	0.07	0.06
Central America	2.59	0.90	-0.07	-0.18	0.00	0.06	0.05
Oceania	1.77	0.78	0.01	-0.06	0.03	0.06	0.06
Polynesia	1.86	0.80	0.09	-0.12	0.00	0.06	0.05
Micronesia	2.35	1.10	0.13	-0.06	0.03	0.07	0.06
Melanesia	2.23	1.38	0.19	-0.21	-0.07	0.05	0.05
Australia/New Zealand	1.64	0.54	-0.08	0.03	0.08	0.07	0.06
Northern America	1.22	0.70	0.11	0.07	0.07	0.06	0.04
Europe	0.57	-0.28	-0.32	0.04	0.08	0.07	0.06
Eastern Europe	0.65	-0.63	-0.49	0.05	0.08	0.06	0.05
Southern Europe	0.58	-0.30	-0.49	0.00	0.08	0.07	0.06
Western Europe	0.53	0.01	-0.16	0.06	0.09	0.08	0.07
Northern Europe	0.39	0.12	-0.09	0.05	0.08	0.07	0.06

E. AFRICA

In the projections to 2050 as well as the long-range projections to 2300, Africa shows distinctive patterns, with faster growth and higher fertility and mortality than other major areas. Are these patterns typical across the continent, or are they due to patterns for some specific region? The United Nations customarily divides the continent into five regions (figure 23). Of these, the three in the "middle" of the continent—Eastern, Middle and Western Africa—are projected to grow vigorously from 2000 to 2050, more than doubling in size. Their growth rates for this period are slightly above that for Africa as a whole. Northern Africa, in contrast, grows less, at 76 per cent over 50 years. Southern Africa, the smallest region, declines, by 8 per cent. The increase in population from 2000 to 2050 in the regions of Eastern, Middle and Western Africa will be twice as large as the increase between 1950 and 2000.

Combined, these three regions of Africa already have the largest share of the continent's population, and this share is growing: from 72 per cent in 2000 to 80 per cent in 2050 to 84 per cent by 2100, the level at which it settles in the long run. Together, they will reach one billion people

Figure 23. Total population, African regions: 1950-2300

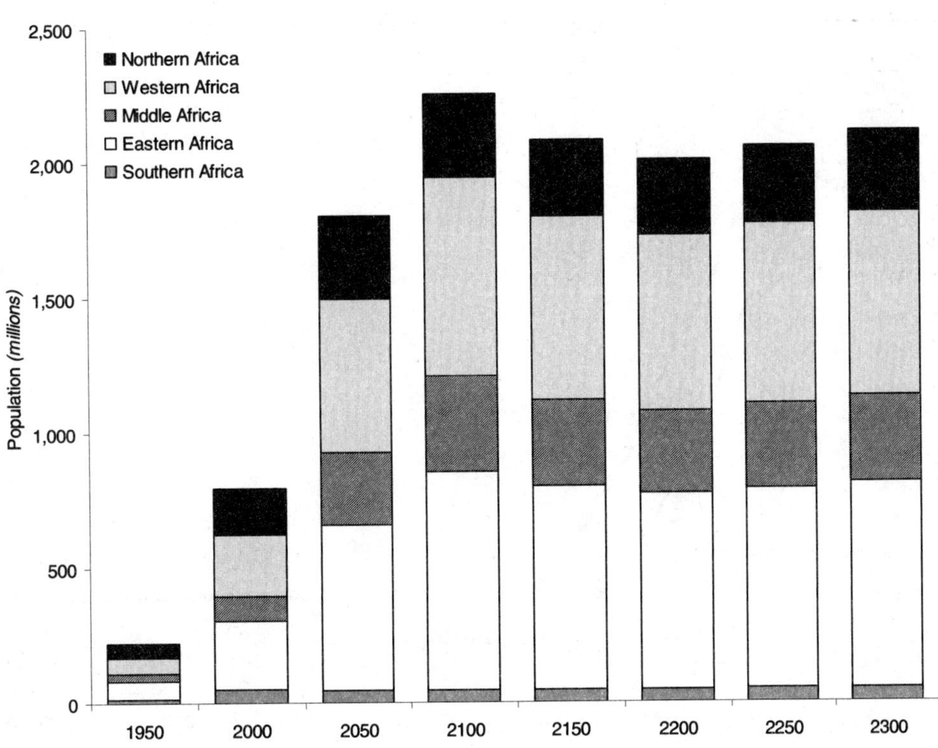

shortly after 2025—it had only 150 million people in 1950—and will be approaching two billion by 2100.

But it will not get there in these projections. Even before 2050, population growth is expected to slow down. Figure 24, in which the 2000-2050 period is set off by vertical lines, shows declining growth rates for these three regions of Africa, though growth rates are even lower within Northern and Southern Africa.

Beyond 2050, population growth substantially moderates in each region—except in a perverse sense for Southern Africa, where a growth rate, still negative by 2050, slowly creeps back to positive levels. As in 2000-2050, Eastern, Middle, and Western Africa are again the three fastest growing regions in the world in 2050-2100, though the pace is much slower. Growth in these three regions does turn negative by 2105 and falls to its lowest level around 2035, about a quarter century after similar turning points for Northern Africa.

Rapid growth in Eastern, Middle, and Western Africa has much to do with high fertility (figure 25). In 1995-2000, these three regions have by far the highest fertility of any region of the world: between 5.9 and 6.4 children per woman, at a time when no other region reaches 4.5. By 2045-2050, these three regions still have the highest fertility, at around 2.5 children per woman, when almost all regions are at 2.0 or below, and Northern and Southern Africa are both at 1.9. By 2145-2150, however, total fertility in Eastern, Middle, and Western Africa has fallen marginally below that in every other region, at 1.91-1.97, versus 2.04-2.09 everywhere else. Given the way fertility is projected, these three African regions will be the last regions with subreplacement fertility, which will not disappear until shortly after 2150. Population growth in these three regions of Africa from 2050 to 2100, however, is still related to high fertility—not entirely contemporaneous high total fertility but also previous high fertility that has produced a young population and consequently many more children.

Figure 24 shows some irregular growth patterns in the recent past, as well as an exceptionally steep fall in the growth rate for Southern Africa. Much of the irregularity, as well as the steep fall,

Figure 24. Average annual rate of population change, African regions: 1950-2300

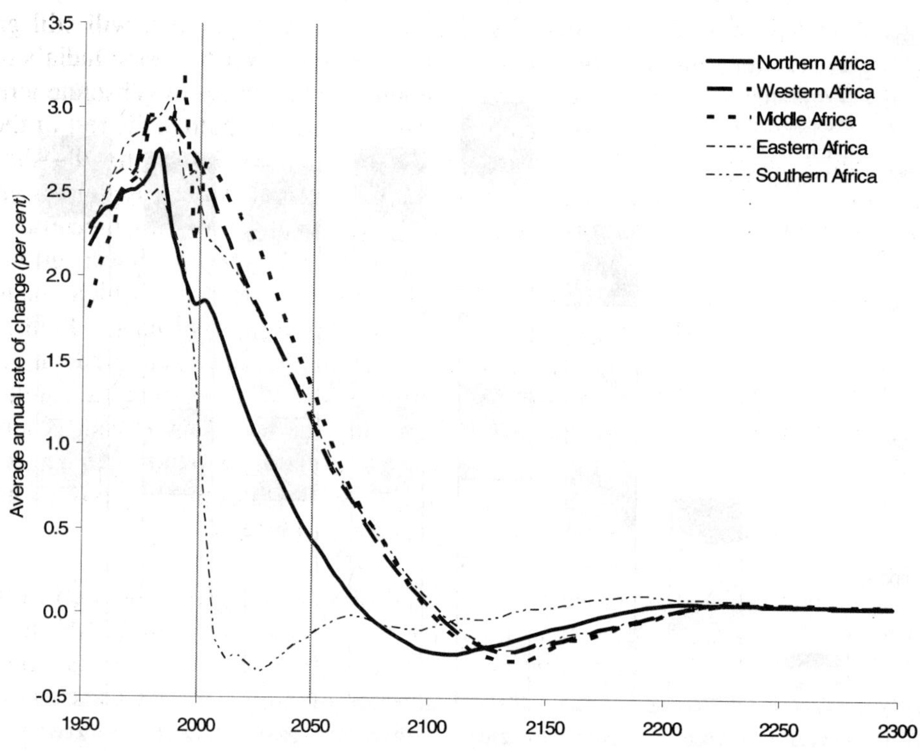

Figure 25. Total fertility, African regions: 1950-2175

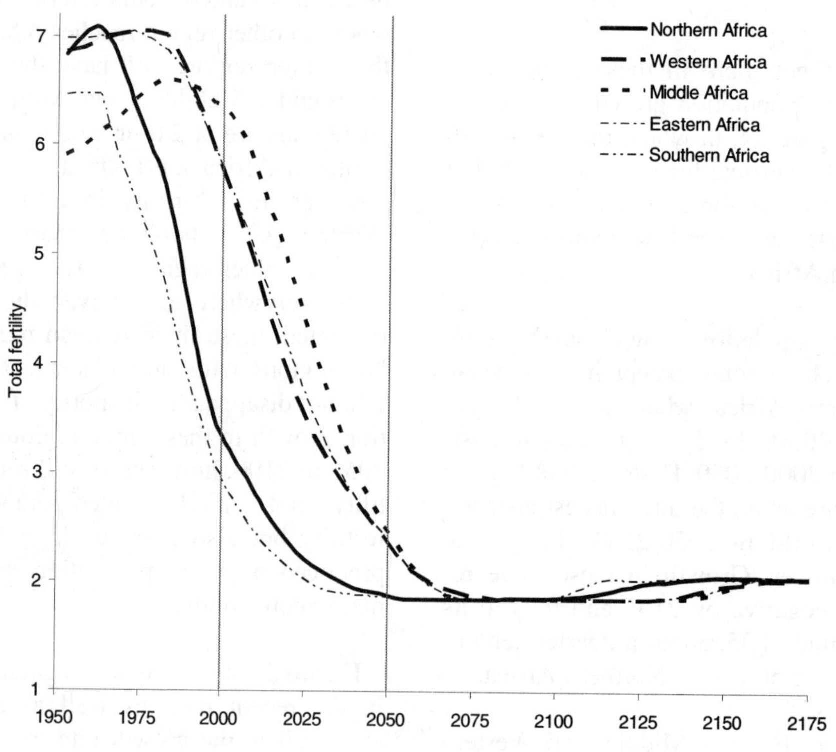

may be ascribed to HIV/AIDS. The projections assume that HIV transmission slows, so the weight of "extra" AIDS mortality is gradually lifted, but not before adding millions of deaths and dragging life expectancy down close to 40 years (figure 26). Only Northern Africa is spared from this effect, which is greatest at the opposite end of the continent, in Southern Africa. Note again that both the projected declines in life expectancy and the pre-2000 declines are derived from epidemic models. The HIV/AIDS epidemic does not entirely account for slower growth in Southern Africa. Substantial fertility decline, earlier than in Eastern, Middle and Western Africa and ahead even of Northern Africa, also plays a part (figure 25).

F. ASIA

Asia is four-and-a-half times as populous as Africa, but by 2050 it will be less than three times as populous. By 2100, it will be 2.2 times as populous, essentially the ratio that will hold till 2300. China and India make up 62 per cent of the major area and therefore are important to distinguish (figure 27). Up to 2050, China's share of the regional population will diminish, though in absolute terms its population will still grow slightly, by 9 per cent over 50 years. India's population, in contrast, will increase in absolute terms by 51 per cent, slightly faster than the rest of the major area. Up to 2050, still faster growth—though short of rates in several African regions—will take place in the remainder of South-central Asia and in Western Asia. Much slower growth will take place in Eastern Asia (which includes, besides China, the Koreas and Japan). Figure 28 suggests, for 2000-2050, an upward gradient in growth rates from east to west and roughly parallel declines in growth. Eastern Asia outside China slips into negative growth around 2015 and China around 2030, while the other regions maintain positive growth past 2050.

Beyond 2050, growth rates converge, and cross over in the decades around 2100. As often seen in these projections, the slowest growing become the fastest growing and vice versa, until the regions converge again close to zero growth. By 2100, India will have 1.46 billion people, or 29 per cent

Figure 26. Life expectancy at birth, African regions: 1950-2300

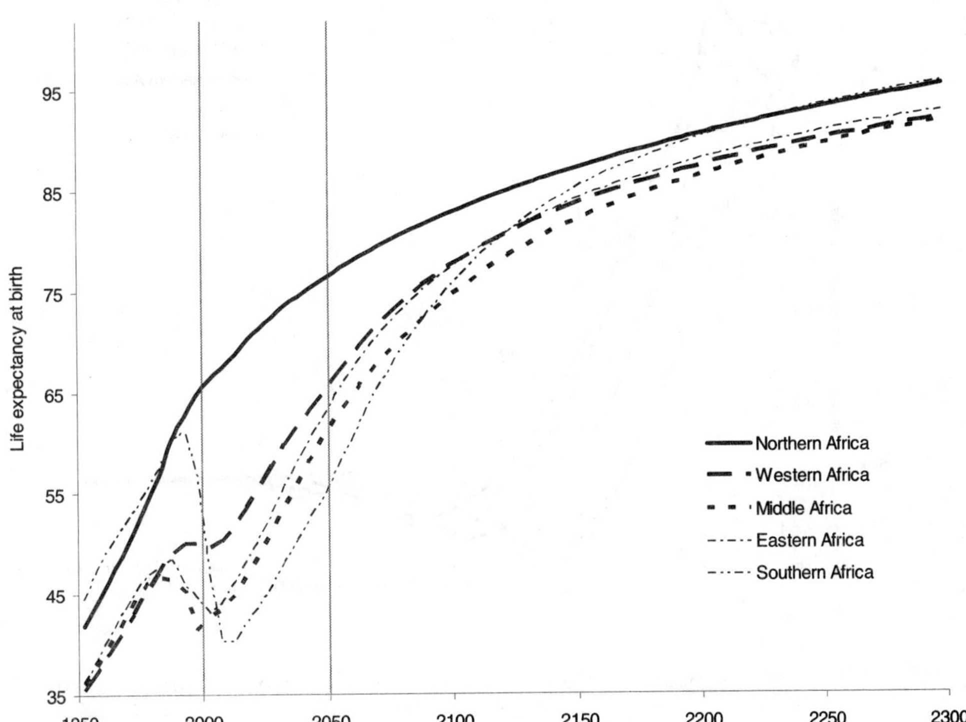

Figure 27. Total population, Asian regions: 1950-2300

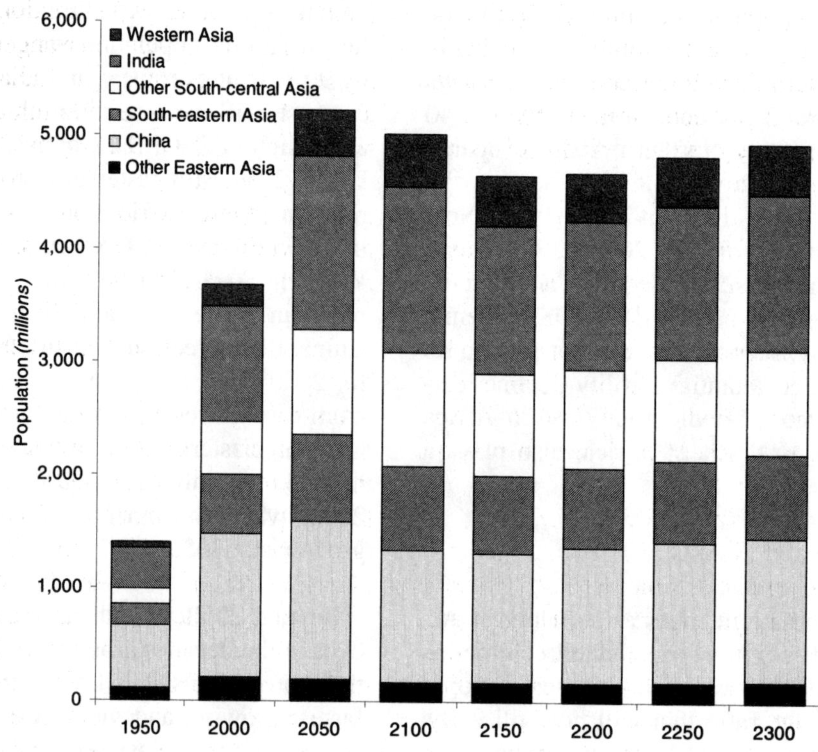

Figure 28. Average annual rate of population change, Asian regions: 1950-2300

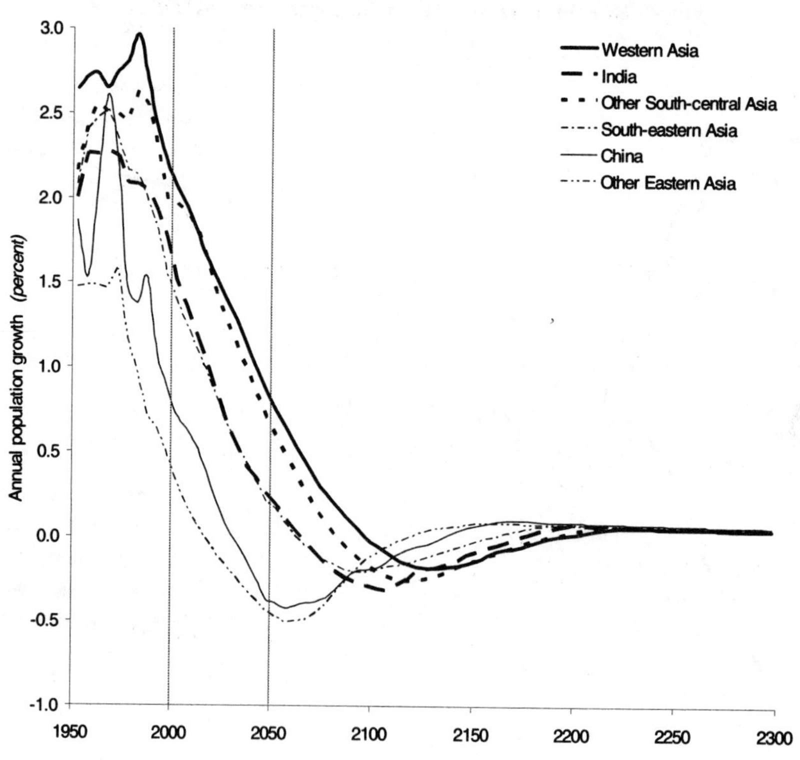

of the Asian population. China will have 24 per cent of the Asian population, South-central Asia outside India 20 per cent, South-eastern Asia 15 per cent, Western Asia 9 per cent, and Eastern Asia outside China 3 per cent. Despite the twists and turns of subsequent growth rates, this distribution will not change much up to 2300.

Unlike growth rates in the 2000-2050 period, the fertility and mortality trends that underlie them are not strictly parallel. Total fertility in Western Asia is somewhat lower than in South-central Asia outside India, but is projected to decline somewhat more slowly (figure 29). Fertility takes the longest to reach 1.85 in Western Asia, where it also takes the longest to recover to replacement level. Life expectancy in Western Asia trails only China and the rest of Eastern Asia, and is projected to overtake China by 2015 (figure 30). But beyond that, gains for Western Asia are slighter. In the long run, China, and especially the rest of Eastern Asia, will maintain a substantial advantage over the rest of the major area. By 2300, life expectancy in the rest of Eastern Asia will be four years longer than in China, while life expectancy in China is at least three years longer than in the other Asian regions. Among these other regions, some rearrangement also takes place. Life expectancy in India, now 2.5 years above that in the rest of South-central Asia, will rise slowly and fall below by 2020, but recover and pass South-central Asia around 2075. In the long run, these two regions, as well as Western Asia and South-eastern Asia, should have life expectancies around 94-96 years.

G. Latin America and the Caribbean

With 8.6 per cent of world population in 2000, Latin America and the Caribbean has a seventh of the population of Asia, and this ratio is projected to hardly change through 2300. Population does grow from 2000 to 2050, from 520 to 768 million, but after 2050, a slight decline sets in. Latin America and the Caribbean can be divided into not quite equal thirds: Brazil (with 30 per cent of regional population in 2050), the rest of South America (36 per cent), and Central America, including Mexico (28 per cent). The remaining 6 per cent of the population in 2050 will be in the

Figure 29. Total fertility, Asian regions: 1950-2175

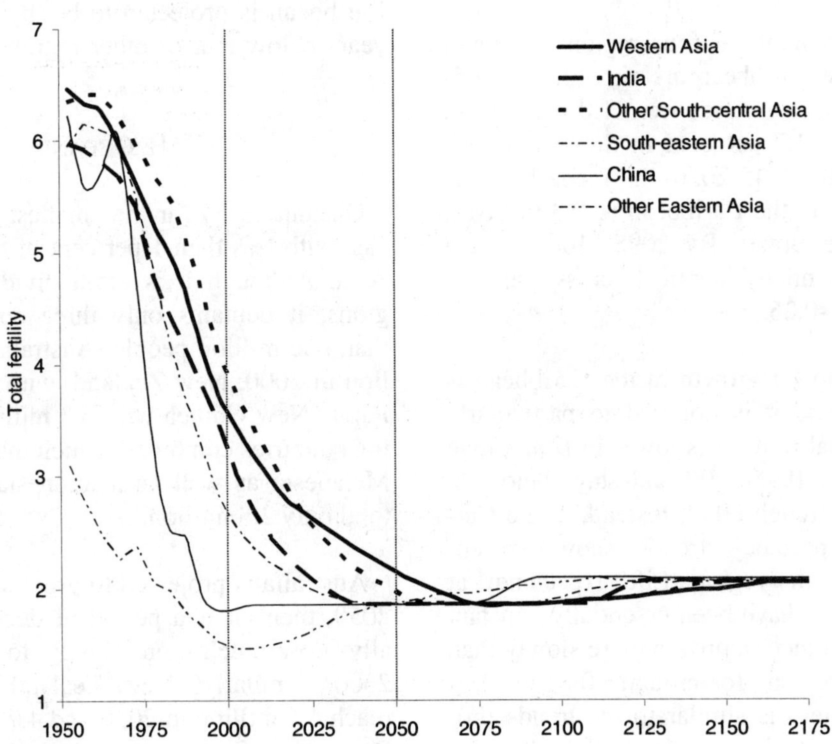

Figure 30. Life expectancy at birth, Asian regions: 1950-2300

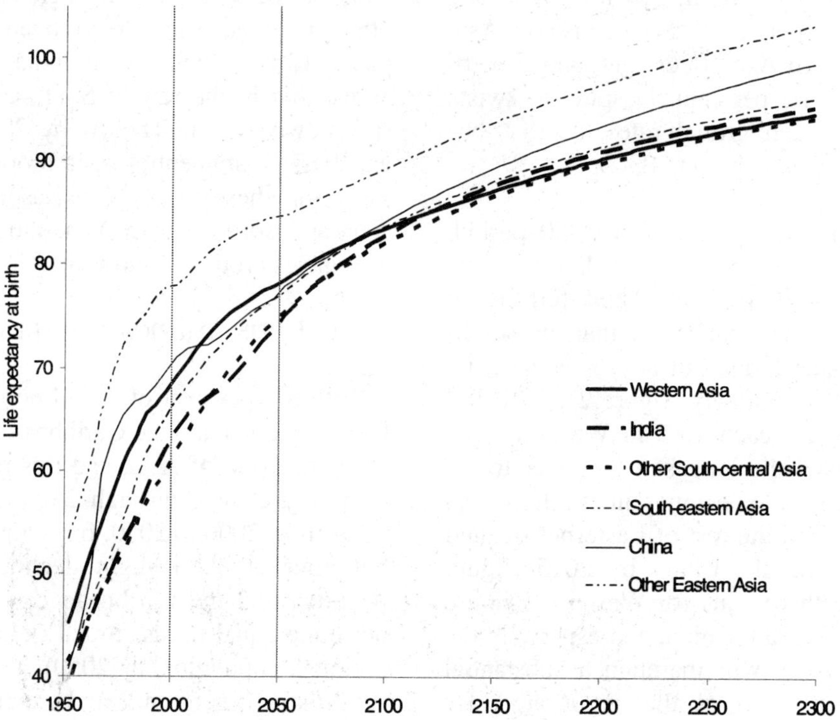

Caribbean (figure 31). This projected division of the population is projected to change little up to 2300.

Growth trends in these four regions of Latin America and the Caribbean are similar. In 1995-2000, the growth rate varies from 1.0 per cent in the Caribbean to 1.7 per cent in South America outside Brazil. By 2045-2050, the range has narrowed from -0.1 in the Caribbean to 0.3 in South America outside Brazil. By 2095-2100, growth rates will be essentially identical across these regions at -0.22 to -0.26.

The slightly slower growth in the Caribbean is of interest because it is not tied to particularly low fertility. Total fertility is lower in Brazil than the Caribbean in 1995-2000 and stays below in the projections through 2050. Instead, in the Caribbean, life expectancy trends show an unusual pattern for the region. Life expectancy at birth is assumed to have been essentially constant in the 1990s, and then improves more slowly than in surrounding regions for around 20 years (figure 32). The pattern is similar to the trends projected for some African regions, though more moderate, and similarly reflects the effects of the HIV/AIDS epidemic. With this shortfall in life expectancy gains, life expectancy at birth in the Caribbean is projected to be, by 2300, 1.3 to 2.0 years below that of other regions of Latin America.

H. OCEANIA

Oceania is by far the smallest of the major areas, with less than 1 per cent of the population of Asia. Although it is often divided into four regions, it contains only three countries of more than one million people: Australia, with 19.2 million in 2000, New Zealand, with 3.8 million, and Papua New Guinea with 5.3 million. The remaining countries combined, which make up the rest of Melanesia as well as Micronesia and Polynesia, total only 2.8 million.

Australia is projected to grow to 25.6 million in 2050, then enter a period of decline and eventually grow much more slowly, to 27.7 million by 2300. Similarly, New Zealand is expected to reach 4.5 million in 2050 and 4.7 million in 2300. Papua New Guinea, on the other hand, is expected

Figure 31. Total population, Latin American and Caribbean regions: 1950-2300

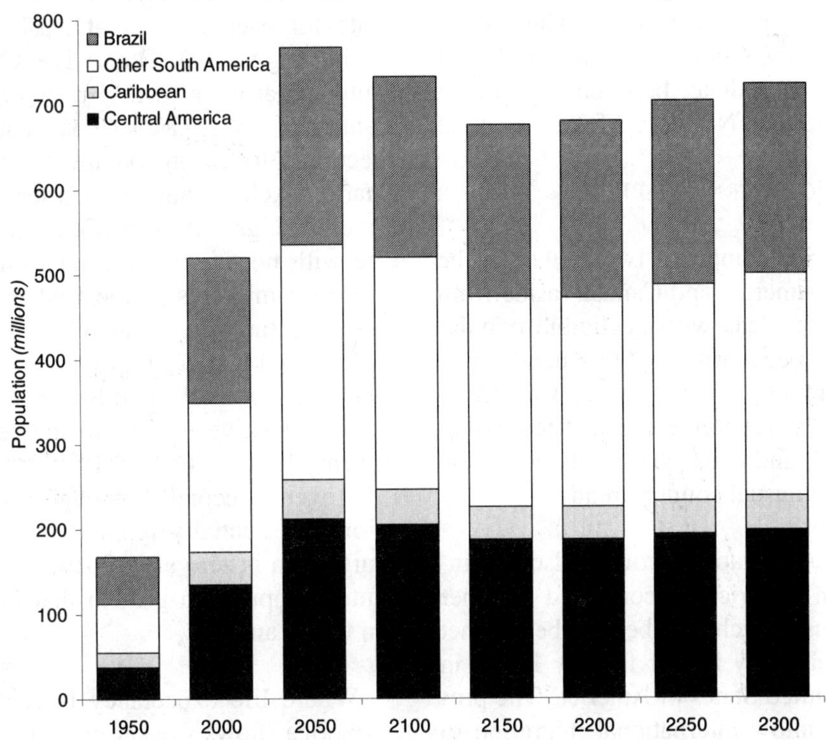

Figure 32. Life expectancy at birth, Latin America and the Caribbean: 1950-2300

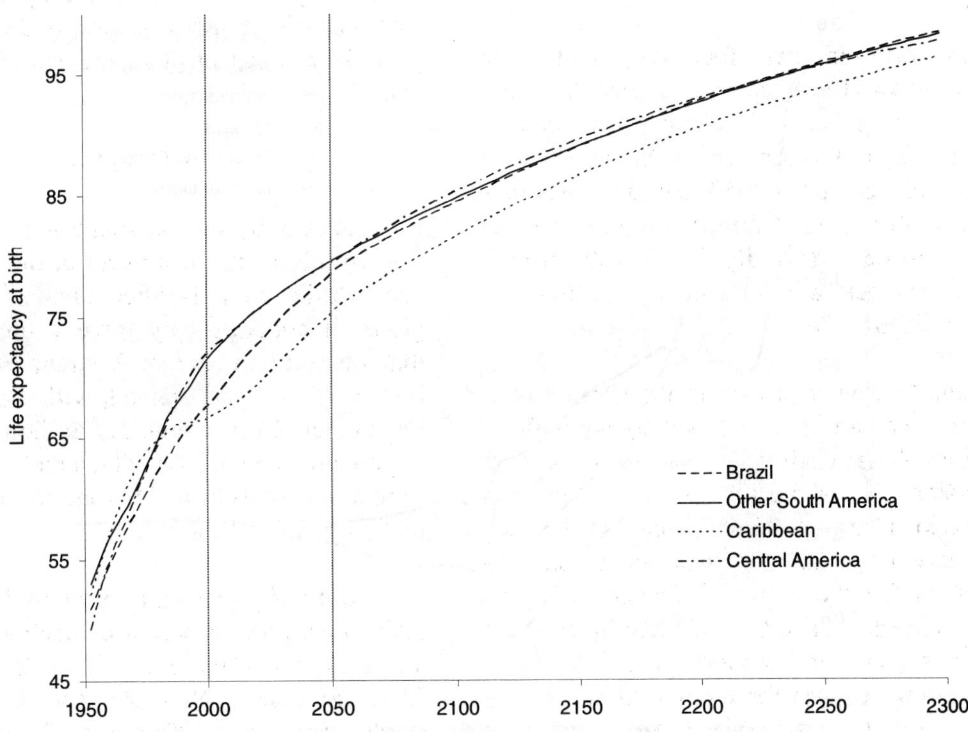

to grow much more rapidly, more than doubling in 50 years to 11.1 million by 2050, but will only be at 11.3 million in 2300. The growth pattern in Papua New Guinea is similar to that of Africa, being intermediate between patterns of sub-Saharan Africa and Northern Africa.

I. Northern America

Northern America comprises two countries, the United States of America and Canada (aside from island countries or areas with negligible population). One of the peculiarities of this major area, that is having trends that are not as smooth as elsewhere, is partly due to the fact that few countries are included, and consequently there is little averaging across unusual country trends.

The absence of negative growth also distinguishes Northern America as compared to other developed regions, which can be ascribed to net migration and relatively higher fertility levels in the case of the United States of America. The projections to 2050 allow international migration to continue largely at current levels. Relative to the alternative of no migration, this raises the growth rate for each country at least half a percentage point (figure 33). Otherwise, Canada would slip into negative growth by 2015 and the United States of America by 2035. The long-range projections, following on the 50-year medium scenario, exclude migration after 2050. Once it is excluded, growth does not revert to what it would be with no migration at all from 2000, however, because migrants in the first half of the twenty-first century are relatively young and help to maintain a higher growth rate. Nevertheless, Canada, but not the United States of America, experiences negative growth in the second half of the twenty-first century and into the first decade of the twenty-second. Although international migration is essentially ignored by assuming that net migration is zero after 2050, it does play a role in future population growth that is worth exploring in future analysis.

Where life expectancy is concerned, Northern America shows weaker gains up to 2050 than any

Figure 33. Average annual rate of population change, with and without migration, Northern America: 1950-2175

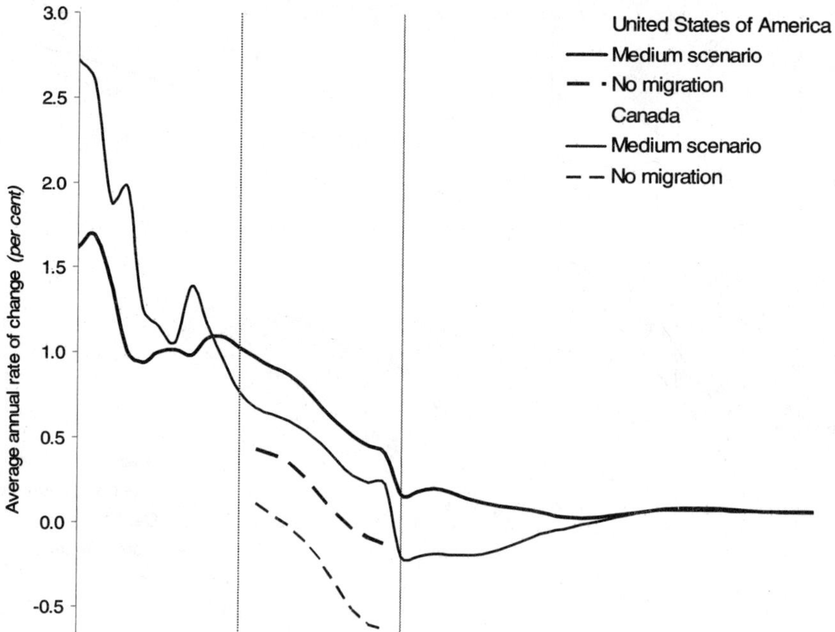

other major area (discounting the relatively short-run impact of HIV/AIDS in Africa) and, in the long run, falls behind Europe. In the United States of America, gains are relatively slow in 2000-2050 (figure 34). Projecting these trends forward gives a pattern of gains that shrink somewhat more rapidly in the United States of America than in other comparable countries. The long-range projections therefore essentially work out implications of the 50-year projections, which in turn are based on historical fluctuations in life expectancy that vary across countries.

J. EUROPE

Europe is at the opposite end of the demographic spectrum from Africa, with not just slow projected growth but actual decline. Europe may be divided into quadrants, in order of decreasing population (figure 35): Eastern and Western, Southern and Northern. Eastern Europe (including Russia) has 42 per cent of the population, as opposed to 25 per cent in Western Europe, but by 2100, and in the long run, they will be about equal with almost a third of the population. Southern Europe has 20 per cent of the population, as opposed to 13 per cent in Northern Europe. By 2100, and in the long run, these two regions too will be equal, at 18 per cent of the population.

This equality between pairs of regions will be achieved because Europe, like Asia, shows a demographic divide between east and west, and a lesser divide between south and north. Population growth in Eastern Europe is now negative, and Southern Europe is projected to join it with zero growth around 2005. Western and Northern Europe, in contrast, are expected to maintain positive growth until around 2025 and 2040, respectively (figure 36). Declines in growth not only come earlier but are also much sharper in Eastern and Southern Europe than in Western and Northern Europe. Were international migration eliminated, zero growth in Western and Northern Europe would come instead much earlier, around 2005. With no migration, the growth trajectories for Western, Northern, and Southern Europe would still be roughly similar but would be pegged at a lower level, but the growth trajectory for Eastern Europe would be little changed. Looking beyond 2050, one sees each region return gradually to zero or slightly positive growth.

Figure 34. Life expectancy at birth, United States of America compared to Japan and Western Europe: 1950-2300

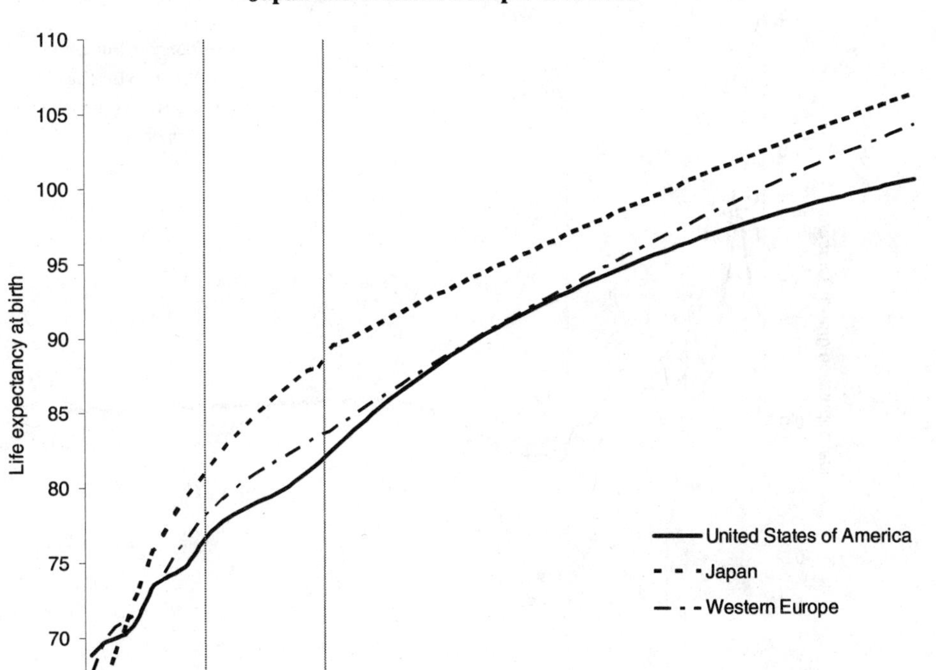

Figure 35. Total population, European regions: 1950-2300

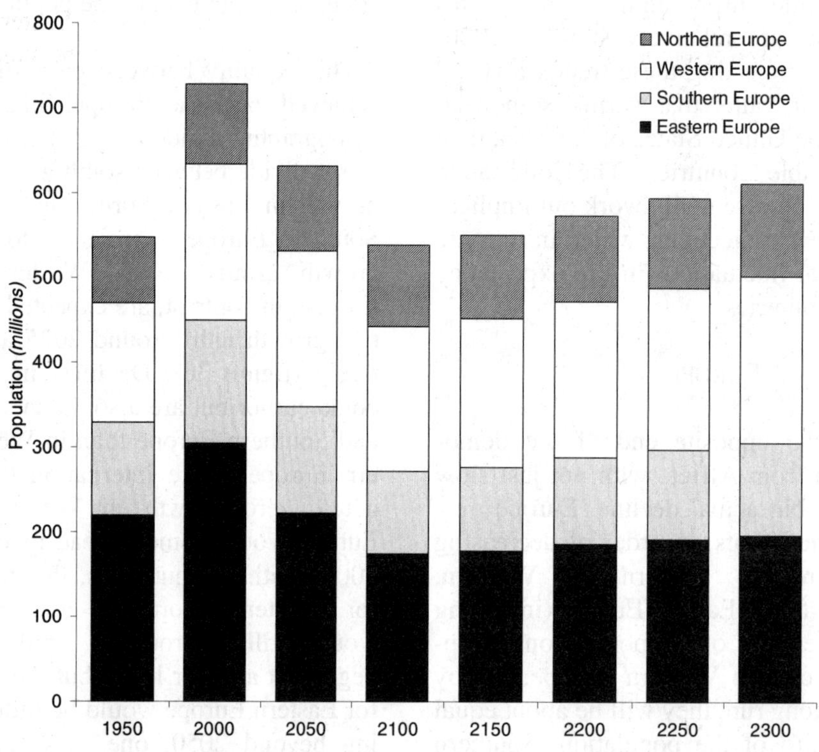

Figure 36. Average annual rate of population change, European regions: 1950-2300

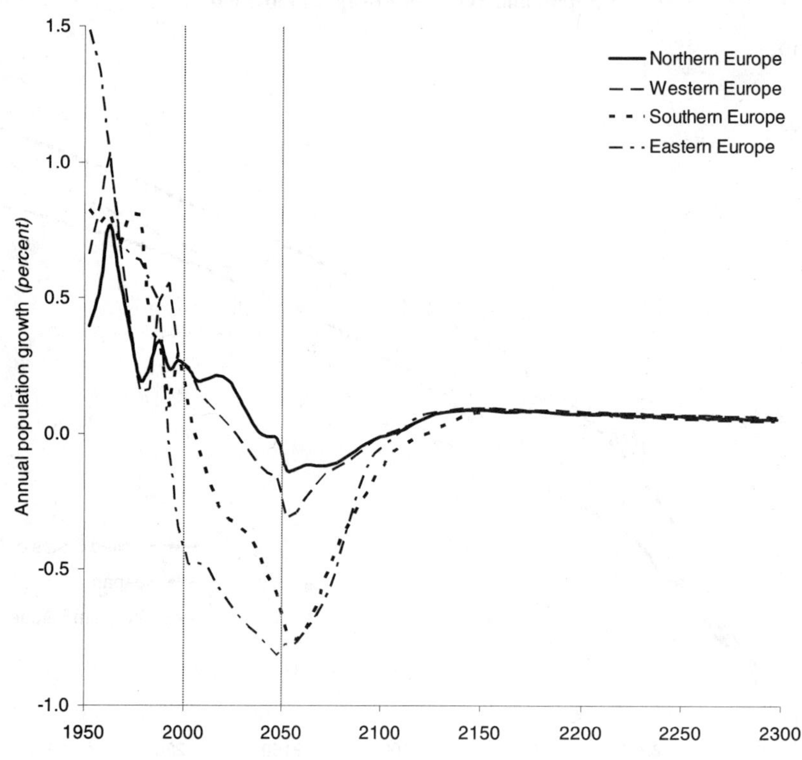

The United Kingdom dominates Northern Europe demographically, with 64 per cent of regional population. Its growth trajectory is about 0.1 points higher than that for Northern Europe as a whole. The region also includes three small Baltic countries with economies in transition: Estonia, Latvia, and Lithuania. Their growth trajectories are radically different, being even more negative than that for Eastern Europe. The remaining European countries with economies in transition are all in Eastern Europe, except for Albania and the successor states to Yugoslavia, which are in Southern Europe. However, growth in Albania and the former Yugoslav republics is not that different from, and actually slightly higher than, growth in Southern Europe as a whole. Southern Europe is dominated by Italy and Spain, whose projected slow growth is reflected in the regional trajectory.

Mortality trends are smooth and roughly similar across European regions (figure 37). Eastern Europe, however, starts with life expectancy at birth almost 10 years lower than the other regions—roughly comparable to the level of China—and will narrow the gap only slightly by 2050—progressing no faster than China. Beyond 2050, some slight divergence emerges, so that, by 2300, life expectancy in Eastern Europe will be about seven years shy of the standard of 104 years to be set by Western Europe.

Projected fertility trends are consistent with the growth trends. Some initial fertility decline further below replacement is expected in this decade, except in Western Europe, where fertility is believed to have hit bottom in the early 1990s and has risen slightly since then (figure 38). Each region is then assumed to reach total fertility of 1.85 by 2045-2050, with Northern and Western Europe progressing along a higher trajectory than Southern and Eastern Europe. Within the following quarter century, fertility is then expected to rise further to replacement level, with Southern Europe lagging behind the other regions.

Long-range fertility in Europe, unlike in most other cases, is expected to be clearly above current fertility. Is it reasonable to expect fertility to rise from current levels? It is impossible to tell, but

Figure 37. Total fertility, European regions: 1950-2175

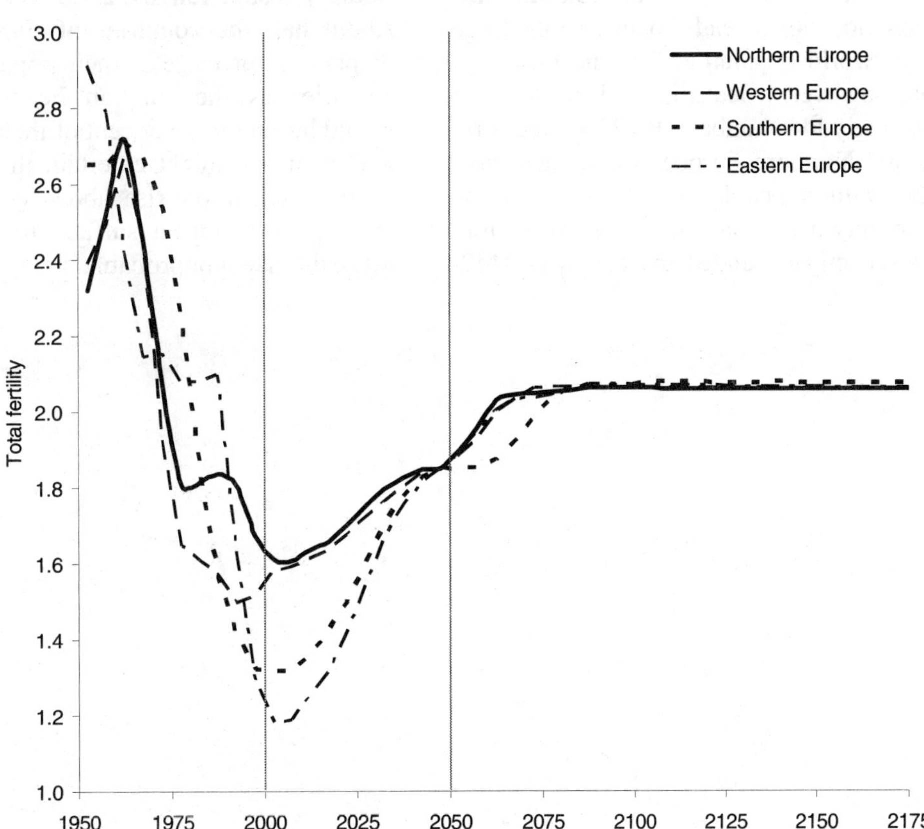

Figure 38. Life expectancy at birth, European regions: 1950-2300

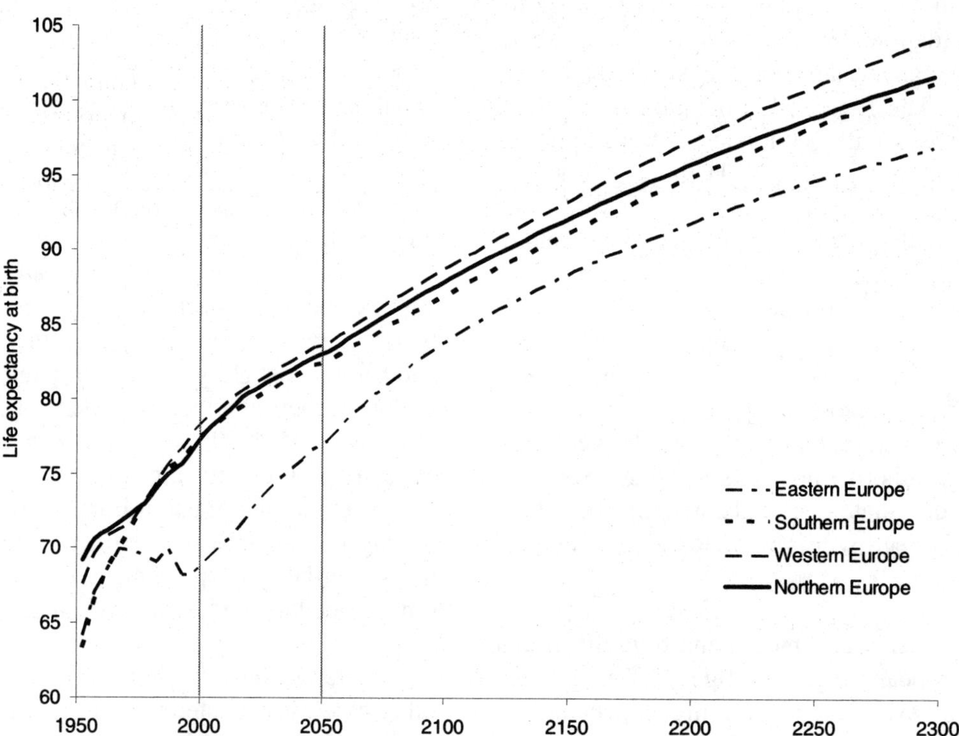

one can consider the implications if it does not. Fertility stays at current levels in the constant projection scenario, which leads to incredibly large numbers for world population. For the European population, however, it leads instead, in the long run, to startlingly low numbers. By 2300, Western, Southern, and Northern Europe would each have only 28-30 million people, and Eastern Europe would have only 5 million. The European Union, which has recently expanded to encompass 452-455 million people (according to 2000 or 2005 figures) would fall by 2300 to only 59 million. About half the countries of Europe would lose 95 per cent or more of their population, and such countries as the Russian Federation and Italy would have only 1 per cent of their population left. Although one might entertain the possibility that fertility will never rise above current levels, the consequences appear sufficiently grotesque as to make this seem improbable.

III. COUNTRY RANKINGS

In looking at regions, a few countries have been touched on, particularly large ones. One can look more systematically at the largest countries, as well as countries that stand out in other respects. This provides an alternative perspective on the projections that illuminates important aspects of long-range possibilities.

A. Size

The six largest countries in 2000, in order, are China, India, the United States of America, Indonesia, Brazil, and the Russian Federation (table 5). Together they cover 51 per cent of world population. By 2050, the six largest will be India, China, the United States of America, Pakistan, Indonesia, and Nigeria. Looking back to 1950, one sees that China, India, the United States of America, and Indonesia have been fixtures among the top six, but the other two have changed and will change. Occupying the other two slots are the Russian Federation and Japan for 1950, Brazil and the Russian Federation for 2000, and Pakistan and Nigeria for 2050.

Similar changes can be observed while looking instead at the ten largest countries. Between 1950 and 2000, Germany, the United Kingdom, and Italy fell out of the top ten, and between 2000 and 2050, the Russian Federation and Japan will fall out. Between 1950 and 2000, Pakistan, Nigeria, and Bangladesh were added to the top ten, and between 2000 and 2050, Ethiopia and the Democratic Republic of the Congo will be added. Countries in more developed regions are being replaced among the largest by countries in less developed regions, especially from Asia, in the recent past, and from Africa, in the next 50 years. This is of course consistent with what one sees in comparing regional growth rates.

Beyond 2050, the countries in the top six will not change, though among them, Nigeria will edge past Indonesia in size. Similarly, the countries in the top ten will be the same in 2100 (and, in the long run in 2300) as in 2050, though Ethiopia and Brazil will change places. Only a few more changes will take place among the top 20 countries, though two are worth noting. The Russian Federation, the last European country among the 20 largest countries by 2050, drops out by 2100 (though it does return as twentieth by 2300, as other countries shrink in population). Egypt is the second largest African country in 2000 (after Nigeria). It will stay among the top 20 worldwide up to 2300, but by 2050 will be passed by Ethiopia and the Democratic Republic of Congo, and by 2100 will also be passed by Uganda and Yemen.

Focusing on the largest countries should not obscure the fact that they carry somewhat less demographic weight over time. As a percentage of world population, the ten largest countries are 62 per cent in 1950, 60 per cent in 2000, 57 per cent in 2050, and 55 per cent in 2100 and 2300. Smaller countries are projected to slowly gain on the larger ones, slightly increasing demographic multipolarity in the world.

B. Growth

Smaller countries have only a slight tendency to grow faster than larger ones. Of the ten countries that grew fastest from 1950 to 2000 (table 6), eight had populations smaller than three million by 2000. However, a more relevant characteristic of this group is that five of the ten are in the region of the Western Asia: the United Arab Emirates, Qatar, Kuwait, Saudi Arabia, and Bahrain (Oman ranks eleventh) All these countries grew at least 3.5 per cent a year over the 50-year period. High fertility was less a factor, in these cases, then immigration.

For 2000-2050, the fastest growing countries are instead projected to be mainly in sub-Saharan Africa and mostly of moderate size, including Niger, Somalia, and Uganda. One Western Asian country—not a main migrant destination—is still near the top of the list, namely Yemen. Growth will also be relatively slower, with no country reaching the level of 3.5 per cent annual growth. For 2050-2100, the list of fastest growing countries is quite similar to that for the previous period, and growth

TABLE 5. TWENTY LARGEST COUNTRIES AND THEIR POPULATIONS, SELECTED YEARS
(millions)

Rank	*1950*		*2000*		*2050*	
1	China	554.8	China	1 275.2	India	1 531.4
2	India	357.6	India	1 016.9	China	1 395.2
3	U.S.A.	157.8	U.S.A.	285.0	U.S.A.	408.7
4	Russian Federation	102.7	Indonesia	211.6	Pakistan	348.7
5	Japan	83.6	Brazil	171.8	Indonesia	293.8
6	Indonesia	79.5	Russian Federation	145.6	Nigeria	258.5
7	Germany	68.4	Pakistan	142.7	Bangladesh	254.6
8	Brazil	54.0	Bangladesh	138.0	Brazil	233.1
9	United Kingdom	49.8	Japan	127.0	Ethiopia	171.0
10	Italy	47.1	Nigeria	114.7	Congo, DR	151.6
11	France	41.8	Mexico	98.9	Mexico	140.2
12	Bangladesh	41.8	Germany	82.3	Egypt	127.4
13	Pakistan	39.7	Viet Nam	78.1	Philippines	127.0
14	Ukraine	37.3	Philippines	75.7	Viet Nam	117.7
15	Nigeria	29.8	Turkey	68.3	Japan	109.7
16	Spain	28.0	Egypt	67.8	Iran	105.5
17	Mexico	27.7	Iran	66.4	Uganda	103.2
18	Viet Nam	27.4	Ethiopia	65.6	Russian Federation	101.5
19	Poland	24.8	Thailand	60.9	Turkey	97.8
20	Egypt	21.8	France	59.3	Yemen	84.4

Rank	*2100*		*2200*		*2300*	
1	India	1 458.4	India	1 304.5	India	1 371.7
2	China	1 181.5	China	1 200.7	China	1 285.2
3	U.S.A.	437.2	U.S.A.	470.0	U.S.A.	493.0
4	Pakistan	408.5	Pakistan	342.5	Pakistan	359.1
5	Nigeria	302.5	Nigeria	268.4	Nigeria	282.8
6	Indonesia	272.8	Indonesia	263.0	Indonesia	276.2
7	Bangladesh	259.9	Bangladesh	232.4	Bangladesh	242.7
8	Ethiopia	222.2	Brazil	208.8	Brazil	222.6
9	Brazil	212.4	Ethiopia	196.6	Ethiopia	206.5
10	Congo, DR	203.3	Congo, DR	173.0	Congo, DR	182.7
11	Uganda	167.1	Uganda	149.0	Uganda	154.5
12	Yemen	144.2	Yemen	126.6	Yemen	129.9
13	Egypt	131.8	Mexico	120.6	Mexico	126.9
14	Philippines	128.8	Philippines	118.5	Philippines	125.4
15	Mexico	128.1	Egypt	117.9	Egypt	124.7
16	Viet Nam	110.2	Viet Nam	107.5	Viet Nam	113.6
17	Niger	98.6	Iran	94.9	Iran	100.7
18	Iran	98.2	Japan	94.5	Japan	100.6
19	Turkey	90.3	Niger	90.8	Niger	93.8
20	Afghanistan	90.3	Turkey	87.5	Russian Federation	91.6

TABLE 6. COUNTRIES WITH THE HIGHEST AND LOWEST AVERAGE ANNUAL RATE OF CHANGE OVER 50-YEAR PERIODS
(per cent)

Rank	*1950-2000*		*2000-2050*		*2050-2100*	
			A. Highest rate			
1	United Arab Emirates	7.40	Niger	3.19	Niger	1.24
2	Qatar	6.29	Yemen	3.09	Yemen	1.07
3	Western Sahara	6.06	Somalia	3.03	Somalia	1.02
4	Kuwait	5.38	Uganda	2.96	Uganda	0.96
5	Djibouti	4.75	Mali	2.70	Burkina Faso	0.86
6	Jordan	4.73	Burkina Faso	2.54	Mali	0.85
7	Brunei Darussalam	3.88	Occ. Palestinian Terr.	2.50	Guinea-Bissau	0.78
8	Saudi Arabia	3.87	Angola	2.50	Angola	0.76
9	French Guiana	3.73	Guinea-Bissau	2.48	Burundi	0.70
10	Bahrain	3.54	Liberia	2.41	Liberia	0.64
			B. Lowest rate			
183	Latvia	0.39	Belarus	-0.57	Republic of Moldova	-0.52
184	Germany	0.37	Armenia	-0.58	Bosnia/Herzegovina	-0.53
185	Portugal	0.35	Lithuania	-0.65	Greece	-0.53
186	Belgium	0.34	Russian Federation	-0.72	Belarus	-0.54
187	United Kingdom	0.33	Guyana	-0.81	Ukraine	-0.55
188	Austria	0.31	Georgia	-0.83	Bulgaria	-0.56
189	Croatia	0.29	Bulgaria	-0.87	Italy	-0.57
190	Czech Republic	0.28	Ukraine	-0.90	Slovenia	-0.61
191	Bulgaria	0.22	Latvia	-1.16	Guyana	-0.69
192	Hungary	0.13	Estonia	-1.46	Armenia	-0.73

rates will be much lower across the board. Beyond 2100, growth rates are quite small, and slight differences in the timing of demographic change essentially determine the rankings.

At the opposite end, among the slowest-growing out of the 192 countries, are various Eastern European countries. In 1950-2000, Hungary, Bulgaria, and the Czech Republic have the slowest growth, though still positive for the whole 50-year period. In 2000-2050, the Baltic states of Estonia and Latvia lead the list, followed by Ukraine, Bulgaria and the Russian Federation, among others, whom are expected to experience negative growth. Altogether, 43 countries out of 192 are projected to have negative growth. In 2050-2100, negative growth should be even more common, affecting 58 per cent of countries, though the largest declines will not be as deep as previously. The slowest growing countries are a mixed group in this period, still including Eastern European countries but also such countries as Guyana and Italy.

Differences in growth rates such as those shown in table 6 can have quite substantial effects. This is illustrated in figure 39 for some of the large countries included in the table. The Russian Federation in 2000 has more than six times the population of Uganda, but by 2050 their populations will be equal. By 2100, the population of Uganda will be twice that of Russia, which will also be smaller than the populations of Yemen and Niger. Interestingly, the range between high and low scenarios for these countries is proportionally smaller than for many other countries, so that the high projection for the Russian Federation for 2100 does not quite reach the low projection for Uganda.

The largest increments to world population come from countries that are both large and relatively fast growing. For 1950-2000, the list of ten countries with the largest increases in population is almost identical to the list of countries that ended up as the largest in 2000. The exceptions were the Russian Federation and Japan, which had

Figure 39. Population trends in selected high-growth and low-growth countries: 1950-2300

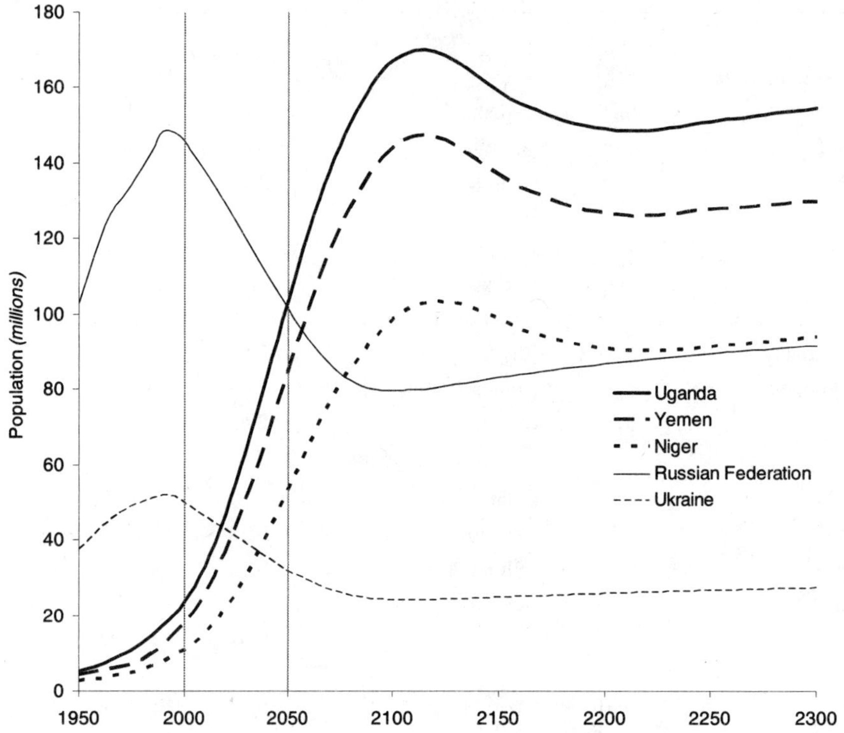

smaller increments than Mexico and the Philippines (table 7). Six countries grew by at least 100 million in 1950-2000, and the ten top countries accounted for 61 per cent of all people added to world population.

In 2000-2050, fewer people will be added to world population: 2.85 billion, as opposed to 3.55 billion in 1950-2000. Eight countries are projected to grow by 100 million or more, the list overlapping substantially with that from the previous period.

For 2050-2100, however, the picture will be substantially different. The increment to world population will be down to 145 million. Countries that add population will add a total of 682 million, but other countries will lose population, the total lost being 537 million. No country will grow by more than 64 million, and only five (as contrasted with 14 in the previous period) will grow by more than 50 million. The top ten list will be led by Uganda, Pakistan, and Yemen. China and India will not be on this list, and in fact will lead the opposite list of those losing population: 214 million lost for China, 73 million lost for India. This list of countries, which will also include Russia, Indonesia, Brazil, Japan, and Mexico, is strikingly similar to the list of the largest countries in the twentieth century.

For a particular country, substantial demographic change, or rapid change, may require significant adjustments, economically, socially, environmentally, and politically. Some indicators of the demographic challenges that countries will need to manage are provided in tables 8 and 9. For the magnitude of potential demographic change, minimum and maximum populations for each country are shown over the period 2000-2300, as well as populations in 2100 (which are generally close to the maximum, for growing countries, although a few pass the 2100 level and are still growing by 2300). Percentage increases from 2000 to 2100 reach 818 per cent for Niger, 700 per cent for Yemen, 658 per cent for Somalia, and 611 per cent for Uganda. Clearly, these countries will look very different if these projections hold. At the other extreme, the population of Estonia, by 2100, will be cut by 62 per cent, of Latvia by 57 per

TABLE 7. COUNTRIES WITH THE LARGEST INCREASES AND DECREASES OVER 50-YEAR PERIODS
(millions)

Rank	*1950-2000*		*2000-2050*		*2050-2100*	
			A. Largest increase			
1	China	720.5	India	514.5	Uganda	63.9
2	India	659.4	Pakistan	206.0	Pakistan	59.8
3	Indonesia	132.0	Nigeria	143.7	Yemen	59.8
4	U.S.A.	127.2	U.S.A.	123.7	Congo, DR	51.7
5	Brazil	117.8	China	120.0	Ethiopia	51.2
6	Pakistan	103.0	Bangladesh	116.6	Niger	45.6
7	Bangladesh	96.2	Ethiopia	105.4	Nigeria	44.0
8	Nigeria	85.0	Congo, DR	103.1	U.S.A.	28.5
9	Mexico	71.2	Indonesia	82.2	Somalia	26.4
10	Philippines	55.7	Uganda	79.8	Mali	24.5
			B. Largest decrease			
183	(No countries with reported decreases)		Bulgaria	-2.8	Spain	-8.2
184			Germany	-3.1	Republic of Korea	-9.2
185			Spain	-3.4	Italy	-11.1
186			South Africa	-3.8	Mexico	-12.1
187			Romania	-4.4	Japan	-19.8
188			Poland	-5.7	Brazil	-20.7
189			Italy	-12.7	Indonesia	-21.0
190			Japan	-17.3	Russian Federation	-21.9
191			Ukraine	-17.9	India	-73.1
192			Russian Federation	-44.2	China	-213.7

cent, of Guyana by 53 per cent, and of Ukraine and Bulgaria by 51 per cent each. Societal adjustments will be needed.

These changes take a century. Quicker societal adjustments are necessary when demographic change is rapid in the short-run, though such demographic changes tend to be more difficult to predict. Table 9 shows the highest and lowest growth rates expected for each country in any period between 2000 and 2300. Most of the largest positive growth rates appear in 2000-2005, while fertility is still high in various countries. The largest negative growth rates appear close to 2050 or beyond 2100, when countries enter a period of below-replacement fertility. European countries tend to show slowest growth earlier, African countries later, except for some Southern African countries where slow growth appears around 2020-2030 because of HIV/AIDS.

Rapid short-run changes are not projected for the majority of countries, but do appear for some. Annual growth in Somalia in 2000-2005, for instance, is estimated at 4.17 per cent, which means that, over five years, population increases by 23 per cent. For the same period, annual growth in Liberia and Timor-Leste is almost as fast at 4.05 and 4.00 per cent respectively. These growth rates are, understandably, higher than the highest for the entire 2000-2050 period (table 6), but they are lower than some for the entire 1950-2000 period. Each of these three countries has recently being embroiled in civil conflict, and substantial net return migration is expected. Since, the long-range projections eliminate migration, one should not expect to see any such rapid, short-run increases in projections beyond 2050.

The most negative growth rates appear in 2045-2050, for Guyana (-2.15 per cent) and Estonia

TABLE 8. POPULATION IN 2000 AND 2100, MINIMUM AND MAXIMUM SIZE UP TO 2300, AND PERCENTAGE CHANGE TO THESE POINTS FROM 2000, BY COUNTRY

	Population (millions)						*Percentage change from 2000 to*		
Country or area	*2000*	*2100*	*Minimum*	*(Year)*	*Maximum*	*(Year)*	*2100*	*Minimum*	*Maximum*
Afghanistan	21.4	90.3	21.4	(2000)	90.4	(2095)	322	0	323
Albania	3.1	3.3	3.0	(2160)	3.7	(2040)	4	-4	19
Algeria	30.2	45.6	30.2	(2000)	49.2	(2060)	51	0	63
Angola	12.4	63.0	12.4	(2000)	63.2	(2105)	409	0	410
Argentina	37.1	51.0	37.1	(2000)	53.9	(2065)	38	0	45
Armenia	3.1	1.6	1.6	(2140)	3.1	(2000)	-48	-50	0
Australia	19.2	24.6	19.2	(2000)	27.7	(2300)	28	0	45
Austria	8.1	6.2	6.2	(2110)	8.1	(2005)	-23	-24	0
Azerbaijan	8.2	10.3	8.2	(2000)	11.0	(2055)	27	0	35
Bahamas	0.3	0.4	0.3	(2000)	0.4	(2050)	20	0	30
Bahrain	0.7	1.2	0.7	(2000)	1.3	(2065)	75	0	91
Bangladesh	138.0	259.9	138.0	(2000)	270.1	(2075)	88	0	96
Barbados	0.3	0.2	0.2	(2125)	0.3	(2025)	-21	-22	6
Belarus	10.0	5.7	5.7	(2115)	10.0	(2000)	-43	-43	0
Belgium	10.3	9.5	9.5	(2105)	11.0	(2300)	-7	-7	7
Belize	0.2	0.4	0.2	(2000)	0.4	(2070)	71	0	82
Benin	6.2	18.7	6.2	(2000)	18.8	(2095)	201	0	202
Bhutan	2.1	6.4	2.1	(2000)	6.4	(2095)	211	0	211
Bolivia	8.3	16.8	8.3	(2000)	17.3	(2080)	102	0	108
Bosnia and Herzegovina	4.0	2.7	2.7	(2125)	4.3	(2015)	-31	-32	8
Botswana	1.7	1.4	1.3	(2065)	1.8	(2005)	-21	-22	4
Brazil	171.8	212.4	171.8	(2000)	233.4	(2055)	24	0	36
Brunei Darussalam	0.3	0.7	0.3	(2000)	0.7	(2075)	109	0	119
Bulgaria	8.1	4.0	3.9	(2120)	8.1	(2000)	-51	-51	0
Burkina Faso	11.9	65.2	11.9	(2000)	66.2	(2115)	447	0	456
Burundi	6.3	27.6	6.3	(2000)	27.8	(2110)	341	0	344
Cambodia	13.1	34.4	13.1	(2000)	34.5	(2090)	162	0	162
Cameroon	15.1	27.0	15.1	(2000)	27.2	(2085)	79	0	80
Canada	30.8	36.2	30.8	(2000)	40.9	(2300)	18	0	33
Cape Verde	0.4	0.8	0.4	(2000)	0.9	(2075)	91	0	98
Central African Republic	3.7	7.5	3.7	(2000)	7.5	(2095)	102	0	103
Chad	7.9	34.6	7.9	(2000)	34.6	(2105)	340	0	340
Channel Islands	0.1	0.1	0.1	(2100)	0.1	(2005)	-22	-22	0
Chile	15.2	21.4	15.2	(2000)	22.2	(2070)	40	0	46
China	1 275.2	1 181.5	1 143.8	(2135)	1 450.5	(2030)	-7	-10	14
China, Hong Kong SAR	6.8	8.1	6.8	(2000)	9.4	(2050)	19	0	39
China, Macao SAR	0.4	0.5	0.4	(2000)	0.6	(2050)	8	0	29
Colombia	42.1	67.5	42.1	(2000)	69.9	(2070)	60	0	66
Comoros	0.7	2.2	0.7	(2000)	2.2	(2095)	211	0	212
Congo	3.4	14.6	3.4	(2000)	14.6	(2105)	322	0	323
Costa Rica	3.9	6.2	3.9	(2000)	6.6	(2065)	58	0	68
Côte d'Ivoire	15.8	30.1	15.8	(2000)	30.4	(2085)	90	0	92
Croatia	4.4	3.2	3.2	(2105)	4.4	(2000)	-27	-27	0

TABLE 8 (*continued*)

Country or area	*Population (millions)* 2000	2100	Minimum	(Year)	Maximum	(Year)	*Percentage change from 2000 to* 2100	Minimum	Maximum
Cuba	11.2	8.2	8.1	(2125)	11.5	(2020)	-27	-28	3
Cyprus	0.8	0.8	0.8	(2145)	0.9	(2035)	1	-4	15
Czech Rep.	10.3	6.6	6.6	(2110)	10.3	(2000)	-35	-36	0
Dem. People's Rep. of Korea	22.3	22.5	21.9	(2135)	25.1	(2040)	1	-2	13
Dem. Rep. of the Congo	48.6	203.3	48.6	(2000)	203.3	(2100)	319	0	319
Dem. Rep. of Timor-Leste	0.7	1.5	0.7	(2000)	1.5	(2080)	108	0	113
Denmark	5.3	4.9	4.9	(2100)	5.6	(2300)	-8	-8	4
Djibouti	0.7	1.7	0.7	(2000)	1.7	(2095)	156	0	156
Dominican Republic	8.4	11.0	8.4	(2000)	12.0	(2060)	32	0	43
Ecuador	12.4	17.9	12.4	(2000)	19.1	(2065)	44	0	54
Egypt	67.8	131.8	67.8	(2000)	136.3	(2075)	94	0	101
El Salvador	6.2	9.7	6.2	(2000)	10.2	(2070)	56	0	64
Equatorial Guinea	0.5	1.5	0.5	(2000)	1.5	(2095)	220	0	221
Eritrea	3.7	12.9	3.7	(2000)	12.9	(2095)	248	0	248
Estonia	1.4	0.5	0.5	(2090)	1.4	(2000)	-62	-62	0
Ethiopia	65.6	222.2	65.6	(2000)	222.3	(2105)	239	0	239
Fiji	0.8	0.9	0.8	(2180)	1.0	(2040)	9	-5	22
Finland	5.2	4.6	4.6	(2100)	5.3	(2300)	-11	-11	3
France	59.3	60.2	59.3	(2000)	68.5	(2300)	1	0	16
French Guiana	0.2	0.4	0.2	(2000)	0.4	(2075)	121	0	130
French Polynesia	0.2	0.3	0.2	(2000)	0.4	(2065)	45	0	54
Gabon	1.3	2.7	1.3	(2000)	2.8	(2085)	118	0	121
Gambia	1.3	3.3	1.3	(2000)	3.3	(2090)	153	0	155
Georgia	5.3	2.7	2.6	(2135)	5.3	(2000)	-49	-50	0
Germany	82.3	73.1	73.0	(2095)	85.3	(2300)	-11	-11	4
Ghana	19.6	43.9	19.6	(2000)	44.2	(2090)	124	0	126
Greece	10.9	7.5	7.4	(2125)	11.0	(2010)	-31	-32	1
Guadeloupe	0.4	0.4	0.4	(2135)	0.5	(2035)	-5	-6	14
Guam	0.2	0.2	0.2	(2000)	0.3	(2075)	60	0	67
Guatemala	11.4	29.4	11.4	(2000)	29.9	(2085)	157	0	162
Guinea	8.1	23.8	8.1	(2000)	23.8	(2095)	193	0	194
Guinea-Bissau	1.4	7.0	1.4	(2000)	7.0	(2110)	410	0	413
Guyana	0.8	0.4	0.3	(2160)	0.8	(2010)	-53	-56	1
Haiti	8.0	12.7	8.0	(2000)	13.3	(2075)	59	0	66
Honduras	6.5	13.3	6.5	(2000)	13.7	(2080)	105	0	112
Hungary	10.0	6.2	6.2	(2100)	10.0	(2000)	-38	-38	0
Iceland	0.3	0.3	0.3	(2000)	0.3	(2040)	6	0	18
India	1 016.9	1 458.4	1 016.9	(2000)	1 557.3	(2065)	43	0	53
Indonesia	211.6	272.8	211.6	(2000)	294.9	(2055)	29	0	39
Iran, Islamic Rep. of	66.4	98.2	66.4	(2000)	106.9	(2060)	48	0	61
Iraq	23.2	68.0	23.2	(2000)	68.4	(2090)	193	0	194
Ireland	3.8	4.5	3.8	(2000)	5.0	(2050)	18	0	31
Israel	6.0	9.8	6.0	(2000)	10.3	(2070)	63	0	70
Italy	57.5	33.8	33.5	(2120)	57.5	(2000)	-41	-42	0
Jamaica	2.6	3.5	2.6	(2000)	3.7	(2060)	34	0	44
Japan	127.0	89.9	89.2	(2115)	128.0	(2010)	-29	-30	1

TABLE 8 (*continued*)

Country or area	Population (millions)						Percentage change from 2000 to		
	2000	2100	Minimum	(Year)	Maximum	(Year)	2100	Minimum	Maximum
Jordan	5.0	10.7	5.0	(2000)	10.9	(2080)	112	0	117
Kazakhstan	15.6	11.7	11.1	(2145)	15.6	(2000)	-25	-29	0
Kenya	30.5	45.8	30.5	(2000)	46.9	(2300)	50	0	53
Kuwait	2.2	4.6	2.2	(2000)	4.9	(2055)	103	0	120
Kyrgyzstan	4.9	6.8	4.9	(2000)	7.3	(2060)	37	0	49
Lao People's Dem. Republic	5.3	12.8	5.3	(2000)	12.9	(2085)	142	0	145
Latvia	2.4	1.0	1.0	(2095)	2.4	(2000)	-57	-57	0
Lebanon	3.5	4.5	3.5	(2000)	5.0	(2055)	30	0	42
Lesotho	1.8	1.6	1.4	(2055)	1.8	(2005)	-8	-23	1
Liberia	2.9	13.5	2.9	(2000)	13.5	(2100)	359	0	359
Libyan Arab Jamahiriya	5.2	9.0	5.2	(2000)	9.5	(2065)	71	0	80
Lithuania	3.5	2.4	2.3	(2085)	3.5	(2000)	-32	-33	0
Luxembourg	0.4	0.7	0.4	(2000)	0.8	(2300)	63	0	89
Madagascar	16.0	61.6	16.0	(2000)	61.7	(2105)	286	0	286
Malawi	11.4	32.8	11.4	(2000)	32.8	(2100)	188	0	188
Malaysia	23.0	39.6	23.0	(2000)	41.2	(2070)	72	0	79
Maldives	0.3	1.0	0.3	(2000)	1.0	(2095)	247	0	248
Mali	11.9	70.5	11.9	(2000)	70.8	(2110)	492	0	495
Malta	0.4	0.4	0.4	(2100)	0.4	(2300)	-3	-3	12
Martinique	0.4	0.4	0.4	(2135)	0.4	(2030)	-3	-4	11
Mauritania	2.6	9.8	2.6	(2000)	9.8	(2100)	269	0	269
Mauritius	1.2	1.3	1.2	(2000)	1.5	(2045)	13	0	24
Mexico	98.9	128.1	98.9	(2000)	140.9	(2055)	29	0	42
Micronesia, Fed. States of	0.1	0.2	0.1	(2000)	0.2	(2085)	62	0	64
Mongolia	2.5	3.4	2.5	(2000)	3.8	(2055)	37	0	52
Morocco	29.1	46.5	29.1	(2000)	48.4	(2070)	60	0	66
Mozambique	17.9	34.4	17.9	(2000)	34.7	(2090)	93	0	94
Myanmar	47.5	60.0	47.5	(2000)	64.7	(2055)	26	0	36
Namibia	1.9	2.9	1.9	(2000)	3.0	(2300)	53	0	56
Nepal	23.5	58.3	23.5	(2000)	58.7	(2090)	148	0	150
Netherlands	15.9	15.9	15.9	(2000)	18.2	(2300)	0	0	14
Netherlands Antilles	0.2	0.2	0.2	(2000)	0.3	(2035)	5	0	18
New Caledonia	0.2	0.4	0.2	(2000)	0.4	(2065)	69	0	80
New Zealand	3.8	4.2	3.8	(2000)	4.7	(2300)	12	0	25
Nicaragua	5.1	12.1	5.1	(2000)	12.2	(2085)	138	0	141
Niger	10.7	98.6	10.7	(2000)	103.2	(2120)	818	0	861
Nigeria	114.7	302.5	114.7	(2000)	302.9	(2095)	164	0	164
Norway	4.5	4.5	4.5	(2000)	5.1	(2300)	1	0	14
Occupied Palestinian Territory	3.2	14.9	3.2	(2000)	14.9	(2105)	368	0	368
Oman	2.6	8.2	2.6	(2000)	8.2	(2095)	214	0	215
Pakistan	142.7	408.5	142.7	(2000)	412.0	(2090)	186	0	189
Panama	2.9	5.1	2.9	(2000)	5.3	(2075)	74	0	81
Papua New Guinea	5.3	12.4	5.3	(2000)	12.5	(2085)	133	0	135
Paraguay	5.5	13.6	5.5	(2000)	13.8	(2085)	148	0	151
Peru	26.0	39.8	26.0	(2000)	42.2	(2065)	53	0	63
Philippines	75.7	128.8	75.7	(2000)	133.4	(2075)	70	0	76

TABLE 8 (*continued*)

Country or area	Population (millions)						Percentage change from 2000 to		
	2000	2100	Minimum	(Year)	Maximum	(Year)	2100	Minimum	Maximum
Poland	38.7	26.1	25.6	(2135)	38.7	(2000)	-33	-34	0
Portugal	10.0	7.3	7.3	(2120)	10.1	(2010)	-27	-27	1
Puerto Rico	3.8	3.1	3.0	(2145)	4.1	(2025)	-19	-21	7
Qatar	0.6	0.8	0.6	(2000)	0.9	(2075)	46	0	53
Republic of Korea	46.8	37.3	36.9	(2115)	50.2	(2025)	-20	-21	7
Republic of Moldova	4.3	2.8	2.6	(2140)	4.3	(2000)	-36	-38	0
Réunion	0.7	1.0	0.7	(2000)	1.0	(2060)	35	0	41
Romania	22.5	14.8	14.8	(2105)	22.5	(2000)	-34	-34	0
Russian Federation	145.6	79.5	79.5	(2100)	145.6	(2000)	-45	-45	0
Rwanda	7.7	20.6	7.7	(2000)	20.6	(2100)	166	0	166
St. Lucia	0.1	0.1	0.1	(2160)	0.2	(2035)	3	-5	16
St. Vincent and Grenadines	0.1	0.1	0.1	(2145)	0.1	(2035)	-3	-6	12
Samoa	0.2	0.3	0.2	(2000)	0.3	(2095)	71	0	71
Sao Tome and Principe	0.1	0.4	0.1	(2000)	0.4	(2090)	172	0	173
Saudi Arabia	22.1	61.3	22.1	(2000)	62.4	(2085)	177	0	182
Senegal	9.4	25.3	9.4	(2000)	25.4	(2090)	169	0	170
Serbia and Montenegro	10.6	7.8	7.6	(2135)	10.6	(2000)	-26	-28	0
Sierra Leone	4.4	11.0	4.4	(2000)	11.5	(2080)	150	0	161
Singapore	4.0	3.6	3.6	(2120)	4.9	(2030)	-11	-11	23
Slovakia	5.4	4.0	3.9	(2135)	5.4	(2015)	-26	-27	1
Slovenia	2.0	1.2	1.1	(2125)	2.0	(2000)	-42	-42	0
Solomon Islands	0.4	1.2	0.4	(2000)	1.2	(2085)	172	0	178
Somalia	8.7	66.1	8.7	(2000)	67.7	(2115)	658	0	676
South Africa	44.0	38.3	37.8	(2130)	45.3	(2005)	-13	-14	3
Spain	40.8	29.1	28.8	(2120)	41.3	(2010)	-29	-29	1
Sri Lanka	18.6	18.7	18.1	(2140)	21.7	(2035)	1	-3	17
Sudan	31.4	65.2	31.4	(2000)	66.1	(2085)	107	0	110
Suriname	0.4	0.4	0.4	(2170)	0.5	(2030)	1	-7	15
Swaziland	1.0	0.9	0.9	(2135)	1.1	(2005)	-9	-12	4
Sweden	8.9	8.1	8.1	(2105)	9.4	(2300)	-8	-8	6
Switzerland	7.2	4.8	4.8	(2110)	7.2	(2000)	-33	-33	0
Syrian Arab Republic	16.6	35.0	16.6	(2000)	36.3	(2075)	111	0	119
Tajikistan	6.1	8.9	6.1	(2000)	9.7	(2065)	47	0	60
TFYR Macedonia	2.0	1.9	1.8	(2140)	2.2	(2035)	-6	-9	9
Thailand	60.9	70.4	60.9	(2000)	77.3	(2045)	15	0	27
Togo	4.6	11.5	4.6	(2000)	11.5	(2095)	152	0	153
Tonga	0.1	0.1	0.1	(2000)	0.1	(2070)	22	0	26
Trinidad and Tobago	1.3	1.1	1.0	(2135)	1.3	(2020)	-18	-20	4
Tunisia	9.5	11.4	9.5	(2000)	12.9	(2050)	20	0	35
Turkey	68.3	90.3	68.3	(2000)	98.1	(2055)	32	0	44
Turkmenistan	4.6	7.2	4.6	(2000)	7.7	(2065)	55	0	65
Uganda	23.5	167.1	23.5	(2000)	170.0	(2115)	611	0	624
Ukraine	49.7	24.1	24.1	(2110)	49.7	(2000)	-51	-52	0
United Arab Emirates	2.8	3.7	2.8	(2000)	4.1	(2040)	30	0	47
United Kingdom	58.7	64.4	58.7	(2000)	73.2	(2300)	10	0	25
United Rep. of Tanzania	34.8	76.7	34.8	(2000)	77.5	(2085)	120	0	123

TABLE 8 (*continued*)

Country or area	Population (millions)						Percentage change from 2000 to		
	2000	*2100*	*Minimum*	*(Year)*	*Maximum*	*(Year)*	*2100*	*Minimum*	*Maximum*
United States of America	285.0	437.2	285.0	(2000)	493.0	(2300)	53	0	73
United States Virgin Islands	0.1	0.1	0.1	(2000)	0.1	(2055)	13	0	22
Uruguay	3.3	3.9	3.3	(2000)	4.2	(2060)	17	0	24
Uzbekistan	24.9	34.4	24.9	(2000)	38.0	(2060)	38	0	53
Vanuatu	0.2	0.5	0.2	(2000)	0.5	(2085)	144	0	148
Venezuela	24.3	40.8	24.3	(2000)	43.1	(2070)	68	0	78
Viet Nam	78.1	110.2	78.1	(2000)	118.5	(2060)	41	0	52
Western Sahara	0.3	0.7	0.3	(2000)	0.7	(2085)	148	0	151
Yemen	18.0	144.2	18.0	(2000)	147.2	(2115)	700	0	717
Zambia	10.4	22.1	10.4	(2000)	22.1	(2105)	112	0	112
Zimbabwe	12.6	12.6	12.0	(2155)	13.7	(2300)	-1	-5	8

(-2.04 per cent). In these cases too, migration is an important factor. In that period, the net migration rate reaches -1.49 per cent in Guyana and -1.15 per cent in Estonia, contributing substantially to negative growth. This also provides an explanation for why the lowest growth rates tend to appear just before 2050. In the 50-year projections, number of net migrants is often held constant, so that, for countries losing population, migrant loss if any becomes proportionally more important in later years. Since, for methodological reasons, migration is eliminated after 2050, loss of migrants often affects growth most just prior to 2050.

Although some substantial short-run changes in growth have been noted, it is worth pointing out that demographic projections of this type are not good at predicting sudden shifts in demographic parameters, as contrasted with smooth long-range trends. Sudden demographic change—demographic quakes due to such factors as waves of migrants that develop with little advance notice, unexpected mortality crises, or environmental catastrophes—have been a major source of projection error in the past and continue to complicate the future prospect.

C. FERTILITY

Fertility tends to progress more smoothly than migration—generally downward until returning to replacement. The highest fertility countries tend to be at the end of the train, in a sense being pulled along after low fertility countries. Figure 40 shows how the proportion of countries with high fertility has steadily shrunk over time and is projected to continue shrinking. In 2000-2005, 56 countries, out of 192, have total fertility of 4.0 or higher. By 2045-2050, the number will be zero. Instead, 139 countries will have total fertility under 2.0. Beyond 2050, however, the progression is not unilinear. The number of countries with fertility below 2.0 will fall, as more and more countries return to a replacement level just above 2.0. But fertility levels of 2.2 or higher are not expected to return.

Back in 1950-1955, the lowest fertility worldwide was evident in Luxembourg, Latvia, and Estonia, with other Western and Northern European countries and Greece rounding out the bottom ten (table 10). For 2000-2005, Hong Kong SAR and Macao SAR, Latvia and other Eastern European countries, and Spain have the lowest fertility. For 2025-2030, Eastern European countries, particularly Armenia, Russia, and Ukraine, are prominent on the list, which is filled out by other European countries and Singapore. By 2050-2055, fully 117 countries are at a total fertility level of 1.85, so the bottom ten are no longer reported.

Throughout the projection, the list of highest fertility countries is filled mainly by countries of sub-Saharan Africa and Western Asia. In 1950-1955, Yemen, Djibouti, and Rwanda had the highest fertility, but the remaining countries in the top 20 included Vanuatu, Honduras, the Philippines, and so on, representing all developing regions. By 2000-2005, the situation has changed, with sub-Saharan Africa dominating the rankings. Niger is at the top of the list, where it remains until 2075.

TABLE 9. HIGHEST AND LOWEST AVERAGE ANNUAL RATE OF POPULATION CHANGE IN ANY FIVE-YEAR PERIOD, BY COUNTRY: 2000-2300
(per cent)

Country or area	*Lowest*		*Highest*	
	Rate	*Period*	*Rate*	*Period*
Afghanistan	-0.408	2135-2140	3.881	2000-2005
Albania	-0.345	2085-2090	0.700	2005-2010
Algeria	-0.268	2095-2100	1.669	2000-2005
Angola	-0.317	2140-2145	3.197	2000-2005
Argentina	-0.258	2100-2105	1.172	2000-2005
Armenia	-1.088	2045-2050	0.089	2175-2180
Australia	-0.100	2060-2065	0.957	2000-2005
Austria	-0.534	2055-2060	0.100	2140-2145
Azerbaijan	-0.217	2085-2090	1.042	2005-2010
Bahamas	-0.234	2090-2095	1.126	2000-2005
Bahrain	-0.395	2095-2100	2.166	2000-2005
Bangladesh	-0.283	2110-2115	2.017	2000-2005
Barbados	-0.672	2045-2050	0.350	2000-2005
Belarus	-0.836	2055-2060	0.099	2150-2155
Belgium	-0.268	2050-2055	0.211	2000-2005
Belize	-0.305	2100-2105	2.061	2000-2005
Benin	-0.259	2130-2135	2.649	2000-2005
Bhutan	-0.282	2130-2135	2.960	2000-2005
Bolivia	-0.328	2120-2125	1.885	2000-2005
Bosnia and Herzegovina	-0.818	2050-2055	1.132	2000-2005
Botswana	-0.666	2030-2035	0.852	2000-2005
Brazil	-0.277	2085-2090	1.241	2000-2005
Brunei Darussalam	-0.288	2095-2100	2.273	2000-2005
Bulgaria	-0.997	2045-2050	0.089	2155-2160
Burkina Faso	-0.241	2145-2150	2.984	2005-2010
Burundi	-0.244	2140-2145	3.298	2005-2010
Cambodia	-0.266	2130-2135	2.403	2000-2005
Cameroon	-0.228	2125-2130	1.829	2000-2005
Canada	-0.199	2050-2055	0.767	2000-2005
Cape Verde	-0.236	2110-2115	2.014	2000-2005
Central African Republic	-0.232	2130-2135	1.475	2005-2010
Chad	-0.280	2135-2140	2.964	2000-2005
Channel Islands	-0.638	2045-2050	0.103	2145-2150
Chile	-0.213	2100-2105	1.225	2000-2005
China	-0.420	2055-2060	0.725	2000-2005
China, Hong Kong SAR	-0.443	2060-2065	1.072	2000-2005
China, Macao SAR	-0.448	2060-2065	0.942	2000-2005
Colombia	-0.292	2115-2120	1.588	2000-2005
Comoros	-0.269	2130-2135	2.833	2000-2005
Congo	-0.240	2135-2140	2.899	2005-2010
Costa Rica	-0.239	2090-2095	1.931	2000-2005
Côte d'Ivoire	-0.249	2130-2135	1.622	2000-2005
Croatia	-0.575	2045-2050	0.096	2145-2150
Cuba	-0.796	2045-2050	0.269	2000-2005
Cyprus	-0.330	2075-2080	0.760	2000-2005

TABLE 9 (*continued*)

Country or area	Lowest		Highest	
	Rate	Period	Rate	Period
Czech Republic	-0.763	2055-2060	0.086	2145-2150
Dem. People's Rep. of Korea	-0.255	2075-2080	0.539	2000-2005
Dem. Rep. of the Congo	-0.296	2135-2140	2.875	2000-2005
Dem. Rep. of Timor-Leste	-0.279	2120-2125	3.996	2000-2005
Denmark	-0.332	2050-2055	0.237	2000-2005
Djibouti	-0.264	2135-2140	1.685	2020-2025
Dominican Republic	-0.377	2110-2115	1.487	2000-2005
Ecuador	-0.287	2105-2110	1.487	2000-2005
Egypt	-0.275	2110-2115	1.991	2000-2005
El Salvador	-0.290	2110-2115	1.551	2000-2005
Equatorial Guinea	-0.271	2125-2130	2.649	2000-2005
Eritrea	-0.270	2130-2135	3.653	2000-2005
Estonia	-2.043	2045-2050	0.096	2145-2150
Ethiopia	-0.240	2135-2140	2.464	2000-2005
Fiji	-0.327	2095-2100	0.980	2000-2005
Finland	-0.338	2040-2045	0.179	2000-2005
France	-0.236	2055-2060	0.472	2000-2005
French Guiana	-0.294	2110-2115	2.534	2000-2005
French Polynesia	-0.242	2095-2100	1.518	2000-2005
Gabon	-0.262	2125-2130	1.853	2005-2010
Gambia	-0.266	2130-2135	2.663	2000-2005
Georgia	-1.173	2045-2050	0.083	2165-2170
Germany	-0.361	2050-2055	0.105	2140-2145
Ghana	-0.232	2125-2130	2.165	2000-2005
Greece	-0.844	2055-2060	0.138	2000-2005
Guadeloupe	-0.444	2045-2050	0.836	2000-2005
Guam	-0.314	2110-2115	1.542	2000-2005
Guatemala	-0.303	2115-2120	2.552	2000-2005
Guinea	-0.287	2130-2135	2.564	2005-2010
Guinea-Bissau	-0.284	2140-2145	2.945	2000-2005
Guyana	-2.146	2045-2050	0.240	2000-2005
Haiti	-0.391	2120-2125	1.319	2005-2010
Honduras	-0.312	2115-2120	2.338	2000-2005
Hungary	-0.683	2045-2050	0.103	2140-2145
Iceland	-0.265	2075-2080	0.792	2000-2005
India	-0.319	2105-2110	1.514	2000-2005
Indonesia	-0.256	2090-2095	1.260	2000-2005
Iran, Islamic Rep. of	-0.272	2080-2085	1.501	2010-2015
Iraq	-0.255	2120-2125	2.681	2000-2005
Ireland	-0.273	2065-2070	1.124	2000-2005
Israel	-0.285	2105-2110	2.023	2000-2005
Italy	-0.951	2055-2060	0.083	2155-2160
Jamaica	-0.281	2095-2100	0.988	2010-2015
Japan	-0.556	2045-2050	0.138	2000-2005
Jordan	-0.237	2110-2115	2.655	2000-2005
Kazakhstan	-0.658	2045-2050	0.261	2010-2015
Kenya	-0.133	2120-2125	1.452	2000-2005

TABLE 9 (*continued*)

Country or area	*Lowest*		*Highest*	
	Rate	*Period*	*Rate*	*Period*
Kuwait	-0.342	2100-2105	3.462	2000-2005
Kyrgyzstan	-0.265	2095-2100	1.401	2000-2005
Lao People's Dem. Republic	-0.280	2120-2125	2.288	2000-2005
Latvia	-1.508	2045-2050	0.097	2150-2155
Lebanon	-0.274	2085-2090	1.563	2000-2005
Lesotho	-0.669	2020-2025	0.450	2080-2085
Liberia	-0.300	2135-2140	4.045	2000-2005
Libyan Arab Jamahiriya	-0.257	2100-2105	1.931	2000-2005
Lithuania	-0.797	2045-2050	0.147	2095-2100
Luxembourg	-0.086	2090-2095	1.319	2000-2005
Madagascar	-0.245	2135-2140	2.842	2000-2005
Malawi	-0.255	2135-2140	2.010	2000-2005
Malaysia	-0.253	2105-2110	1.925	2000-2005
Maldives	-0.239	2125-2130	2.981	2000-2005
Mali	-0.276	2140-2145	3.174	2005-2010
Malta	-0.211	2045-2050	0.416	2000-2005
Martinique	-0.293	2045-2050	0.558	2000-2005
Mauritania	-0.256	2135-2140	2.976	2000-2005
Mauritius	-0.236	2075-2080	0.957	2000-2005
Mexico	-0.302	2090-2095	1.452	2000-2005
Micronesia, Fed. States of	-0.299	2120-2125	1.293	2025-2030
Mongolia	-0.327	2095-2100	1.395	2005-2010
Morocco	-0.245	2105-2110	1.620	2000-2005
Mozambique	-0.271	2130-2135	1.751	2000-2005
Myanmar	-0.265	2100-2105	1.284	2000-2005
Namibia	-0.145	2125-2130	1.415	2000-2005
Nepal	-0.296	2125-2130	2.228	2000-2005
Netherlands	-0.260	2050-2055	0.500	2000-2005
Netherlands Antilles	-0.267	2080-2085	0.831	2000-2005
New Caledonia	-0.280	2100-2105	1.919	2000-2005
New Zealand	-0.154	2050-2055	0.769	2000-2005
Nicaragua	-0.315	2120-2125	2.426	2000-2005
Niger	-0.262	2155-2160	3.619	2000-2005
Nigeria	-0.244	2130-2135	2.533	2000-2005
Norway	-0.270	2050-2055	0.429	2000-2005
Occupied Palestinian Territory	-0.281	2135-2140	3.574	2000-2005
Oman	-0.285	2130-2135	2.927	2000-2005
Pakistan	-0.324	2125-2130	2.438	2000-2005
Panama	-0.287	2105-2110	1.843	2000-2005
Papua New Guinea	-0.263	2125-2130	2.218	2000-2005
Paraguay	-0.319	2120-2125	2.374	2000-2005
Peru	-0.292	2105-2110	1.496	2000-2005
Philippines	-0.248	2105-2110	1.792	2000-2005
Poland	-0.661	2065-2070	0.080	2165-2170
Portugal	-0.661	2055-2060	0.129	2000-2005
Puerto Rico	-0.571	2045-2050	0.516	2000-2005
Qatar	-0.298	2105-2110	1.536	2000-2005

TABLE 9 (*continued*)

Country or area	*Lowest*		*Highest*	
	Rate	*Period*	*Rate*	*Period*
Republic of Korea	-0.625	2060-2065	0.567	2000-2005
Republic of Moldova	-0.695	2070-2075	0.083	2175-2180
Réunion	-0.168	2090-2095	1.448	2000-2005
Romania	-0.701	2050-2055	0.100	2140-2145
Russian Federation	-0.876	2050-2055	0.118	2125-2130
Rwanda	-0.211	2130-2135	2.163	2000-2005
St. Lucia	-0.398	2045-2050	0.777	2000-2005
St. Vincent and Grenadines	-0.380	2045-2050	0.582	2000-2005
Samoa	-0.294	2125-2130	1.133	2010-2015
Sao Tome and Principe	-0.241	2125-2130	2.489	2000-2005
Saudi Arabia	-0.270	2115-2120	2.918	2000-2005
Senegal	-0.259	2130-2135	2.394	2000-2005
Serbia and Montenegro	-0.471	2065-2070	0.090	2170-2175
Sierra Leone	-0.535	2120-2125	3.804	2000-2005
Singapore	-0.737	2050-2055	1.694	2000-2005
Slovakia	-0.610	2060-2065	0.086	2165-2170
Slovenia	-0.902	2055-2060	0.078	2160-2165
Solomon Islands	-0.327	2120-2125	2.877	2000-2005
Somalia	-0.258	2145-2150	4.171	2000-2005
South Africa	-0.372	2025-2030	0.592	2000-2005
Spain	-0.763	2060-2065	0.211	2000-2005
Sri Lanka	-0.314	2070-2075	0.813	2000-2005
Sudan	-0.282	2125-2130	2.170	2000-2005
Suriname	-0.602	2045-2050	0.796	2000-2005
Swaziland	-0.425	2030-2035	0.798	2000-2005
Sweden	-0.241	2050-2055	0.102	2005-2010
Switzerland	-0.734	2040-2045	0.085	2140-2145
Syrian Arab Republic	-0.271	2110-2115	2.378	2000-2005
Tajikistan	-0.331	2100-2105	1.454	2010-2015
TFYR Macedonia	-0.311	2070-2075	0.508	2000-2005
Thailand	-0.235	2070-2075	1.010	2000-2005
Togo	-0.232	2125-2130	2.344	2000-2005
Tonga	-0.332	2045-2050	0.965	2000-2005
Trinidad and Tobago	-0.549	2045-2050	0.343	2000-2005
Tunisia	-0.341	2075-2080	1.070	2000-2005
Turkey	-0.254	2090-2095	1.419	2000-2005
Turkmenistan	-0.280	2100-2105	1.537	2000-2005
Uganda	-0.261	2145-2150	3.555	2005-2010
Ukraine	-1.112	2045-2050	0.094	2145-2150
United Arab Emirates	-0.315	2100-2105	1.937	2000-2005
United Kingdom	-0.081	2070-2075	0.323	2015-2020
United Rep. of Tanzania	-0.253	2125-2130	1.929	2000-2005
United States of America	0.035	2105-2110	1.028	2000-2005
United States Virgin Islands	-0.294	2085-2090	0.869	2000-2005
Uruguay	-0.261	2100-2105	0.715	2000-2005
Uzbekistan	-0.320	2085-2090	1.511	2000-2005
Vanuatu	-0.315	2125-2130	2.431	2000-2005

TABLE 9 (*continued*)

Country or area	Lowest		Highest	
	Rate	Period	Rate	Period
Venezuela	-0.301	2100-2105	1.858	2000-2005
Viet Nam	-0.231	2090-2095	1.348	2000-2005
Western Sahara	-0.236	2120-2125	2.554	2000-2005
Yemen	-0.290	2145-2150	3.570	2010-2015
Zambia	-0.214	2135-2140	1.476	2010-2015
Zimbabwe	-0.164	2020-2025	0.490	2000-2005

Figure 40. Percentage distribution of countries by total fertility level: 1950-2150

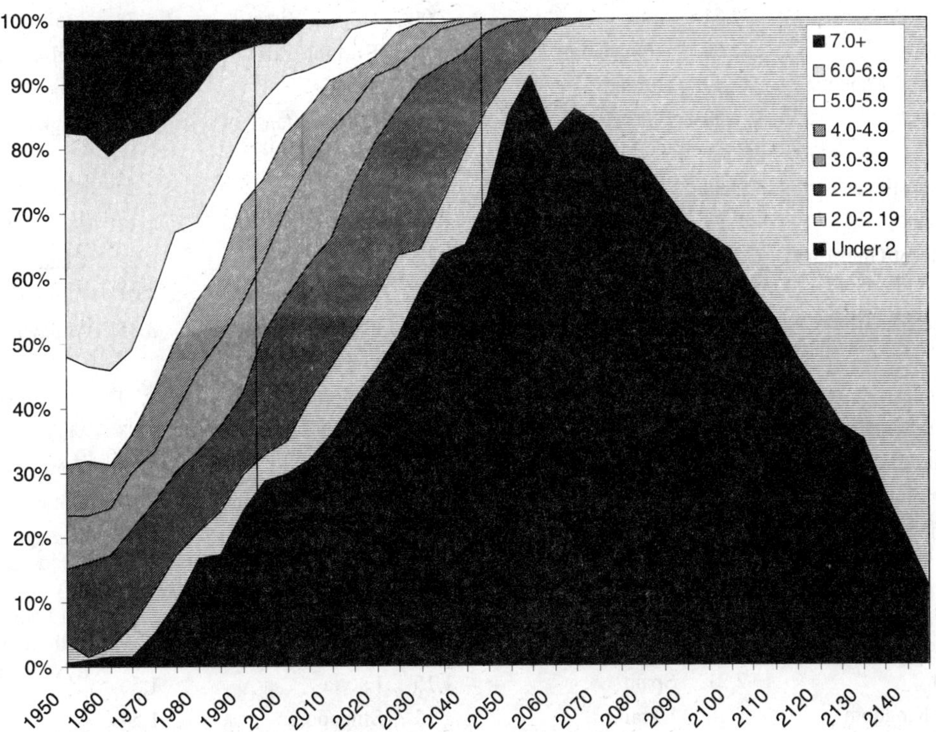

Aside from Yemen and Afghanistan, all the rest in the top 20 are in sub-Saharan Africa. In 2025-2030 and 2050-2055, Yemen and Afghanistan are still among the top 20, but all the rest continue to be in sub-Saharan Africa. They are scattered throughout the broad middle of the continent, from Mauritania and Ethiopia in the north to Angola and Madagascar in the south. The rapid growth seen earlier for sub-Saharan Africa (mainly in Eastern, Middle and Western Africa) clearly is rooted in this high fertility. As notable, however, is the projected substantial fertility decline—though over relatively long time scales—among these high fertility countries. By 2075, fertility will be at replacement level or lower even in Niger.

The trend in Niger is illustrated in figure 41, where it is contrasted with Latvia (which is consistently among the lowest fertility countries), and alternative high and low projections are also shown. Though Nigerien fertility is higher than that of any other country in the 50-year projections, it also shows a steep fall, eventually intersecting with slightly rising Latvian fertility around 2075. Beyond that point, Nigerien fertility falls further to 1.85, given the projection assumptions, and eventually returns to replacement level after about a hundred years. Latvian fertility does not fall below replacement because it has already been below replacement earlier. High and low scenarios provide what look like somewhat narrow bands

TABLE 10. COUNTRIES WITH THE HIGHEST AND LOWEST TOTAL FERTILITY, ESTIMATES AND MEDIUM SCENARIO, SELECTED PERIODS

Rank	*1950-1955*		*2000-2005*		*2025-2030*		*2050-2055*	
			A. Highest total fertility					
1	Yemen	8.20	Niger	8.00	Niger	6.06	Niger	3.35
2	Djibouti	7.80	Somalia	7.25	Somalia	5.14	Yemen	2.82
3	Rwanda	7.80	Angola	7.20	Yemen	5.09	Somalia	2.72
4	Afghanistan	7.70	Guinea-Bissau	7.10	Angola	5.07	Angola	2.68
5	Niger	7.70	Uganda	7.10	Mali	4.91	Burkina Faso	2.62
6	Vanuatu	7.60	Yemen	7.00	Uganda	4.87	Uganda	2.60
7	Kenya	7.51	Mali	7.00	Guinea-Bissau	4.78	Mali	2.59
8	Honduras	7.50	Afghanistan	6.80	Burkina Faso	4.69	Guinea-Bissau	2.57
9	Dominican Republic	7.40	Burundi	6.80	Liberia	4.56	Liberia	2.50
10	Jordan	7.38	Liberia	6.80	Afghanistan	4.52	Afghanistan	2.49
11	Occ. Palestinian Terr.	7.38	Congo, DR	6.70	Burundi	4.45	Burundi	2.46
12	Nicaragua	7.33	Burkina Faso	6.68	Congo, DR	4.37	Congo, DR	2.36
13	St. Vincent/Grenadines	7.33	Chad	6.65	Chad	4.25	Chad	2.31
14	Samoa	7.30	Sierra Leone	6.50	Sierra Leone	4.01	Ethiopia	2.31
15	Tonga	7.30	Congo	6.29	Congo	3.85	Malawi	2.29
16	Philippines	7.29	Ethiopia	6.14	Ethiopia	3.79	Sierra Leone	2.23
17	Algeria	7.28	Malawi	6.10	Malawi	3.73	Mauritania	2.22
18	Somalia	7.25	Equatorial Guinea	5.89	Mauritania	3.49	Congo	2.17
19	Kuwait	7.21	Guinea	5.82	Equatorial Guinea	3.34	Djibouti	2.17
20	Micronesia, FS	7.20	Mauritania	5.79	Djibouti	3.30	Madagascar	2.17
			B. Lowest total fertility					
1	Greece	2.29	Czech Republic	1.16	Republic of Moldova	1.58	(117 countries with total fertility of 1.85)	
2	Switzerland	2.28	Armenia	1.15	Spain	1.58		
3	Sweden	2.21	Spain	1.15	Latvia	1.56		
4	United Kingdom	2.18	Ukraine	1.15	Singapore	1.54		
5	Germany	2.16	Russian Federation	1.14	Italy	1.54		
6	Austria	2.09	Slovenia	1.14	Austria	1.54		
7	Channel Islands	2.07	Bulgaria	1.10	Belarus	1.53		
8	Estonia	2.06	Macao, China	1.10	Ukraine	1.50		
9	Latvia	2.00	Latvia	1.10	Russian Federation	1.49		
10	Luxembourg	1.98	Hong Kong SAR	1.00	Armenia	1.48		

around the medium fertility trend but in the long run can produce substantial population growth or decline.

D. MORTALITY

Unlike fertility, life expectancy is projected as showing monotonic increase. There are exceptions, but they all occur in the 50-year projections. All 17 cases of life expectancy decline in fact involve declines prior to 2015. Each case is an African, Caribbean, or Central American country severely affected by HIV/AIDS.

Figure 42 shows some extreme cases, where life expectancy is concerned. Japan has the highest life expectancy in 2000-2005, at 81.6 years for females and males combined, and will stay highest up to 2300, by which time life expectancy will reach 106.3 years. Sierra Leone, in contrast, has

Figure 41. Total fertility in Niger and Latvia, estimates and three scenarios: 1950-2300

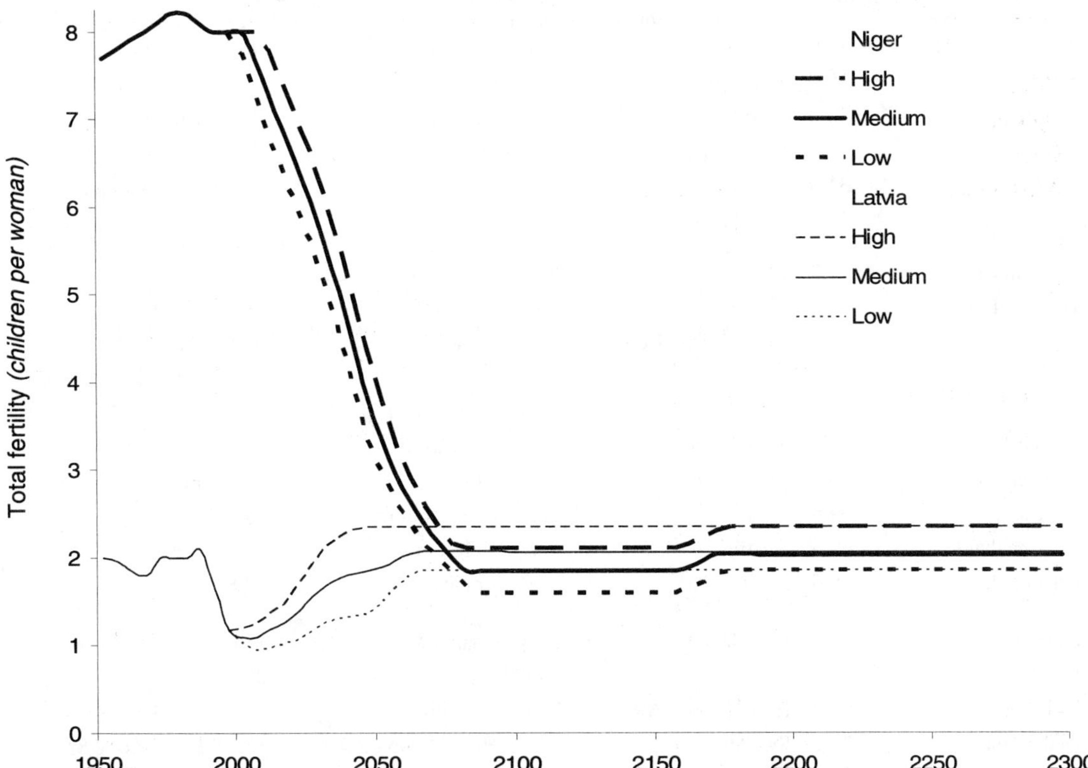

the third lowest life expectancy in 2000-2005, at 34.2 years, and will be lowest of all for an extended period from at least 2100 to 2250, even though, by 2300, it will reach 88.6 years. The other two countries illustrate relatively slow and relatively rapid increases in life expectancy. From 2050 to 2300, life expectancy rises less in Suriname, by 15.5 years, than in any other country, and rises most in Botswana, by 50.3 years The increase for Botswana is large because of a postulated preceding decrease as a result of HIV/AIDS. The projections show similarly large increases in life expectancy after 2050 for other countries, especially in Southern Africa, where HIV/AIDS produces a substantial preceding decline.

The ten countries with the lowest life expectancy in 2000-2005 are all severely affected by HIV/AIDS and are predominantly in the Southern Africa region or the somewhat broader Southern African Development Community (SADC). Sierra Leone is a notable exception in not being in or close to Southern Africa (table 11). By 2100, life expectancy will double in some of these countries, but Southern Africa and SADC will still be the dominant presence on the list. By 2150, however, they will make up only half the list and will gradually drop off it thereafter. Sierra Leone, Liberia, and Mali will dominate the list (with life expectancies below 90 years), and such Asian countries as Yemen, Timor Leste, and Afghanistan will be added.

The opposite list, of countries with the highest life expectancy, consists primarily of European countries, though Japan leads this list throughout the projection period. In 2000-2005, the list also includes Hong Kong SAR, Canada, Israel, and even Martinique, but these non-European countries do not keep up, and only Japan and the Republic of Korea stay on the list in the long run. By 2300, 31 countries will have life expectancies over 100. At these high levels, differences between countries at the top will not be large, and improvement will be slow. When one looks at rates of growth in life expectancies from 2050 to

TABLE 11. COUNTRIES WITH THE LOWEST AND HIGHEST LIFE EXPECTANCY AT BIRTH, SELECTED PERIODS

Rank	*1950-1955*		*2000-2005*		*2050-2055*		*2100-2105*	
			A. Lowest life expectancy at birth					
1	Timor-Leste, DR	30.0	Zambia	32.4	Swaziland	46.4	Sierra Leone	66.4
2	Sierra Leone	30.0	Zimbabwe	33.1	Botswana	46.6	Zimbabwe	67.9
3	Angola	30.0	Sierra Leone	34.2	Lesotho	47.5	Swaziland	68.5
4	Gambia	30.0	Swaziland	34.4	Zimbabwe	48.2	Botswana	72.1
5	Guinea	31.0	Lesotho	35.1	Sierra Leone	54.2	Mozambique	72.8
6	Mozambique	31.3	Malawi	37.5	Zambia	54.9	Malawi	73.2
7	Afghanistan	31.9	Mozambique	38.1	Mozambique	56.4	Zambia	73.3
8	Burkina Faso	31.9	Rwanda	39.3	Kenya	56.7	Liberia	73.4
9	Niger	32.2	Cen. African Rep.	39.5	Namibia	56.8	Angola	73.4
10	Chad	32.5	Botswana	39.7	South Africa	58.4	Cen. African Rep.	75.0
			B. Highest life expectancy at birth					
183	United Kingdom	69.2	Switzerland	79.1	Norway	84.5	Norway	89.5
184	Switzerland	69.2	Martinique	79.1	Malta	84.5	France	89.6
185	Australia	69.6	Israel	79.2	Luxembourg	84.6	Germany	89.7
186	New Zealand	69.6	Australia	79.2	Belgium	84.6	Belgium	89.8
187	Channel Is.	70.6	Spain	79.3	France	84.8	Luxembourg	89.8
188	Denmark	71.0	Canada	79.3	Spain	85.0	Spain	89.8
189	Sweden	71.8	Iceland	79.8	Macao, China	85.0	Malta	90.0
190	Iceland	72.0	Hong Kong SAR	79.9	Sweden	85.3	Sweden	90.0
191	Netherlands	72.1	Sweden	80.1	Hong Kong SAR	85.5	Hong Kong SAR	90.1
192	Norway	72.7	Japan	81.6	Japan	89.3	Japan	93.3

Rank	*2150-2155*		*2200-2205*		*2250-2255*		*2295-2300*	
			A. Lowest life expectancy					
1	Sierra Leone	75.0	Sierra Leone	81.1	Sierra Leone	85.5	Liberia	87.4
2	Liberia	79.5	Liberia	83.1	Liberia	85.6	Mali	87.6
3	Zimbabwe	79.7	Mali	83.9	Mali	86.1	Sierra Leone	88.6
4	Swaziland	80.4	Malawi	85.4	Congo	87.7	Congo	89.1
5	Malawi	80.9	Congo	85.7	Yemen	88.1	Yemen	89.4
6	Mali	81.0	Afghanistan	85.9	Timor-Leste, DR	88.3	Timor-Leste, DR	89.8
7	Angola	81.2	Angola	86.0	Malawi	88.4	Malawi	90.3
8	Mozambique	81.6	Timor-Leste, DR	86.2	Afghanistan	88.6	Cambodia	90.3
9	Afghanistan	81.9	Yemen	86.2	Cambodia	88.9	Afghanistan	90.6
10	Congo, DR	82.2	Zimbabwe	86.4	Angola	89.4	Bangladesh	91.7
			B. Highest life expectancy					
183	Hong Kong SAR	93.9	Norway	97.7	Austria	101.1	Republic of Korea	103.6
184	France	93.9	France	97.8	Republic of Korea	101.3	Austria	104.1
185	Republic of Korea	94.2	Republic of Korea	98.1	France	101.4	France	104.3
186	Spain	94.3	Belgium	98.3	Belgium	101.7	Belgium	104.5
187	Belgium	94.3	Sweden	98.3	Sweden	102.0	Sweden	105.0
188	Sweden	94.3	Spain	98.4	Spain	102.1	Spain	105.2
189	Luxembourg	94.4	Luxembourg	98.6	Luxembourg	102.3	Luxembourg	105.3
190	Germany	94.4	Germany	98.7	Germany	102.5	Germany	105.4
191	Malta	94.9	Malta	99.2	Malta	102.9	Malta	105.7
192	Japan	97.0	Japan	100.4	Japan	103.6	Japan	106.3

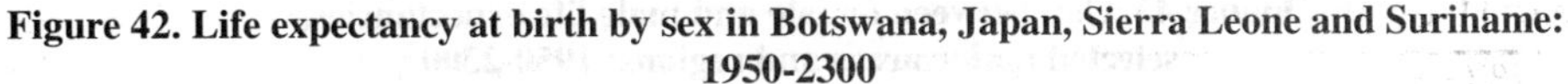

Figure 42. Life expectancy at birth by sex in Botswana, Japan, Sierra Leone and Suriname: 1950-2300

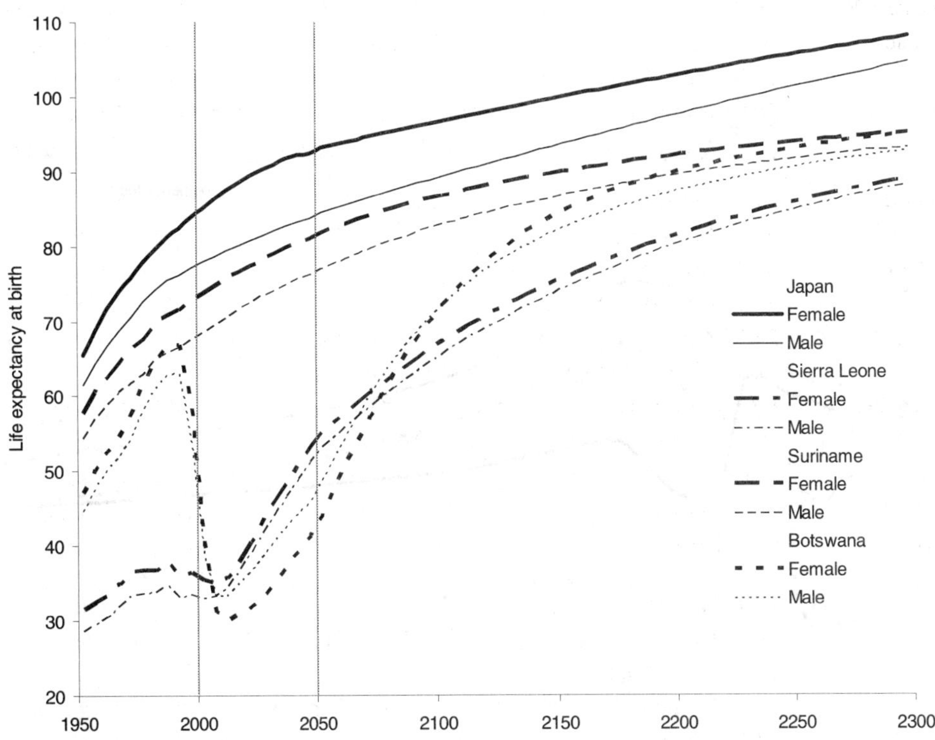

2300, European countries take the bottom positions.

In the long term, improvements in life expectancy come mainly from reducing mortality at advanced ages, not at younger ages. Mortality at young ages declines to low levels early in the projections. From 2000 to 2050, infant mortality in less developed regions falls from over 60 deaths per thousand to 23.5 per thousand, and by 2100 to less than 10 per thousand (6.7 for 2195-2200). By 2100, under-five mortality will also be under 10 deaths per thousand (7.9 in 2195-2200). This will still be above rates in more developed regions at that time but will be sufficiently low so that possible additional gains at these ages will have little overall effect on life expectancy. Similarly, for adults in middle age, few additional gains against mortality will be possible once the effects of HIV/AIDS have been wrung out of the system. Rising life expectancies beyond 2100, therefore, will come mainly from extending life at the oldest ages.

In the long run, females are expected to maintain an advantage in life expectancy over males. As figure 42 illustrates, this advantage is greater at higher levels of life expectancy. At lower levels, as in Sierra Leone, life expectancies are more nearly equal. Figure 43 provides an additional perspective. It shows three major areas—Europe, Asia, and Africa—and one region of each of the latter two. The large advantage that females have in Europe, 8.1 years in 2000-2005, declines to 5.9 years in 2050-2055 and to 2.8 years in 2295-2300. In Africa, the female advantage is only 2.1 years in 2000-2005, will be unchanged in 2050-2055, and will drop to 0.9 years by 2295-2300. However, between 2000 and 2050, the female advantage will not stay constant but will first decline, as HIV/AIDS produces higher female mortality, and then increase again. This is illustrated dramatically for Southern Africa, where, around 2025, females will actually be at a disadvantage, with life expectancies three years shorter than males. Asia, and South-central Asia especially, exhibits a strikingly different trend. The female advantage will grow

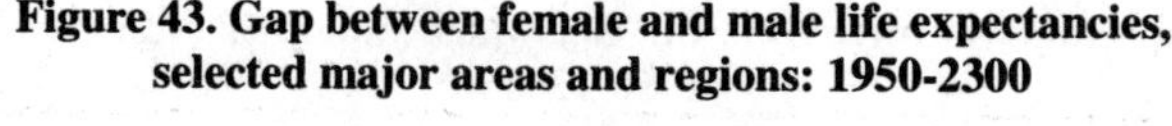

Figure 43. Gap between female and male life expectancies, selected major areas and regions: 1950-2300

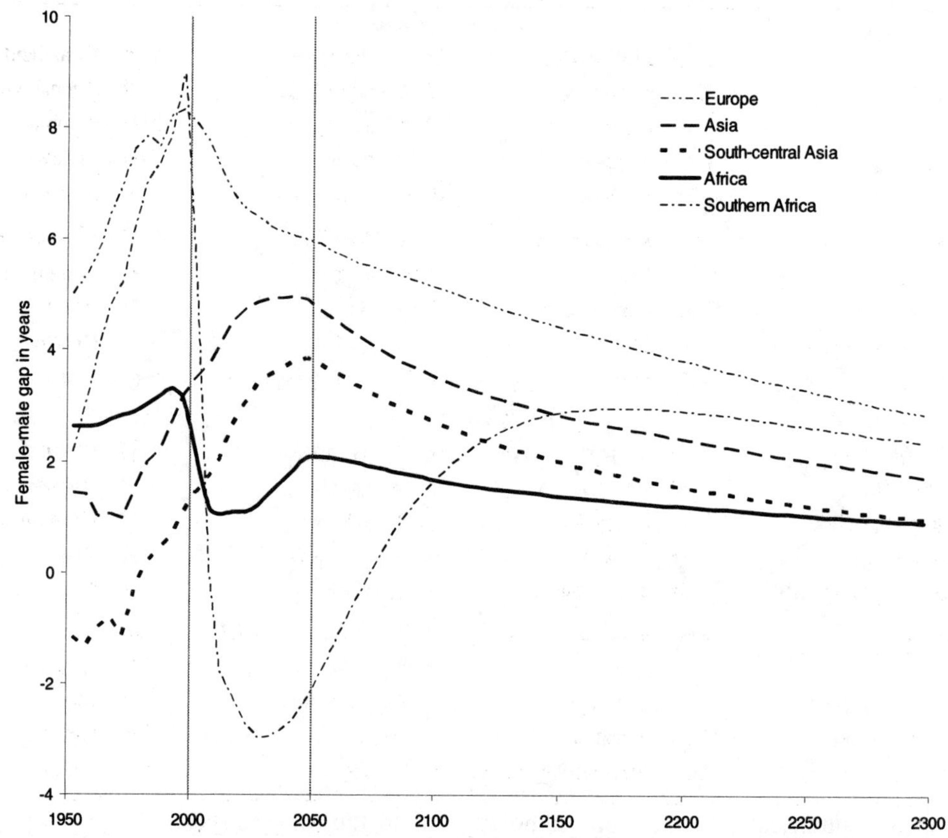

from 3.5 to 4.7 years in South-central Asia (including India) in the 50-year projections before declining in the long run to 1.7 years.

In 2000-2005, the ten countries where the female advantage is smallest (or the male advantage greatest) are a mix of South-central Asian countries and African countries severely affected by HIV/AIDS (table 12). By 2050, the African countries take over the list entirely. Not until 2250 is a country from outside Africa, Pakistan, added. The greatest female advantage, in contrast, is now in countries of the former Soviet Union, which indicates not female robustness but problems with relatively high male mortality. This will change, and eventually at the top of this list will be a mix of countries: Japan, the U.S. Virgin Islands, Puerto Rico, and countries of Southern and Western Europe.

Mortality rankings, and actually ranking on many demographic indicators, are substantially affected by the HIV/AIDS epidemic, even though HIV transmission is assumed to begin a sustained decline by 2010.

TABLE 12. COUNTRIES WITH THE SMALLEST AND LARGEST GAP BETWEEN FEMALE AND MALE LIFE EXPECTANCIES, SELECTED PERIODS

Rank	*1950-1955*		*2000-2005*		*2050-2055*		*2100-2105*	
			A. Smallest gap					
1	Maldives	-2.50	Zimbabwe	-1.12	Botswana	-4.38	Swaziland	-1.23
2	Pakistan	-2.50	Maldives	-0.80	Swaziland	-2.99	Zimbabwe	-1.11
3	Bangladesh	-1.60	Zambia	-0.65	Zimbabwe	-2.97	Zambia	-0.09
4	Sri Lanka	-1.52	Nepal	-0.50	Lesotho	-2.66	Malawi	0.02
5	India	-1.37	Pakistan	-0.30	South Africa	-1.76	Botswana	0.10
6	Nepal	-1.00	Afghanistan	0.30	Namibia	-1.74	Mozambique	0.39
7	Afghanistan	-0.30	Malawi	0.36	Zambia	-1.32	Cameroon	0.51
8	Iran, Islamic Rep. of	-0.01	Côte d'Ivoire	0.39	Kenya	-1.27	Namibia	0.55
9	TFYR Macedonia	0.05	Niger	0.56	Malawi	-0.61	Nigeria	0.73
10	Yemen	0.30	Guinea	0.70	Mozambique	-0.30	Kenya	0.86
			B. Largest gap					
183	Turkmenistan	6.90	Hungary	8.32	Belarus	6.60	Portugal	5.57
184	Azerbaijan	7.60	Brazil	8.58	France	6.62	Slovenia	5.61
185	Hong Kong SAR	7.71	Puerto Rico	8.94	Ukraine	6.64	Réunion	5.67
186	Georgia	7.90	Ukraine	10.00	Lithuania	6.76	Puerto Rico	5.71
187	Rep. of Moldova	8.00	Lithuania	10.13	Estonia	6.81	France	5.75
188	Ukraine	8.44	Estonia	10.30	U.S. Virgin Islands	7.04	Latvia	5.78
189	Kyrgyzstan	8.50	Belarus	10.47	Latvia	7.10	Argentina	5.97
190	Belarus	8.90	Latvia	10.60	Argentina	7.19	Brazil	6.05
191	Kazakhstan	10.20	Kazakhstan	11.08	Brazil	7.91	U.S. Virgin Islands	6.51
192	U.S. Virgin Islands	12.67	Russian Federation	12.28	Japan	8.68	Japan	7.39

Rank	*2150-2155*		*2200-2205*		*2250-2255*		*2295-2300*	
			A. Smallest gap					
1	Swaziland	0.36	Tanzania, UR	0.63	Tanzania, UR	0.47	Tanzania, UR	0.37
2	Malawi	0.48	Malawi	0.65	Guinea	0.57	Pakistan	0.50
3	Zambia	0.55	Guinea	0.65	Nigeria	0.57	Nigeria	0.51
4	Zimbabwe	0.61	Nigeria	0.66	Burkina Faso	0.65	Guinea	0.52
5	Mozambique	0.71	Zambia	0.69	Pakistan	0.65	Burkina Faso	0.58
6	Nigeria	0.75	Cameroon	0.75	Malawi	0.66	Rwanda	0.59
7	Cameroon	0.76	Burkina Faso	0.76	Zambia	0.67	Sudan	0.60
8	Guinea	0.79	Mozambique	0.77	Cameroon	0.67	Senegal	0.60
9	United Rep. of Tanzania	0.89	Djibouti	0.80	Sudan	0.68	Cameroon	0.61
10	Burkina Faso	0.93	Côte d'Ivoire	0.80	Benin	0.69	Benin	0.61
			B. Largest gap					
183	Finland	4.90	Italy	4.38	Italy	3.87	Italy	3.45
184	Italy	4.92	Brunei	4.45	France	3.92	France	3.48
185	Switzerland	4.93	Switzerland	4.46	Switzerland	4.00	Japan	3.50
186	Luxembourg	4.95	France	4.46	Luxembourg	4.01	Luxembourg	3.60
187	France	5.06	Luxembourg	4.48	Brunei	4.06	Switzerland	3.61
188	Albania	5.08	Portugal	4.60	Portugal	4.11	Portugal	3.68
189	Portugal	5.08	Albania	4.67	Albania	4.18	Albania	3.70
190	Puerto Rico	5.23	Puerto Rico	4.85	Japan	4.25	Brunei	3.70
191	U.S. Virgin Islands	5.91	Japan	5.19	Puerto Rico	4.50	U.S. Virgin Islands	4.16
192	Japan	6.24	U.S. Virgin Islands	5.28	U.S. Virgin Islands	4.66	Puerto Rico	4.20

IV. POPULATION DENSITY

Since world population in 2300 is projected not to vary much from 2050 levels, one might expect long-range projections to add little of interest about the pressure of people on resources. Nevertheless, these long-range projections do raise issues that are not evident in the 50-year projections. Population is not constant beyond 2050, but will rise, decline, and rise again; growth and decline may destabilize any static balance with resources, even if, in the long run, population does not increase. Pressure on resources may come not just from the number of people at any one time but from the cumulative weight of numbers. Resources of possible concern vary, not simply between renewable and non-renewable but also in their sensitivity to actual numbers of people or population concentration in urban agglomerations that grow faster than population totals. Pressure on resources may lead to technological change, which may or may not be sufficient to solve the problem. And all these factors vary, of course, as do projected demographic paths, by region and country.

These complex considerations are beyond the scope of this report, but one can consider the balance between population and one constant resource—land area. Land area is not entirely fixed, but over the time scales considered does not vary much. Land area is used as defined by the Food and Agriculture Organization (2004), which excludes major inland lakes and rivers.

In 2000, population density, or the ratio of people to land area, varies considerably across major areas, from 119.3 persons per square kilometer in Asia to 3.7 persons per sq. km. in Oceania. In the 50-year projections, density increases in all major areas except Europe, the increases being quite substantial for Asia and Africa (figure 44). In the long-range projections, Asia and Latin America and the Caribbean reach maximum projected density in 2065 and Africa in 2100, after which some decline takes place. All major areas then have slowly rising densities from at least 2200, but only Europe and Northern America eventually exceed earlier densities toward the end of the projection. Regional densities in 2100 provide a rough indication of the prospects over the following two centuries, over which period densities do not fall more than 10 per cent below 2100 figures or rise by more than 15 per cent.

These results are derived from the medium projection scenario. High and low scenarios naturally produce quite different densities. Density would increase or decrease steadily beyond 2050, reaching either four times the level or a quarter to a third of the level in the medium scenario.

In the medium scenario, the variation across major areas is actually less than the variation within them (table 13). The regions of Oceania, for instance, range in density in 2100 from 3.6 persons per sq. km. in Australia/New Zealand to 503.6 in Micronesia. Similar variation, though not as extreme, appears everywhere else (figure 45). In Asia, Eastern Asia excluding China has 74.8 persons per sq. km., in 2100, whereas India has 490.5. The figure for India is unusual; higher densities usually appear for smaller regions. In contrast to variation in density levels, density trends tend to be quite similar, with density usually increasing to a local maximum relatively early in the projection period, declining, and rising again.

Across countries, as across regions, there is a tendency for smaller land areas to be related to higher densities. For 2100, the most dense countries or areas are the city-states or city-territories, of Macao SAR, Hong Kong SAR, and Singapore. Figure 46 shows how countries with larger land areas tend to have lower densities in 2100, and also identifies countries that are outliers where this trend is concerned. For 2100, three large South Asian countries—Bangladesh, Pakistan, and India—appear relatively dense, as do a variety of countries from other regions. At the opposite extreme, Guyana, Mongolia, and Botswana will have only two persons per sq. km. in 2000. A number of the least dense countries have extensive deserts or other land of limited habitability.

Figure 44. Density, major areas: 1950-2300

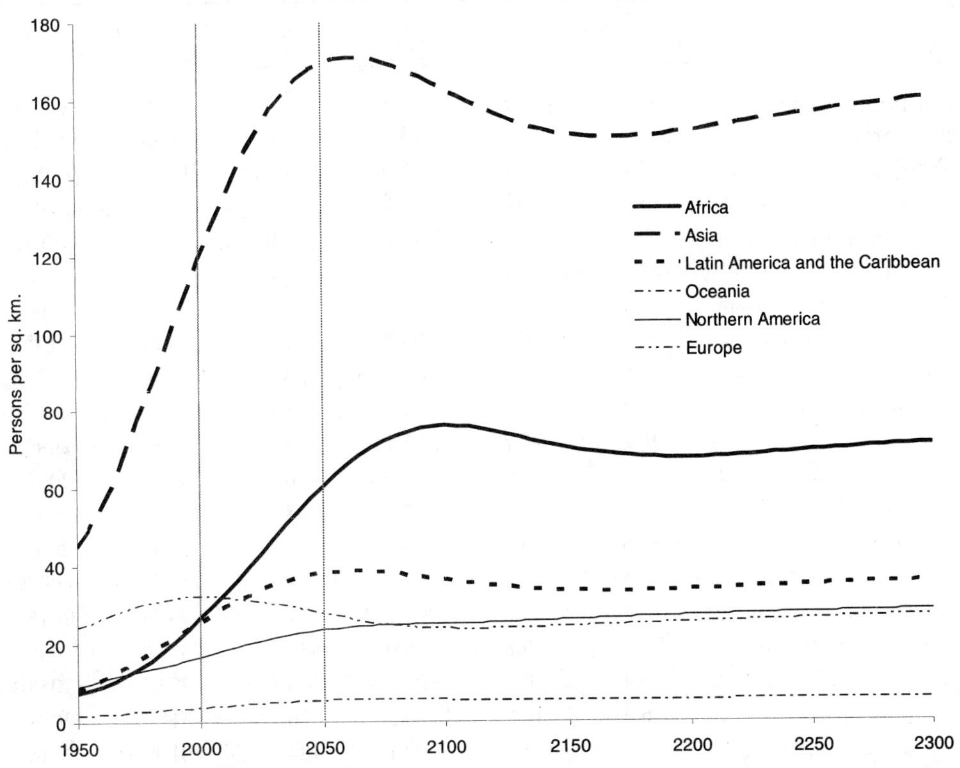

Figure 45. Density in relation to land area by region and selected countries: 2100

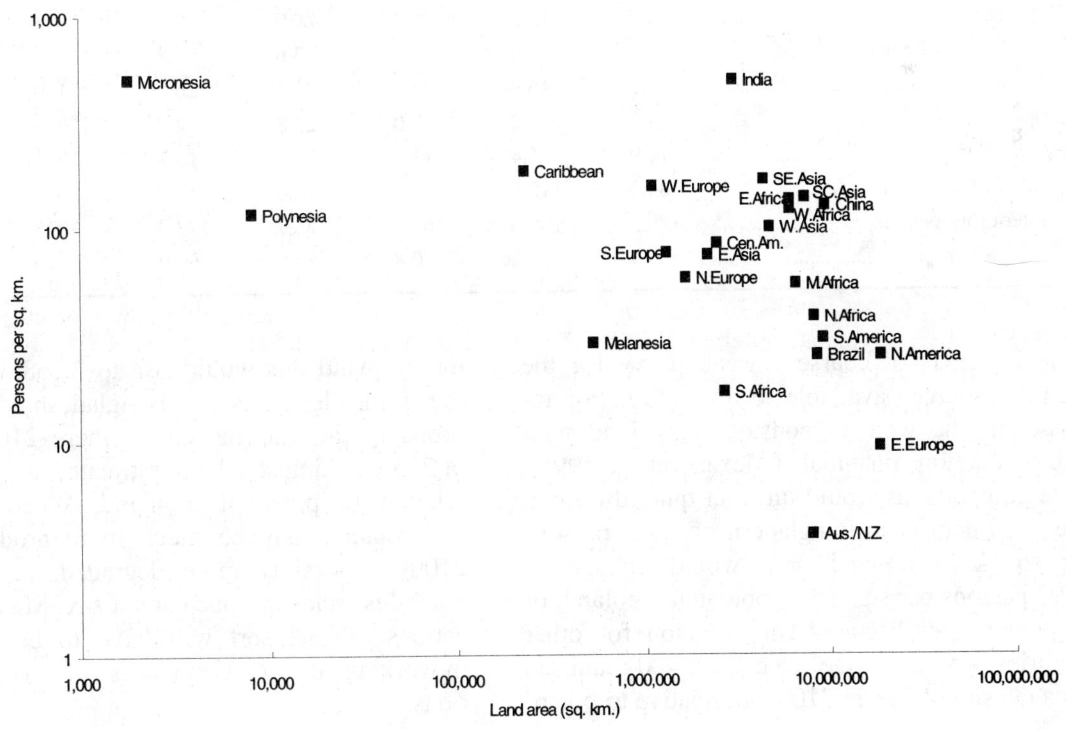

TABLE 13. DENSITY IN PERSONS PER SQUARE KILOMETER OF LAND, BY MAJOR AREA AND REGION: 1950-2300

Major area and region	*1950*	*2000*	*2050*	*2100*	*Maximum up to 2150*	*Year of maximum*	*2300*
World	19.3	46.5	68.4	69.5	70.7	(2075)	68.8
More developed regions	16.4	24.0	24.6	22.8	25.0	(2030)	25.7
Less developed regions	21.2	60.5	95.6	98.5	100.2	(2080)	95.5
Africa	7.5	26.8	60.8	76.1	76.1	(2100)	71.3
Southern Africa	5.9	19.0	17.5	17.0	19.6	(2005)	18.8
Eastern Africa	10.8	41.7	101.5	133.6	134.0	(2105)	125.8
Middle Africa	4.1	14.3	41.0	54.7	54.7	(2100)	49.5
Western Africa	10.0	37.3	94.1	121.4	121.6	(2105)	112.8
Northern Africa	6.6	21.4	37.7	38.2	39.6	(2075)	36.6
Asia	45.3	119.3	169.2	162.7	170.8	(2065)	160.2
Western Asia	10.8	40.8	85.1	100.4	100.4	(2095)	94.7
India	120.3	342.0	515.1	490.5	523.8	(2065)	461.4
Other South-central Asia	19.3	64.1	127.4	138.1	140.4	(2085)	126.1
South-eastern Asia	40.8	119.3	176.0	168.5	178.1	(2060)	169.5
China	59.5	136.7	149.6	126.7	155.5	(2030)	137.8
Other Eastern Asia	53.8	95.2	90.1	74.8	98.1	(2015)	82.7
Latin America and the Caribbean	8.3	25.8	38.0	36.3	38.6	(2065)	35.8
Brazil	6.4	20.3	27.6	25.1	27.6	(2055)	26.3
Other South America	6.5	19.3	30.5	30.2	31.5	(2070)	28.9
Caribbean	74.4	164.6	200.1	184.0	201.1	(2045)	178.5
Central America	15.3	55.9	87.5	84.4	89.6	(2065)	81.6
Oceania	1.5	3.7	5.4	5.4	5.5	(2075)	5.7
Polynesia	29.7	75.1	112.1	117.3	118.8	(2080)	116.9
Micronesia	84.1	272.6	471.8	503.6	505.5	(2085)	528.8
Melanesia	4.3	13.2	26.4	29.0	29.3	(2085)	26.4
Australia/New Zealand	1.3	2.9	3.8	3.6	3.8	(2050)	4.1
Northern America	9.2	16.9	23.9	25.3	26.2	(2150)	28.5
Europe	24.2	32.2	28.0	23.8	32.2	(2000)	27.0
Eastern Europe	11.9	16.4	11.9	9.4	16.7	(1990)	10.6
Southern Europe	84.1	112.5	96.9	76.0	112.9	(2005)	84.5
Western Europe	129.5	168.6	169.5	156.7	173.8	(2025)	180.6
Northern Europe	46.9	57.2	60.8	58.0	60.9	(2040)	65.9

Land area is of course a weak proxy for the natural resources available to a country. For instance, if one were to consider only land with crop production potential (Alexandratos, 1995), some comparisons would turn out quite different. The 2100 density in Bangladesh of 1,997 persons per sq. km. of land area would change to 2,793 persons per sq. km. of potential cropland, or 28 persons per hectare. The situation for other countries would change even more. Afghanistan has a density of 138 in 2100, but relative to potential cropland this would rise to 2,768, essentially the same level as in Bangladesh. Yemen is probably the extreme case, where 2100 density of 273 would instead be estimated as 17,071 in relation to potential cropland. Whether potential cropland may be much more productive by 2100 or possibly more degraded, or somehow much less relevant, one cannot say. Many complications of this sort will have to be addressed in working out consequences of these projections.

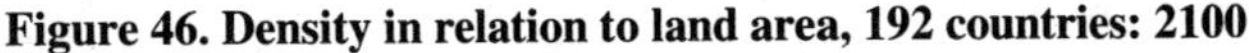

Figure 46. Density in relation to land area, 192 countries: 2100

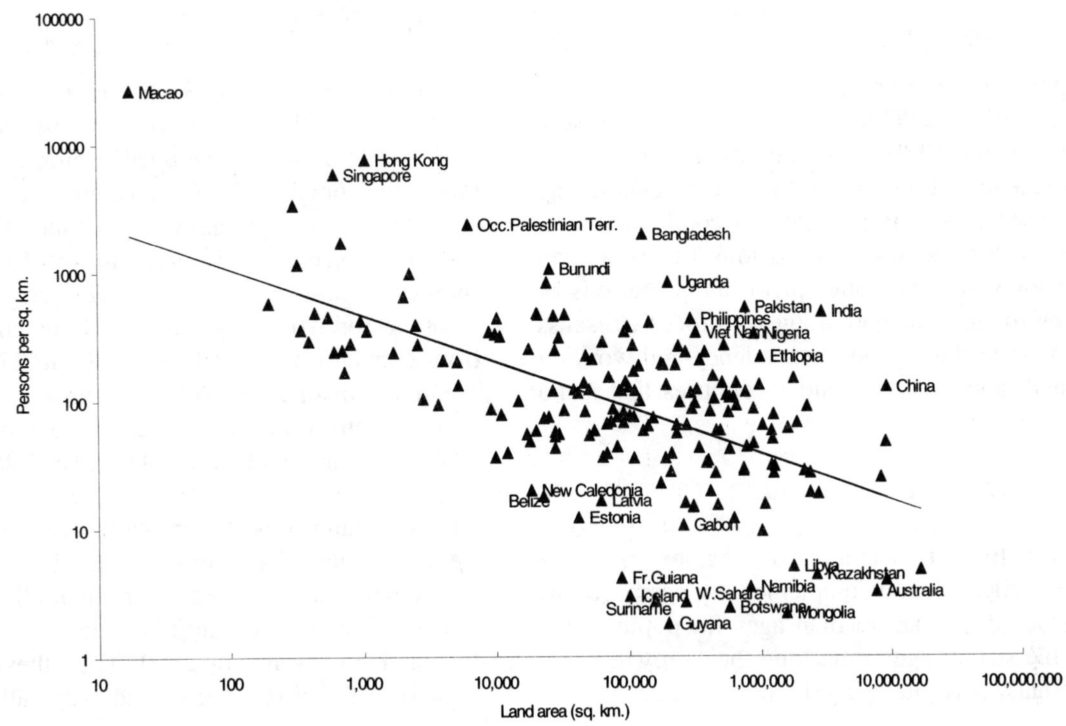

V. AGEING POPULATIONS

Apart from coping with population size, growth, and decline, countries will have to cope with substantial ageing of their populations. This process, a consequence of falling fertility and lengthening life expectancies, is expected to continue indefinitely. The following sections look first at ageing in major areas, then attempt to define periods or phases for the population ageing process, discuss the ages at which young dependency and working life end, and finally consider countries that stand out.

A. MAJOR AREAS

Alternative indicators for ageing provide slightly different and complementary perspectives. Considered first are median ages for populations, then the size of age groups and their growth rates, and finally percentage distributions by age.

The median age of 37.3 years in more developed regions in 2000 is well above the median age of 24.1 years in less developed regions, but both more developed and less developed regions can expect these median ages to rise (figure 47). In the 50-year projections, the median age for Europe rises ten years, from 37.7 to 47.7 years. The median age for Africa rises almost as much, though from a much lower level, from 18.3 to 27.5 years. The other major areas are all intermediate between these extremes, and their median ages converge, so that they are all close to 40 years by 2050.

In long-range projections beyond 2050, trends are somewhat more complex. Median ages for some major areas cross over, and all medians eventually converge, until they are all between 44.7 and 46.1 years in 2150. Then they diverge again over the next 50 years and eventually follow

Figure 47. Median age, major areas: 1950-2300

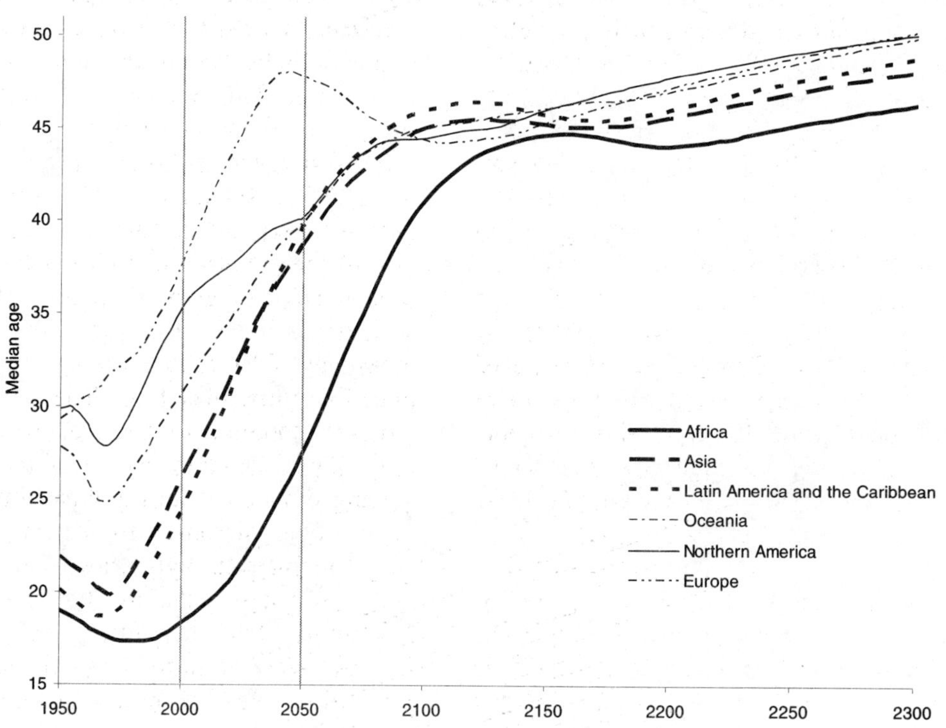

largely parallel paths. By 2300, median ages in Europe and Northern America are at half the life expectancy, or just over 50 years, 1.4 years above median ages in Latin America and the Caribbean, 2.1 years above those in Asia, and 3.9 years above those in Africa. Entire populations with half their members over 50 may seem, today, unusually old. This is of course a very long-range projection, but note that Europe is expected to be almost at this level, with a median age of 47.7 years, by 2045.

Median age rises not simply because of growth for older age groups but also because of some declines in size for younger age groups. It is useful to focus initially on broad age groups: those of working age, conventionally defined as 15-64 years, and the "dependent" population aged 0-14 years and 65 years and older. Even with this drastic simplification, the pattern of age-group growth and decline over time is complex and not easily described (table 14). Generally, declines are projected for those aged 0-14 years as well as for those aged 15-64, but not in all periods nor for all major areas. Some declines are large, though they are produced by relatively small annual changes. For instance, a 27 per cent decrease in the population aged 0-14 years in Europe from 2000 to 2050 is equivalent to an average growth rate of only -0.6 per cent annually, and a contrasting increase, in the same period, of 48 per cent in Africa involves an average growth rate of 0.8 per cent annually. For those aged 0-14 years, declines appear earlier, for those 15-64 years later, sometimes preceded, in both cases, by substantial increases. Declines are not synchronized across major areas, as seen earlier for overall population change. Declines start in Europe, generally move through other major areas, and eventually affect Africa. By 2175, declines in the size of age groups under 65 years are essentially over in all countries. (This point comes much earlier for the majority of countries.) From this point, too, age groups under 65 are essentially stationary and unchanging in size in each country.

This is not the case for the population aged 65 years and older. This group is not affected by decline, expect in Europe between 2050 and 2100. In fact, this older age group more than quadruples in size in Africa, Asia, and Latin America and the Caribbean between 2000 and 2050 and continues to grow thereafter. The 2000-2050 growth rate for this age group is 2.4 per cent annually worldwide, 3.0 per cent annually in less developed regions.

The population 80 years old and older, which is a part of this age group, is relatively small worldwide and increases even faster, at 3.4 per cent annually worldwide in 2000-2050. In raw numbers for 2000, those 80 years old and over are 37 million in more developed regions, 32 million in less developed regions. The 50-year projections take their numbers up to 113 million and 265 million, respectively. By 2300, they are projected at 267 million in more developed regions and 1.26 billion in less developed regions.

The subgroup of those who are 100 years old and older increase even faster in 2000-2050, at 6 per cent annually worldwide. In actual numbers, they rise from only 170,000 worldwide in 2000 to 17.6 million by 2100, meaning that millions already born will be around to see the turn of the century. By 2300, they will be 162 million.

The large changes in the size of age groups affect the balance across ages, though proportions do not change as dramatically as raw numbers. Consider first more developed and less developed regions. Under the assumptions of the 300-year projections—largely constant fertility in the long run and mortality at younger ages falling to low levels—younger age groups (figure 48 shows ages 0-14, 15-29, 30-44, and 45-59) eventually become similar in size and decline in parallel as a proportion of the population. Both more developed and less developed regions show this pattern. The age structure is like a cake with added layers (of increasingly older cohorts) being piled on top, one after the other, over time. The lower layers (the younger cohorts) shrink proportionally, though only slightly, from the weight of the added layers, staying about equal among themselves. The added layers come, of course, from rising life expectancies, which increasingly determine the age composition of the population. When the effects on population of fertility differences between countries disappear from the projections, by 2225, the proportion at each age becomes almost perfectly correlated, across countries, with life expectancies.

TABLE 14. POPULATION IN BROAD AGE GROUPS AND PERCENTAGE CHANGE OVER LONG PERIODS: MAJOR AREAS

Major area	Millions, 2000	Percentage change 2000-2050	2050-2100	2100-2300	Millions, 2000	Percentage change 2000-2050	2050-2100	2100-2300
	0-14				*15-64*			
World	1 828	-1.9	-17.0	-5.8	3 823	49.3	-6.0	-13.0
More developed regions	219	-12.4	-0.6	-0.3	804	-11.4	-11.9	1.0
Less developed regions	1 609	-0.5	-19.0	-6.6	3 019	65.4	-5.2	-14.8
Africa	340	47.7	-21.8	-12.9	430	174.0	20.6	-19.9
Asia	1 119	-13.2	-17.4	-4.0	2 345	43.8	-13.0	-12.5
Latin America and the Caribbean	166	-16.3	-18.2	-2.2	326	50.1	-14.7	-11.5
Oceania	8	3.3	-9.5	-3.1	20	44.0	-9.0	-7.7
Northern America	68	16.4	1.2	-0.4	209	32.5	-5.4	1.6
Europe	127	-26.7	-2.2	-0.2	493	-26.6	-16.5	0.5
	65 and older				*80 and older*			
World	419	238.4	55.9	31.2	69	446.0	104.8	97.6
More developed regions	171	84.8	-0.9	45.5	37	207.1	20.8	96.0
Less developed regions	248	344.0	72.2	28.8	32	716.9	140.6	98.0
Africa	26	376.8	259.4	43.8	3	586.9	480.8	162.0
Asia	216	307.3	45.8	25.2	29	660.9	102.9	86.8
Latin America and the Caribbean	28	390.7	44.3	20.2	5	673.0	116.1	64.3
Oceania	3	187.9	41.4	36.7	1	310.8	72.5	101.5
Northern America	39	135.8	43.2	43.1	10	230.8	70.6	92.4
Europe	107	64.7	-18.0	49.5	21	182.8	2.1	106.4

Figure 48. Distribution of population by age, more developed and less developed regions: 1950-2300

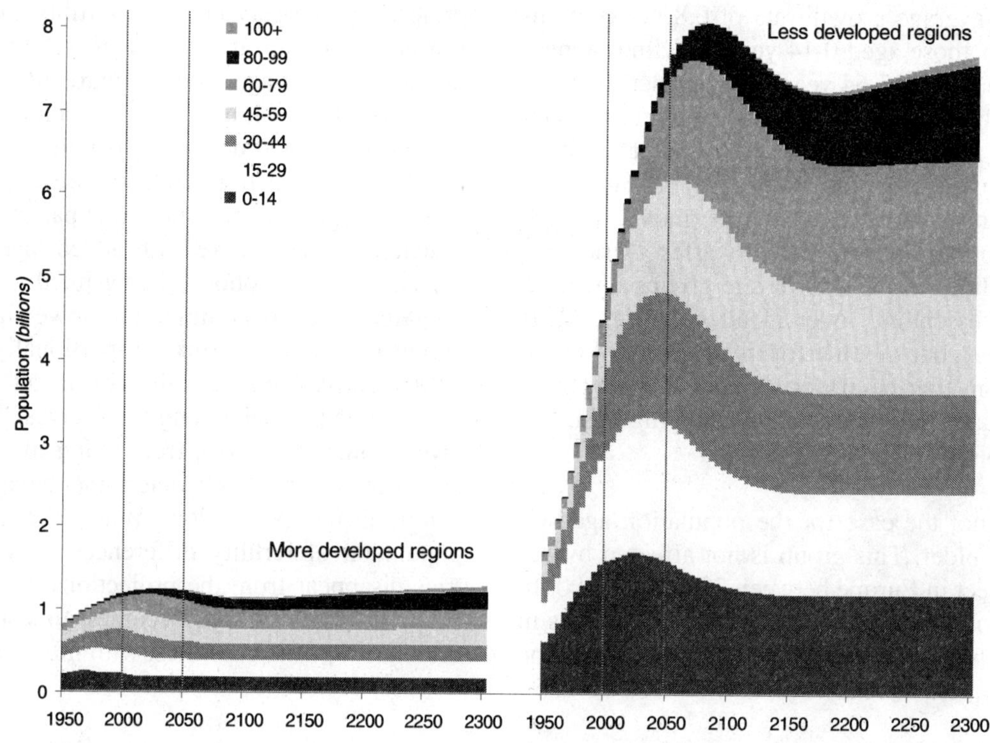

By 2300, more developed and less developed regions have roughly similar distributions, at least at younger ages. In more developed regions, 14.9 per cent of the population is in each 15-year age group up to age 59, as compared with 15.7 per cent in less developed regions. However, since life expectancies still differ, the oldest age groups continue to differ, with 20.9 per cent of the population being 80 years or older in more developed regions, as contrasted with 16.4 per cent in less developed regions.

Major areas that initially look very different in age structures do gradually come to resemble each other with the large changes shown for age groups. Still, complete convergence of age structures does not occur in these projections (table 15). In 2000, children and youth aged 0-14 years are 43 per cent of the population in Africa but only 17 per cent of the population in Europe (figure 49). The gap is reduced to 28 per cent versus 15 per cent by 2050, at the same time that other major areas converge at around 18 per cent. Africa and Europe also converge, though not until 2105.

For other age groups, the major contrast is also between Europe and Africa. Between 2000 and 2050, people aged 15-64 years increase in Africa from 54 to 65 per cent and decrease in Europe from 68 to 57 per cent. Beyond 2050, these trends reverse, but a gap remains by 2100 and continues through 2300. By 2100, Africa will have 63 per cent of its population in working ages, as contrasted with 56 per cent in Europe. Both percentages decline through 2300 roughly in parallel. Other major areas show intermediate levels over time.

In 2000, people 65 years old and over are 15 per cent of the population in Europe, 3 per cent of the population in Africa. By 2100, both percentages rise substantially and the gap closes somewhat—27 versus 20 per cent. But by 2300 the contrast still remains—35 per cent versus 30 per cent. As is obvious from growth rates, this older population is

Figure 49. Distribution of population in three broad age groups, major areas: 1950-2100

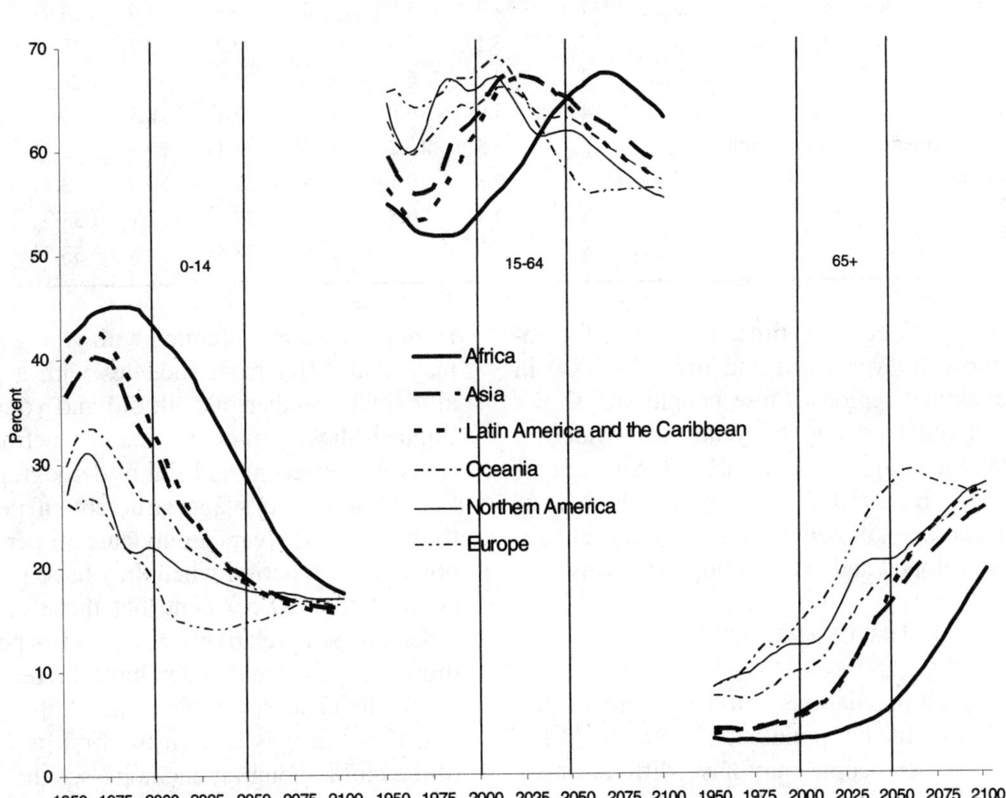

TABLE 15. PERCENTAGE IN DIFFERENT AGE GROUPS, BY MAJOR AREA: 1950-2300

Age group and Major area	*1950*	*2000*	*2050*	*2100*	*2150*	*2200*	*2250*	*2300*
0-14 years								
World	34.3	30.1	20.1	16.4	16.5	16.5	16.0	15.6
More developed regions	27.4	18.3	15.7	16.9	16.4	15.7	15.3	14.9
Less developed regions	37.6	33.0	20.8	16.4	16.5	16.6	16.1	15.7
Africa	42.0	42.7	27.8	17.4	16.4	17.0	16.6	16.2
Asia	36.5	30.4	18.6	16.0	16.6	16.5	16.0	15.6
Latin America and the Caribbean	40.0	31.9	18.1	15.5	16.5	16.3	15.8	15.4
Oceania	29.9	25.8	18.1	16.3	16.3	16.0	15.5	15.0
Northern America	27.2	21.6	17.7	16.9	16.3	15.7	15.3	15.0
Europe	26.2	17.5	14.8	17.0	16.5	15.9	15.4	14.9
15-64 years								
World	60.5	63.0	64.0	59.2	56.0	54.7	53.3	52.0
More developed regions	64.8	67.4	58.4	55.5	54.4	52.4	50.8	49.5
Less developed regions	58.5	61.9	64.9	59.7	56.2	55.1	53.7	52.4
Africa	54.8	54.1	65.4	63.1	57.7	56.3	55.2	53.9
Asia	59.4	63.7	64.5	58.5	55.7	54.7	53.2	51.9
Latin America and the Caribbean	56.3	62.6	63.7	57.0	54.4	53.9	52.4	51.1
Oceania	62.8	64.4	62.8	56.9	54.6	53.2	51.5	50.0
Northern America	64.6	66.1	61.8	55.3	54.1	52.2	50.9	49.8
Europe	65.6	67.8	57.3	56.1	55.0	52.8	51.1	49.7
65+ years								
World	5.2	6.9	15.9	24.4	27.5	28.8	30.7	32.3
More developed regions	7.9	14.3	25.9	27.7	29.3	31.9	33.9	35.6
Less developed regions	3.9	5.1	14.3	23.9	27.2	28.2	30.1	31.8
Africa	3.2	3.2	6.8	19.5	25.9	26.7	28.2	29.9
Asia	4.1	5.9	16.8	25.5	27.7	28.8	30.9	32.5
Latin America and the Caribbean	3.7	5.5	18.2	27.5	29.1	29.7	31.8	33.5
Oceania	7.3	9.8	19.1	26.8	29.1	30.9	33.1	35.0
Northern America	8.2	12.3	20.5	27.7	29.6	32.1	33.9	35.2
Europe	8.2	14.7	27.9	26.9	28.5	31.3	33.5	35.4

itself getting older over time. Consider, for instance, those 80 years old and over. In 2000 in more developed regions, these people are 22 per cent of all older people (65 years and older); in less developed regions, they are 13 per cent of older people. By 2030, they are more than half of all older people—59 and 51 per cent respectively in more developed and less developed regions.

B. HISTORICAL PERIODS

All projected populations will have a mix of different generations, but populations with large proportions of older people may have different economic emphases and require different institutions from populations saturated with young people, and may also differ from societies with a proportionally small number of both old and young. To distinguish these situations, one can define three periods in the recent and future demographic evolution of a society's age structure: a period when those under 15 years are at least 30 per cent of the population; a period when they have fallen permanently under 30 per cent, but those 65 years and older are still relatively few; and a period when those 65 years and older have increased permanently to at least 15 per cent of the population. The focus here is less on the first period, the age of the child, though it encompasses the majority of societies in 2000, but more on the middle period, which is labelled the demographic window. The third period, or the third age, if you like, is an extended period in these projections that would be worth subdividing into shorter periods if more information and insight were available about how social dynamics evolve in older populations.

The specific cutting points between periods are set somewhat arbitrarily and obviously assume that the dependency burdens and social implications of large proportions of older persons are not equivalent to those of similar proportions of youth. With these cutting points, the three periods almost always follow in sequence. In only two countries (Argentina and Timor-Leste) does the proportion aged 0-14 years fall below 30 per cent and then rise above it again. In both cases it falls permanently below 30 per cent within 15-25 years, and the later point is taken as the dividing point between periods. Similarly, in only four countries or areas (Austria, the Channel Islands, Denmark, and Germany) does the proportion aged 65 years and older rise above 15 per cent and then fall below it—only to rise permanently above 15 per cent in 15-20 years. Again, the later point is taken as the critical one.

Societies who have entered the demographic window have proportionally large working-age populations and relatively light dependency burdens, and therefore the demographic potential for high economic growth. This period (though not defined precisely as it is here) has been characterized as a "demographic window" of great economic possibilities, because of the bonus of a favourable age structure (e.g., Bloom, Canning, and Sevilla, 2003). Whether the economic potential is realized depends on a variety of complementary considerations, such as the quality of this workforce, the availability of complementary resources, the nature of government policy, and the structure of international competition. Whether the demographic window also confers other economic advantages, such as greater entrepreneurship and risk-taking, is more speculative. Conceivably, the preceding period, the child decades, might have an advantage in this. The child decades also feature larger potential numbers of young households with higher consumption needs. Nor are prospects during the third age necessarily bleak. Societies that build up their human, institutional, and other capital over the demographic window phase and develop fiscally sound institutional arrangements, particularly intergenerational ones, could enter the third age with the prospect for continued high productivity. The demographic balance among generations does not dictate societal prospects, though it provides particular opportunities and challenges.

The demographic window phase starts in 1950 or earlier for Europe as a whole—the data considered here do not go back earlier—and comes to an end in 2000. Because population is projected by quinquennia, the period might actually last up to four years longer (and in theory start up to four years earlier, if a starting date were specified), but greater precision was not attempted. Figure 50 shows not only the length of this period in each major area but also the dependency ratio, the ratio of dependents to working-age population (multiplied by 100) during the period. During the demographic window phase, this ratio is roughly between 40 and 60 (as contrasted, say, with 92-96 in 2000 in Eastern, Middle and Western Africa). For Europe as a whole, the dependency ratio starts at 52 in 1950 (at least the portion of them observed), rises to 56, and finally falls to 48. This pattern is not typical. In most cases, the dependency ratio declines during the demographic window phase, hits a minimum, and starts to rise as the demographic window phase ends.

Other regions show staggered periods of high worker potential, given the way demographic change sweeps across the world in various directions. For Northern America, with higher fertility and migration, the demographic window phase comes later than in Europe, in 1970-2015, during which the dependency ratio drops from 62 to 49. Asia and Latin America and the Caribbean both pass through the demographic window later but at the same time, in 2005-2040, and with a similar pattern for dependency ratios. Africa enters the demographic window even later, in 2045, and exits in 2080. Oceania is a complex case (figure 51). Australia and New Zealand go through the demographic window at about the same time as the United States of America and Canada, and the dependency ratio shows a steep decline, as for the United States of America, as well as a continuing decline after a brief reversal, as for Canada. In contrast, Melanesia, Micronesia, and Polynesia

Figure 50. Dependency ratio during the demographic window phase, major areas

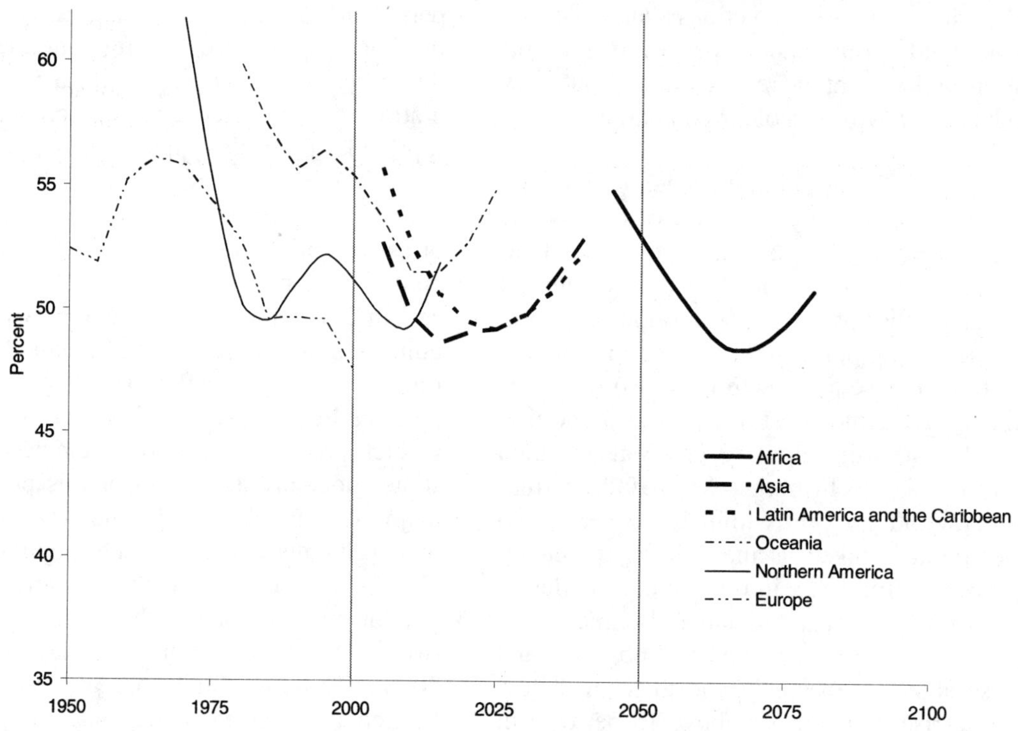

Figure 51. Dependency ratio during the demographic window phase, regions of Oceania and Northern American countries

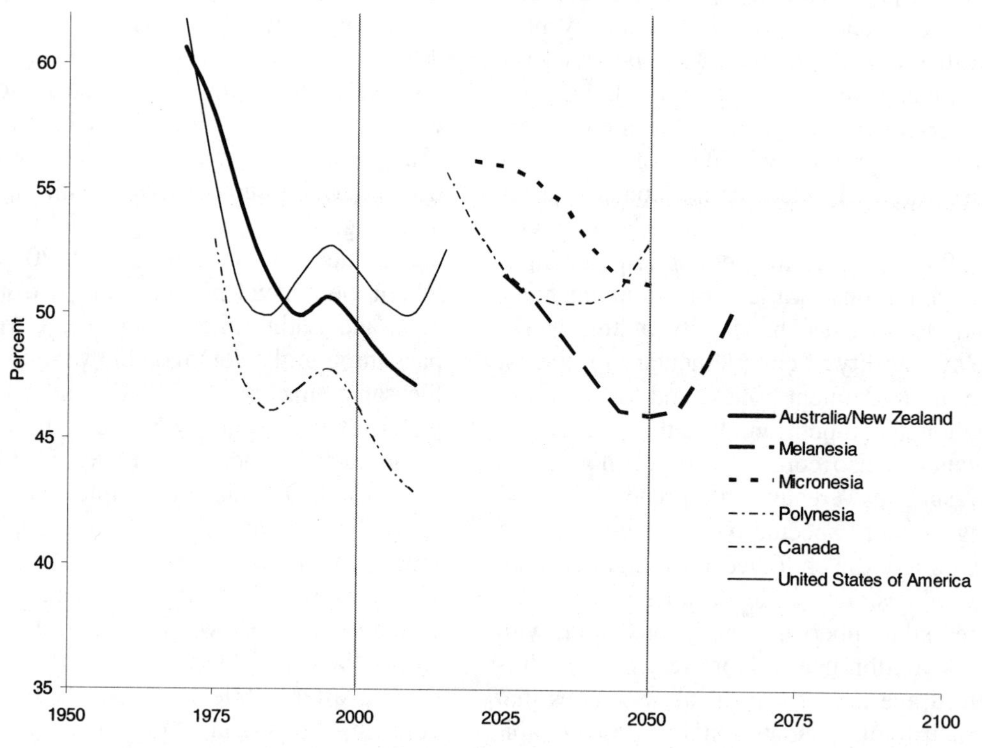

enter the demographic window much later, in a pattern typical of less developed regions.

Patterns for regions on other continents generally resemble those for the continents as a whole, though some patterns are distinctive (table 16). In Europe, Eastern Europe stands out, with longer demographic window phases, lasting up to 2015, and the dependency ratio falling as low as 39. In Asia, the pattern for Eastern Asia aside from China (meaning mainly Japan and the Koreas) resembles that for more developed regions, with the demographic window phase coming early and ending by 2000. China goes through the demographic window a little later but earlier than the rest of Asia. In Africa, the Eastern, Middle and Western African regions clearly enter the demographic window latest of all, not starting until 2050 or 2055.

C. Dependency thresholds

One arbitrary aspect of the definition of three periods is the specific age limits that define dependency. It is commonly assumed that young dependency ends at age 15, though youth certainly do not begin working everywhere at this age. Some may start earlier, but in modern societies the start of working life appears increasingly delayed beyond 15 by extended education. The commonly accepted age to start old dependency is 65 years, though older people do not retire everywhere at that age, and may need to less often in the future given the health improvements presumably underlying rising life expectancies. One can ask the question about historical periods differently. If one wanted young dependents to be less than 30 per cent of the population, and old dependents less than 15 per cent, what age limits would be sufficient to accomplish this? At what age would youth have to enter the labour force, and at what age would old people be able to retire, for a country to maintain the worker potential represented by the demographic window?

In more developed regions as a whole in 2000, youth could avoid working until age 23, and young dependents would still be under 30 per cent of the population. Old people could not retire until age 65 if old dependents were to stay under 15 per cent of the population (figure 52). These ages are labelled dependency thresholds and vary with the population age structure, in contrast to the fixed thresholds of 15 and 65 years generally used in calculating dependency ratios. Variable dependency thresholds have reasonable values when countries are in or close to the demographic window, but can get unusually high or low further out.

Back in 1950, the variable young dependency threshold in more developed regions was 16 years, and the variable old dependency threshold was 57 years. Old people could have retired by age 57 according to the societal criterion used, though many may not have done so. Not doing so, of course, would have added to their societies' worker potential in that year. For 2050, the dependency thresholds in more developed regions rise to 27 and 75 years. If old dependents are not to exceed their current proportion in the population, retirement ages would have to rise ten years between 2000 and 2050, and working lives would be delayed and lengthened, by six years. If age 74 is considered too old to work, more developed regions as a whole would require a substantial transformation—characterized as the movement from the demographic window phase to the third age—in which old dependents become increasingly prominent in the population.

In less developed regions, variable dependency thresholds are substantially lower. In 2000, they are 13 and 50 years. Since having children start working at age 13 is undesirable, the implication can be drawn that less developed regions as a whole—though not necessarily individual countries—cannot escape being in the age of the child, cannot at this time mobilize a sufficiently large workforce to enter the demographic window phase. These low ages suggest, in addition, that there could be demographic pressure for children to work. For 2050, dependency thresholds in less developed regions rise to 21 and 65 years, about what they are in more developed regions in 2000.

Dependency thresholds vary across major areas largely as one would expect. They are quite low in Africa: 9 and 44 years in 2000, and still only 16 and 55 years by 2050, suggesting that Africa is inescapably stuck in the age of the child for several decades. Dependency thresholds are quite high in Europe: 24 and 65 years in 2000, rising to

TABLE 16. START AND END YEAR OF THE DEMOGRAPHIC WINDOW PHASE AND CORRESPONDING DEPENDENCY RATIO, BY MAJOR AREA AND REGION, ESTIMATES AND MEDIUM SCENARIO

	Demographic window		*Dependency ratio*		
Major area and region	*Start*	*End*	*Start*	*Minimum*	*End*
World	2005	2045	55.4	52.4	55.6
More developed regions	Pre-1950	2000	54.4	48.4	48.4
Less developed regions	2010	2050	54.3	52.2	54.2
Africa	2045	2080	54.8	48.5	50.8
Southern Africa	2020	2070	56.3	47.4	53.2
Eastern Africa	2050	2085	53.4	46.6	50.5
Middle Africa	2055	2090	51.4	44.6	50.1
Western Africa	2050	2085	52.9	47.8	51.5
Northern Africa	2020	2050	52.6	47.3	50.8
Asia	2005	2040	52.7	48.6	52.9
Western Asia	2020	2060	55.3	53.7	54.7
India	2010	2050	54.8	47.4	49.4
Other South-central Asia	2025	2060	54.5	47.7	50.8
South-eastern Asia	2010	2045	50.2	46.4	50.9
China	1990	2025	49.8	39.6	46.1
Other Eastern Asia	1970	2000	54.9	43.9	44.9
Latin America and the Caribbean	2005	2040	55.7	49.2	52.4
Brazil	2000	2035	52.7	45.7	49.9
Other South America	2010	2040	55.0	51.4	52.7
Caribbean	2000	2030	57.6	52.3	54.9
Central America	2015	2040	52.9	48.5	50.9
Oceania	1980	2025	59.9	51.5	54.9
Polynesia	2015	2050	55.6	50.4	52.9
Micronesia	2020	2050	56.1	51.2	51.2
Melanesia	2025	2065	51.6	45.9	50.4
Australia/New Zealand	1970	2010	60.6	47.2	47.2
Northern America	1970	2015	61.7	49.3	51.9
Europe	Pre-1950	2000	52.4	47.5	47.5
Eastern Europe	Pre-1950	2015	53.0	38.6	40.6
Southern Europe	Pre-1950	1995	54.5	46.9	46.9
Western Europe	Pre-1950	1990	50.4	47.2	47.6
Northern Europe	Pre-1950	1985	51.5	51.5	52.6

29 and 75 years in 2050. These threshold ages are higher by 3-5 years than those for Northern America.

Over the long run, the young dependency threshold will rise, to 25-28 years by 2100 across regions, and to 27-30 years by 2300 (table 17). The old dependency threshold will also rise, toward possibly unrealistic levels: 70-77 years by 2100, and 80-87 years by 2300. Whether people will be both able and willing to work to these ages in the future seems unlikely at present, which may imply that societies will not be able to avoid shifting to third-age social and institutional arrangements, whatever those turn out to be.

Note however that, should retirement ages actually rise in accordance with the variable old dependency threshold, the post-retirement period will not necessarily be any shorter for most people. Between life expectancy and retirement defined by the old dependency threshold in 2000, the average difference worldwide is 12 years (see table 17). This shrinks by 2050 to 9 years, but in the

TABLE 17. DEPENDENCY THRESHOLD AGES AND POST-RETIREMENT DURATION, BY MAJOR AREA AND REGION, SELECTED YEARS

Major area and region	*1950*	*1975*	*2000*	*2025*	*2050*	*2075*	*2100*	*2200*	*2300*
				Young dependency threshold[a]					
World	12	11	14	18	22	25	26	27	28
More developed regions	16	18	23	27	27	27	26	28	30
Less developed regions	11	10	13	17	21	25	27	27	28
Africa	9	9	9	12	16	21	25	26	27
Asia	11	10	14	19	23	26	27	27	28
Latin America and the Caribbean	10	10	14	19	24	27	28	27	29
Oceania	15	14	17	21	24	26	27	28	29
Northern America	16	17	21	23	24	26	26	28	30
Europe	17	18	24	30	29	27	26	28	30
				Old dependency threshold[a]					
World	52	51	54	61	66	71	74	79	83
More developed regions	57	61	65	70	75	77	78	82	87
Less developed regions	49	47	50	58	65	70	73	78	82
Africa	46	44	44	47	55	63	70	76	80
Asia	49	48	52	60	67	72	75	79	83
Latin America/Caribbean	48	47	50	60	69	74	77	80	84
Oceania	56	55	58	65	70	74	76	81	86
Northern America	58	60	62	68	71	74	77	82	86
Europe	57	62	65	70	75	77	77	82	87
				Post-retirement duration based on retiring at threshold[b]					
World	-6.2	7.9	11.8	9.6	8.7	8.9	9.0	13.0	14.3
More developed regions	8.7	11.4	11.0	9.2	7.5	8.9	10.7	13.9	14.9
Less developed regions	-8.9	8.8	13.4	10.3	9.2	8.9	8.8	12.9	14.2
Africa	-8.3	3.5	6.0	9.7	11.7	10.3	8.8	12.1	13.8
Asia	-9.2	9.4	14.9	11.9	9.5	9.1	9.2	13.3	14.3
Latin America/Caribbean	2.9	15.3	19.9	15.7	10.8	8.3	8.3	12.9	14.2
Oceania	4.0	11.7	15.7	13.4	12.0	10.5	10.6	13.5	14.8
Northern America	11.1	12.9	15.4	11.8	11.4	11.4	11.2	14.1	15.0
Europe	7.6	9.8	9.0	7.9	5.7	7.4	10.3	13.7	14.8
				Post-retirement duration based on retiring at 65 years					
World	-20.0	-6.1	0.0	4.6	9.7	14.0	17.4	26.2	31.3
More developed regions	0.0	6.8	10.3	14.1	16.8	19.9	22.7	30.7	36.2
Less developed regions	-25.6	-9.3	-2.1	2.9	8.6	13.2	16.7	25.5	30.6
Africa	-28.3	-17.8	-15.5	-9.0	0.7	7.9	12.8	23.0	28.0
Asia	-25.4	-7.6	1.4	6.7	11.4	15.3	18.3	26.6	31.6
Latin America/Caribbean	-15.1	-3.0	4.9	10.0	13.8	16.8	19.5	27.6	33.1
Oceania	-5.6	1.6	8.7	13.0	16.0	18.7	21.2	29.3	35.3
Northern America	3.4	7.5	11.9	14.5	16.9	20.2	23.2	30.9	35.5
Europe	-0.7	6.2	8.7	12.7	15.7	18.9	21.6	29.9	35.9

[a] The young dependency threshold is the age at which dependency must end if young dependents are to be limited to less than 30 per cent of the population. The old dependency threshold is the earliest possible retirement age if old dependents are to be limited to less than 15 per cent of the population.

[b] Calculated as the difference between life expectancy and the retirement threshold age.

Figure 52. Dependency thresholds, life expectancy at birth, and expected working life, more developed and less developed regions: 1950-2050

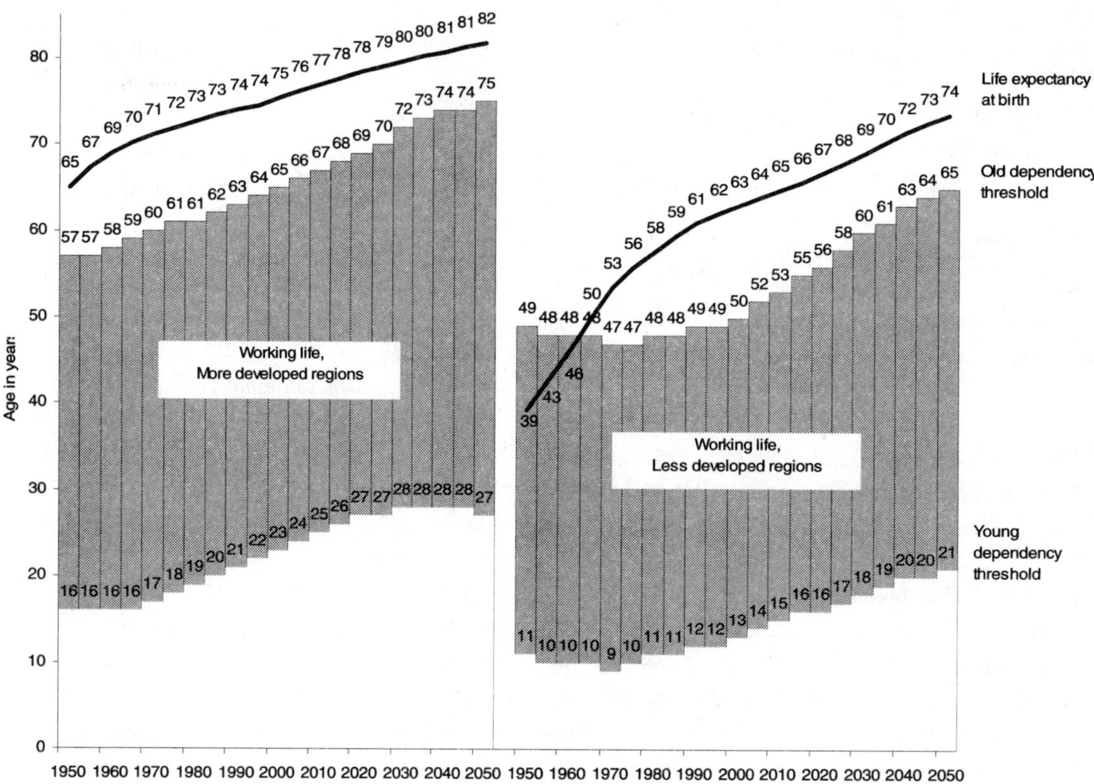

long run rises, by 2300, to 14 years. Under the contrary assumption that retirement age is fixed indefinitely at 65 years, the average worldwide gap between life expectancy and retirement age is only two weeks in 2000 but reaches 10 years in 2050 and 31 years in 2300.

D. Countries

Individual countries are easiest to compare with regard to median ages. While median ages rose, in most regions, between 1950 and 2000, they fell in Africa. This is reflected in falling medians among the ten countries with the lowest median age (table 18). In 1950, this list of the countries with the youngest populations included some far-flung island states, but from 2000 on, the list is almost exclusively African. From 2000 on also, median ages even among these youngest countries show increases, initially quite dramatic ones.

In the relatively short run, both fertility and mortality contribute to countries having particularly young populations. The countries with the youngest populations tend to be those with high fertility. In addition, HIV/AIDS-related mortality can reduce the adult population. In the longer run, slower decline in mortality at advanced ages keeps the older population from growing faster. Between 2000 and 2050, the list of youngest countries shows some rearrangement but little turnover, with only one country being replaced. But between 2050 and 2100, six countries are replaced, all by Southern African or neighbouring Southern African Development Community countries severely affected by HIV/AIDS. Over the following decades and centuries, these countries fall out of the list again, until only one—Malawi—is left by 2250. From 2200 to 2300, Liberia, Mali, and Sierra Leone are the three youngest countries (in varying order) and a few non-African countries—Yemen, Afghanistan, and Cambodia—also appear on the list. Especially in the later years of the projections, the list is increasingly similar to that of the countries with the lowest life expectancies.

Between these youngest countries and the oldest countries, the gap in median ages is especially

TABLE 18. COUNTRIES WITH THE LOWEST AND HIGHEST MEDIAN AGES, SELECTED YEARS

Rank	*1950*		*2000*		*2050*		*2100*	
			A. Lowest median age					
1	St. Vincent/Grenadines	15.4	Uganda	15.1	Niger	20.0	Swaziland	35.8
2	Tonga	15.5	Niger	15.1	Angola	22.0	Zimbabwe	36.0
3	Djibouti	16.5	Mali	15.4	Somalia	22.1	Botswana	37.1
4	Samoa	16.6	Yemen	15.4	Yemen	22.3	Niger	37.7
5	Fiji	16.6	Burkina Faso	15.5	Uganda	22.5	Lesotho	38.1
6	Rwanda	16.7	Burundi	15.8	Mali	22.6	Zambia	38.7
7	Botswana	16.8	Somalia	16.0	Burkina Faso	22.7	Malawi	38.8
8	Vanuatu	16.8	Angola	16.3	Guinea-Bissau	23.1	Liberia	39.1
9	United Rep. of Tanzania	16.9	Congo, DR	16.5	Liberia	23.3	Angola	39.2
10	Iraq	17.0	Liberia	16.6	Burundi	23.4	Mali	39.4
			B. Highest median age					
183	Norway	32.7	Croatia	38.9	Greece	51.3	Bahrain	46.9
184	Switzerland	33.3	Greece	39.1	Armenia	51.5	Hong Kong SAR	47.0
185	Sweden	34.3	Belgium	39.1	Czech Republic	51.7	Qatar	47.0
186	France	34.5	Bulgaria	39.1	Spain	51.9	Brunei Darussalam	47.0
187	United Kingdom	34.6	Finland	39.4	Singapore	52.0	U.S. Virgin Islands	47.2
188	Luxembourg	35.0	Sweden	39.6	Estonia	52.3	Uruguay	47.2
189	Germany	35.4	Germany	39.9	Italy	52.4	Kuwait	47.2
190	Belgium	35.6	Switzerland	40.2	Latvia	53.0	Japan	47.4
191	Channel Islands	35.7	Italy	40.2	Slovenia	53.1	Israel	47.6
192	Austria	35.8	Japan	41.3	Japan	53.2	Costa Rica	47.8

Rank	*2150*		*2200*		*2250*		*2300*	
			A. Lowest median age					
1	Zimbabwe	41.1	Sierra Leone	41.1	Liberia	42.5	Liberia	43.6
2	Swaziland	41.2	Liberia	41.6	Sierra Leone	42.6	Mali	43.7
3	Botswana	42.5	Mali	42.1	Mali	42.8	Sierra Leone	44.2
4	Liberia	42.6	Zimbabwe	42.2	Congo	43.6	Congo	44.4
5	South Africa	42.7	Swaziland	42.3	Malawi	43.8	Yemen	44.6
6	Dem. Rep. of Korea	42.8	Malawi	42.5	Yemen	43.9	Timor-Leste, DR	44.8
7	Sierra Leone	43.1	Timor-Leste, DR	42.8	Timor-Leste, DR	43.9	Malawi	45.0
8	Malawi	43.1	Congo	42.8	Afghanistan	44.2	Cambodia	45.1
9	Mali	43.2	Mozambique	43.1	Cambodia	44.2	Afghanistan	45.2
10	Republic of Moldova	43.4	Angola	43.4	Angola	44.4	Angola	45.7
			B. Highest median age					
183	Jordan	47.1	Norway	48.4	Austria	50.2	Republic of Korea	51.7
184	Papua New Guinea	47.1	France	48.5	France	50.3	Austria	51.9
185	Oman	47.1	Sweden	48.7	Republic of Korea	50.4	France	52.0
186	French Guiana	47.2	Belgium	48.7	Belgium	50.6	Belgium	52.1
187	Nicaragua	47.3	Republic of Korea	48.7	Sweden	50.6	Sweden	52.3
188	Samoa	47.4	Spain	48.7	Spain	50.6	Spain	52.4
189	Occ. Palestinian Terr.	47.4	Luxembourg	48.8	Luxembourg	50.7	Luxembourg	52.4
190	Colombia	47.5	Germany	48.9	Germany	50.9	Germany	52.6
191	Israel	47.7	Malta	49.1	Malta	51.0	Malta	52.7
192	Japan	48.0	Japan	49.8	Japan	51.5	Japan	53.0

large up to 2050. In 2050, the medians in the youngest countries are 20-23 years, as opposed to over 50 years in the oldest countries. The gap narrows subsequently to about 10 years or less. However, if one focuses on the oldest portion of the population, the contrasts are quite striking. Liberia, the youngest country from 2250 on, can be contrasted with Japan, the oldest country (figure 53). By 2300, the proportion 65-79 years old is actually slightly higher in Liberia than Japan, but the proportion 80-99 years old in Liberia is just over half that in Japan, and the proportion 100 years old and older in Liberia is only 0.06 per cent, as opposed to 7 per cent in Japan. Substantial contrasts at the oldest ages therefore remain up to the very end of these projections.

Japan leads the list of oldest populations virtually throughout the three centuries of the projections, though not historically, just as it leads the list of countries with highest life expectancies (see table 11). In 1950, the ten oldest countries were all Western or Northern European. In 2000, Japan enters and leads the list. In 2000 also, a couple of Southern European and a couple of Eastern European countries are added in 2000, and substantial turnover on the list continues after that. By 2050, Japan is still on the list, with 36.5 per cent of its population 65 years or older, and half of these 80 years or older. Also on the list are still the two Southern European countries, but every other country is replaced. For 2100, all but Japan are replaced again, and, by 2150, all but Japan and Israel (added in 2100) are replaced yet again. Finally, by 2200, European countries return to the list—a somewhat similar set to those with the oldest populations in 1950—though Japan continues to have the oldest population of all. Two factors are responsible for turnover in the rankings. First, the fact that median ages tend to converge, particularly at higher levels, makes rankings somewhat unstable. Second, the projected fall and then rise in fertility comes early in Europe, relative to other major areas, and while fertility recovers to replacement in Europe, other major areas are moving toward lower fertility and therefore, temporarily, greater population ageing.

By 2200, the list of oldest countries is virtually identical to the list of countries with the highest life expectancies. Through 2300, there is little further change in the list. By 2300, the Japanese population 65 years and older will be only a slightly larger proportion of the population than in 2050 (38.7 per cent), but those 80 years or older will be close to two-thirds of this group.

Countries with the oldest populations naturally enter the demographic window first, and countries with the youngest populations last. This was shown for Europe, where countries have entered the demographic window starting in 1950 or earlier. This is generally true country by country, except for a few, notably Albania and Ireland. Countries in Africa, in contrast, will wait up to 70 years to enter the demographic window. The last will be Niger (2070), preceded by Somalia (2065). Except for Yemen, all ten countries entering the demographic window in 2060 or later are in Eastern, Middle or Western Africa. Of the 12 countries entering in 2050 and 2055, all are in sub-Saharan Africa, except for Afghanistan. Table 19 shows when each country enters the demographic window. This period generally stretches for 30-40 years.

Figure 53. Percentage of population at older ages, Japan and Liberia: 1950-2300

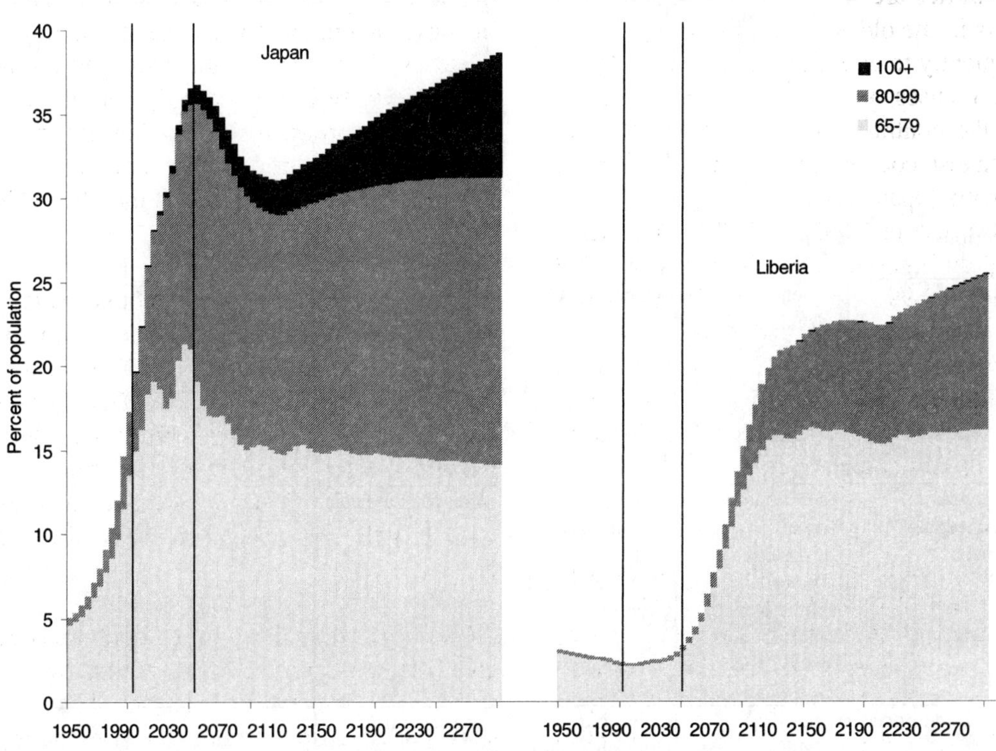

TABLE 19. STARTING DATE FOR ENTERING THE DEMOGRAPHIC WINDOW PHASE BY COUNTRY, CLASSIFIED BY MAJOR AREA

Date	*Africa*	*Asia*	*Latin America and the Caribbean*	*Oceania*	*Northern America*	*Europe*
Pre-1950			Uruguay			Austria, Belgium, Bulgaria, Channel Is., Croatia, Czech Rep., Denmark, Estonia, France, Germany, Greece, Hungary, Italy, Latvia, Lithuania, Luxembourg, Netherlands, Norway, Portugal, Romania, Russian Fed., Serbia and Montenegro, Slovenia, Spain, Sweden, Switzerland, Ukraine, United Kingdom
1965		Japan		Australia		Finland
1970					United States of America	Belarus, Malta, Poland, Slovakia
1975		China-Macao SAR, Cyprus, Georgia, United Arab Emirates		New Zealand	Canada	Republic of Moldova

TABLE 19 (*continued*)

Date	*Africa*	*Asia*	*Latin America and the Caribbean*	*Oceania*	*Northern America*	*Europe*
1980		China-Hong Kong SAR, Singapore	Barbados, Netherlands Antilles			Bosnia and Herzegovina, Iceland, TFYR Macedonia
1985		Dem. People's Rep. of Korea, Qatar, Rep. of Korea	Cuba, Guadeloupe, Martinique, Puerto Rico			Ireland
1990	Mauritius	China	United States Virgin Is.			
1995	Réunion	Armenia, Israel, Kazakhstan, Kuwait, Sri Lanka, Thailand	Argentina, Chile			
2000		Bahrain	Bahamas, Brazil, Trinidad and Tobago	New Caledonia		Albania
2005	Libyan Arab Jamahiriya, Tunisia	Azerbaijan, Brunei Darussalam, Indonesia, Islamic Rep. of Iran, Lebanon, Turkey, Viet Nam	Costa Rica, Guyana, Jamaica, St. Lucia, St. Vincent and Grenadines	French Polynesia		
2010	Algeria, Morocco	India, Kyrgyzstan, Malaysia, Mongolia, Myanmar, Turkmenistan, Uzbekistan	Colombia, Dominican Rep., Ecuador, Mexico, Panama, Peru, Suriname, Venezuela	Fiji, Guam		
2015	South Africa	Philippines, Tajikistan	El Salvador, French Guiana			
2020	Egypt, Western Sahara	Bangladesh, Jordan, Syrian Arab Rep.	Belize	Tonga		
2025	Cape Verde	Dem. Rep. of Timor-Leste, Saudi Arabia	Bolivia, Honduras	Fed. States of Micronesia		
2030	Gabon, Ghana, Sao Tome and Principe, Sudan	Lao People's Dem. Rep., Nepal, Oman	Guatemala, Haiti, Nicaragua, Paraguay	Papua New Guinea, Samoa, Solomon Islands, Vanuatu		
2035	Comoros, Côte d'Ivoire, Gambia, Kenya, Senegal	Bhutan, Cambodia, Iraq, Maldives, Pakistan				
2040	Cameroon, Nigeria, Togo, United Rep. of Tanzania					

TABLE 19 (*continued*)

Date	*Africa*	*Asia*	*Latin America and the Caribbean*	*Oceania*	*Northern America*	*Europe*
2045	Benin, Botswana, Central African Rep., Djibouti, Equatorial Guinea, Eritrea, Guinea, Madagascar, Mauritania, Namibia, Rwanda	Occupied Palestinian Territory				
2050	Ethiopia, Mozambique, Sierra Leone, Swaziland, Zimbabwe	Afghanistan				
2055	Chad, Congo, Dem. Rep. of the Congo, Lesotho, Malawi, Zambia					
2060	Angola, Burkina Faso, Burundi, Guinea-Bissau, Liberia, Mali, Uganda	Yemen				
2065	Somalia					
2070	Niger					

NOTE: Countries go through a period labelled here the demographic window, when the proportion of children and youth under 15 years falls below 30 per cent and the proportion of people 65 years and older is still below 15 per cent.

VI. CONCLUSION

These projections were introduced as an attempt to work out the long-range demographic implications of the 50-year projections in the *2002 Revision* of the United Nations population figures. Long-range trends are examined partly as a way to reflect on the situation and trends in our own time. The picture beyond 2050, though it is based on what goes before, involves some interesting twists and turns. Population growth falls and rises, and population totals in 2300, at least for the world as a whole, end up close to where they are expected to be in 2050. This result is not obvious from 50-year projections, and is at least one new finding from long-range projections.

Long-range projections also show regions and countries changing in absolute and relative size, growth, density, median ages, fertility, and mortality. All country populations age, but at different rates and with different timing; demographic homogeneity is not achieved even after three centuries. Without recapitulating the projected trends already described, it bears emphasizing that 50-year projections cannot sufficiently work out all these demographic implications of earlier trends.

A. Consequences

Given the demographic implications that have been drawn out, do any long-range threats emerge to human welfare? Since the focus here is on describing the demographic trends rather than assessing economic, social, political, environmental, or other consequences, this question is not answered but rather posed for others to consider. There are certainly aspects of these projections that could suggest a need for societal responses. Perhaps growth, as estimated, will be too rapid in some countries, or population decline too severe, or the long-range population and the density it implies too much of a burden. Perhaps some countries are ageing too fast given the institutional structures to deal with this issue, or too slowly so that young dependents continue to drain economic resources and receive inadequate preparation to become fully productive. Many varied aspects of these projections are worth examining from the perspective of whether societies are prepared to deal with populations of such size, growth rates, or composition.

What does not happen in these projections, the demographic events projected not to occur, could also in a different way pose social challenges. For instance, the projections assume that HIV transmission slows progressively from 2010, and that mortality therefore does not stay at elevated levels in the affected countries. From what is known of previous epidemics, such an assumption appears reasonable, but how it will come to pass is not yet clear. Although forecasters may assume a forthcoming end to the epidemic, those who must bring this about cannot simply make such an assumption but must work diligently to bring it about. One counts on such efforts, and their success, in making these projections.

Similarly, the substantial fertility declines still to come, especially in Africa, should help, eventually, to tame the rapid growth that still continues in such areas of the less developed regions. The projections are not meant to say that, if everyone sits back and relaxes, such fertility decline will happen on its own. Rather, the projections count on continuing effort similar to that in the historical record for other countries. While there is a need to assess whether and how societies can live with the consequences of projected population trends, there is also a need to assess how societies can ensure that the more sanguine aspects of these projections actually come to pass.

B. Limitations

Also important to keep in mind are the limitations of these projections. Some of these limitations can be specifically described and might in principle be mitigated in the future. For instance, there is the problem of international migration, which has essentially been assumed away after 2050, because of the difficulty of anticipating migration flows that far in advance. Alternative possibilities could be modelled but have not been so far. There is also the difficulty of determining levels and properly modelling trends in mortality in some less developed regions, especially in Africa, because of the inadequacy of the data. Subsequent work should address such issues as these.

More difficult issues concern matters that are inherently difficult to settle. It is not possible to know if the units chosen for projection—mainly 192 countries or areas and various groupings of them with much smaller entities—will continue to exist as such. The emergence of new nations in the last few decades, as well as consolidation of previously separate states, suggest that the stability of nations should not be taken for granted. Focusing on individual countries, these projections also risk being upended by national crises, such as outbreaks of civil strife or new epidemics or environmental emergencies, which could produce short-run catastrophic mortality or large, unpredictable migrant movements. Such crises have been the major source of error in past country projections and undoubtedly will interrupt future trends. Perhaps most critical is what level of fertility to assume for the long run. Three possibilities are defined and used in alternative scenarios, but which is most likely, it is difficult to say. The main argument that might be made is a reverse argument—that the resulting population looks too large or too small—and this is clearly not a satisfactory basis unless one assumes that societies will be regulating their size and growth closely in future centuries.

One difficult but inescapable question is how long distinctive country patterns can be expected to persist. Here, different assumptions have been made for different parameters, eliminating country differences in migration by 2050, allowing fertility to converge along distinctive paths until complete equality in 2175, and permitting life expectancy alone among the components to be different between countries indefinitely, though it is forced to come close to converging. Beyond a certain point, country projections are increasingly homogeneous, except at the oldest ages, where life expectancy still produces contrasts. While this could be considered a substantial limitation, there does not appear to be a good way to maintain country contrasts, which undoubtedly will be produced, in the future, by factors that are not yet evident today. One could of course terminate the projections before 2300, but earlier trends still appear to have demographic implications into the twenty-third century.

C. The long view

These projections, because of their length, are necessarily drawn in broad strokes, abstracting, in a sense, from transient events. To put the projected trends in the broadest possible context, one might consider how population has grown since the 18th century (Durand, 1974) and how these projections to the end of the twenty-third century compare. Figure 54 shows how the twentieth century, especially the second half of it, was an exceptional period of substantial population growth, which carries over into the twenty-first century. By the end of the twenty-first century, however, a more sedate pattern of growth harking back to the eighteenth and nineteenth centuries is re-established—at least in the medium projection scenario.

But this is not the final word. If one looks instead at growth rates (figure 55), the exceptional growth in the twentieth century still stands out, and carries over into the twenty-first century. However, the medium scenario shows growth, after the twenty-first century, that is noticeably slow, only a tenth of the rate in the eighteenth or nineteenth centuries. It is the high scenario instead that marks a return to growth rates of the eighteenth and nineteenth centuries.

These projections suggest, therefore, that world population, after moving through the demographic transition from high, and relatively balanced, birth and death rates to low rates, will not necessarily return to the old equilibrium. If the medium scenario is correct, future population growth will be slower than it has been at any point since the Industrial Revolution, and if the low scenario is correct population decline will ensue. If the high scenario is correct, future population growth rates will resemble earlier rates before the demographic transition, but population will continue to grow substantially to unprecedented levels. In each case, the projections suggest that a new demographic era will unfold toward the end of this century.

Figure 54. World population, estimates and three scenarios: 1700-2300

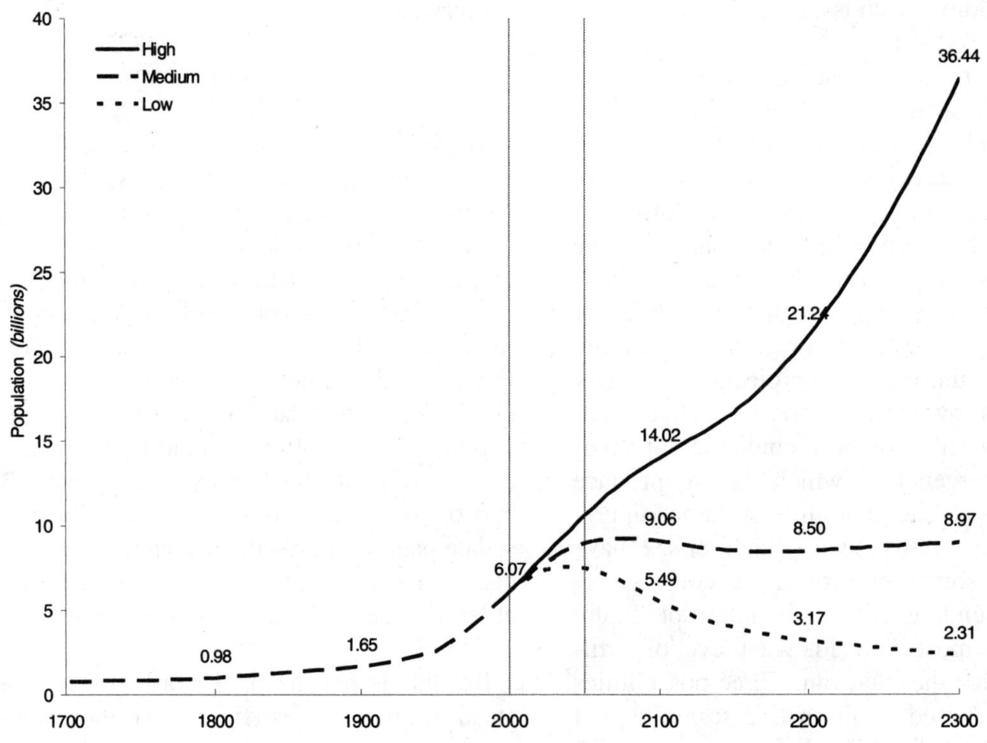

Figure 55. Average annual rate of change of the world population, estimates and three scenarios: 1700-2300

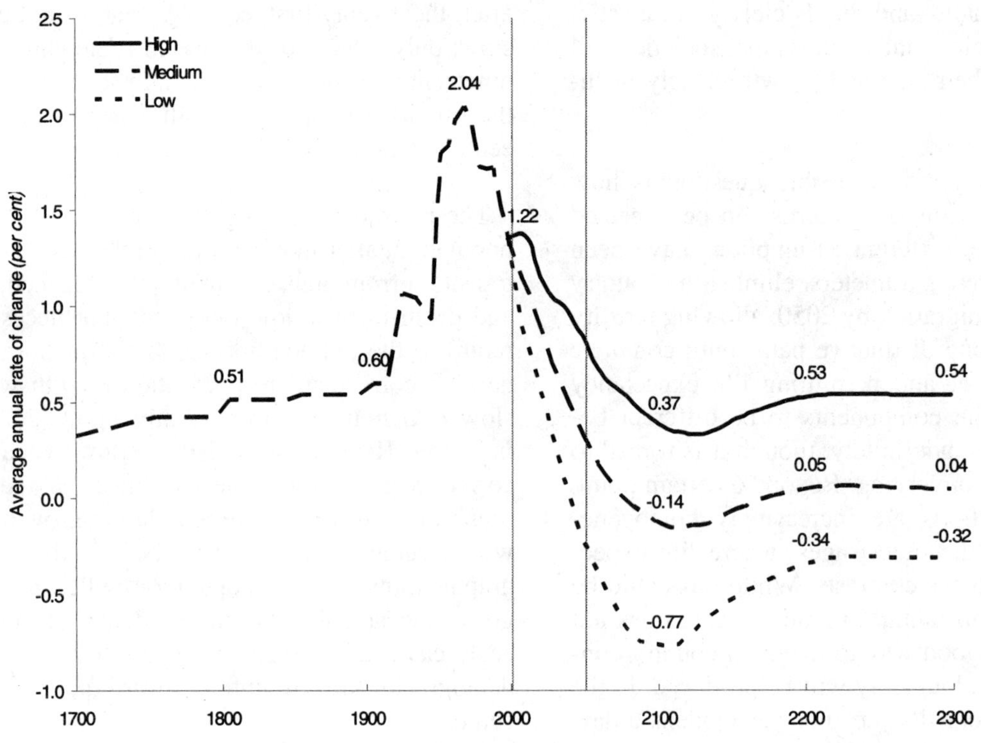

References

Alexandratos, Nikos, ed. (1995). *World Agriculture: Towards 2010.* An FAO Study. Rome: Food and Agriculture Organization.

Bloom, David E., David Canning and Jaypee Sevilla (2003). *The Demographic Dividend: A New Perspective on the Economic Consequences of Population Change*. Santa Monica, CA: RAND.

Coale, Ansley J., and Ellen E. Kisker (1990). Defects in data on old-age mortality in the United States: New procedures for calculating mortality schedules and life tables at the highest ages. *Asian and Pacific Population Forum*, vol. 4, No. 1.

Durand, John D. (1974). *Historical Estimates of World Population: An Evaluation.* Philadelphia: Population Studies Center, University of Pennsylvania.

Food and Agriculture Organization (2001). FAOSTAT: FAO Statistical Databases. At http://apps.fao.org/default.jsp.

Lee, Ronald D., and Lawrence R. Carter (1992). Modeling and forecasting U.S. mortality. *JASA: Journal of the American Statistical Association,* vol. 87, No. 419, pp. 659-675.

National Research Council (2000). *Beyond Six Billion: Forecasting the World's Population.* Washington, D.C.: National Academy Press.

Thatcher, A. R., V. Kannisto, and J. W. Vaupel (1998). *The Force of Mortality at Age 80–120.* Monographs on Population Aging, vol. 5. Odense: Odense University Press.

United Nations (1999a). *World Population Prospects: The 1998 Revision,* vol. I, *Comprehensive Tables* (United Nations publication, Sales No. E.99.XIII.9).

__________ (1999b). *World Population Prospects: The 1998 Revision,* vol. II, *Sex and Age Distribution of the World Population* (United Nations publication, Sales No. E.99.XIII.8).

__________ (2000a). *Long-range World Population Projections: Based on the 1998 Revision* (United Nations publication, Sales No. E.00.XIII.8).

__________ (2000b). *World Population Prospects: The 1998 Revision,* vol. III, *Analytical Report* (United Nations publication, Sales No. E.99. XIII.10).

__________ (2001a). *World Population Prospects: The 2000 Revision,* vol. I, *Comprehensive Tables* (United Nations publication, Sales No. E.01.XIII.8).

__________ (2001b). *World Population Prospects: The 2000 Revision,* vol. II, *Sex and Age Distribution of the World Population* (United Nations publication, Sales No. E.01.XIII.9).

__________ (2002). *World Population Prospects: The 2000 Revision,* vol. III, *Analytical Report* (United Nations publication, Sales No. E.01.XIII.20).

__________ (2003a). The impact of HIV/AIDS on mortality. Paper prepared for the Workshop on HIV/AIDS and Adult Mortality in Developing Countries, New York, 8-13 September.

__________ (2003b). *World Population Prospects: The 2002 Revision,* vol. I, *Comprehensive Tables* (United Nations publication, Sales No. E.03.XIII.6).

__________ (2003c). *World Population Prospects: The 2002 Revision,* vol. II, *Sex and Age Distribution of the World Population* (United Nations publication, Sales No. E.03.XIII.7).

__________ (forthcoming). World Population Prospects: The 2002 Revision, vol. III, Analytical Report (United Nations publication).

Notes

[1] While some statistics are for five-year periods, for convenience charts occasionally report them for specific years, either assuming that the period level applies to each year in the period or interpolating where possible. The *2002 Revision* (United Nations, 2003b, 2003c, 2004) or the annex to this report can be consulted for precise figures.

[2] Japan is considered more developed but is included in Asia in the figure. Oceania combines the more developed countries of Australia and New Zealand and less developed Melanesia, Micronesia, and Polynesia.

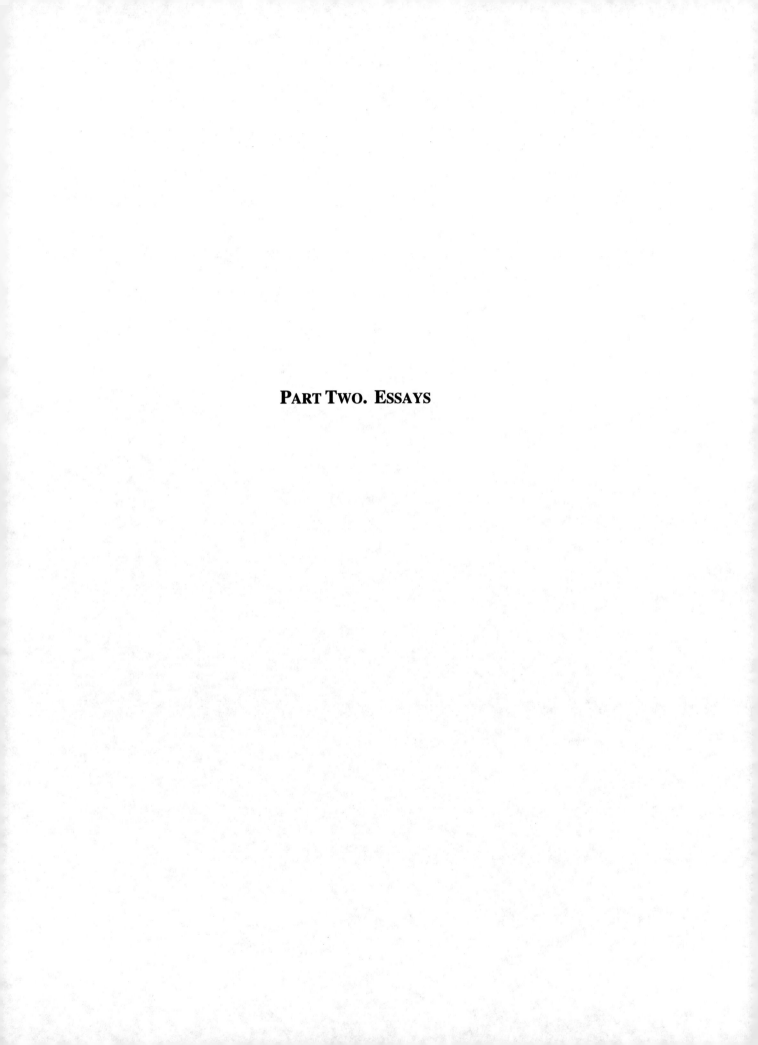

Part Two. Essays

I. TOWARDS AN UNDERSTANDING OF THE EMOTIONS IN THE POPULATION OF 2300

*Alaka Malwade Basu**

INTRODUCTION

It is a curious thing that the one research discipline in which one would expect 'heart-over-head' issues to be a central feature of the behavior it seeks to understand has virtually nothing to say on the subject of emotions. This disinterest is particularly intriguing at a time when even the most rational of all the social sciences, economics, has also caved in to the idea of non-rational (as opposed to irrational) decision-making being an important part of economic behavior.

Whereas we demographers, who deal with births and deaths and marriages and movements – the very stuff of the most highly charged literature and poetry – spend all our time on the costs and benefits of childbearing and on pull versus push factors in migration, and on the insurance versus replacement effects of child mortality. This seems to be a very incomplete way to study demography, as well as a loss of opportunity to let the discipline contribute to our understanding of 'sociocultural experience from the perspective of the persons who live it' (Lutz and White, 1986).

There is very little to go on, but in this paper I try to scour the demographic literature, and the literature from related disciplines, to explore the interrelationships between emotions and demographic behavior. I then try to extrapolate from these results to speculate on the impact on emotions of the births and deaths and the distribution of these births and deaths in 2300.

I believe this exercise is at least as valuable as the exercise of speculating on the economic and social conditions that the population of 2300 will bring with it. If things like changing dependency rates, changing mortality from catastrophic factors like HIV/AIDS, an unimaginable rise in the population of centenarians, are important concomitants of these population projections, surely one major reason for their importance is related to the 'happiness' levels that they imply. Indeed, an unstated concern with generating happiness underlies the social science project of improving the world - if what a better quality of life resulted in was increased emotional misery, it is doubtful that we would seek this quality of life[1].

While demography has been largely silent on the question on emotions, other social sciences, anthropology and sociology in particular, are now beginning to burst with 'emotions' studies that go beyond the traditional interest in the subject in psychology (indeed, the subject has also finally crept into the cynical discipline of economics). In the next two sections, I turn to some of these disciplines to identify those aspects of the emotions literature that are most relevant to a preliminary investigation of emotions and demographic outcomes.

DEFINITIONS

What, first of all, do we mean by 'emotions'? In a major review of the subject in sociology, Thoits (1989) distinguished emotions from feelings, affects, moods and sentiments. The first two are less specific than 'emotions', the last two are more specific. Feelings refer to physical states (such as hunger or fatigue) as well as emotional states. Affects refer to positive and negative evaluations of something (like/dislike). Emotions may be linked to these two for being culturally delineated types of feelings or affects.

At the other end, moods are more chronic than emotions and less clearly tied to a provoking situation. While sentiments may be defined as referring to 'socially constructed patterns of sensations, expressive gestures, and cultural meanings organized around a relationship to a social object, usually another person … or group such as a family" (Gordon, 1981; cited in Thoits, 1989).

*Department of Sociology, Cornell University, Ithaca, New York.

But perhaps emotions are better understood analytically by the larger process of which they are a part. Reviewing the literature on emotions in the different social sciences, this process is best captured as follows:

ELICITOR	→	PHYSIOLOGICAL RESPONSE	→	COGNITION/EXPERIENCE	→	SOCIAL ACTION

A few words on each of these components of the process:

Elicitors: These are the situations or events that provoke an emotional response. In the anthropological and sociological literature, they are also called triggers or stimuli (see, Lutz and White, 1986; Thoits, 1989), all words that are self-explanatory. They can be of any and many kinds, but in the context of the present paper, we define them as demographic. In turn, by 'demographic', we mean both demographic events (such as births, deaths and marriages) as well as demographic situations (such as population densities, age distributions and the like).

Physiological response: The physiological basis of emotional experience is a relatively recent intermediate variable in the social scientist's interest in the link between elicitors and emotions. But it is now central to an understanding of this process and the neurosciences (see Damasio, 1994; Berezin, 2004). In turn these physiological changes may remain at the level of appetites or visceral responses like thirst, hunger or sleepiness (Elster, 1999; LeDoux, 1996) or they may be followed by what may be called the recognition and experience of an emotional state. They may or may not also be followed by a stimulus to rational thought and action (Massey, 2001).

Cognition/Experience: Once the physiological response to an emotional trigger occurs, it has to be translated into a recognizable emotion. There is a large literature in all the relevant social sciences on how universal these emotions are; that is, across cultures and across time, do the same elicitors stimulate the same kind of emotional response? The answer to this question is especially salient to the present paper because it is speculating on emotions in the twenty-third century. That is, the question here is whether only the elicitors (the demographic facts) will be different in 2300 or both the elicitors as well as the elicitor-emotion relationship will be qualitatively different.

Wading through some of the discourses on this theme of the cultural construction of emotions, one is more conscious of the disagreements and the hair-splitting than of any resolution of the issue. If there is a consensus, it seems to be arrived at by accommodating both positions – that some emotions are universal, while others are culturally mediated. The best known study of universal emotions (or at least universally expressed emotions) is Ekman's (1982) demonstration that particular patterns of facial muscle movements are universally (that is, by people of diverse cultural backgrounds) recognized as expressing what he called the six 'core' emotions – happiness, surprise, fear, anger, disgust and sadness. Other emotions might be more culturally grounded.

Similarly, Kemper (1987) identifies four primary emotions – fear, anger, depression and satisfaction – from which secondary emotions like love, guilt, gratitude and pride are derived. In this framework, the universally common feeling of the core emotion is given a social meaning that is more contextual and defines both the label given to an experienced emotion as well as its external manifestation.

This cultural/social definition of an emotion is the result of what anthropologists and sociologists call 'emotional socialization', a term that becomes particularly significant to demographically pertinent emotions such as mother-love, desire, and grieving (as I discuss in a later section).

This culturally and socially mediated identification of a particular combination of elicitor and physiological state with an emotion is believed to affect the recognition of an emotion as well as its outward expression. There are two aspects to this – the cognition or the subjective *experience* of an emotional state, and the *expression* of that state. To turn to the latter first, the consensus is that societies differ in what may be called 'display rules' or 'expression norms' (Hochschild, 1979; Ekman, 1982) which regulate emotion behavior. To give a very simple example, most cultures have norms about the appropriate way to express sympathy for another's loss, or to receive such sympathy at the time of one's loss – behavior outside these norms is occasion for small or large social sanctions. There is a growing literature on this 'disciplining' of the emotions by larger entities than the individual experiencing the emotion. While different societies may have fairly similar rules about how an emotional state is best expressed, these rules may also differ widely (the large differences in mourning rituals catalogued by anthropologists being a good example of this variation).

By the same token, there are believed to be implicit 'feeling rules' or 'emotion norms' that culturally prescribe the appropriate range, intensity and duration of 'private feelings' (as distinct from the expression of these feelings) in given situations (Thoits, 1989). Levy (1984) coined the terms 'hypocognized' and 'hypercognized' to describe the tendencies of different cultures to mute or emphasize the conscious recognition of an emotion. However, one can go too far in this kind of cultural determinism and it might be closer to the truth to say that emotion and culture are not merely the same thing; culture might affect the expression of an emotion but not necessarily the actual experience of it (Shweder, 1993). That is, the elicitor-emotion relation may be relatively hard-wired, even if ways of dealing with the relationship are culturally constrained.

Social Action: This is the last link of the chain in which emotions are embedded. It refers to the response to an emotion in the form of some kind of social action. That is, from the social scientist's point of view, we are interested in the outcome of an emotional state for society as well as for the individual. Emotions that are completely internalized, that are experienced with no subsequent effect on the individual or anyone else, are as uninteresting as they are rare. So, by definition, an emotion is something that results in some consequences, whether planned (see, for example, Frank, 1993) or uncontrolled.

For the purposes of the present paper (and that too tangentially), we will only look at the demographic consequences for emotions in 2300 and not on the impact of the emotions on demographic events at that time. However, it is probably all very circular, with demographic events and emotions reinforcing one another, so perhaps not much will be lost by this partial exercise in the following sections.

TOWARDS AN EMOTIONAL LANDSCAPE FOR THE POPULATION OF 2300

This section is going to be almost as speculative as the 2300 projections themselves. It is bad enough that we know next to nothing about the relations between demographic situations and the emotions in the contemporary world. To extrapolate from this little knowledge to think about a world 300 years from now might be a foolhardy undertaking. But all that I do in this paper is make some suggestions for approaching the question, not come up with any answers myself.

As already mentioned, there are two perspectives from which one can approach this analysis. On the one hand, one could look at the potential impact of the emotions on demographic behavior and on the other, one could look at the potential impact of demographic factors on emotions. In the second case, one would need to take some position on the universality and immutability of emotions. As discussed above, this is a contentious subject, but even without getting into these distinctions, a case could be made for different emotional states of the world (in terms of both the nature and the intensity of expressed and/or felt emotions) arising out of different demographic regimes.

It is the direct relationship between emotions and demographic regimes and demographic events that I want to explore here. I do not consider relationships that are mediated by other structural factors like political systems (for example, it appears from the literature that democracy is good for happiness, except that the Russians do not seem to feel the same way after the fall of communism (Veenhoven, 2001). That is, I will consider only those variables that are central in a standard textbook of demography.

Thus, in the next few pages, I briefly look at the possible emotional implications of the 2300 (medium) population scenario. The population variables that I look at may be grouped into two categories – micro-level population 'events' like births, deaths and marriages and macro-level population 'parameters' like age and geographic distributions. And the emotions I consider are those that the current limited literature purports as having a potential relationship with these population variables.

POPULATION DENSITY AND DISTRIBUTION

To take the simplest example of a demographic change that must accompany the change in numbers between now and 2300, all other things being equal (that is, in the absence of living facilities on the moon), population densities will certainly rise. There will certainly be more people per square mile then than there are now – to give the United Nations' exact projections, the medium range population increase should result in nine billion people compared to six billion today. That is a 50% rise in numbers, made even more significant for the uneven distribution of this growth. While the more developed regions (MDRs henceforth) will register no change in overall population densities, population density will double in the less developed regions (LDRs) and almost triple in the least developed countries.

To speculate on the implications of this change for emotions, one would need to think about the role of factors such as crowding in raising levels of different kinds of emotions, both positive and negative. These include the emotions of aggression, anger, perhaps excitement, and perhaps even a sense of belonging. There is also the complementary question of the emotions engendered in sparsely inhabited spaces, emotions such as fear, depression, perhaps excitement, perhaps even a sense of well-being.

The literature on this subject suggests that on the whole, the crowding that must accompany population increase will be damaging to the emotional well being of the population in 2300. For example, Hammond (1988) has theorized that social stratification and social differentiation will be positively associated with population density because of emotional factors. He argues that social bonds depend on positive emotional (or affective) arousal and that people seek to maximize this arousal. However, human affective resources are limited and so they must limit the numbers of others to whom they are thus attached. The choice of these others, in a crowded environment, will most likely be based on easily identifiable common characteristics like race and age and language, thereby increasing social differentiation[2].

In a similar vein, Fleming et al (1987), discuss the stress resulting from the loss of a sense of control in dense surroundings, especially if the density includes a greater measure of anonymity – measured in their study by the prevalence or not of shops in residential areas. The sense of insecurity engendered in crowded locations possibly also accounts for the experimental finding that threatening faces 'pop' out of crowds to be noticed and felt threatened by (Hansen and Hansen, 1988). It is almost as if we are somehow biologically attuned to look out for these signals of threat in dense environments.

However, all these findings refer to the contemporary developed world, where notions of space and privacy have bred parallel emotions of stress and fear when space and privacy are invaded. It is less frequent in accounts of the city in the past in the developed world as well as contemporary developing countries. Here, it appears that the anonymity is what gives the crowded city its emotional excitement, its sense of new opportunity. These differing world-views are important if we are to speculate on the impact of increased density in 2300. Whether this increase contributes to increasingly stressed lives will be contingent on the underlying 'emotion norms' that have developed in adaptation to changing economic and ecological conditions. After all, as Massey (2001) discusses, historically there has been a relation between increasing group size and a refinement of the emotions to increase what may be called social intelligence.

All these issues become more pertinent given the expected distribution of the population of the future. As the United Nations (2001) forewarns, by 2007, for the first time in history, more than half of all human beings will live in cities. Presumably, this proportion can only be higher by 2300.

At the micro-level too, there is a small 'crowding' literature that suggests that psychological distress is greater in densely packed homes (see, for example, Evans et al, 1996). But here our predictions for the future will have to counterbalance the shortage of public and private space due to 9 billion people occupying the space now occupied by six billion, along with the increased residential space possible with smaller and smaller completed family sizes.

Unless, of course, the space crunch leads to more multigenerational households than at present. This possibility is real not only because of the sheer increase in numbers but because of the changed age distribution in the world of 2300. If life expectancy is projected to rise to 97 years for females and 95 years for males during this time, there will be a great number of old people around to be cared for. This, given our current patterns of old age care and the already visible trends in public resources for such care, implies more multigenerational households. This has consequences for the interpersonal emotions that I bring up in a later section on the family; here it is worth mentioning that the literature on stress and household crowding might have something to offer as well.

BIRTHS

The central interesting feature of the 2300 population projections is the assumption that by this time replacement level fertility will have been reachieved in all parts of the world, but only after they have undergone a century or so of subreplacement fertility. While one might quarrel with this assumption, it is useful from our present point of view for it allows us to extrapolate on the emotional state of the world using contemporary information on low birth societies.

To begin with, one can extrapolate to say that, by 2300, all parts of the world will be characterized by childbearing for purely psychic reasons[3]. This is believed to be the primary rationale for childbearing only in the low fertility contemporary world according to various value-of-children surveys and the summaries of the evidence in sources like Bulatao and Lee (1983). This means that the 'happiness' or satisfaction derived from children will be an important determinant of fertility. Conversely, one can ask what the happiness levels will be in a society with low childbearing. That is, will parenthood in general and motherhood in particular be a source of emotional gratification or will the replacement level fertility instead increase the opportunity costs of and thus emotional resentment about children?

This is not as harsh a question as it sounds. The Social History literature is now awash with studies of the cultural construction of the positive emotions associated with motherhood and wifehood (see, for example, the societal construction of happy motherhood through the institution of Mother's Day described in Hausen, 1984).

If these emotions are subdued in the postmodern below-replacement fertility achieving populations of Europe today (see, for example, Van de Kaa, 2001), then it means that the rise in fertility that is projected for 2300 must come with increased childbearing for non-psychic reasons and/or with a reinstatement of the emotional benefits of childbearing.

These non-psychic reasons can be of various kinds related to state sponsored attempts to raise fertility that are already underway in much of the developed world (see, for example, Chamie, 2004). Such state encouragement might well result in raising the economic benefits of children and have a positive impact on fertility in the same way as it is supposed to do through the economic benefits of children in high fertility but poor societies. But to be sustainable, all evidence thus far suggests that childbearing will have to be encouraged through a revalidation of emotions like mother love and mother-child bonding or, in this post-postmodern age in 2300, parent love and parent-child bonding.

One can think of other non-familial emotions being called to the service of renewed replacement fertility. Emotions such as nationalism, religious duty, self-sacrifice, have all been evoked to control childbearing (in either direction) in the past and there is no reason for the woman of 2300 to not once more be prey to their appeal.

Incidentally, one might also speculate about the changed emotional experience of childbearing itself (i.e. the emotions experienced through a pregnancy and delivery) in the low fertility world of 2300. With fewer births than today, will the typical in the less developed regions woman stop being as blasé as she is believed be about each conception? Arguably, childbearing will no longer be just a normal part of a good day's work; but will there now be a new kind of emotional socialization that invests each pregnancy with all kinds of symbolic and material significance? Conversely, might the rarity of pregnancy increase the fear of it and lead to more resolute attempts to prevent another one? These are all unanswerable questions with our current empirical knowledge but they do raise interesting questions for the sociology of emotion in childbirth. For current attempts to grapple with the question, see, for example, Jeffery and Jeffery, 1998; Patel, 2000. These diametrically opposed interpretations of the emotional experience of childbearing in North India are particularly important for the methodological issues they raise about interpreting emotional states from outward behavior.

Deaths

Once we are past the horrors of the HIV/AIDS epidemic and if we do not have to contend with new forms of unnatural death (both these things are implied in the 2300 projections), the emotional experience of death should be a qualitatively different experience from that of today, at least in the less developed regions of the world.

This will happen for several reasons. In the case of infant, child and young adult mortality, there will be fewer absolute numbers of deaths to be exposed to because of fewer births as well as lower mortality rates. Those premature deaths that do occur will be caused by more unexpected things like accidents and violence as compared to the fevers and infections of today. And with smaller family sizes all round, the social and institutional supports to help with the experience of premature death will have to be quite different from today.

Similar arguments can be made about the reduced exposure of children to parental death (except of course that there will not be fewer absolute numbers of parents per child). As for deaths among the old, naturally these will not be reduced in number, given that we must all die some day. But they will certainty often come late enough for the typical adult to spend many more years than today without being exposed to such deaths. Similarly, they may also often occasion some sense of emotional relief, especially if the increased longevity is not proportionately accompanied by reduced morbidity and disability.

This overall reduced exposure (if one measures exposure as either the risk of experiencing the loss of a loved done in a given year or to the risk of losing a loved one 'before his time' so to speak) can have emotional consequences that we do not have enough research as yet to anticipate. But one can make some educated guesses from the converse observation that, in high mortality societies, even if the grief experienced after a death is no smaller than in low mortality societies, coping mechanisms are certainly somehow robust. In her discussion of historical and cross-cultural differences in the experience of grief, Loffland (1985) concludes that the intensity and duration of grief depend on how much has been invested in the relationship, the mortality rate of the group, norms about the expression of feelings and the private space that individuals have to indulge their feelings.

One can situate the 'celebration' of infant death described by Scheper-Hughes (1992) for the favelas of Brazil, in which the dead child is equated with an innocent angel in such a framework. These 'coping' norms can sometimes become proactive enough to be self-fulfilling. That is, they might hasten premature death through too much helpless anticipation of it. But it might be a mistake to infer from this behavior, as Loffland seems to do, that expressed emotions and behavior are a direct representation of 'experienced' emotions and especially of complicated emotions like love (on this, see Basu, 1994; Basu, 1997).

To turn to the experience of grief in 2300, one can see that, following Loffland's framework, the overt expression of grief as well as the mourning rituals that might be in place by then may well be more intense and prolonged than they are today due to changes in at least three of the four determinants of grief. However, much more research is needed on the possible changes in the personal meaning of death and the internal sorrow that will come in its wake in 2300. Perhaps such research will conclude that the old saw that life is cheap in high mortality societies might be just that – an old saw.

MARRIAGE

If there is one institution that will continue to change radically in the coming centuries, it must be marriage. The rumblings of change are already loud enough for us to see today and include both the attraction of marriage to groups who do not subscribe to the idea that marriage is primarily for childbearing (same sex couples, for example) as well as the retreat from marriage by those who bear the responsibility for childbearing. What does this imply for the emotional content of conjugal relationships? That this has been changing radically over time is suggested by the scores of books and papers on the changing meaning of the family and the emotions associated with it. Most of this literature refers to the western conjugal unit but might nevertheless have lessons for the non-western households that will form the bulk of the households in 2300.

The ideology of love in particular has undergone a sea change, a change that is still fraught with contradictions and conflicts which might find some kind of resolution in the next 300 years. As several writers have argued, the first changes began in the 1800s in the shift from agrarian to capitalist economies and an increased gender division of labor. The home came to mean more and more an emotional haven from the outside world for the male (Stone, 1977; Stearns and Stearns; 1986; Swidler, 1980; Cancian, 1987), with the wife being expected to be the emotional cushion against this world. This arrangement required the emotional socialization[4] of conjugal relationships and the idea of romantic love was culturally promoted to resolve the cultural contradiction between a youth focussed on self-actualization and autonomy and an adulthood that needed to be all about commitment and self-sacrifice. Traditional love myths were also needed to resolve the growing contradiction in the nineteenth and twentieth centuries between the continued need for women's commitment to the home and their growing interest in the world outside the home. This growing interest was spurred by lower birth rates, a growing consumerism and increasing labor force opportunities (Thoits, 1989) – all changes of a profoundly demographic kind and all changes that should extend into the future.

An initial stage in the increasing conflict between these gender-prescribed roles and these changing demographic conditions has probably involved a rise in domestic violence. Domestic violence is today a major concern of demographic research, but it tends to be too bland in its analysis. It too easily attributes domestic violence to unequal gender relations that allow and perpetuate the one-sided use of violence and abuse; without noting how in fact it is sustained not just by unequal power but also by an emotional socialization that confuses domestic violence with erotic love and sometimes even with romantic love. Qualitative analyses of such a frequent conflation of violence with love are beginning to emerge in fiction (see, for example Doyle, 1996) as well as social science research (see, for example, Geetha, 1998) probing the emotional basis of the collaboration of women in the perpetuation of domestic violence.

As Geetha (1998) and Cancian (1987) suggest rather hopefully, the next stage might be a less gender based emotional vocabulary of conjugal love that is characterized by an androgynous form of interdependence in love that allows the mutual expression and satisfaction of emotions such as desire and affection. If we are indeed headed in such a direction, then 2300 may well see a new equilibrium in which demographic changes in marriage and fertility are associated with more and not less gender equality in the cultural determinism of emotions. There is much optimism about and activism among social scientists for such gender equality in areas like the marketplace, the law and domestic responsibility. But they have far too little to say on these changing emotion cultures that have as important implications for human welfare as job opportunities and equal inheritance.

KINSHIP

If there is one stark conclusion in the 2300 population projections, it is the major shift in age distributions worldwide by that time. In the median projections, the proportion of the population aged 60 and over will rise to 41 per cent in the more developed regions (from 19 per cent in 2000) and to 37 per cent in the less developed regions (from 8 per cent today). These are enormous increases by any reckoning and must result in major shifts in the emotional responsibilities of those entrusted with the care of the oldest of these old. Such care giving requires more than a sense of duty, it requires an emotional commitment that goes well beyond the call of duty. That such emotional commitment can (or must) be culturally and socially constructed is evident from Hochschild's (1983) landmark study of the training for 'emotional labor' in certain service sector occupations like nursing and airline stewardesses. A major part of this training consists of learning to control one's own feelings while enhancing the positive feelings of others. In the short term, such training might do little more than change the emotion *display* rules of a profession, with little change in underlying emotions as feelings. But in the longer-term cultural socialization which defines kinship affects, it is probable that care-giving emotions become sufficiently internalized for the old to be well looked after within the family. One certainly hopes for the sake of the future old and disabled that this kind of emotional labor becomes as commonplace as it currently is in the upbringing of children.

In particular, I would speculate that emotional bonds between generations once removed (grandchildren and grandparents) will change drastically by 2300. The existing literature on this relationship is small and focussed on certain groups (such as African Americans) and certain situations (primarily the situation of grandparents bringing up grandchildren, see, for example, de Toldeo and Brown, 1995; Cox, 2000). But we need much greater understanding of the prospects for a reversal of this inter-generational flow of emotional resources.

Some clues about the demographic determinants of these bonds emerge from the existing literature. For example, one of the repeatedly important influences of grandparent-grandchild closeness appears to be the frequency of contact between the two (for example, Lin and Harwood, 2003; Mills et al, 2001) – a frequency that can be expected to increase as life expectancies rise as well as crowding increases. Both these demographic factors will likely change living arrangements in the direction of greater contact between these alternate generations. The frequency of contact might also be assumed to increase at the low fertility levels projected for 2300, when grandparents might substitute for siblings in affective ties.

CONCLUSION

This is admittedly a highly speculative paper. Given the paucity of research on demography and the emotions even in the contemporary world, it might seem unduly ambitious to even think of the emotional state of the world in 2300. But perhaps such speculation about the future might be one way of increasing attention to the present.

I have tried in this paper to suggest that a study of the emotional implications of demographic behavior is an important subject in its own right, for both academic reasons as well as to satisfy the social science imperative of understanding and changing the world for the better.

But this is also an extremely difficult area to study and perhaps that is what largely explains the low research interest in it. An important part of any attempt to develop a body of knowledge on the subject will need to be focussed on research methodology. Anthropology, sociology and, in more recent times, economics, have proposed some directions. But demographers will need to go well beyond the usual demographic research tool – the large scale survey – to shed any real light on the matter. At the same time, demography is also the social science discipline to which the study of emotions must be natural, dealing as it does with births, deaths, marriages and movements. For that reason, perhaps a research project on emotions might eventually have more of an impact in demography, one which will also contribute better to other disciplines' endeavors to understand the subject matter.

References

Basu. A.M. (1992). *Culture, The Status of Women and Demographic Behavior –Illustrated with the Case of India.* Oxford: Clarendon Press.

_________ (1994). How Pervasive Are Sex Differentials in Childhood Nutritional Levels in South Asia? *Social Biology,* vol. 40, Nos. 1-2, pp. 25-37.

_________ (1997). Underinvestment in Children: A Reorganization of the Evidence on the Determinants of Child Mortality. In *The Continuing Demographic Transition,* Jones, Douglas, Caldwell and D'Souza, eds. Oxford: Clarendon Press, pp. 307 331.

Berezin, M. (2004). Emotions and the Economy. In *Handbook of Economic Sociology,* Smelser & Sweberg, eds. 2nd edition. Russell Sage Foundation and Princeton University Press (forthcoming).

Bulatao, R.A., and Lee, R.D. (1983). *Determinants of Fertility in Developing Countries.* New York: Academic Press, vols. 1 and 2.

Cancian, F.M. (1987). *Love in America: Gender and Self-Development.* Cambridge: Cambridge University Press.

Chamie, J. (2004). Low Fertility: Can Governments Make a Difference. Session 105: International Responses to Low Fertility. Presented at the Annual Meeting of the Population Association of America, April 2, 2004.

Cox, Carole B., ed. (2000). *To Grandmother's House We Go and Stay: Perspectives on Custodial Grandparents.* New York, NY: Springer Publishing Company.

Damasio, A.R. (1994). *Descartes' Error: Emotion, Reason, and the Human Brain.* New York: Harper Collins.

de Toldeo, Sylvie and Deborah Edler Brown (1995).*Grandparents as Parents: A Survival Guide for raising a Second Family.* New York: The Guilford Press.

Doyle, R. (1996). *The Woman Who Walked Into Doors.* New York: Viking.

Ekman, P., ed. (1982). *Emotions in the Human Face.* Cambridge: Cambridge University Press, 2nd edition

Elster, J. (1999). *Strong Feelings: Emotion, Addiction and Human Behavior.* Cambridge: The MIT Press.

Evans, G.W. (1996). The role of interior design elements in human responses to crowding. *Journal of Personality & Social Psychology,* vol. 70, No.1, pp. 41-46.

Fleming, I et al. (1987). Social density and perceived control as mediators of crowding stress in high-density residential neighborhoods. *Journal of Personality & Social Psychology,* vol. 52, No.5, pp. 899-906.

Frank, R.H. (1993). The Strategic Role of the Emotions: Reconciling Over-and Undersocialized Accounts of Behavior. *Rationality and Society,* vol. 5, No.2, pp. 160-184.

Geetha, V. (998). On Bodily Love and Hurt. In *A Question of Silence, The Sexual Economies of Modern India,* Nair & John, eds. London and New York: Zed Books, pp. 304-331.

Gordon, S.L. (1981). The Sociology of Sentiments and Emotion. In *Social Psychology: Sociological Perspectives,* M. Rosenburg and R.H. Turner, eds. New York: Basic Books, pp. 562-592.

Hammond. M. (1989). Affective maximization: A new macro-theory in the sociology of emotions In *Research Agendas in the Sociology of Emotions,* Kemper, ed. Albany, NY: SUNY Press.

Hansen, C., and D. Hansen (1988). Finding the face in the crowd: An anger superiority effect. *Journal of Personality & Social Psychology,* vol. 54, No.6, pp. 917-924.

Hausen, K. (1984). Mothers, sons, and the sale of symbols and goods: The 'German Mother's Day' 1923-33. In *Interest and Emotion,* Medick and Sabean, eds. Cambridge: Cambridge University Press, pp. 317-413.

Hochschild, A.R. (1979). Emotion Work, Feeling Rules, and Social Structure. *American Journal of Sociology,* vol. 85, pp. 551-575.

_________ (1983). *The Managed Heart: The Commercialization of Human Feeling.* Berkeley, California: University of California Press.

Jeffery, P. et al. (1998). *Labour Pains and Labour Power: Women and Child Bearing in India.* London: Zed Books.

Kemper, T.D. (1987). How many emotions are there? Wedding the social and autonomic components. *American Journal of Sociology,* vol. 93, No.2, pp. 263-289.

LeDoux, J. (1996). *The Emotional Brain: The Mysterious Underpinnings of Emotional Life.* New York: Simon and Schuster.

Levy, R.I. (1984). Emotion, Knowing, and Culture. In *Culture Theory: Essays on Mind, Self, and Emotion,* Shweder and Levine, eds. Cambridge: Cambridge University Press, pp. 217-234.

Lin, M., and J. Harwood (2003). Accommodation Predictors of Grandparent-Grandchild Relational Solidarity in Taiwan. *Journal of Social and Personal Relationships,* vol. 20, No. 4, pp. 537-563.

Lutz, C. and G.M. White (1986). The Anthropology of Emotions. *Annual Review of Anthropology,* vol. 15, pp. 405-436.

Massey, D. (2002). A Brief History of Human Society: The Origin and Role of Emotion in Social Life. *American Sociological Review,* vol. 67, No.1, pp. 1-29.

Mills, T. et al. (2001). Adult Grandchildren's Perceptions of Emotional Closeness and Consensus with Their Maternal and Paternal Grandparents. *Journal of Family Issues,* vol. 22, No. 4, pp. 427-455.

Patel, T. (2000). The Silent Subject: Childbirth and the Sociology of Emotion. *Sociological Bulletin* (India), vol. 49, No. 2, pp. 179-192.

Thoits, P. (1989). The Sociology of Emotions. *Annual Review of Sociology,* vol. 15, pp. 317-342.

United Nations (2001). *World Urbanization Prospects: The 1999 Revision.* (United Nations publication, Sales No. E.01.XIII.11).

Van de Kaa, D.J. (2001). Postmodern Fertility Preferences: From Changing Value Orientation to New Behavior. *Population and Development Review,* Supplement to vol. 27, pp. 290-331.

Veenhoven, R. (2001). Are the Russians as Happy as they say they are? *Journal of Happiness Studies,* vol. 2, No. 2, pp. 111-136.

NOTES

[1] Philosophy, especially German philosophy, has been more skeptical than the more robust social sciences on this score. This pessimism embraces both the idea of the possibility of human happiness, as well as the desirability of it.

[2] In less crowded situations, there will be less need to exercise such choice in affective social relations.

[3] To say this is not to say that in high fertility societies, psychic reasons for childbearing are not important, a misleading conclusion sometimes drawn in the literature. As discussed in Basu (1992), they may often be even more important in poverty situations in which there are few emotionally gratifying alternatives to childbearing. In a survey of slum dwellers in Delhi there was a significant positive relationship between the number of living children and self-perceived happiness with life even though the questions on happiness were not asked in the context of children.

[4] Such socialization took up and continues to take up (with less and less success today) a great part of the efforts of all kinds of institutions – schools, the mass media, marriage manuals, popular entertainment, religious authority.

II. AN INTERGENERATIONAL RATIONALE FOR FERTILITY ASSUMPTIONS IN LONG TERM WORLD POPULATION PROJECTIONS

*Herwig Birg**

A. INTRODUCTION AND FRAMEWORK OF THE ANALYSIS

The analysis of fertility and generative behaviour usually concentrates on persons, couples, families, social communities, ethnic groups, nations or generations. These individuals and groups are examples for various decision making units with different objective functions and specific constraints for their generative behaviour. In this contribution, the elementary units for fertility decisions are generations. Generations may be regarded as the most natural units of making fertility decisions because the mere existence of any generation depends on the fertility decisions of the preceding ones.

There are many emotional, cultural, social and economic interactions between the behavioural units making fertility relevant decisions. This is especially true for generations which are very intensively connected by family ties, by kinship and by the societal and institutional regulations like the financial arrangements in the educational system, the health system and the pension system. Fertility theories differ very much according to the kind of the explanatory variables taken into account in the approaches of the various scientific disciplines like the economic theory of fertility, the anthropological-sociological fertility theories and the demographic theories, e.g. the transition theory and the biographic theory of fertility which tries to combine the explanatory power of different disciplines in an holistic approach.[1] Even more relevant than these distinctions, which emphasize the theoretical characteristics of the underlying scientific approaches, is the methodological question of whether the generations are treated as separate single units, which make their fertility decisions independently from each other by maximizing their objective functions separately or whether they are regarded as *one trans-generational* decisions making unit constituting a chain of consecutive generations.

In this contribution, the fertility analysis of generations is based on two concepts: The first is denoted as the *"chain of generations concept"* in which the successive generations are linked by intergenerational financial transfers. The corresponding chain of successive generations constitutes the decision making unit for fertility decisions. In the second concept, denoted as the *"single generation concept"*, fertility is analysed in the framework of a model including intergenerational transfers in the same way as in the chain of generations concept, but treats each generation as a separately acting unit which tries to maximize its objective function independently from the actions of the preceding and of the succeeding generations.

B. THE THEORETICAL CONCEPT[2]

Most models of optimal population growth and fertility are developed by economists in the framework of neoclassical economic theory. These models are based on the objective functions of optimum per capita output, consumption and on central economic variables like the interest rate and the rate of savings. Contrary to these neoclassical models, which are based on restrictive economic concepts like production and utility functions, the subsequent models use more general notions.[3] The assumptions made are as follows:

(1) Every generation in the sequence of generations is linked both to the preceding and to the succeeding one by way of intergenerational transfers. During childhood and youth, each generation starts out as a recipient of material support from it's parent's generation. During it's mid-phase, each generation provides material support to two

* Bielefeld University, Germany.

other generations, i.e. to it‘s children and to it‘s parents who have now grown old. Finally, it enters the third phase during which it in turn is a net recipient of assistance from its children who have now entered the mid-phase. Special assumptions on the length of the three phases are not made. Furthermore, it is not necessary to make explicit assumptions on the life expectancy of the generations or on the relative length of the three phases (see figure 1).

(2) The relative sizes of the generations in demographic terms are significant for the balance between the support received and given during an entire life-course. This raises the question of how significant the size of a particular generation, as determined by the birth rate, will be for the ratio of assistance received to assistance given. Let the following be the notation used to analyse this relationship:

Gx = the size of generation x

Gx-1 = the size of generation x's parental generation

Gx+1 = the size of generation x's children's generation

αx = the services rendered and assistance given by generation x per head of its children's generation

βx = the services rendered and assistance given by generation x per head of its parents' generation

The value of the services rendered and assistance given by generation *x* to it‘s children's generation can be obtained by multiplying the size of its children's generation by the services per head of that generation, i.e. by the expression ${}_xG_{x+1}$. Likewise, the services and assistance rendered to the parental generation is ${}_xG_{x-1}$. That means that generation *x* provides a total amount of service and assistance

Figure I. Intergenerational transfers in a chain of generation

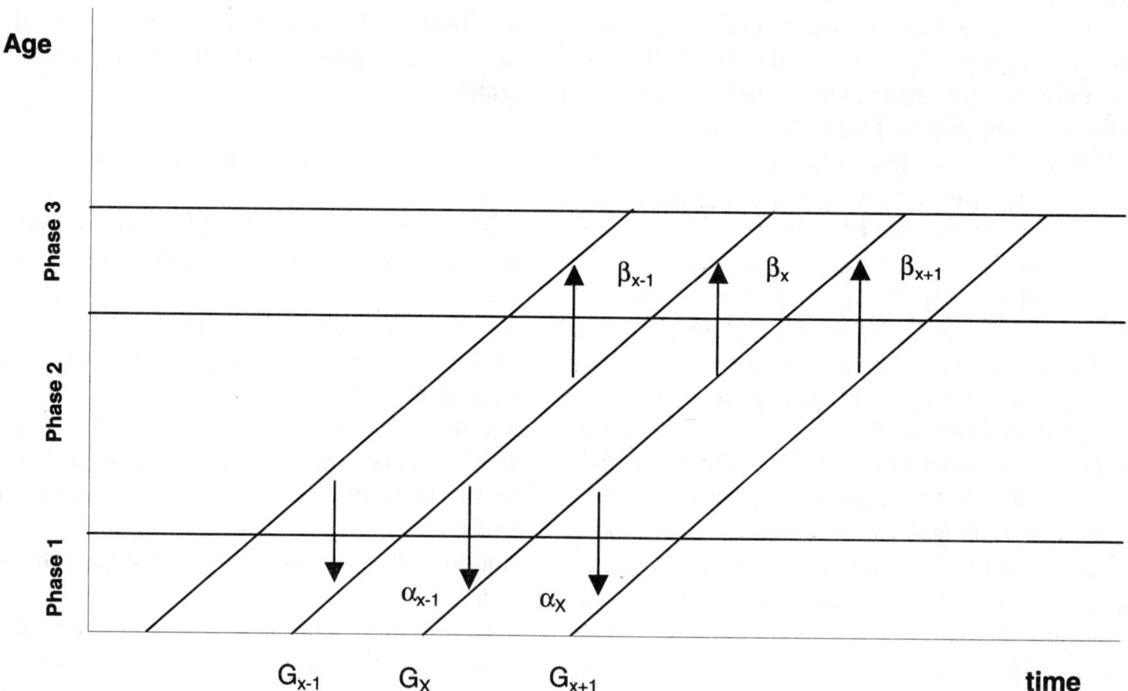

to other generations of

$$\alpha_x G_{x+1} + \beta_x G_{x-1} \quad (1)$$

Correspondingly, generation x in turn will receive a total of

$$\alpha_{x-1} G_x + \beta_{x+1} G_x \quad (2)$$

from its predecessor and successor generations.

The services/assistance given or received (or) have the index x appended to them because each generation can potentially have its own approach to these activities.

(3) The ratio of the services/assistance received and given to or by generation x is referred to as the "intergenerational transfer quotient Tx for generation x":

$$T_x = \frac{\alpha_x G_{x+1} + \beta_x G_{x-1}}{\alpha_{x-1} G_x + \beta_{x+1} G_x} \quad (3)$$

The basic assumption made is that each generations objective function is to minimize its transfer quotient T_x.

C. Fertility in the "Chain of Generations Model"

The transfer quotient depends on the sizes of the three generations of G_{x-1}, G_x and G_{x+1}. To minimize the transfer quotient for generation x is not a trivial problem. For example, one important aspect of a favourable quotient for generation x is that the number of its children, i.e. G_{x+1} should not be too large. However, because the same argument applies to all generations, including the preceding one G_{x-1}, generation x's size when in the denominator of the transfer quotient would be all the smaller, making its transfer quotient less favourable, the more the parental generation G_{x-1} kept down the number of children it had for the sake of improving its own transfer quotient. In other words, this is a trans-generational, dynamic optimization problem.

The problem can best be expressed by asking what ratio between the generations G_{x-1}, G_x and G_{x+1} will yield the optimum, i.e. the lowest, transfer quotient. The numerical ratio between two consecutive generations is termed the net reproduction rate (NRR). Since any particular NRR always relates two generations to one another, the three generations involved in the transfer quotients can be represented by two net reproduction rates, as follows:

$$\frac{G_{x+1}}{G_x} = NRR_x \quad (4a)$$

$$\frac{G_x}{G_{x-1}} = NRR_{x-1} \quad (4b)$$

By substituting these expressions into the definitional equation (3) for the transfer quotient, we obtain:

$$T_x = \frac{\alpha_x NRR_x + \beta_x \dfrac{1}{NRR_{x-1}}}{\alpha_{x-1} + \beta_{x+1}} \quad (5)$$

To begin with, let us seek to establish the optimum value of the transfer quotient when net reproduction rates and the "assistance output" rates and specific to the generations are equal, i.e. when

$$NRR_x = NRR_{x-1} = NRR \quad (6a)$$

$$\alpha_x = \alpha_{x-1} = \alpha \quad (6b)$$

$$\beta_x = \beta_{x+1} = \beta \quad (6c)$$

In this case, instead of equation (5) we have the simplified expression

$$T = \frac{\alpha NRR + \beta \dfrac{1}{NRR}}{\alpha + \beta} \quad (7)$$

The net reproduction rate yielding the optimum, i.e. lowest, value for the transfer quotient is found by setting the derivative of T with respect to NRR to zero. The result is:

$$NRR^{opt} = \sqrt{\frac{\beta}{\alpha}} \tag{8a}$$

Substitution of NRR^{opt} from equation (8a) into equation (7) yields the optimal value of the transfer quotient:

$$T^{opt} = \frac{2\sqrt{\alpha\beta}}{\alpha + \beta} \tag{8b}$$

The dependence of the transfer quotient upon the net reproduction rate as expressed in equation (7) is portrayed graphically in figure 2. As the net reproduction rate increases, the transfer quotient initially falls, as the support provided to the older generation is spread among more people in the middle generation. However, because the effort they need to make for the young generation also increases as a result, the optimum value of the transfer quotient is reached with a net reproduction rate of exactly one. For all NRR figures above that, the transfer quotient increases in proportion.

The conclusions which can be drawn from this outcome are directly apparent from the equation (8a) showing the optimum NRR and from equation (8b) showing the optimal transfer quotient:[4]

Figure 2. Dependance of the International Transfer Quotient upon the Net Reproduction Rate

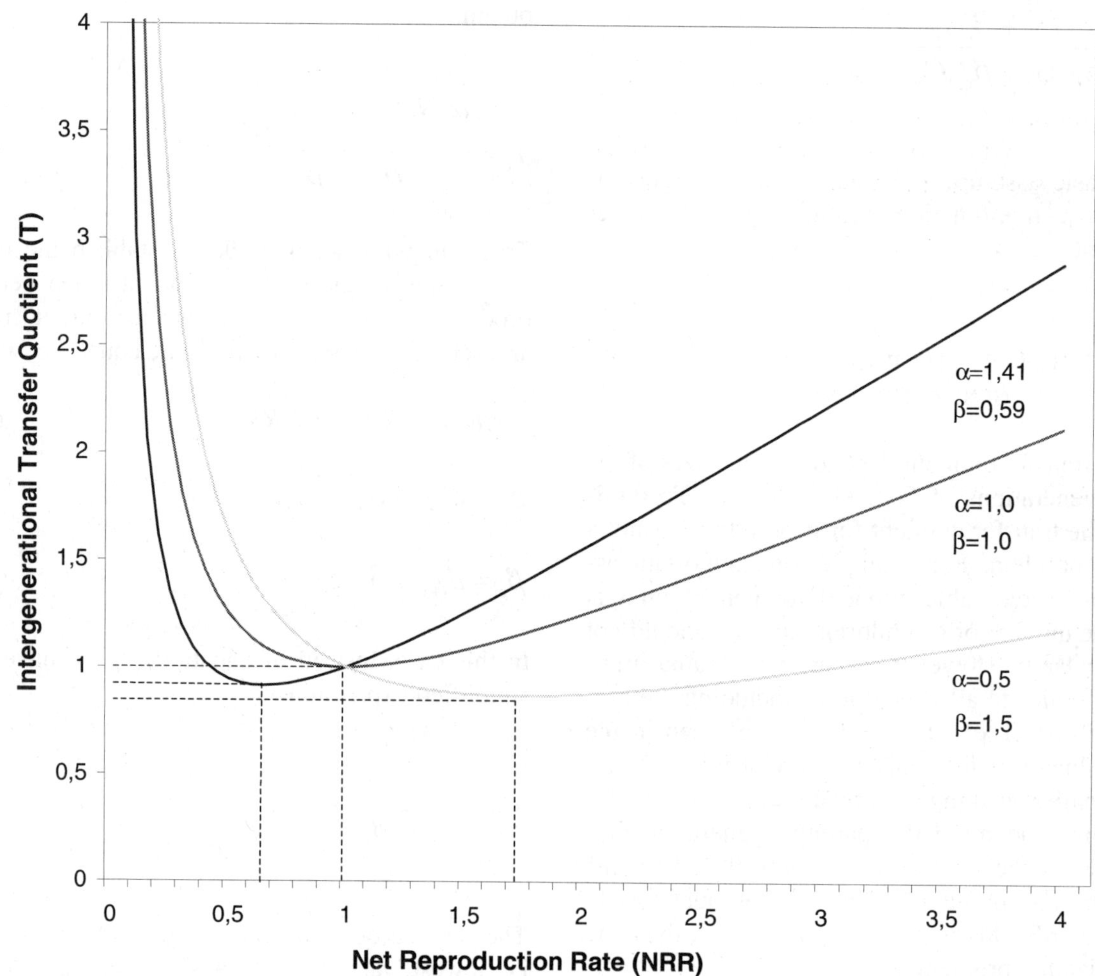

(a) A country's optimum net reproduction rate does *not* depend on the actual level of per capita assistance provided to the succeeding generation (α) or to the older generation (β), but on the ratio of the latter to the former (β/α) So if both forms of support are larger in country B than in country A by the same margin, there will be no affect on the optimum net reproduction rate.

(b) The larger the amount of assistance provided per capita to the younger generation (α) relative to that provided per capita to the older generation (β), the lower the optimum net reproduction rate will be, and vice versa.

(c) If the value of the assistance given to the younger and older generations is equal on a per capita basis (α=β), the optimum net reproduction rate = 1, regardless of the actual amount of support transferred from generation to generation: thus the population will remain constant without any need for immigration or emigration.

(d) If the assistance given to the young generation is greater than that given to the older one ($\alpha>\beta$), the optimum net reproduction rate < 1, which means the population will decline if there is no net immigration.

(e) If the assistance given to the young generation is less than that given to the older one ($\alpha<\beta$), the optimum net reproduction rate > 1, which means the population will grow if there is no net emigration.

(f) The social and economic power to determine the relative amounts of per capita assistance given to the young and the old normally lies with the generation in the middle which is active in the working world. It is to the advantage of this active generation if it keeps a damper on the amount of assistance given to the young per head while favouring assistance to the old, particularly since this generation has already left it‘s own phases of childhood and youth, in which it was a recipient, whereas its phase of old-age when it will again require support still lies ahead. Consequently, in any society, like numerous developing countries, which does not protect children from being exploited by the middle generation (e.g. by prohibiting child labour or passing laws for the benefit of children and young people, say on school provision), one would expect the balance of assistance provided to shift in favour of the older generation, making $\beta>\alpha$, and the optimum net reproduction rate > 1, resulting in persisting population growth. Figure 2 outlines these links by examining three examples:

Example 1 (less developed countries):

α = 0.50
β = 1.50
NRRopt = 1.732

Numerous developing countries with high net reproduction rates correspond to example 1.

Example 2 (stationary populations and world population as a whole):

α = 1.00
β = 1.00
NRR_{opt} = 1.00

This example represents an ideal case in which a population remains constant when viewed net of migratory flows. It‘s net reproduction rate is 1.00 (approx. 2 children eventually reaching adult age and reproducing themselves per woman).

Example 3 (more developed countries):

α = 1.41
β = 0.59
NRR_{opt} = 0.65

The figures in example 3 were chosen so as to reflect roughly the circumstances in a developed country like Germany today. In this case, the net reproduction rate is 0.65. Please note that the optimum net reproduction rate depends solely on the *ratio* of α to β, and not on the absolute value of either parameter. That being the case, the figures shown in the example for α and β do not actually have to agree with the *absolute* parameters existing in the real world but only with their relative values. One may conclude from this example that the objective of maintaining a constant population, with a net reproduction rate of 1.0, without the need for net immigration will be unattainable as long as the assistance provided to the younger generation (per head of that generation) is greater than that given, per head, to the older generation. Is the per capita inter-generational transfer in favour of the younger generation lower or higher than that in favour of the older generation? The answer cannot be found simply by examining statistics on family or household income and expenditure, for these figures are, firstly, themselves influenced by government policy on families, and secondly, they fail to take into account any of the government services and infrastructure provided to the younger or to the older generation. What is needed is an assessment which takes in all real payments or transfers of assistance, so that would have to include such items as expenditure on the educational system etc. The same naturally applies to the support given to the older generation. Many of the real provisions made by the state are economic quantities which cannot be directly captured in statistical information, but they can certainly be empirically estimated using statistics as a basis, though the necessary research input is high.

Another issue to be addressed in this theoretical treatment is that of what effects can be expected to be generated if an ever-greater proportion of the transfers per head of the younger or older generation are no longer made by individuals or families, but by society as a whole or by government bodies. Suppose the sum of individual services (α^i) and societal services (α^s) per head of the younger generation is constant, and likewise for the services to the older generation:

$$\bar{\alpha} = \alpha^i + \alpha^s \qquad \alpha^i = \bar{\alpha} - \alpha^s \tag{9}$$

$$\bar{\beta} = \beta^i + \beta^s \qquad \beta^i = \bar{\beta} - \beta^s \tag{10}$$

Let us further assume that the members of the middle generation only bear their individual share of the services given, although they have been, or will later be, recipients both of the individual and of the societal assistance given to younger and older people. Based on these assumptions, the numerator of the transfer quotient, showing the services or assistance given out, will only contain the individual items, whereas the denominator will show both the individual and societal transfers received by the same generation during its lifetime:

$$T_x = \frac{\alpha^i NRR_x + \beta^i \dfrac{1}{NRR_{x-1}}}{\left(\alpha^i + \alpha^s\right) + \left(\beta^i + \beta^s\right)} \tag{11}$$

Here too, let us begin by assuming a net reproduction rate which remains constant from generation to generation (NRRx-1 = NRRx = NRR), yields the following optimum net reproduction rate, where the transfer quotient is at a minimum:

$$NRR^{opt} = \sqrt{\frac{\bar{\beta} - \beta^s}{\bar{\alpha} - \alpha^s}} \tag{12}$$

The derivation of the optimum net reproduction rate is based on legally and culturally defined standards for the assistance provided, per capita, to the younger or older generation. If these findings are applied to the situation, say, in Germany, the following statements can be made:

Summary (with reference to a more developed country like Germany):

(I) The greater the proportion of the assistance provided (per capita) to people in the late old-age phase of the life-cycle which is borne by society at large or by the state, the lower the optimum net reproduction rate will be, all other factors being equal. In Germany, for example, the birth rate began to decline at the time a collective insurance programme for old-age pensions was introduced (in the Bismarckian social reforms of the 1890s), thus backing up this finding. Of course, one should not take that to mean that the introduction of a state social insurance scheme was the only factor behind the fall in the birth rate in the 20th century.

(II) The greater the proportion of the assistance provided (per capita) to children and young people which is borne by society at large or by the state, the higher the optimum net reproduction rate will be. It is this functional relationship which nurtures the hope in industrial countries that it will be possible to raise the net reproduction rate substantially with the help of government policy towards families.

(III) Whether the net reproduction rate is greater than, equal to or less then unity, or in other words whether the population net of migration will grow, remain constant or shrink in the long term, depends on the ratio between the portion of per capita assistance provided by society at large to the older generation and the portion of per capita assistance it provides to the younger generation.

(IV) For example, the introduction of nursing-care insurance in Germany in 1995 has raised the proportion of per capita services to the older sections of the population which is borne by society or at least collectively, the effect of which is to lower the optimum net reproduction rate. So in a population like Germany's which is shrinking since 1972 without net immigration, the introduction of nursing-care insurance for senior citizens will mean that net immigration needs to be even higher than it already was in order to maintain a constant population. (In the early 1990tees the number of refugees asylum seekers and other immigrants was above one million per annum and above the number of births so that Germany's population grew despite of the birth deficit.)

Nursing-care insurance thus intensifies the cause of the low birth rate and of the aging of Germany's population, which is the actual reason for introducing the insurance scheme in the first place. From the purely demographic point of view, the measure is counter-productive, apart from which it breaches the principles laid down in the Federal Constitution Court's much-publicized judgement of July 7, 1992 (on pension rights for the women who had worked to clear the rubble in Germany's cities after the World-War-II bombings), because it increases still more the transfer payments made by families with several children to pensioners with few or no children, instead of reducing this "inverse solidarity".

D. Fertility in the "single generation model"[5]

So far, we have set out to establish the optimum net reproduction rate on the basis of the functional relationship between the NRR and the intergenerational transfer quotient, while assuming that the net reproduction rate sought or obtained will be equal in all generations. In other words, we imagined that what might be termed a "chain of generations" existed as the focus of people's actions, linking the different sections of the population together in a community of consecutive generations giving assistance and reciprocating it.

Let us now drop this rather idealistic conception in favour of a more realistic view, enquiring what the optimum number of children per woman will be if the focus of action is not the community of generations but a single one, generation x. So the new question posed is: What are the optimum patterns of reproductive behaviour and family structure in terms of the transfer quotient for the generation under examination if it seeks solely to optimize the benefits to itself?

Taking generation x's point of view in isolation, the outcome of this seems to be directly apparent from equation (5). The only quantities which generation x can influence in a bid to minimize its transfer quotient are the number of children it has, the amount of assistance it provides per head of its children (αx) and the amount of assistance it provides per head to its parent's generation (βx) The generation x's transfer quotient will be at an optimum when its net reproduction rate NRRx, the amount of assistance αx provided per child and the amount of assistance per head provided to the parental generation βx are all at their lowest. In contrast to the outcome of the trans-generational optimization problem considered prior to this one, the transfer quotient seems now to be at its lowest, when the number of children per woman is zero. But this simple outcome is only valid for a rather unrealistic condition. In the following it will be demonstrated that the result is more complicated.

The central assumptions made in this argument are that generation x's transfer quotient is independent of the values of α and β and independent of the net reproduction rate of the preceding and succeeding generations. Which net reproduction rate is optimal, if these assumptions do not hold? To answer this question four cases will be distinguished:

Case 1: Equal values of α for all generations and generation specific values of β_x and NRR_x,

Case 2: equal vaues of β for all generations and generation specific values of α_x and NRR_x,

Case 3: equal values of α, equal values of β and generation specific net reproduction rates NRR_x, and

Case 4: equal net reproduction rates for all generations and generation specific values of α_x and β_x.

In the following it will be shown that in these four cases the problem of the single generation model equals the problem treated in game theory: There is no way for a single generation x to optimize its transfer quotient independently from the preceding and succeeding generations.

Case 1

In case (1) the central assumption and the equation for the transfer quotient are given by the equations:

$$\alpha_x = \alpha_{x-1} = \alpha \tag{13}$$

$$T_x = \frac{\alpha NRR_x + \beta_x \dfrac{1}{NRR_{x-1}}}{\alpha + \beta_{x+1}} \tag{14}$$

The optimal value of T_x is found setting the partial derivative of T_x with respect to α to zero:

$$\frac{\delta T_x}{\delta \alpha} = \frac{NRR_x(\alpha + \beta_{x+1}) - (\alpha NRR_x + \beta_x / NRR_{x-1})}{(\alpha + \beta_{x+1})^2} = 0 \tag{15}$$

The condition for the minimum of T_x derived from (15) is:

$$NRR_x \cdot NRR_{x-1} = \frac{\beta_x}{\beta_{x+1}} \tag{16}$$

Substitution of NRR_x from equation (16) into equation (14) yields the optimal value of the transfer quotient:

$$T_x^{opt} = \frac{\alpha NRR_x + NRR_x \cdot \beta_{x+1}}{\alpha + \beta_{x+1}} = NRR_x \tag{17}$$

The interpretation of equations (16) and (17) yields: It is not possible for generation x to minimize T_x by a low value for its net reproduction rate independently from the value of the net reproduction rate of generation x+1 since according to equation (16) NRR_x and NRR_{x+1} are not independent. If in equation (16) NRR_x is decreased, NRR_{x-1} has to be increased so that the minimum of T_x can not be reached simply by a decrease of NRR_x.

Case 2

In case (2) the basic assumption and the corresponding transfer quotient are given by equations (18) and (19):

$$\beta_x = \beta_{x-1} = \beta \tag{18}$$

$$T_x = \frac{\alpha_x NRR_x + \beta \frac{1}{NRR_{x-1}}}{\alpha_{x-1} + \beta} \tag{19}$$

Setting the partial derivative of Tx with respect to β to zero

$$\frac{\delta T_x}{\delta \beta} = \frac{(\alpha_{x-1} + \beta) / NRR_{x-1} - (\alpha_x NRR_x + \beta / NRR_{x-1})}{(\alpha_{x-1} + \beta)^2} = 0 \tag{20}$$

The condition for the minimum of Tx derived from (20) is:

$$\alpha_x NRR_x = \frac{\alpha_{x-1}}{NRR_{x-1}} \tag{21}$$

Substitution of NRRx from equation (21) into equation (19) yields the optimal transfer quotient:

$$T_x^{opt} = \frac{\frac{\alpha_{x-1}}{NRR_{x-1}} + \frac{\beta}{NRR_{x-1}}}{\alpha_{x-1} + \beta} = \frac{1}{NRR_{x-1}} = \frac{\alpha_x}{\alpha_{x-1}} NRR_x \tag{22}$$

Interpreting these equations the result is the following. The transfer quotient of generation x is low, if NRR_x is low, but according to condition (21) a decrease of NRR_x is not possible without an increase of NRR_{x-1}. If generation x-1 minimizes its own transfer quotient by a low NRR_{x-1} the net reproduction rate of generation x-2 has to be increased and so on. As in case (1) the conclusion of case (2) is that there is no way for a single generation to achieve its optimal transfer quotient independently from the preceding and the succeeding generations.

Case 3

The following assumptions are made:

$$\alpha_x = \alpha_{x-1} = \alpha \qquad (23a)$$

$$\beta_x = \beta_{x-1} = \beta \qquad (23b)$$

Using the definition

$$\gamma = \alpha + \beta \qquad (24)$$

the transfer quotient is

$$T_x = \frac{(\gamma - \beta)NRR_x + \dfrac{\beta}{NRR_{x-1}}}{\gamma} = \left(1 - \frac{\beta}{\gamma}\right)NRR_x + \frac{\dfrac{\beta}{\gamma}}{NRR_{x-1}} \qquad (25)$$

Setting the partial derivative of Tx with respect to γ equal to zero

$$\frac{\delta T_x}{\delta \gamma} = -NRR_x + \frac{1}{NRR_{x-1}} = 0 \qquad (26)$$

we obtain the condition for the minimum of Tx:

$$NRR_x \cdot NRR_{x-1} = 1 \qquad (27)$$

Substitution of NRRx-1 from equation (27) into equation (25) yields:

$$T_x^{opt} = NRR_x \qquad (28)$$

The interpretation of equations (27) and (28) results in the same conclusions as in the cases (2) and (3).

Case 4

In this case the basic assumption is that the net reproduction rates of the generations are equal but the values of the α's and β's are different:

$$NRR_x = NRR_{x-1} = NRR \tag{29}$$

$$T_x = \frac{\alpha_x NRR + \beta_x \dfrac{1}{NRR}}{(\alpha_{x-1} + \beta_{x+1})} \tag{30}$$

Setting the partial derivative of T_x with respect to NRR equal to zero:

$$\frac{\delta T_x}{\delta NRR} = \frac{\alpha_x - \beta_x \dfrac{1}{NRR^2}}{\alpha_{x-1} + \beta_{x+1}} = 0 \tag{31}$$

yields the optimal net reproduction rate

$$NRR^{opt} = \sqrt{\frac{\beta_x}{\alpha_x}} \tag{32}$$

and the optimal transfer quotient

$$T_x^{opt} = \frac{2\sqrt{\alpha_x \cdot \beta_x}}{\alpha_{x-1} + \beta_{x+1}} \tag{33}$$

The interpretation of these equations is: Generation x cannot minimize its transfer quotient simply by decreasing the values αx and βx independently from the preceding and succeeding generations, because a corresponding decrease of αx-1 and βx+1 in equation (33) would cause a rise of Tx.

E. Conclusion for the world population as a chain of generations

The general result of the interpretations of the four cases based on the single generation model is: For a single generation x, it is not possible to optimize its own benefits without any regard for what would happen if other generations acted in the same way. A specific generation can only reach its optimal fertility if the preceding and the succeeding generations also practice optimal fertility rates. A more general conclusion is: If the different generations chose to violate the universal ethical principle laid down in Immanuel Kant's *categoric imperative* - they cannot achieve their optimal transfer quotient and optimal fertility. If they acknowledge this principle they would act like a *community* or *chain of generations*, all of which would experience the optimum successively. But even if this principle would cause an in-built tendency to an optimal level of the net reproduction rate, the value of the reproduction rate can be less than one or more than one. *The level of the net reproductions rate would be one only in the ideal case that the amount of support given by a generation per head of its children's generation equals exactly the amount of support given per head of it's parent's generation.* This result can be interpreted as a rationale for fertility assumptions in long term world population projections if the world population is regarded as a chain of generations which tries to achieve an optimal solution of its dynamic intergenerational optimization problem.

NOTES

[1] Typical examples: Becker, G.S., *A treatise of the family*, Cambridge: Harvard University Press, 1981; Caldwell, J.C., *Toward a restatement of demographic transition theory*. In: Population and Development Review, Vol. 20, No. 4, Sept./Dec. 1976; Mackenroth, G., *Bevölkerungslehre*, Berlin 1953; Chesnais, J.C., *The demographic transition - stages, patterns and economic implications*, Oxford 1992; Birg, H., Flöthmann, E.-J., Reiter, I., *Biographic analysis of the demographic characteristics of the life histories of men and women in regional labour market cohorts as clusters of birth cohorts*. In: Becker, H.A. (Ed.), Life histories and generations, Vol. I, University of Utrecht, Faculty of Social Sciences, Utrecht 1991.

[2] This part is an extended version of the model published in Birg, H., *World Population Projections for the 21st Century - Theoretical Interpretations and Quantitative Simulations"*, Frankfurt/: Campus and New York: St. Martin's Press, 1995, Chapter 3.3, p. 67f.

[3] Examples for the type of models with non overlapping or overlapping generations all based on the philosophy of economic utility functions on which this paper does not build on are: Samuelson, P.A., *The optimum growth rate for population. And: Optimal social security in a life-cycle growth model.* Both contributions in: International Economic Review, Vol. 16, No. 3, 1975, p. 531-544. Arthur, B. and McNicoll, G., Samuelson, Population and Intergenerational Transfers. In: International Economic Review 19, p. 241-246. Lee, R.D., Fertility, Mortality and Intergenerational Transfers. In: Ermisch and Ogawa (Eds.), *The Family, the Market, and the State in Aging Societies*, Oxford University Press, 1994.

[4] The results are similar to those of the model of J. Bourgeois-Pichat which is based on more restrictive assumptions of the theory of stable population. See: *"Charge de la population active"*. In: Journal de la societé de statistique de Paris, Paris, Année 91, 1950, p. 94f. An extended version of the model of Bourgeois-Pichat has been developed by Höhne, H.-G.: *"Optimale Bevölkerungs-wachstumsrate - Eine Modifikation der Approximation von Bourgeois-Pichat"*. In: G. Buttler, H.-J. Hoffmann-Novotny and G. Schmitt-Rink (Eds): Acta Demographica, Heidelberg, 1991, p. 15-38.

[5] I am grateful for the fruitful comments made by Jürgen Schott, Technical University of Dresden, on the general model which encouraged me to extend the original version in this contribution.

III. THE IMPLICATIONS OF THE UNITED NATIONS LONG-RANGE POPULATION PROJECTIONS

*John C. Caldwell**

The attempt to project population growth over the coming three centuries to 2300 may seem at first sight to be outrageous. Yet it is also necessary because it allows population change to be placed in perspective, and is needed as a guide for population policy decisions that may have to be made in the near future. The attempt is little braver than the United Nations projections for the next 50 years, which are incorporated as the first half-century of the long-term projections. Indeed, according to the medium projection, that first 50 years covers the whole of world population growth over the next 300 years or perhaps a very much longer period. As we shall see, our final focus will be less on future population numbers than on future fertility rates and on the narrow width over which they will have to range.

The projections, as is inevitable in a necessarily mechanistic approach, move forward after 2050 in a smooth way. The real future population will probably have a greater tendency to undulate as population policies are implemented or withdrawn. One reason for policy actions is as a reaction to population projections. It is hard to doubt that the influential United Nations projections from 1951 onward changed national and international population policies and ultimately population growth itself. All the projections have been within the framework of demographic transition theory and so far population change has vindicated that theory.

This analysis concentrates on the consequences of the projections and rarely attempts to question the assumptions. Nevertheless, insofar as the assumptions determine the consequences, it should be noted that the *2002 Revision* showed more extreme fertility variations for the next 50 years than the new long-range projections thereafter. Thus the gap between the low and high scenarios for 2045-50 is from a total fertility of 1.54 to one of 2.50, but after another hundred years this closes to 1.85 - 2.35 (with the medium total fertility then at replacement level). This convergence takes into consideration demographic realities, for, if the assumptions for the next fifty years were to continue in place, thereafter low and high projections imply population implosion and explosion of such horrific extents that avoiding them would necessarily become overriding national and international political policy. Much of the earlier discussion will concentrate on global numbers. Such an approach has become increasingly necessary as evidence accumulates that populations and their activities found anywhere may contribute to destabilizing our atmosphere which is common to all parts of the earth's surface.

A. DEMOGRAPHIC TRANSITION

Classical demographic transition theory as outlined by Thompson (1929) and Notestein (1945) envisaged countries, as they became industrialized, successively experiencing a fall in mortality, consequent greatly increased population growth, and finally the growth period coming to an end as the population implements fertility control. There was an often unstated assumption (shown in graphs) that the end of the transition would be like its beginning, stationary population. In truth, zero population growth did not quite describe the pre-industrial world, for global numbers had probably trebled in the two millennia up to 1700, but at an average annual rate of natural increase of less than 0.05 per cent. Nor did growth easily come to a halt again, for at the beginning of the twenty-first century the oldest industrialized countries, Britain and Belgium still had small positive rates of natural increase.

The second half of the twentieth century showed that individual countries did not have to wait for industrialization to begin the process of demo-

*Demography and Sociology Program, Australian National University, Canberra, Australia.

graphic transition. It was only necessary for them to be part of an industrializing world—a global economy—with rising individual incomes and levels of education, and falling mortality. The Western Industrial Revolution, and the scientific everywhere. This led to global population growth rates previously unknown, and subsequently and consequently to the spread of fertility control. Already population growth is slowing, with the annual rate of increase having dropped from over two per cent in the late 1960s to about 1.2 per cent at the end of the twentieth century.

The consequence is that we are now in the middle of the key century of global demographic change, 1950–2050, and in an increasingly better position to judge the shape of that change. According to the medium projection, that hundred years will see the world adding 6.4 billion to its numbers, almost three-quarters the magnitude of the final near-stationary population of the year 2300. By the end of the twentieth century we were already five-ninths of the way through that hundred years' colossal climb. The medium projection is in accord with classic transition theory with an annual growth rate during the last half of the twenty-third century of only 0.05 per cent. Even the two other major projections produce very modest annual rates of change during that time period compared with recent experience: the low projection an annual decline of 0.31 per cent, and the high projection a rise of 0.54 per cent.

B. The parameters of growth

To understand the projections and their implications we must first briefly examine the assumptions incorporated in them. A single mortality assumption is plotted with almost linear recent gains in life expectancy continuing throughout the twenty-first century and then slackening, nearly reaching an asymptotic value in 2300. Even so, the global life expectancies by 2300 are 95 years for men and 97 for women. The highest projected level is for Japanese women of 105 years (compared with 85 now) and the lowest is for Sierra Leonean men at 89 years (compared with under 40 now). These are startling levels but the growing number of centenarians already in our midst suggest that such levels are realistic for 300 years into the future. The possibility of such advances and technological revolutions that were part of it, did not succeed even in its countries of origin in substantially reducing mortality until almost the end of the nineteenth century, and yet within another 50 years death rates were falling nearly against mortality suggests that fertility levels will not be the only significant determinant of old age dependency.

Net international migration is set at zero after 2050. This would have seemed nonsensical 20 years ago, but growing resistance by the electorates of many developed countries to new settlers suggest that the assumption could be close to the truth. Two qualifications should be made. The first is that there may be free movement in such supranational areas as the European Union although net flows may be low. The second is that some countries with persistent below-replacement fertility levels may seek immigrants to stabilize their numbers.

Probably the single most important aspect of the new projections is the fertility assumptions and their implications. Those assumptions cover a surprisingly narrow band and yet produce astonishingly different results. Attention is focussed here on the more plausible fertility assumptions: medium, high and low. The other two projections, constant fertility and zero growth, exhibit a degree of artificiality, and, in any case, zero growth differs little from the medium projection and constant fertility is utterly implausible in view both of recent experience and its passing of the 100 billion mark before the end of the twenty-third century.

The main three projections mirror at first present trends, with fertility exhibiting continued falls at first, but then followed by rises, with stability after 2175. Our prime focus will be on what happens after this date because that demonstrates the long-term situation which in the real world could easily begin long before then. The medium scenario from 2175 posits fertility at replacement level with long-term stability around 9 billion, a figure first approximately reached as early as 2045. The low scenario exhibits an eventual total fertility of 1.85 children per woman and a global population slowly sinking from 7.5 billion in 2075 to 2.3 billion in 2300 and then continuing to fall at

0.3 per cent per annum. This would mean a further halving in the following quarter of a millennium with a 2550 world population back to the level of 1850. The high scenario is finally characterized by a total fertility of 2.35 children per woman and a 2300 population of over 36 billion increasing by 0.54 per cent annually.

We do not know what will ultimately prove to be a sustainable global population. It is unlikely to be constituted by a stationary population because continued rises in real per capita income would place continually rising pressure on resources. By the 1990s world population growth was no higher than per capita income growth, both around 1.4 per cent per annum, and henceforth per capita income growth is likely to exert greater pressure on the environment and resources than population growth. The latter falls, according to the medium projection, to almost zero in the second half of the twenty-first century, leaving economic growth alone to exert ever-increasing pressure on the environment. It is of course possible that the economy can so readjust itself that the additional pressures it exerts are not proportional to its growth. Alternatively, the maximum stable population may well be one that is slowly declining so as to offset continued rises in per capita income.

One point should be noted. The relatively modest populations projected for 2050, with low, medium and high scenarios at 7.4 billion, 8.9 billion and 10.6 billion, respectively, and the modest peak populations for the low and medium scenarios of 7.5 billion and 9.2 billion are heavily dependent on continuing fertility falls across the developing world towards sub-replacement fertility over the next half century. This, in turn, depends on continuing economic and social globalization, with all countries eventually becoming consumer societies.

C. Population growth

The single clearest message to come from the projections is that the high scenario is untenable and that such a path of population growth must not be allowed. This is an extraordinary implication. A total fertility ultimately settling at only 2.35 children per woman would yield a global population of 36 billion by 2300. This population figure would be ecologically unsustainable except perhaps with extremely poor populations, a situation which needs to be avoided and, in any case, probably implies such limited technological advance that a population of that size could not be fed. This is not a high fertility level: in the post-war era the United States was above it until the late 1960s, Italy until the early 1970s and Ireland until the early 1980s. Regional fertility in the developing world is still above that level—mostly well above—except in Eastern Asia.

Surprisingly, the low scenario is by no means implausible. It posits a 2100 population of 5.5 billion people, only 27 per cent or two billion persons below the peak, over two generations earlier, and equal to global population in the early 1990s. What would render such a population acceptable is that some sensitive national populations are projected to be higher in 2300 than is commonly thought. Some low projections for 2300 of this type are the following: Germany, 31 million (and still 40 million in 2200), France, 22 million, United Kingdom, 26 million and the United States, 153 million. This would be achieved with a final total fertility of 1.85 children per woman, admittedly well above total fertility rates in much of contemporary Europe, but not greatly above what might be termed the "intrinsic total fertility rate", the rate corrected for the transient impact of rising maternal age at birth. The medium projection is probably our best guess at the future and accordingly we will now examine it at greater length, specifically its regional implications.

D. Sub-global population projections

The projections continue to be divided into "more developed regions" and "less developed regions", the former being constituted by North America, Europe, Australia, New Zealand and Japan. The apparent implication is that the industrialized world will be swamped as its numbers remain virtually stationary over the next three centuries, falling as a fraction of the world's population from 20 per cent in 2000 to 14 per cent in 2300. The further implication is that this would put a brake on industrial growth and rise in incomes. The reality is that this comparison demonstrates little more than that the analytical categories are increasingly meaningless. The last half-century has witnessed the "Asian Tigers" catching up with the "developed world" in real per capita income, and Malaysia, Thailand and South America equalling Eastern Europe. The next hundred years may well witness the Asian giants, China and India, and many other countries doing the same.

More meaningful is a comparison of major regions. There is more stability here than is often thought. According to the medium projection, the next three centuries will witness Northern America, Oceania and Latin America holding their own, as does Asia after 2100. Over the three centuries Northern America's proportion moves from 5.2 to 6.0 per cent, Oceania stays at 0.5 per cent, Latin America and the Caribbean go from 8.6 to 8.1 per cent, and Asia from 60.6 per cent to 55.4 per cent in 2100 and 55.1 per cent in 2300. The major loser is Europe, falling from 12.0 to 6.8 per cent, and the major gainer is Africa, rising from 13.1 to 23.5 per cent. Northern America, largely because the United States has at present relatively high fertility, is seen as moving in numbers from 43 per cent of that of Europe in 2000, to 71 per cent in 2050, 88 per cent in 2100, and to exceed Europe by 14 per cent in 2300.

The projected figures for sub-Saharan Africa are the most problematic, climbing from 10 per cent of the world's population in 2000 to 17 per cent in 2050 and to 21 per cent in 2100 before remaining constant at around one-fifth of the global population. The population of sub-Saharan Africa is multiplied by 2.4 in the first half of the twenty-first century and by 3.1 over the whole century to reach almost two billion in 2100 (the whole world's population in 1920). That is likely to happen because three-quarters of this growth is projected to occur within the first half of the twenty-first century (half of that growth being attributable to females already born) and is based firmly on current conditions: a late fertility transition, still mostly in urban areas, and current total fertility rates close to six outside Southern Africa. That the transition may be even later than has hitherto been feared is shown by the most recent figures for Nigeria, which contains almost one-fifth of the population of sub-Saharan Africa. The total fertility recorded by the 1990 Demographic and Health Survey (DHS) was 6.0 and that for the 1999 DHS was 5.2, apparently evidence of the kind of persistent fall in fertility that characterized the early stages of transition in many countries in other parts of the developing world. But the 2003 DHS found a total fertility of 5.7 children per woman and agreed with the suspicion voiced in the report on the 1999 survey that the 1999 survey was unreliable (National Population Commission 2000, 2003). Nigeria's annual rate of natural increase may still be close to three per cent in spite of very considerable efforts put into the national family planning programme, and 38 per cent of women surveyed in 2003 having at least secondary education and 32 per cent being in urban areas. Similarly, the 2003 DHS for Kenya shows a cessation of fertility decline with a 2000–2002 total fertility of 4.9 children per woman instead of the medium projection's figure for 2000–2005 of 4.15 children per woman.

It seems scarcely possible that sub-Saharan Africa could feed two billion people. It lacks the alluvial soils of the great riverine basins of Asia and volcanic soils are largely confined to parts of East Africa that are already densely settled (Rwanda's population density is over 800 persons per square mile, a comparable Asian density being that of Sri Lanka). Water resources are largely in the wrong places: the Congo River is nowhere near good irrigable soils; the much less voluminous Niger River does flow through good savannah grassland soils but its water available for irrigation is mostly already employed.

Problems will also face the more arid parts of southwest Asia, especially in the longer term as oil resources are depleted and consequently the capacity to import food and distil seawater is reduced. The major projected population increases are over the next 50 years, with Saudi Arabia climbing from 22 to 55 million. But supporting 55 million people in 2050 with significant remaining oil reserves may be simple compared with providing for a similar number in 2100 or 2300 when oil is but a memory in terms of reserves and possibly international demand. Iran's problems are fewer because of a fertility transition largely completed in the late twentieth and early twenty-first centuries. Thus, while over the period 2000–2050 Saudi Arabia's population is projected to increase by 150 per cent, the increase in Iran is only 60 per cent. But even this addition to the population may raise problems in a country already experiencing water shortages.

Asia's developing giants are also of great interest. China is shown over the next 50 years as increasing its population by 120 million (9 per cent), India by 515 million (51 per cent), Indonesia by 82 million (39 per cent), Pakistan by 206 million (144 per cent), and Bangladesh by 117 million (85 per cent). More contentiously these populations are attained partly because the total fertility in the medium scenario is constrained not to go below 1.85 before returning to replacement level after a century. It is quite possible that China and India, and possibly Pakistan and Bangladesh, will keep their national family programmes in place and not only encourage total fertility to fall below 1.85 but would aim at achieving a considerable period of declining population. It might also be noted that analysis carried out after the projections were constructed shows that Pakistan has belatedly and very recently experienced quite steep fertility decline and may not differ as markedly from India and Bangladesh in its pattern of future growth as the projections suggest (Feeney and Alam, 2003).

Equally interesting is the future of Europe in that it is not projected to approach extinction. The whole continent according to the medium scenario will fall in population by 13 per cent by 2050 but by only 16 per cent by 2300. This is the product of rises in Northern Europe (6 per cent by 2050 and 16 per cent by 2300) and Western Europe (one per cent and 7 per cent), while Southern Europe falls moderately (14 per cent and 25 per cent) and Eastern Europe steeply (27 per cent and 35 per cent). These differences depend greatly on the situation in 1995–2000 and eventually may not prove to be so great. For instance, it seems unlikely that Germany and Italy, which differ little now in estimated completed cohort fertility, would exhibit respectively population declines of four per cent and 22 per cent by 2050 and a gain of four cent contrasted with a fall of 34 per cent by 2300.

Nevertheless, the European lesson is important for it shows that many of the countries that have provided policy leadership in the past may not be facing population decline, or at least sufficiently serious decline, to make it likely that they will put much effort into devising deliberate policies for raising fertility. They may, as will be discussed later, bring into being new social welfare policies that have a potential for either raising fertility or preventing its further decline. Thus population is projected to rise over the next half century by 5 per cent to 12 per cent in Sweden, Netherlands, France and the United Kingdom, and by 19 per cent to 44 per cent in New Zealand, Canada, Australia and the United States. Nor is a fall of four per cent over that period likely to galvanize the German government or electorate.

Although the focus of this essay is on the consequences of the projections and not on the probability of their being right, one issue is of such central importance that it should be briefly treated. That issue is the likelihood that the poor countries of Asia and the very poor ones of sub-Saharan Africa can reach below-replacement level fertility in the coming century. Clearly the rich, highly urbanized countries of Europe with most women working outside the home can do so. In fact, they already have achieved such levels. China has also fallen below replacement level, but with a somewhat coercive family planning programme of a type not found elsewhere. But can this be achieved in South Asia, let alone Nigeria or the Congo?

In regard to South Asia, the medium scenario shows total fertility rates reaching 1.85 in Sri Lanka, India and Bangladesh in 2045–2050, and in Pakistan in 2095–2100. An analysis restricted to Sri Lanka, India and Bangladesh, relying on projections of female education and infant mortality, supplemented by anthropological findings, concluded that Sri Lanka had already reached replacement level, that India was likely to do so by 2020 and Bangladesh by 2030, all dates consonant with the medium projection (Caldwell and Caldwell, 2003). The delayed onset of Pakistan's fertility transition, 15 years after Bangladesh and a generation after India, suggested that its achievement of replacement fertility might well wait until the late twenty-first century. But the new data and analysis indicate that Pakistan's attainment of replacement fertility may not be far behind that of India and Bangladesh. There will probably be some gap, the product of Pakistan's lower levels of girls' schooling and higher infant mortality rates (possibly related phenomena). In Africa it might be noted that no sudden fertility declines are forecast: neither Nigeria nor the Democratic Republic of the Congo attains a total fertility of 1.85 children per woman until near the end of the twenty-first century. Such an achievement then or earlier is certainly implied by a total fertility now of 3.0 children per woman in Southern Africa, 4.1 in Ghana and 4.9 in Kenya.

How, then, is it possible that poor countries could be characterized within another 50 years by below-replacement fertility necessitating a large number of one-child families and possibly a significant number of childless women when this was not true of the wealthy countries of Europe until the 1970s and is still not true of the United States? Part of the answer is the continued fall of infant and child mortality rates with many fewer deaths than the West achieved at the same real income levels. Part of the explanation is the continued rise of educational levels, especially of females. Part also is the work of family planning programmes and the positive attitudes of governments and social elites to small families. But much arises from the globalization of the world economy and of the spread of the consumer society. For instance, families in poorer countries now aspire to own cars at much lower real income levels than was the case in the West. This has two effects: first it places a premium on restricting the number of consumers in the family, and secondly it encourages wage earning by wives as well as husbands. The move towards all women working for incomes places additional pressure to limit childbearing. It allows women to support themselves and so marry later, and it leads to competition for women's time and energy between working and raising children. This is aggravated in more patriarchal societies where men undertake few household tasks and little child care, as has been argued for Mediterranean Europe which first achieved total fertility rates under 1.3 (McDonald 2000). It is significant that the Mediterranean model approximates the situation in much of Asia and Africa and probably explains why Japan, South Korea and Taiwan all exhibit fertility levels almost as low as those of the Mediterranean.

E. Age structure and dependency

The impact of sustained low fertility on age structure will be immense and will alter the nature of our societies and their economies. The projections define aged as being over 60, seemingly an unnecessarily low cut-off point for working life but one in keeping with retirement age in contemporary Europe. The proportion over 60 years is largely a product of the fertility level although life expectancy is also a determinant. The present span of that proportion is from around five per cent in Africa to 20 per cent in Europe, with the world exhibiting a 10 per cent level.

The upper level is revealed by Europe, Northern America and Oceania where the proportion over 60 years continues to rise all the way to the year 2300 when it stands at about 40 per cent. Although there is a continuing rise (albeit with a trough as well), in Europe three-quarters of the eventual total rise occurs between 2000 and 2050, and only one-quarter in the following 250 years. In contrast, in Africa the next 50 years will see only one-sixth of the full rise occurring before 2050, but two-thirds by 2100.

When children (under 15 years) and the old (60+ years) are added and expressed as a ratio to those of working age the movement is not quite as great because, as fertility falls, not only does the aged proportion rise but the proportion of children falls. Thus Europe in 2000 is characterized by 18 per cent children and 20 per cent old, giving a total proportion of dependents of 38 per cent. In 2050 those proportions are projected to be 15, 35 and 50 per cent and in 2300, 15, 40 and 55 per cent. Thus, during the next 50 years the fall in the proportion of children will offset the rise in the proportion aged by around one-fifth but thereafter the effect is negligible.

The first point is that in the West families are not likely to appreciate this offsetting. The reason is that the aged do not usually live within the family and are largely supported by Governments through taxation, while children once born are part of the family and deserving of support, just as are the children's parents, from family income left over after taxation. The situation is different in such low-fertility Asian countries as Japan and Singapore where most aged parents live with their adult children and their grandchildren. The Asian Governments hope to retain this family structure, partly because it limits expenditure from taxation, and partly because it is financially more efficient. But evidence from Japan shows that the proportion of the old living with their children is declining slowly. The nuclear family of parents and their dependent children is emotionally strengthening to the exclusion of all others (grandparents, cousins, nephews, nieces), especially the spousal tie. The movement of adult children for work elsewhere in the country also changes residential arrangements.

The second point is that the cost of supporting each aged person is greater than that of supporting a child by, according to one calculation, a ratio of five to three. Much of this additional cost arises from higher health costs, especially among the very old and in the period before death. Additionally, many aged persons—most in the West—live in separate accommodation and not with their children. This arrangement is necessarily more expensive, especially when additional services, such as specialized health care, are added.

The third point is that in one sense the published tables minimize future dependency problems by taking the work span to start at 15 years. In the richest countries most 15–19 year olds are now full-time students rather than workers, and long before 2300 this will probably be the case throughout the world for 20–25 year olds as well. There will, however, be two counteracting forces. One is the probability that a healthier, longer-living population, mostly employed in areas not requiring strenuous physical activity, can remain working long after age 60 or even 65. The other is that, with continuing growth in economic productivity, a smaller proportion of working persons—say 50 per cent in 2100 or 45 per cent in 2300, compared with 62 per cent now in Europe—will easily be able to support the whole population. Even now in Western and Central Europe the economy cannot provide employment for all persons up to 60 years of age.

F. The contrast between the different scenarios

So far the analysis has been largely confined to the implications of the medium scenario, which is likely to be the approach also of most government analysis. The question is whether the low and high scenarios are also plausible. To begin answering that question, the table below presents the total fertility (the only variable taking different paths in the different scenarios) and the resultant populations.

The variation in this initial quinquennium (2000-2005) is surprising given that it is almost coincident with the time of construction of the *2002 Revision* (as is shown by the population estimates). In passing, it might be noted that now (2004) it seems likely that total fertility for the first quinquennium of the twenty-first century will be around 2.8, half way between the medium and high projections. All scenarios begin in 2000 at higher fertility levels than experienced subsequently because the fertility transition in some parts of the world is still in its earlier stages. During the twenty-first century they are further apart than they are from 2100 onward when the gap

Assumptions about total fertlity and consequent world population, low, medium and high scenarios, 2000–2300

		2000-2005	*2045-2050*	*2095-2100*	*2195-2200*	*2295-2300*
Assumed total fertility	Low	2.48	1.54	1.67	1.85	1.85
	Medium	2.69	2.02	1.91	2.05	2.05
	High	2.90	2.50	2.17	2.35	2.35
		2000	*2050*	*2100*	*2200*	*2300*
Resulting population (billions)	Low	6.1	7.4	5.5	3.2	2.3
	Medium	6.1	8.9	9.1	8.5	9.0
	High	6.1	10.6	14.0	21.2	36.4

between the low and high scenarios is only half a child. This is a very modest range compared with the experience of single industrialized countries over the second half of the twentieth century when the extreme range of quinquennial total fertility variations was typically one child in Western Europe and two children in the English-speaking countries of overseas European settlement.

In the short-run there is no real global problem. The population range in 2050 will be only from 7.4 to 10.6 billion, numbers which at first can certainly be fed and, given proper safeguards, are not likely to cause a major upset to such global systems as the atmosphere. Nevertheless, the low and high projections have by 2050 already obtained a demographic and behavioural momentum which will not be changed easily, and which in the longer run will be either physically or politically unsustainable. Given our present evidence on such matters as global warming, ozone holes and increasing water shortages in drier countries, the move shown by the high projection towards 14, 21 and then 36 billion seems impossible. In the longer run even the nine billion people of the medium projection, richer than now, might prove to be destabilizing to global systems or incompatible with the way people want to live. However, a global population falling as in the low projection to five, three and then two billion would probably portend to many the fear of human extinction, unless it became clear that with larger populations their desired consumption levels could not be sustained. This fear of extinction would be especially the case in individual countries. Italy is forecast by the low projection to lose 33 million people, and to reduce its population to 42 per cent of its present size by 2100 and to 23 per cent by 2300. My task is to comment on the consequences of the projected populations rather than their constructions, but I should add here that the proposition that by 2300 Italy and Spain might have fewer than one quarter of their present populations, while Germany and France retain almost 40 per cent of theirs, seems to place too much weight on the probably transient demographic problems of the Mediterranean world in the early twenty-first century.

These considerations might seem to render the medium projection by far the most plausible and the only one salient for consideration. The dense, rich, highly educated and urbanized population of Western Europe, not facing the traumatic shocks of Eastern Europe or the perhaps transient problems of Southern Europe, has a current total fertility of 1.6 and seems unlikely to rise much higher in the foreseeable future. It seems hard to believe that the populations of China or India when they reach this level of affluence with many of their people, living in cities far bigger than London, Paris or Berlin, at population densities in their more populated provinces greater than in present Western Europe, will have a higher total fertility than contemporary Western Europe. If they do not, global population may follow the low projection path until 2100 and thereafter continue at a constant level but lower than the medium projection.

There is an assumption built into the projections that Governments and their peoples will react against the threat of lower populations much as they reacted against the threat of population explosion in the 1960s and later. Nothing else explains the eleven per cent jump in fertility in the three main projections after 2100. Yet, as we will see in the next section, that assumption, especially as it applies to the general population, may well be wrong. The parallel with the opposite movement in the 1960s and 1970s may not be close.

G. Reactions and policies

Government policies in an industrialized world could raise fertility if that became the ideology of the mass of the population as well. The precedent is the fall in the fertility of the industrialized countries from the 1960s when the conviction came that it was in keeping with the world's needs to restrict fertility. However, this fitted in with other trends and desire so well that it is impossible to assign to each its share in promoting the 40 per cent decline in the fertility of developed countries which characterized the rest of the twentieth century. There was better contraception. Married women were moving into employment, much of it full-time, and there were difficulties in both working and simultaneously bearing and raising children. The high-consumption society had spread from the United States to the rest of the developed world and the expenditure of time and money on children competed with other ends. Concepts of maturing and travelling before becoming a parent gained further ground, and sexual activity's tie with marriage was weakened. Marriage rates declined and age at marriage rose. Being a spouse or partner became a more important role than being a parent.

Nothing on this scale could possibly occur so as to raise fertility. Large families would continue to be at odds with wives working, with married couples travelling or "finding themselves", and with the acquisition of good housing in a preferred location filled with appropriate possessions. Children's education and family health services will probably become more expensive as privatization erodes universal public schooling and welfare state health services. Environmental movements will continue to advocate halting or reversing population growth and may have increasingly better data to support their case.

Nevertheless, Governments, especially those where population growth is halting or threatening to reverse, are likely to try to raise fertility levels. One way will be by inspirational speeches and writings praising parenting and motherhood and appealing to demographic patriotism. Some will probably oppose mothers of young children working and attempt to change industrial law or taxation regulations to make working outside the home less rewarding. Once official statistics are recording a sustained fall in population numbers, and this becomes a continuing emotive theme in the media, attitudes opposing childlessness or single-child families may become widespread. So may respect for more long-lasting and stable conjugal relationships. But there is nothing in the nature of developing industrial society to assist this process.

Nor, in most countries will the statistical warnings come early enough to change societal attitudes and so prevent population decline. For instance, Europe's fertility rates have been below long-term replacement levels for almost 30 years and the total fertility rate is around 1.4 and yet population growth has only recently ceased and population decline according to the medium projection will not exceed 0.5 per cent per annum for another 30–40 years.

Furthermore, the demographic ideologies generated will not all be in favour of higher fertility and national population stabilization. This is shown by the relative silence of the developed world's Governments about below-replacement fertility in contrast to attitudes in Europe towards global high fertility during the two decades from 1965. Most First World Governments are deeply conscious that they have promoted family planning programmes in the Third World over the last half century and feel that a pro-fertility campaign at home might at the best smack of hypocrisy and at worst discourage national family planning programmes in poor countries. The latter is not a trivial point for, according to the medium scenario world population growth will not peak for another three-quarters of a century. More to the point, that of the less developed regions will not peak until 2080 with a population two-thirds again as great as at present, while the population of the least developed countries is projected not to peak for another hundred years at more than three times the present level. Governments will probably not act decisively to raise fertility if the environmental movement, which is much more likely to have grass-roots appeal than an official pro-natalist stance, can produce convincing evidence that ecological imbalance is accelerating. Governments are unlikely to react as they did during the 1930s when it was clear that numbers might count in future wars, because now nuclear weapons and a military unipolar world make the situation very different.

This is not, however, the whole story as is shown by precedent. As movement towards the welfare state in most of the West gathered momentum during the 1930s and early 1940s, to come to fruition after the Second World War, an essentially social justice movement was supported by many on the grounds that help to families should help to raise fertility from the very low levels of the Depression of the 1930s. The very different world that came into being after the Second World War had such a demographic impact that it became impossible to determine whether family support schemes played a significant role in attaining higher fertility levels. The much more comprehensive programmes of Eastern Europe from the 1960s, especially in countries like the former Czechoslovakia and the Democratic Republic of Germany, were more openly directed at raising fertility, but also had a social justice rationale. They undoubtedly had some success, but at a cost that no open-market democracy could fund, and to an extent that could not ultimately be measured because they were ended prematurely by the fall of communism.

McDonald (2002) provides a comprehensive list of measures that might be employed to raise fertility, some already having been tried in Western Europe and a majority in socialist Eastern Europe. They include direct bribes such as taxation rebates for children and payment to families according to number of children as well as subsidized housing and other help for those marrying young; assistance by legislation or persuasion in women's employment to make it more compatible for both them and their husbands with raising a family—maternity and paternity leave, better and cheaper child care, compatible schooling and working hours, childbearing contributing towards rather than against work tenure and promotion, flexible working hours and more part-time employment; and social change: gender equality in the home especially with regard to housework and childcare, pro-child societies and work places. Most of the second and third group will come into being because of support from larger coalitions of interests than the pro-fertility lobby as society begins to adjust itself to a situation where all adults normally work. As much will be done under the rationale of social justice for children as for their mothers and some steps will be a recognition of the contribution of single mothers to population growth.

H. THE FUTURE POPULATION PATH: THE MOST PLAUSIBLE SCENARIO

Taking all the above considerations into account, which is the most plausible scenario? It has long been safest to rely on the medium scenario and its usually successful predictions support this approach. But this was constructed at the most for 50 years, not for three centuries. On the face of it, it seems just as absurd projecting the population of 2300 from a 2000 starting point as it would be for William Petty or Gregory King to have successfully constructed population projections to the end of the second millennium. This probably is not the case, for they could not have foreseen the Industrial Revolution and its likely final impact: almost everyone living in towns and working outside agriculture, the diminishing value of children, the passing of the need for families or even marriages as the basic building block of society, and such a dramatic decline in mortality as to make deaths rare before old age (rare even in infancy), and with the eventual attainment of a life expectancy of one hundred years quite likely. We are also beginning to understand something about the ability of the earth's systems to withstand pressures, although we know less about possible technological fixes to prevent disequilibrating tendencies.

The most important demonstrations of the projections is the very narrow range in the longer run that fertility can exhibit. There are, however, fewer constraints in the short run even though some of the paths may be recklessly heedless of the more distant future. Several points can be made. It now seems likely that the global total fertility in 2000–2005 will be close to that of the higher projection, not far short of 2.8. Nevertheless, that level is not necessarily incompatible with fertility over the next four decades falling as fast as the medium projection postulates. Bottoming out at 1.85, as in the medium projection, seems quite likely, a level which appears to be similar to the present levels of completed cohort fertility found in Europe (with the exception of crisis-ridden Eastern Europe). All projections show a moderate fertility rise early in the twenty-second century with the medium projection attaining replacement fertility. This rise presumably reflects the result of change in societal attitudes and government action. This seems a late date for such an achievement in the developed world, for one would imagine that it would happen there earlier or not at all. Nevertheless, my own feeling is that by 2100 world consensus would see Governments struggling strongly to reach replacement fertility almost regardless of cost.

The world population will probably reach close to its maximum within the lifetime of many people now living. The low and medium scenarios show all-time maximum populations being reached in 2040 and 2075 respectively, the latter being less than one per cent above the 2050 population. Those maxima are 9.0 billion for the medium scenario and 7.5 billion for the low scenario.

Ironically, the long-term situation is clearest. Global population probably will not spontaneously, or by government intervention, be allowed to go higher than 14 billion for 2100 as in the high scenario. The rest of that scenario, showing population reaching 36 billion in 2300 is almost certainly irrelevant. The high fertility path is unlikely to be followed short of a nuclear war decimating the human race. Similarly, global numbers are unlikely to be allowed to go below 5.5 billion, as in the low scenario for 2100 and certainly not to the 2.3 billion given for 2300. There is one caveat here. If atmospheric change and global warming, or any other potentially catastrophic attack on world systems, cannot be stabilized, population decline is likely to be allowed, even to be encouraged, until stability can be reached. Apart from these considerations, the very long-term global fertility level is unlikely to exhibit a total fertility differing much from 2.05 children per woman. My guess is that population numbers will be somewhere between 8 billion and 12 billion, although both total fertility and global population may oscillate within those bounds in a way that projections cannot predict. There will continue to be a demand for population projections and their findings will continue to influence Governments, society and reproductive ideologies. They may indeed be the driving force behind oscillations.

References

Caldwell, Bruce K., and John C. Caldwell (2003). Below – replacement fertility: determinants and prospects in South Asia. *Journal of Population Research,* vol. 20, No. 1, pp. 19–34.

Feeney, Griffith, and Iqbal Alam (2003). New estimates and projections of population growth in Pakistan. *Population and Development Review,* vol. 29, No. 3, pp. 483–492.

Kenya Bureau of Statistics et al. and Measure DHS +/ORC Macro (2003). Kenya Demographic and Health Survey, 2003: Preliminary Report. Nairobi.

McDonald, Peter (2000). Gender equity, social institutions and the future of fertility. *Journal of Population Research,* vol. 17, No. 1, pp. 1–16.

McDonald, Peter (2002). Sustaining fertility through public policy: the range of options. *Population* (English edition), vol. 57, No. 3, pp. 417–446.

Nigeria National Population Commission and Measure DHS+/ORC Macro (2003). Nigeria Demographic and Health Survey, 2003: Preliminary Report. Abuja.

Notestein, Frank W. (1945). Population: the long view. In *Food for the World,* Theodore Schultz ed. Chicago: University of Chicago Press, pp. 36–57.

Thompson, Warren S. (1929). Population. *American Journal of Sociology,* vol. 34, No. 6, pp. 959–975.

IV. COMPARING LONG-RANGE GLOBAL POPULATION PROJECTIONS WITH HISTORICAL EXPERIENCE

*Joel E. Cohen**

In 2003, the Population Division of the United Nations released projections of the world's population from the year 2000 to the year 2300 (United Nations, 2004). The purpose of this note is to compare the projected ratios of population size over intervals of one, two and three centuries with the historically observed ratios of population sizes over intervals of one, two and three centuries during the last two millennia.

In addition to the global population projections, the Population Division projected many demographic details, such as age structure for every existing country for the next three centuries. This note does not attempt to examine these details. Such details could in principle be examined by analogs of the methods used here for the global population projections.

Table 1 shows the Population Division's projections according to five scenarios. This note analyzes the low, medium, high, and constant-fertility scenarios, and ignores the zero-growth scenario.

Table 2 shows 21 estimates of the world's population in years divisible by 100 (excepting year 1) for the last 2,000 years. The estimates for all years except years 100 and 300 came from the United States Census Bureau (2003). For each year in which the United States Census Bureau low estimate differed from the United States Census Bureau high estimate (all years except year 2000), a single estimate was obtained by taking the geometric mean of the low and high estimates. The geometric mean was used here because random variation in population sizes is typically log-normally distributed. The estimate for the year 100 is the geometric mean of the estimates for the years 1 and 200. The estimate for the year 300 is the geometric mean of the estimates for the years 200 and 400. The geometric mean was again used here because it gives the correct estimate at a midpoint in time if population growth is exponential between the earlier and the later date. Both uses of the geometric mean reflect the multiplicative mechanism of population variation and growth.

Table 2 also shows the ratio of the current population to the population one, two, or three centuries earlier. There are 20 ratios for population change over an interval of one century, 19 ratios for population change over two centuries, and 18 ratios for population change over three centuries. The frequency distributions of these historical ratios (approximated as histograms, minima and maxima in table 3) provide a background against which the anticipated future ratios (table 4) of the long-range population projections of the United Nations Population Division can be considered.

For the low scenario, all three projected 100-year ratios, namely 0.90, 0.58 and 0.73, are lower than the smallest 100-year ratio observed in the last 2,000 years. The last two of the three 200-year ratios and the last one of the three 300-year ratios are also lower than the smallest of the observed 200-year and 300-year ratios, respectively. The low-scenario projection is lower than recent historical experience, even for the coming century, and increasingly in future centuries.

All the ratios of the medium scenario fall within the range of historical experience.

For the high scenario, the 200-year ratio of 2100 and the 300-year ratios for 2100 and 2200 are larger than the largest observed ratios for 200 years and 300 years, respectively. The high scenario projection is higher than recent historical experience, especially beyond the next century.

The constant-fertility projection differs from the other scenarios. It is intended as a what-if exer-

* Laboratory of Populations, Rockefeller University and Columbia University, New York.

TABLE 1. EVOLUTION OF THE POPULATION OF THE WORLD ACCORDING TO THE DIFFERENT SCENARIOS, 2000-2300

Year	Population (billions)				
	Low	*Medium*	*Zero-growth*	*High*	*Constant*
2000	6.1	6.1	6.1	6.1	6.1
2050	7.4	8.9	8.9	10.6	12.8
2100	5.5	9.1	9.1	14.0	43.6
2150	3.9	8.5	8.5	16.7	244.4
2200	3.2	8.5	8.3	21.2	1 775.3
2250	2.7	8.8	8.3	27.8	14 783.0
2300	2.3	9.0	8.3	36.4	133 592.0

Source: United Nations, Department of Economic and Social Affairs, Population Division, World Population in 2300 (ESA/P/WP.187).

TABLE 2. HISTORICAL ESTIMATES OF WORLD POPULATION
(in millions)

Year	Population			Ratio		
	Lower	*Upper*	*Geometric mean*	*100 years*	*200 years*	*300 years*
1	170	400	261			
100			240	0.92		
200	190	256	221	0.92	0.85	
300			209	0.95	0.87	0.80
400	190	206	198	0.95	0.90	0.82
500	190	206	198	1.00	0.95	0.90
600	200	206	203	1.03	1.03	0.97
700	207	210	208	1.03	1.05	1.05
800	220	224	222	1.06	1.09	1.12
900	226	240	233	1.05	1.12	1.15
1000	254	345	296	1.27	1.33	1.42
1100	301	320	310	1.05	1.33	1.40
1200	360	450	402	1.30	1.36	1.73
1300	360	432	394	0.98	1.27	1.33
1400	350	374	362	0.92	0.90	1.17
1500	425	540	479	1.32	1.21	1.19
1600	545	579	562	1.17	1.55	1.42
1700	600	679	638	1.14	1.33	1.76
1800	813	1125	956	1.50	1.70	2.00
1900	1550	1762	1653	1.73	2.59	2.94
2000	6071	6071	6071	3.67	6.35	9.51

Source: For "Lower" and "Upper" columns: United States Census Bureau 2003. Historical estimates of world population. http://www.census.gov/ipc/www/worldhis.html, accessed 10-Dec-03. Remaining columns are calculated here.

NOTE: Estimates for years 100 and 300 are geometric means of estimates for prior and following centuries. "Ratio" shows population for the current year divided by the population one, two or three centuries earlier. The ratios for 100 years earlier in the years 100 and 200 (namely, 0.92) are necessarily identical because of the use of the geometric mean; likewise for the years 300 and 400 (ratios 0.95).

TABLE 3. FREQUENCY HISTOGRAMS OF RATIOS IN TABLE 2

Bin	100 years		200 years		300 years	
	Frequency	Cumulative %	Frequency	Cumulative %	Frequency	Cumulative %
0	0	0.0	0	0.0	0	0.0
1	7	35.0	5	26.3	4	22.2
2	12	95.0	12	89.5	12	88.9
4	1	100.0	1	94.7	1	94.4
8	0	100.0	1	100.0	0	94.4
16	0	100.0	0	100.0	1	100.0
minimum ratio	0.92		0.85		0.80	
maximum ratio	3.67		6.35		9.51	

Source: Table 2.

NOTE: Bin 1 counts the number of ratios less than or equal to 1.00; e.g., of the 20 ratios over one century, 7 were less than or equal to 1. Bin 4 counts the number of ratios that exceeded 2.00 (the next lower bin limit) and were less than or equal to 4; for example of the 20 ratios over one century, exactly 1 ratio (namely, 3.67, the ratio of the population in 2000 to that in 1900) exceeded 2 and was less than or equal to 4.

TABLE 4. RATIOS OF PROJECTED POPULATIONS IN YEARS 2100, 2200 AND 2300 TO (ACTUAL OR PROJECTED) POPULATIONS 100, 200 OR 300 YEARS EARLIER, ACCORDING TO THE LOW, MEDIUM, HIGH AND CONSTANT-FERTILITY SCENARIOS
(in millions)

		Year		
		2100	2200	2300
Low	Population	5 491	3 165	2 310
	100 years	0.90	0.58	0.73
	200 years	3.32	0.52	0.42
	300 years	5.74	1.92	0.38
Medium	Population	9 064	8 499	8 972
	100 years	1.49	0.94	1.06
	200 years	5.48	1.40	0.99
	300 years	9.48	5.14	1.48
High	Population	14 018	21 236	36 444
	100 years	2.31	1.51	1.72
	200 years	8.48	3.50	2.60
	300 years	14.66	12.85	6.00
Constant-fertility	Population	43 600	1 775 300	133 592 000
	100 years	7.18	40.72	75.25
	200 years	26.38	292.42	3064.04
	300 years	45.59	1 074.24	2 2004.94

Source: Tables 1 and 2.

cise rather than as a realistic possibility. Every projected ratio greatly (and unrealistically) exceeds the largest historically observed ratio for each interval of one, two or three centuries. A continuation of present levels of fertility, in combination with the other assumptions concerning mortality and migration in the long-range projections, would lead to increments of population size far, far greater than any within historical experience.

In conclusion, the medium scenario of these long-range projections calls for changes in population size that fall well within historical experience over the last two millennia. The ratios of population change anticipated in the low scenario and the high scenario fall below and above historical experience, respectively. This conclusion does not argue that either scenario is unrealistic. As table 2 shows, the 100-year ratio for year 2000, namely 3.67, was more than twice the 100-year ratio for the nineteen preceding centuries. The rise of population in the twentieth century was unprecedented. The global fall in fertility since 1965 was also unprecedented. All that can be concluded is that the high and low scenarios fall outside of historical experience. Unprecedented events are not unprecedented in demography.

I acknowledge with thanks the support of United States National Science Foundation grant DEB 9981552, the assistance of Kathe Rogerson, and the hospitality of Mr. and Mrs. William T. Golden during this work.

References

United Nations (2004). World Population in 2300 (ESA/P/WP.187). New York.

United States Census Bureau (2003). Historical estimates of world population. http://www.census.gov/ipc/www/worldhis.html, accessed 10-Dec-03.

V. WORLD POPULATION IN 2300: A CENTURY TOO FAR?

*David Coleman**

A. INTRODUCTION

Once more the United Nations Population Division has boldly gone where few demographers have dared to go before. Previous United Nations projections were very daring when they went from 50 years to 150 years. Now all that has been left in the shade by projections up to 2300, which will provoke even more intense interest because of the focus on countries as well as major regions. The Population Division, in sticking its neck out in this way, has exposed itself to many obvious criticisms. There is much to argue about and to disagree with in the scenario assumptions. But they have performed a valuable service in showing on a comparative basis the implications in the very long run for human populations of various reasonable ranges of demographic parameters. Three centuries of development, with two or three fertility transitions, allows two or three more or less stable population distributions and trajectories to emerge, although the continuing improvement in mortality built into the projections never permits a perfectly stable structure to emerge. All that helps to focus attention in the inevitable geographical shifts in population, ultimately of considerable political and military importance, that will unfold in the future, both between major regions and also within them. The long view inevitably also raises fundamental demographic questions of whether there are any lower limits to fertility in developed societies, or any upper limits to human lifespan.

B. ASSUMPTIONS

It may be appropriate to start with a recapitulation of the scenario assumptions with some comments on them.

The main *medium scenario* assumes that the total fertility rate (TFR) will fall below replacement level and remain there for 100 years, after which it returns to replacement and remains there until 2300. The *high scenario* assumes that the TFR after 2050 is 0.25 higher than in the medium scenario and remains at 2.35 instead of falling to replacement level. The *low scenario* assumes the TFR to be 0.25 lower than in the medium scenario and then remains constant at 1.85 instead of returning to replacement. The *zero-growth scenario* uses the same TFR as the medium scenario until 50 years after fertility has fallen to replacement level. Then the number of births is adjusted to match the number of deaths, ensuring zero growth (i.e. the scenario does not cut off increases in mortality, but reduces fertility in step with it). Finally a *constant fertility scenario* maintains fertility constant during the whole period at the level estimated for 1995-2000.

Different regions, and difference countries within those regions, achieve these targets at different times over the period. But by 2200 almost exact convergence on replacement rate is achieved in all major regions and more controversially, fertility has converged everywhere to the narrow range of 1.85 – 2.09. Even by 2045-50 fertility in the world as a whole, and all major regions has fallen below replacement except for Africa (2.4) with Middle Africa (2.6) as the highest of all. All TFRs are below 3 by 2050, most below 2.5, many below 2.0. All TFRs are found between 1.85 and 2.08 by 2100 and between 2.02 and 2.08 by 2300. Only a very few countries are projected not to have fallen below A net reproduction rate (NRR) of 1.0 by 2050. Almost all are in sub-Saharan Africa except for Afghanistan (2055) and Yemen (2070), including Somalia, Ethiopia, Democratic Republic of the Congo and Niger, the latest of all (2075). Not surprisingly these countries are destined to make the most spectacular relative and absolute increases in population, some rising from demographic obscurity to reach the top 12 or so of national populations by 2300 (United Nations, 2004, table B.14) and becoming the powerhouses of population growth in the later part of the period.

[1] University of Oxford, Oxford, United Kingdom.

The assumption on sub-replacement fertility fits the conclusions reached by the United Nations Expert Group meeting of 2002.[1] There, a panel of demographic wise persons agreed that there were no convincing reason why the fertility decline observed in all but 14 countries should conveniently end when it had fallen to 2.1. Therefore sub-replacement fertility was on the horizon, in general, for the world. However, the Population Division makes two more big jumps -namely to assume that their conclusion, reasonable in general, will apply in detail to all countries, however unpromising, and also—an even bigger jump—that it will then more or less uniformly rise again to 2.05+/-0.2 and stay there forever. That was not foreseen, or discussed in the earlier meeting, the horizon for which ended at 2050.The previous consoling assumption is thereby reinstated after a century's delay. A diversity scenario is surely called for here, with elements of the 'low' scenario in some regions (e.g. Europe) and a higher one elsewhere (e.g. tropical Africa).

One intriguing feature of the medium scenario is the long time spent at sub-replacement fertility (during different calendar years for different countries) which is then followed by a return to replacement, presumably for ever after. It is not unreasonable to assume some recovery of fertility for purely technical reasons after a decline. Many populations may have an underlying norm of about 2 surviving children. Their sub-replacement fertility in the immediate post-transition phase may be attributable to marked tempo delays which in the case of third-world populations might take mean age at first birth from near 20 to near 30 over some decades. Insofar as some births delayed may eventually materialise, period fertility rates should recuperate somewhat, as they are in some European countries and are predicted to do in others – an assumption built in to many population projections. However this recuperation is almost nowhere assumed to take European fertility back to replacement rate in the short term and may well not do so for some third world populations either. If it does, then it is likely to do so over the course of one or two decades, not a complete century. That is a very long time for sub-replacement fertility to persist. If it did so, any process of recuperation would be completely exhausted in such a long period of time. Social and economic structures, and fertility norms, would have adjusted to such low fertility rates over a century and it is difficult to see why the birth rate should then ever subsequently increase except as the result of some specific feedback—perhaps a population policy—against the reality or prospect of population decline. But feedbacks of that kind are specifically excluded from this set of projections.

The *high scenario* seems to be potentially realistic only for a minority of third-world countries that have not yet begun the fertility transition or where that transition may become stalled for a long time. There is no guarantee that all countries will acquire really low fertility, and some have been 'stuck' at the theoretically transient and unstable level between 2 and 3 children for a long time; for example the semi-developed countries of Uruguay and Argentina since the 1950s. There is no reason why they should remain the only examples. On the other hand, TFRs rising to 2.35 seems out of the question for Europe and most of the rest of the low-fertility developed world. On this high scenario several billionaire countries are added to the current shortlist of China and India– Bangladesh, Brazil, Pakistan, Nigeria, and the United States of America. The populations of Yemen and Viet Nam, (18 million and 78 million respectively in 2000) rise to exceed 400 million by 2300.

The *low scenario*, therefore, seems more appropriate for at least some European countries, especially those that experience period levels of fertility described as 'lowest – low' usually defined as being at the level of TFR=1.3 or lower (Kohler and Billari, 2002), and currently prevalent in Southern and Eastern Europe. In fact a TFR of 1.85 is somewhat higher than that used in most national long-term projections in such low fertility areas, although in national terms, 'long-term' seldom means more than 50 years. In one of the few longer-term European projections published, the TFR in the United Kingdom is not projected to rise above 1.75 (Shaw, 2001), although this author thinks that is a little too conservative. Chinese populations, overseas and in China itself, also seem to be potential candidates for persistent very low fertility, and some other Asian populations might fall into the same category. The medium scenario of the official Japanese 2000 – based population projections envisage rising TFRs only in a miniscule amount, from 1.35918 in 2000 to 1.38726 in 2050 (National Institute, 2002, appendix table 1) a level of pessimism that seems unrealistic. However, for unexplained reasons after nearly 80 years of sub-replacement fertility, the TFR is deemed to rise to 2.07 for the period 2050–2100.

The *zero-growth scenario* is an odd contrivance that incorporates the only form of interaction or feedback in the whole set. Here the TFR follows the medium scenario until 50 years after replacement is reached, after which the number of births and therefore the TFR, is adjusted to match the number of deaths to eliminate natural increase (It is not entirely clear what illustrative function this scenario is meant to illustrate, and it is based on a very precise kind of feedback mechanism In the very long run, presumably as survival tends to infinity, fertility tends to zero so that at immortality, the TFR = zero. However, no tendency of that kind is apparent in the data. This gives a constant 8.3 billion population from 2175 till 2300; somewhat less than that of the medium scenario.

Finally the *constant fertility scenario* keeps fertility at the same level as in 2000. After 300 years of natural increase this yields a world population with an exciting number of trillions – 133.6 to be exact (that is 133.6 x 10^{12}), of which the developed world comprises just 0.6 billion or less than 0.0005 per cent of the then world total. This scenario yields some remarkable trillionaire countries: by 2300 Burkina Faso would have 3.5 trillion people, Angola 8.5 trillion, Afghanistan 4.2 trillion, Chad 2.6 trillion, Democratic Congo 16.3 trillion, Ethiopia 7.6 trillion, Niger 23.6 trillion, Nigeria 7.4 trillion, Somalia 8 trillion, Uganda 18.6 trillion and Yemen 8.5 trillion; the least of these therefore holding 1000 times more than the total world population (6.1 x 10^{6}) at present.

Also unlikely, but perhaps less unlikely, are some of the results from Europe. Some, after all, have despaired of any substantial future increases in the fertility rates of some European countries and here the Population Division makes that come true. In this scenario, Europe's overall population falls from 728 million to 90 million; little more than the total population at its mediaeval peak before the Black Death. In the same scenario, Eastern Europe shrinks to near-disappearance at 5 million—perhaps the total around the fifth century. The other regions fall to between 28 million and 30 million each. As in all other scenarios, Northern Europe gains ground relatively speaking over all other parts.

Many of the regions in this constant fertility scenario have the initially baffling property of rising TFRs, some to considerable levels. This arises because the population balance shifts over the decades and centuries to the progeny of higher-fertility populations. These gain ground over lower fertility groups and those with below–replacement fertility drift down towards extinction. In the longest run only those populations with above-replacement fertility will survive and those with the highest fertility will eventually predominate, however numerically insignificant they may initially be. Regions without any sub-populations with above replacement fertility will continue to decline, those with at least one such will eventually recover. Thus Northern Europe would increasingly become Irish, Norwegian and above all—and eventually entirely—Icelandic. In Southern Europe the only national population with above-replacement fertility is Albania. Thus on this scenario the future is Albanian, duly reflected in the rapid increase of Southern European fertility to above-replacement levels in the latter part of this scenario (figure 1). This concept is familiar from the population dynamics of minorities (Steinmann and Jaeger, 2000) but seldom demonstrated on the international level.

To a considerable extent the latter part of most of the projections, with their stable fertility levels near or on replacement level, serve more to consolidate the differentials and trajectories established in the first 50 years or so. That is when the big shifts in rank order and the membership of the top ten most populous nations is sorted out. There is great sensitivity in the long term to precise level of assumptions. In favouring relatively high stable levels of sub-replacement fertility, and a return to replacement, these projections to that extent inflate the likely future population of the developed world in particular.

Figure 1. Projection of European regions to 2300, total fertility rate constant (2000-2005 level) within each country

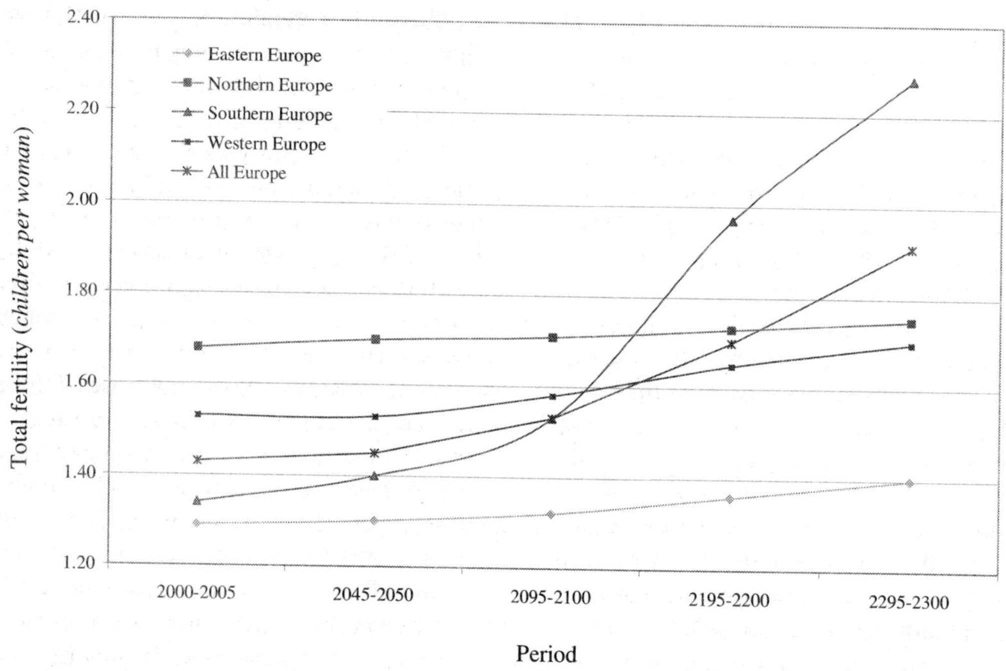

C. FERTILITY VERSUS MORTALITY

One of the curious features of the set of scenarios is the asymmetry of assumptions given to fertility and mortality. All the variants are based on different assumptions on fertility levels and trends. None is based on any variation in mortality. This is rather strange, given the greatly increased prominence given to mortality and its variation in population projection in recent years, and the growing controversy surrounding the likelihood of its falling to very low levels or not. In relation to population ageing in the developed countries such as France (Calot and Sardon, 1999), for example, mortality trends are taking over the major role in current and near-future population ageing. Fertility trends have remained relatively unchanged since the roller-coaster years of the baby-boom and bust of the 1950s and the 1970s and an increasing consensus of demographers argues against any future substantial increase in European birthrates from current sub-replacement levels (Lesthaeghe and Willems, 1999; Frejka and Sardon, 2003). In the Population Division's projections the variation attributed to mortality variants is a substantial fraction of that attributed to fertility variation and it may be argued that in respect of the developed world at least, the level of uncertainty is in fact greater. For example, although fertility variants in projections often include a high fertility variant, in the developed world at least this seems to be inserted more for the sake of symmetry than for the sake of realism. It would be very difficult to find any demographers willing to bet on an increase of the birth rate in the developed world to 2.35, the level posited there in the 'high fertility' scenario. Yet there is very great uncertainly attached to the future level of mortality in developed and developing countries in both directions and whether there is, or is not, any final limit to the improvement of life expectation.

Opinion is polarised between two camps engaged in an unusually lively debate (Wilmoth, 2001). The one points to the impressive continued improvement in expectation of life in recent decades, not just from the elimination of mortality at younger ages but more importantly from the continued reduction of mortality at all ages among older people. It is certainly true that most official projections of mortality have been far too pessimistic for some decades (Murphy, 1995). An 'optimistic' viewpoint is particularly encouraged by the discovery that mortality among the oldest-old appears to follow a flatter, non-Gompertz trajectory which apparently opens the possibility of survival into old ages previously unimagined, at least in scientific circles (Robine and Saito, 2003). Here, model fitting to time-series of survival curves can provide a very favourable future outlook for long survival although at a declining rate (Lee and Carter, 1992; Oeppen and Vaupel, 2002) with no real prospect of a final absolute limit.

The other offers persuasive counter-arguments: the astonishing reductions in age-specific mortality rates that the more optimistic model-based projections of survival require, with their need for commensurate and at present medically unimaginable radical reductions in major causes of death (Olshansky and Carnes, 1996, Olshansky and others, 2001). On this view current improvement in survival are a transient experience dependent on the long survival of privileged cohorts selected in earlier life in a temporarily favourable risk environment enabling mortality to be postponed. Problems already being accumulated in younger cohorts, notably the epidemic of obesity in developed countries, may prevent this promise being realized, a problem heralded by the recent relative failure of death-rates to improve much among women in some of the richest developed societies such as Denmark and the Netherlands.

This great dimension of scientific uncertainty is ignored in these projections, which adopt a model decidedly on the optimistic side, or at least one leading to optimistic conclusions in the long run. The Lee-Carter model adopted here (Lee and Carter, 1992) extrapolates long-term historical patterns of mortality decline which allows age-specific death rates to decline exponentially without limit, and provides confidence interval for the estimates. It incorporates no information on medical, behavioural or social influences on mortality. In the United States of America context, this method projected an expectation of life for both sexes based on the trend of death rates 1933 to 1987 of 86.05 years by 2065, considerably more than the official United States projection for 2050 current in 1992 of 80.5. The latter is clearly far too pessimistic given the rate of change and the fact that the level for 2001 (both sexes) was already 77.2.

The Lee-Carter approach is recognized as a major advance in mortality projection. But its adoption over such a long time-span does rather imply the endorsement of the views of one camp in the survival debate rather than those of the other. The Lee-Carter model has probably never been used in a mortality projection over quite such a long period of time. By the end of the projection period here – 2300 expectation of life has reached just over 100 in the most favoured regions. It is projected to reach 104 years for males and 108 for females in Japan, here still strongly in the lead despite misgivings already expressed elsewhere about its staying power, based on trends in the 1990s (Wilmoth, 1998) which do not fit a Lee-Carter extrapolation very well. The high values projected by the Population Division may, of course well come to pass or even with hindsight be regarded as conservative. However, although a number of authors have commented on the technical possibility of their models yielding such expectations of life, none has been so bold to endorse that figure as a projection.

It would therefore have greatly helped the scenarios presented here if variation would have been introduced into the mortality patterns as well as into the fertility levels. That would have recognised the great importance of mortality variation and allowed us to estimate the extent to which growth and ageing in the middle and later parts of the scenarios are due to continued mortality change. In the nature of the Lee-Carter model, mortality keeps on improving over the course of the 300 years, albeit at a declining rate, while the fertility levels are fixed here for centuries at a time. Without alternative mortality scenarios, the sensitivity of these projections to the mortality assumption, in numbers, age-structure and dependency, cannot be gauged.

D. The end of migration

In all scenarios international migration declines to zero after 2050. Given the long-term nature of these projections, it is a surprising assumption and one with particular influence on the developed world, both in Europe and in Northern America, where for decades net inward migration (immigration) has been making substantial contributions to population numbers (Salt, 2003). The projection of migration is, of course, even more difficult than that of fertility. So many influences affect it: economic, demographic, social and political, in both sending and receiving countries. The proposed independent variables are themselves at least in part beyond prediction. In the past, European national projections almost invariably posited a rapid decline in net immigration to zero, partly in order not to contradict national government policy to minimise inflows, partly because of the difficulty of working out what would happen in the future, if not zero. Previous projections of the Population Division also follow this pattern.

Some national governments no longer accept this position. In the United Kingdom at least, the government since 1997 has reversed its formerly restrictive stance and adopted a pro-immigration policy in which the Home Secretary has declared that he 'saw no obvious upward limit to the level of immigration'. In the last few years official projections by the United Kingdom's Government Actuary's Department have partly caught up with reality and with official policy and now incorporate constant net inward migration for the duration of the projection (103,000 per year in the 2002 based projections), mostly to 2050 although a few have been made to 2100 (Shaw, 2001). In the latest projections for the United Kingdom, net immigration (projected at a level considerably lower than the actual current annual level of 154,000) accounts for 83 per cent of the additional 5 million people expected to live in the United Kingdom up to 2031. Net immigration accounts for the greater part of population growth in many western European countries and prevents decline in Italy, Germany and Greece. The United States projections, both by the Bureau of the Census (1996) and by others (Smith and Edmonston, 1997), also assume constant immigration continuing at a high constant level for the duration of the projection period—usually 2050—without any diminution. So do those of a number of other developed countries (e.g. Alders, 2001). In view of the comments above it is obviously risky to make any generalisation about future migration levels.

However it could reasonably be argued that one underlying guarantor of substantial net inward migration to developed countries will persist, even if the sources and the exact level cannot be determined. That is, the continuation of marked economic and demographic disparities between the North and South, and the continuation of political unrest in the South. The future concentration of population growth in the poorest countries, envisaged by these projections, makes it even more likely that disparities provoking emigration pressure will persist beyond 2050 in many parts of the world. Economic disparities between North and South—tenfold or more—have not diminished since the 1960s; in some areas they have expanded. Demographic regimes have diverged even further despite the inception of fertility transition in the majority of poor countries. Many countries, and important sections of the populations of others, will move out of the third world and into the developed realm in the next century, including much of the East Asian and Chinese population. But this will be far from complete for many. Pakistan, Bangladesh and India will by themselves comprise nearly two billion people. The majority will be poor. Many already have connections in the West to facilitate chain migration. The Population Division's projections themselves show us where new future migration pressure is likely to come—the poorest-poor countries with the slowest fertility transition, whose rapid growth, perpetuating poverty, is charted in these projections: Ethiopia, Somalia, Niger, Nigeria, even Yemen. Their growth will contribute most of global population growth as the projection progresses. It will continue well into the twenty-second century and in some cases into the twenty-third. Some have chain—migration connections, others have still to make them. Mass migration, or at least migration pressure, is thus unlikely to end in 2050. In the absence of new effective policies to stem it, migration will continue to make substantial contributions to population both in Northern America and in Western Europe.

E. Feedback

In projections of this duration, all kinds of fundamental questions that can be ignored in shorter projections begin clamouring for attention. One was briefly suggested above; patterns of migration are affected by governments wishing to limit or increase flows according to various interpretations of their national interest and the view on the desirability of existing levels. Other population policies, to limit fertility in the third world, are tacitly already taken into consideration. They have substantially influenced the empirical trajectory of fertility decline and presumably will continue to do so. More interesting are the possibilities for policy feedbacks on low fertility countries to encourage the birth-rate and environmental pressures of a harsher unplanned kind on some of the poorest and fastest-growing countries, especially those in arid areas where water shortage is likely to become a problem. Family welfare considerations of an enlightened kind are increasingly likely to enjoy support from more explicitly pronatalist concerns as the implications of very low fertility for population decline and ageing become apparent. As the shadow of the past fades into the distance European countries will become less inhibited in proposing demographically—aware family and workforce policies. However it may be that the Population Division in choosing fertility values for these scenarios, pitched rather higher than most analysts might expect –at least for the next 50 years—have pre-empted the population planners in giving them a fertility level otherwise difficult to attain.

More interesting is the question of the sustainability of some of the poor-country populations that emerge from the projections. Can their environment, or any imaginable economic growth, enable the Yemen to sustain a population of 147 million in 2100, Somalia to maintain 68 million , Afghanistan 90 million, Pakistan 409 million, Democratic Republic of the Congo 209 million or Uganda support 167 million? If not, what will the people do: emigrate, die or promote a much faster fertility transition? Few demographers will want to risk repeating the experience of the Club of Rome in building complex feedbacks on minimal data (Cohen, 1999). However projections on such a long-term, with such implications, oblige us to think about inter-relationships between variables and constraints (Sanderson, 1999).

F. WHAT EUROPEAN POPULATION DECLINE?

Europe has grown accustomed to being told by its transatlantic partners that it faces little but marginalisation, decline, ageing and decay unless it agrees to import tens of millions of foreigners or adopt a more robust attitude to fertility (or a more careless one, according to Frejka and Kingkade, 2003). While demographic marginalisation and ageing is inevitable, the medium scenario projection offers a slightly more optimistic future than other projections, even offering the hope of modest demographic recovery. The dramatic decline in overall 'European' numbers from 728 million to 538 million inhabitants is mostly accounted for by the steep decline in numbers in Eastern Europe, demographically dominated by the Russian Federation, Ukraine and Romania, all with very low birth rates and high death rates. The first two of those are far from being integrated into the 'Western' part of Europe on any economic, political or demographic criteria, having havered for centuries between Westernising and Slavophile inclinations.

A more conventional and realistic 'European' picture is given by the trajectory of Northern, Western and Southern Europe below. The first two of those suffer little decline until 2100, after which fertility is projected to pick up. Southern Europe's decline to 2100 is more impressive (figure 2). The first 100 years of this scenario suggests that it is not very meaningful to talk about 'European' demography when both its recent past (Coleman, 2002) and its medium-term projected future are so diverse. National and United Nations projections, for example, show little fall and even some increase in the numbers of 20-24 year olds for the next 50 years in Norway, United Kingdom and France, even without the recent fertility rises in the latter case (including immigrants, of course), contrasted with a marked falling away in the same age-groups in Germany, Italy and Spain.

Among individual countries, Germany falls only from 82 million to 73 in 2100 then rises to 85.3 by 2300. Sweden's decline is very modest: 8.8 million to 8.1. The United Kingdom keeps growing, reaching 66 million in 2050 (about a million more

Figure 2. Population of European regions projected to 2300, United Nations medium scenario
(millions)

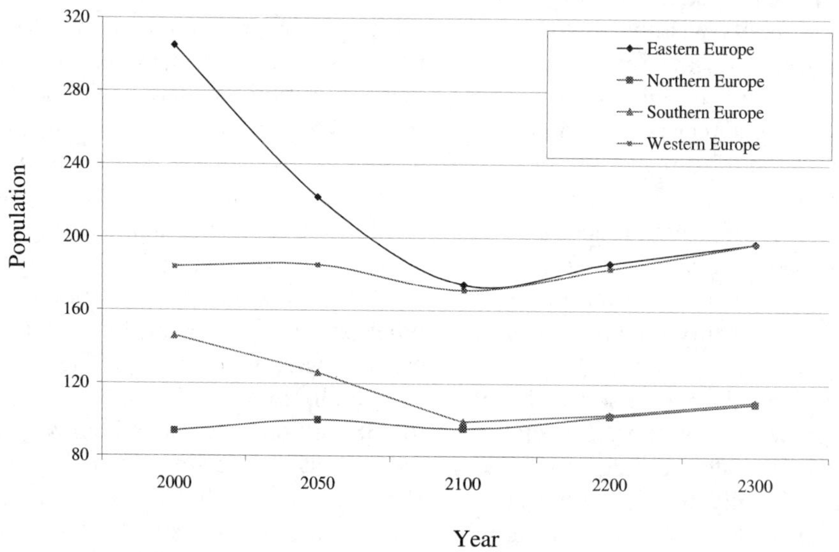

than the official projection) and 73 million in 2300, slightly ahead of France, while Italy drops out of the European premier league altogether. Denmark hardly changes at all, while Belgium sticks at 10 million to 11 million, providing perhaps the longest-range justification of any population projection; Verhulst's logistic predicted in 1847 that its ultimate population would be 9.44 million (Schtickzelle, 1981, p 553). In Eastern Europe Bulgaria's experience is typical, halving from 8.1 million to a low 4.0 million in 2100, but then, like Romania, recovering somewhat.

Central European countries such as the Czech Republic do better, but two of the Baltic States are reduced to near-vestiges; Estonia down to 0.52 million and Latvia falling from 2.3 million to 1.0 million in 2100.

However this better than expected future (for some) is to a large degree dependent on relatively high (although mostly sub- replacement) assumptions about TFR levels in the first 100 years followed by a recovery to replacement fertility after that, thus tending to stabilise the position while falling mortality permits further growth. In the shorter run at least the lower fertility scenario, showing the consequences if fertility does not recover to more than 1.85 children per woman, may be more appropriate (figure 3). With the absence of migration, it certainly offers more exciting examples of decline. Even here, European variety persists. Even on the low scenario some European countries do not decline that much—the population of the United Kingdom only halves in 300 years; from 58.7 million down to 26.2, doing better than France—not the outcome expected from the current French fertility advantage. Only modest decline is projected for countries such as Norway by 2100, while Belgium, which begins with the same population as Belarus, ends up, though much diminished, with twice the number. Current and projected variety would probably better be fitted by running different regions, and different countries, in different scenarios rather than imposing a one-size-fits all policy over all periods of time. Hence the need for a systems approach using feedbacks. Different countries need no more have the same fertility trajectory than they need to have the same fertility level.

G. Naturally a disaster?

The implications of all this are very interesting. The issue of population ageing perhaps needs no more discussion. On population size, the view from E 44th Street tends to echo that of Proverbs XIV, 28: 'In the multitude of the people is the king's honour; but in the want of people is the destruction of the prince'. Population growth is good for General Motors and for the United States, its end a problem and its reversal a disaster. This may

Figure 3. Population of European regions projected to 2300, United Nations low fertility scenario
(millions)

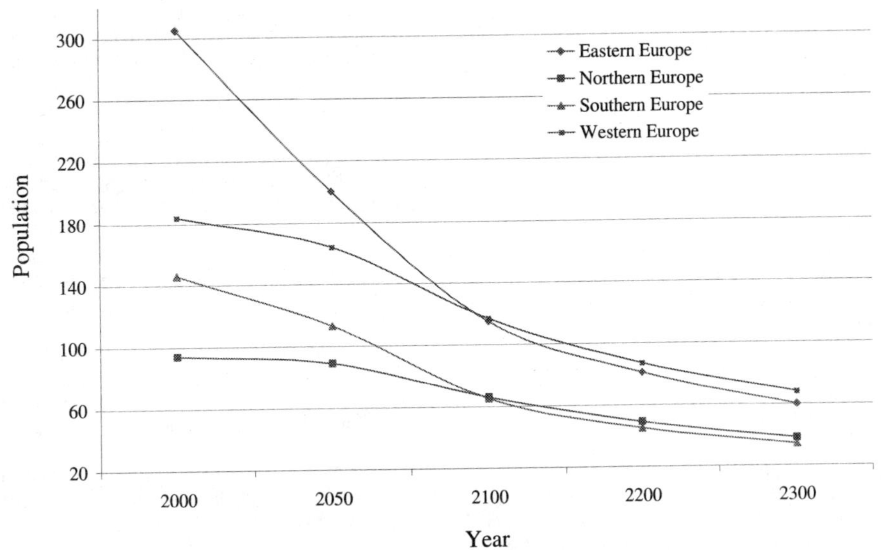

be true and Europeans may be the first in modern times to find out. But the proposition is by no means universally accepted, especially in the more overcrowded parts of Western Europe. There is no relationship between population growth or size, and income per head in the Western world. Actual decline is another matter. We have hardly any modern experience and its theory has hardly been looked into since the time of Reddaway, although the early mediaeval experience seems to have been beneficial.

There has been little recent official comment, but the United Kingdom's Royal Commission on Population (1949) and its Population Panel (1973) felt that the end of population growth would moderate problems of food imports and balance of payments and 'ease the solution of a number of social and economic problems'. The Netherlands has long considered itself over-populated; up to the 1950s it sought, like the United Kingdom, to encourage emigration to ease domestic population pressure. That remains part of the rationale for the moderation of immigration. Even in the United States a Congressional Committee saw some advantages in an end to growth, although not in decline. In crowded countries, population growth is regarded as a major source of environmental degradation, the reduction of biodiversity and the destruction of countryside; so on environmental grounds the prospect of population decline is usually welcomed. Even though the definition of 'optimum' population size has proved elusive, Australian environmentalists, arguing from considerations of sustainable 'environmental footprint' desire a population of 10 million, not the present 19 million although more demographically-informed opinion suggests 25 million.

While decline brings problems, it may be argued that a small stable population, if ever achieved, has advantages. Problems of overcrowding are ameliorated and environment protected. Unsatisfactory infrastructure, hastily constructed to cope with growth, can be demolished. Labour shortage will reduce unemployment, moderate inequality and promote capital substitution as wages rise. With international trade and alliances, globalized markets and regional security transcend frontiers. European countries have lost territory and (in most cases) the corresponding population over the last century (United Kingdom, Germany, Austria), without harming their standard of living.

Malthus was right about the beneficial effects of labour shortage for labourers; his anxieties about failure of demand may not apply in a world of international trade and accelerating individual consumption. One of the many merits of these projections is that they underline the need for much more research on these issues, which for some populations may be nearer than they think.

REFERENCES

Alders, M. (2001). Allochtenprognose 2000-2050 de toenamevan het aantal niet-westerse allochtonen nader bekeken. *Maandstatistiek van de bevolking*, 2001/4, pp. 29-33.

Calot, G., and J.-P. Sardon (1999). Les facteurs du vieillissement démographique. *Population*, vol. 54, No. 3, pp. 509 - 552.

Cohen, J. E. (1999). Should Population Projections consider 'Limiting Factors' and if so, how? In *Frontiers of Population Forecasting. Supplement to volume 24 of Population and Development Review,* W. Lutz, J. W. Vaupel and D. A. Ahlburg. New York: Population Council, pp. 118 - 138.

Coleman, D. A. (2002). Populations of the Industrial World - A Convergent Demographic Community? *International Journal of Population Geography,* vol. 8, pp. 319 - 344.

Frejka, T., and W. Kingkade (2003). US Fertility in International Comparison: An Exploration to Aid Projections. In *The Direction of Fertility in the United States,* US Bureau of the Census. Alexandria, Virginia: Council of Professional Associations on Federal Statistics, pp. 55 - 150.

Frejka, T., and J.-P. Sardon (2003). *Childbearing Prospects in Low-Fertility Countries. A Cohort Analysis*. Dordrecht: Kluwer.

Kohler, H. P., F. C. Billari and others (2002). The emergence of lowest-low fertility in Europe during the 1990s. *Population and Development Review,* vol. 28, No. 4, pp. 641 - 680.

Lee, R. D., and L. R. Carter (1992). Modeling and Forecasting U. S. Mortality. *Journal of the American Statistical Association,* vol. 87, No. 419, pp. 659 - 671.

Lesthaeghe, R., and P. Willems (1999). Is low fertility a temporary phenomenon in the European Union? *Population and Development Review*, vol. 25, No. 2, pp. 211 - 228.

Murphy, M. (1995). The Prospect of Mortality: England and Wales and the United States of America, 1962 - 1989. *British Actuarial Journal,* vol. 1, No. II, pp. 331 - 350.

National Institute of Population and Social Security Research (2002). *Population Projections for Japan: 2001 - 2050 with long-range projections 2051-2100.* Tokyo: National Institute of Population and Social Security Research.

Oeppen, J., and J. Vaupel (2002). Are there limits to Human Life Expectancy? *Science,* vol. 296, No. 5570, pp.1029 – 1031.

Olshansky, J., B. A. Carnes and others (2001). Prospects for Human Longevity. *Science,* vol. 291, Nos. 1491 - 1492.

Olshansky, J., and B. A. Carnes (1996). Prospects for extended survival: a critical review of the biological evidence. In *Health and Mortality among Elderly Populations,* G. Caselli and A. D. Lopez, eds. Oxford: Oxford University Press, pp. 39 - 58.

Robine, J.-M., and Y. Saito (2003). Survival Beyond 100: The Case of Japan. In *Life Span: Evolutionary, Ecological and Demographic Perspectives,* J. R. Carey and S. Tuljapurkar, eds. New York: Population Council, pp. 208 - 228.

Salt, J. (2003). Current *Trends in International Migration in Europe*. Strasburg, Council of Europe. http://www.coe.int/T/E/Social_Cohesion/Migration/Documentation/Publications_and_reports/Salt's%20report%202003-1.pdf.

Sanderson, W. C. (1999). Knowledge can improve Forecasts: A Review of Selected Socioeconomic Population Projection Models. In *Frontiers of Population Forecasting,* Supplement to volume 24 of Population and Development Review, W. Lutz, J. W. Vaupel and D. A. Ahlburg, eds. New York: Population Council, pp. 88-117.

Shaw, C. (2001). United Kingdom Population Trends in the 21st Century. *Population Trends,* No. 103, pp. 37 - 46.

Steinmann, G., and M. Jaeger (2000). Immigration and Integration: Non-linear Dynamics of Minorities. *Journal of Mathematical Population Studies,* vol. 9, No. 1, pp. 65 - 82.

Schtickzelle, M. (1981). Pierre-François Verhulst (1804 – 1849). La première découverte de la fonction logistique. *Population,* vol. 36, pp. 540-555.

Smith, J. P., and B. Edmonston, eds. (1997). *The New Americans. Economic, Demographic and Fiscal Effects of Immigration.* Washington, D. C.: National Academy Press.

United Nations (2002). *Expert Group Meeting on Completing the Fertility Transition.* http://www.un.org/esa/population/publications/completingfertility/completingfertility.htm and /Summaryofcountrypapers.pdf

United States Bureau of the Census (1996). *Population Projections of the United States by Age, Sex, Race and Hispanic Origin 1995 - 2050. Current Population Reports P25-1130.* Washington, D. C.: US GPO.

Wilmoth, J. (1998). Is the pace of Japanese mortality decline converging toward international trends? *Population and Development Review,* vol. 24, No. 3, pp. 593-600 and 670-671.

Wilmoth, J. (2001). How long can we live? A Review Essay. *Population and Development Review*, vol. 27, No. 4, pp. 791-800.

NOTE

[1] The United Nations Expert Group Meeting on Completing the Fertility Transition, New York, 11-14 March 2002.

VI. POPULATION FUTURES FOR THE NEXT THREE HUNDRED YEARS: SOFT LANDING OR SURPRISES TO COME?

*Paul Demeny**

Some 50 years ago John Hajnal, in a characteristically insightful article (Hajnal, 1955), considered the prospects for population forecasts. On matters other than practical procedures and techniques he argued three main points:

1. that population projections in the future as in the past will often be fairly wide of the mark—as often as simple guesses would be;

2. that, nevertheless, the frequent preparation of projections will continue;

3. that a projection can be useful as a piece of analysis even if its accuracy is low.

World Population in 2300 (United Nations, 2004), reporting on the proceedings of a December 2003 expert group meeting on long-range population projections and presenting the results of a new set of United Nations population projections, bears out Hajnal's argument. Among his three propositions, the validity of the second is the most obvious. There has been a veritable outpouring of demographic projections during the last 50 years, prepared by various international organizations and national agencies, as well as by independent analysts. Among these, the United Nations Population Division's now biennially revised projections are by far the most detailed, best known, and most widely used. This well-deserved prominence reflects the Division's unparalleled access to national data, its in-house analytic experience and resources, and its willingness to draw on outside expertise whenever that might usefully complement its own. The most recent of the biennial projections, the *2002 Revision* (United Nations, 2003a), is the immediate predecessor of *World Population in 2300,* and indeed the former provides the year 2000 to 2050 component for the new set of long-term projections covering the next 300 years.

This new set is not just one among the many. It is distinguished from the routine by an exceptionally brave ambition: to draw a picture of plausible demographic futures up to the year 2300 and to do so in extraordinary detail: country-by-country according to the political map of the early twenty-first century.

The wisdom of venturing so far ahead in time to obviously uncertain territory will be, no doubt, questioned by many. Most historians, including historians of demographic change, would agree that we cannot fully explain the past. How can we then tell what the remote future will bring, let alone do so in minute numerical detail? But the criticism of the ambition is not justified. Three hundred years is a time span long in individual human terms, but short by historical standards. It is not the cosmic distance of H. G. Wells' fictional *Time Machine*, or Charles Galton Darwin's book, published in 1953, *The Next Million Years.* Backtracking 300 years would bring us to 1700—a year that may be thought of as marking the dawn of modernity—but the time elapsed since that date covers only a small fraction of recorded human history. It is a fraction, however, from which at least some relevant lessons, including demographic lessons, can be drawn for the future. The ultimate goal of science is prediction. Attempting to chart demographic futures for the next 300 years is an eminently legitimate and worthwhile enterprise. No one has better credentials to make such an attempt than the United Nations Population Division.

A surprise-free future?

Following its long-established pattern, United Nations population projections are elaborated in several variants. Presenting these in user-friendly numerical detail and also in printed form—providing country-level information along with their various regional aggregates and showing numerous demographic variables of interest at closely-spaced time intervals—imposes obvious limitations on the number of variants that can be

* Population Council, New York.

offered. In the practice of the biennial projections that meant essentially three variants, incorporating different assumptions about the parameter considered least predictable yet most influential in setting future population numbers: fertility. In addition, some subsidiary illustrative exercises, such as projections assuming constant fertility or zero migration, usually complemented the trinity of "high," "medium," and "low" variants. In practice, however, these three were never quite equal. Any user-survey could readily demonstrate the overwhelming attention paid to the medium projections.

World Population in 2300 follows the practice of earlier and less extravagant United Nations projections in offering a "medium" fertility variant, bracketed by "high" and "low," and supplements that dominant trio with two additional illustrative sets. Austerity dictates that the characterization of fertility level be consistent throughout the projection period—"high" is high and "low" is low, and in between lies "medium." With reasonably modest hypothetical differences between the paths traced by fertility over time, the deviations in terms of total population size generated by the end of a 50-year time span conveniently stay within plausible limits. What plausible limits are, of course, is in the eye of the beholder, but few would dispute that the United Nations' 2002 revisions for 2050—offering a global medium population figure of 8.9 billion, bracketed by a low of 7.4 billion and a high of 10.6 billion—provide a range that is sufficiently narrow to yield meaningful information. To be sure, each of these figures is the result of what, using the late Herman Kahn's label, may be described as surprise-free, and of course none more so than the one in the middle. The future time paths of the governing variables are smooth; if there are any gentle bumps in the projected population figures, they are an inheritance from past demographic disturbances that left a mark on the age structures from which the projections start. With just three projection variants this could hardly be different: orderly and gradual change must rule.

But a pattern of differences maintained consistently into a future far more remote than just the next five decades inevitably produces major deviations in projected population numbers. The title of the press release that announced the results of the new long-range projections highlighted the likely global population in 2300 as 9 billion. In other words, it replicated virtually the exact message that a press release announcing the 2002 revisions would have identified as the likely global total for 2050, that is to say, a full 250 years earlier. Surprise-free 2300 global population future indeed: the news broadcast by the medium projection for the two and a half centuries beyond 2050 is that there is no news; there is, grosso modo, homeostasis. Less comfortingly, what brackets that projected 9 billion "medium" population figure according to the "low" and "high" projections conveys information that is distressingly vague: the 2300 global population, we are told, will be between 2.3 and 36.4 billion. And this massive difference is the result of remarkably modest differences in the assumed fertility parameters. Total fertility rates, after transitory phases that by fiat are largely completed by the end of the present century, settle down at replacement level in the medium projection, bracketed by rates that are only 0.25 children lower or higher in the low and high projection variants.

Each of these variants incorporates the same—again, very much surprise-free, very much business-as-usual—assumptions as to the future evolution of mortality. Practical considerations support that choice. Complicating the picture by assuming alternative mortality scenarios would have increased the complexity of the projection results beyond levels tolerable for most users. It is evident, however, that introduction of multiple assumptions on the plausible future course of mortality would have widened the range of uncertainty signaled by the global totals, and, even more, would have left a mark on such characteristics of the projected population as structure by age and, plausibly, also by sex. There are wide disagreements among experts about how and how much human mortality might change in the next three centuries. Some hold a less sanguine view about the likely pace of progress in longevity than even the rather cautious assumptions incorporated in the United Nations projections. Others foresee far greater gains in survival rates. Taking these possibilities into account would have created higher "high" and lower "low" figures for 2300.

Since the United Nations does not designate any particular figure within the interval bracketed by its high and low projection as its best guess for 2300 (not even the 9 billion trumpeted by the press release), the global actual total in 2300 will be wide of the mark. This bears out Hajnal's first proposition.

More gratifyingly, the projections up to 2300 also demonstrate the truth of Hajnal's third point—about analytical usefulness, regardless of ex-post accuracy. For anyone contemplating the demographic future in the next three centuries, the United Nations projections *are* an eminently useful device. They provide reference marks for outcomes under well-specified conditions, hence stimulate and help organize thinking about the immense variety of possible alternative scenarios and their likely results. The three major alternatives numerically worked out in the United Nations' set serve as a broad frame within which, and also beyond which, mental exercises can heuristically scan patterns that break with the assumption of "no surprises" and, at least qualitatively or through back-of-the-envelope calculations, trace demographic futures that could be quite different from the smooth, gently rising or falling, curves presented by the frame.

This point is well illustrated by the United Nations projection set itself. Beyond the basic "high," "low," and "medium" trio, a complementary projection variant provides the outcome resulting from an unabashedly counterfactual assumption: that of keeping fertility levels constant at their year 2000 value. The United Nations of course does not suggest that in 2300 the so-called less developed regions might contain 133 trillion persons—the figure arrived at—while the population of the more developed regions will stand at a paltry 600 million, that is, a minuscule fraction of the colossal global total. The impossibility of sustaining fertility at its present levels especially where those levels happen to be high and, equally, the glaring anachronism inherent in freezing the labels of those two "regions" would have been evident to those who computed the scenario. Presenting the numerical result of this counterfactual finger-exercise makes a point about the unsustainability of certain present-day demographic patterns. It is a point laden with theoretical as well as policy implications.

The reference above to two broad regional groups within the global total is a reminder of the special recipe through which the populations of these large aggregates were projected. Heroically, the United Nations proceeded to treat virtually all member states of that organization, along with some territories, as equals, whether the country's name was India (projected 2300 population in the medium variant 1.372 billion) or Tonga (projected 2300 population 112 thousand). In and by themselves these country projections can be treated similarly to the global one: they provide outcomes under a limited set of well-specified assumptions, hence can serve as a frame of reference in contemplating demographic futures country-by-country. When the countries are aggregated to yield regional and eventually global totals, one would expect that those totals are more solidly based than their component parts, since variations in the latter, up and down, average out.

But here we encounter a peculiarity of the United Nations long-range projections—a peculiarity that also applies to the familiar biennial series. Once the governing assumptions are specified for each country or group of countries—in practice, whether fertility follows a high, low, or medium path—aggregating country figures into regional and eventually the global total assumes that countries go in lock-step: all follow, simultaneously, high, low, or medium trajectories. As in the choice of the number of alternative fertility and mortality assumptions, practical considerations must have dictated this procedure. It is a procedure, however, that the user should be aware of, and mental exercises in probing alternative futures should constantly challenge the assumption of trajectories that go in lock-step. Countries proceeding on the same type of path—say, high or low—however different the initial conditions and the assumed tempo of demographic change over time, is just one of the many alternative possibilities. It is also necessary to envisage patterns within which the component parts follow different trajectories: some traveling on a "high," others on a "low" path and, of course, various such combinations. Clearly, depending on the particular mixes, the resulting aggregates will exhibit different relative weights of their country units even if the aggregate totals turn out to be similar.

A defense of the "lock-step" assumption might invoke the notion that demographic patterns are converging the world over: countries are more and more likely to exhibit similar demographic behaviors. This argument has some validity. What may be termed high fertility—say, anything above a total fertility rate of 2.5—is unsustainable in the long run under conditions of low mortality. Hence, if low mortality is to be sustained, high fertility must fall. Prospective fertility differences among countries as a result are bound to be reduced in absolute terms over time. Nevertheless, there is much empirical evidence that qualifies this loosely defined phenomenon of convergence. And such qualifications apply not only to the twentieth century, during which demographic changes occurred at an especially variegated and unequal tempo country-by-country, but also to present-day and to plausibly expected future demographic experience. For example, in 1900 the Philippines and Hungary both had a population of 7 million. One hundred years later, the Philippines had a population of 76 million and Hungary had 10 million—a spectacular combination of what the United Nations might describe as a "high" and a "low" growth path. Countless similar, if perhaps less striking comparisons could be cited.

The issue of course is not simply differential population growth, explainable in terms of differences in the proximate determinants of that variable, but the qualitative characteristics of the time paths followed and, in the present context, the expected pattern of future change. To illustrate the point with reference to the two countries just cited, the United Nations 2002 medium projections (and, by construction, also the new 300-year United Nations projections up to the middle of the present century) foresee a 2050 Philippines population of 127 million. The corresponding "lock-step" figure for Hungary is 7.6 million. But what if the trajectories differed between the two countries? The Philippines might follow a "high" path (because total fertility would sink from its 2000 level of 3.43 to "only" 2.35 by mid-century) that would yield a 2050 population of 154 million, while Hungary might follow a "low" path (because its 2000 total fertility of 1.17 would *rise* only to 1.35 by 2050), yielding 6.8 million. Such a combination—and a myriad of other intermediate combinations, including the reverse variant: Philippines "low," Hungary "high"—can by no means be excluded. But *World Population in 2300* allows for no such eventuality even though the implications for the global and regional totals with respect to the relative population sizes of the constituting units could be far-reaching. It is left for the careful user to ponder the possible effects of countries or regions traveling on different demographic trajectories.

Thus, the governing assumption of the "medium" projection—global fertility eventually settling at replacement level—is more reasonably seen as a weighted average: one resulting from a distribution of country-by-country fertility levels characterized by substantial differences, hence, over time, yielding a shift—continuous or perhaps fluctuating—in relative country population weights. Such a pattern could well occur even within country groupings that exhibit similar economic, political, and cultural characteristics, a fact amply demonstrated by, among other examples, persisting historical and present-day fertility differences within the countries of the European Union. Current fertility within the countries of the EU 25 is below replacement level, but, despite a high degree of cultural and socioeconomic similarity, differences in fertility levels are sufficiently marked for population growth prospects to differ substantially. The likelihood of this happening between broad regional population aggregates displaying much greater contrasts in cultural, political, and economic characteristics is correspondingly greater. For example, the plausibility of assuming lock-step progress on the same trajectory—whether high, medium, or low—by Europe in contrast to North America, or by Europe in contrast to neighboring North African and West Asian countries, or by India in contrast to China, is far from obvious. Relaxing that assumption could have major long-term consequences for relative regional population totals in the coming three centuries.

A likely consequence of such differential patterns of fertility change country-by-country would be a discernible impact on the patterns and magnitudes of international migratory flows. Those patterns and magnitudes are influenced by numerous factors, but the emergence of relative demographic vacuums and pressure points is certainly one among them, and by no means the least important. The assumption, incorporated in the long-term projections up to 2300, that beyond 2050 international migration can be disregarded is prima facie implausible. The United Nations demographers of course were well aware of this, but evidently felt helpless in arriving at numerically specifiable migration rates that could be grounded in the experience of past patterns of international migration, hence that would withstand scrutiny. The stance is understandable within the terms of the overall construct of the long-term projections, even though it yields a jarring discontinuity as even major current, and up to 2050 projected, international migration flows fall suddenly to zero as the year 2050 arrives. Critics predictably will have a field day in objecting to that abrupt freeze of permanent cross-border population movements. Others will rightly object to the equally implausible if implicit assumption of frozen international boundary lines for the next 300 years—an assumption arguably bordering on the bizarre. The United Nations' likely answer to such criticisms will be that such critics would have a standing only if they could propose a more acceptable set of assumptions. That is a task not many would care to undertake.

But the point, again, is not the need for incorporating additional complications and adornments in the numerical projections that set out a no-surprise demographic future for the long term. What *is* needed is a constant insistence that the construct of the long-term projections is a stylized one: not intended to be a prediction, not even a prediction of alternative futures. What the United Nations offer to its clients is a way to think about coming demographic developments: a frame of reference that users must fill with substance.

Surprises: Pleasant and unpleasant

By the criteria of its basic input characteristics, the core trio of the United Nations projections up to 2300 could be justly characterized as optimistic to a fault. Mortality improves everywhere, but the changes, in comparison to those experienced during the last century, are supposed to be modest. Radical changes in biomedical technology that would push average life expectancy well beyond 100 years are not part of the scenario. Thus, the potential curse of populations with extreme senescence is assumed away. Also excluded are from the post-2050 future mortality setbacks, even temporary ones, ignoring numerous warning signs clearly present in the contemporary world. Posited fertility changes are also a model of conservatism: the medium scenario envisages convergence to replacement levels everywhere, albeit at differing speeds. This leads to a global stationary population, or, rather, one creeping up in size very slowly through an accretion of the very old, as that category is currently defined. The bracketing scenarios, in terms of total fertility rates, differ from the middle one, up or down, by only a quarter child, thus assuming away the possibility of precipitous population decline or rapid population growth. As to migration, the 190-odd territorial units of today's world are preserved for the next 300 years and their borders, past the middle of the twenty-first century, are crossed only by temporary migrants—presumably just tourists or business travelers. Changes in each of these characteristics, if any, especially after 2050, are assumed to be slow—indeed nearly imperceptible year-after-year and even decade-after-decade, and by the twenty-third century virtually nil.

If these surprise-free long-term scenarios, especially the one articulated in the medium projection, sound too good to be true in comparison to the demographic dramas and dislocations of the twentieth century, they probably are. Paradoxically, the coming-true of their end-of-history outcomes, even if they are in harmony with a near-consensus in expert opinion, could be called a historical surprise par excellence.

The dominant voices in that expert consensus foresee a peaking of the global population in the second part of the present century, followed by a slow decline—a pleasant soft-landing to a slowly decaying quasi-stationary state, underpinned by spreading and ultimately generalized economic affluence. This image corresponds, roughly, to that depicted by the United Nations' low variant, or to something between the low- and the medium-variant projections. The governing influence that underlies that view is the European and Japanese experience. It provides the paradigm of the demography of the postindustrial society, prefiguring the demographic behavior of those still on lower rungs of their socioeconomic transformations. Such relative backwardness is seen as temporary, since the recipes for advancement toward the yearned-for material comforts are at hand, are readily applicable, and will yield the hoped-for results. With economic gains—essentially, rising incomes per capita—come the changes that reshape social values and behavioral mores in ways already observable among the pioneers in the so-called second demographic transition. Fertility settles at or slightly below replacement level. Should it have a tendency to settle well below that level, creating a top-heavy age structure to which even advanced industrial societies would be unable to adjust, policy interventions would be triggered, providing timely correction.

According to this soft-landing scenario, much of that transition to demographic decompression will take place in the present century, and much of it during the coming five decades. But before eventless demography supposedly sets in at around mid-century, much demographic turbulence will be unavoidable—indeed, turbulence not unlike that experienced in the past 50 years. It could prove to be less than benign. Population momentum virtually guarantees that 3 billion or so persons will be added to the population of the poorer countries. Absorbing this demographic growth will make the convergence to the affluent vanguard of countries more difficult and slower than what would be otherwise possible, undercutting the potency of the economic welfare ingredients expected to propel spontaneous fertility decline and rising survival rates. Thus, while the prospects for substantial economic progress are encouraging in much of the less developed world, the economic gap measured in absolute per capita terms between the rich and the poor countries is not only likely to remain wide but to further widen in the present century. Perceived relative economic deprivation is commonly seen as just as potent a force in generating lower birth rates as is economic improvement pure and simple. Although assumptions about socioeconomic factors are not explicitly spelled out in the United Nations population projections, such anticipated changes may underlie the assumption that by 2050 average fertility will be below replacement level in the countries classified today as less developed, even if that category excludes China. Plausible as that assumption may seem today, it could well turn out that it underestimates the strength of countervailing cultural influences: influences inherited from the past or newly emerging as a reaction against materialistic postindustrial values. If so, fertility decline from levels still relatively high will be slower than envisaged, population growth will be correspondingly greater, and the shift in the relative population weights between the countries of high affluence and the countries of relative poverty will be sharper. In any event, demand for outmigration in relatively poor countries is likely to intensify, and the potential for demographically fueled international conflicts will increase, not implausibly going beyond the economic. And some countries and large subnational regions still characterized by high fertility, with perhaps as much as one-fifth of the global population total, may be entirely unable to travel the classic path of the demographic transition driven by economic forces. Malthusian pressures and adjustments in these parts of the world may thus darken the optimistic tableau of gradual and peaceful progress toward an affluent low-fertility world—depicted in the United Nations long-term projections as largely achieved by the middle of the present century.

Nor are the affluent postindustrial pioneers certain to live up to the role assigned to them in the surprise-free, soft-landing scenario. The United Nations medium projections implicitly assume that the trend toward lower birth rates that resulted in fertility levels well below replacement in many countries in Europe and in Japan will elicit negative feedbacks that by the middle of the twenty-first century will bring fertility back to near-replacement levels everywhere—specifically to a total fertility rate of 1.85. This may happen; it is possible to speculate about a variety of mechanisms that might bring about such a reversal. But *positive* feedbacks are equally plausible, reinforcing a tendency for further falls in fertility. As population aging progresses as a result of low birth rates and rising life expectancy, individuals—men and women alike— seeking to provide for their old-age security have an increasing incentive to accumulate human capital and savings and to acquire pension rights. The result may be longer education, greater labor force participation of women, and later and more restrictive procreation. The deus ex machina usually invoked as capable of tipping the uncertain balance of competing forces affecting fertility in the socially preferred direction—up, toward replacement level—is deliberate pronatalist population policy. But the experience in this domain thus far is anything but encouraging, and states already fiscally overcommitted in sustaining pension and health care systems will have great difficulty in improving on that record. In affluent low-fertility countries, the option of allowing more immigrants will likely be preferred to costly subsidizing of the home-production of children. That solution, plausibly requiring massive migration flows, raises potentially major social and geopolitical problems of its own.

Thus, the base from which population trends will continue beyond 2050 may look quite different from the one depicted by the United Nations medium projection, with repercussions not compatible with the presumed business-as-usual demographic patterns of the following 250 years.

Finally, factors not connected with or only remotely related to individual demographic behavior or population policy intent may also upset the quietude depicted in the United Nations long-term projections. In trying to take account of such forces when drawing up population futures, demographers would of course venture on territory beyond their professional expertise. But at least acknowledging them is necessary because doing so provides a much-needed cautionary note in taking business-as-usual population projections even remotely at face value.

On this score, calamities of nature come first to mind. The kind of celestial collisions that extinguished the dinosaurs and could well do the same to humans occur so rarely—apparently there were three such instances in the last 300 million years—that they perhaps would not deserve even a footnote in an exercise presenting 300-year projections. But, given its documented past frequency and severity, the possibility of abrupt climate change certainly would rate a mention in speculating about population trends over three centuries. The major concern here is not gradual global warming, to which modern industrial societies could adjust at a tolerable cost, and from which even net benefits for world agriculture might ensue, but possible major temperature drops, such as occurred some 12,000 and 8,000 years ago, lasting many decades or even centuries. These occurred *without* the involvement of human agency. In the future they might, additionally, be triggered by human-induced global warming affecting oceanic currents and causing a chain reaction of adverse weather changes. This could lead to a major reduction in carrying capacity through diminished food production, water shortages, disruption of energy supplies, global conflicts in competition for scarce resources, and ultimately to massive population loss. This last possibility, with or without climate change, may also be the consequence of unforeseen worsening of the epidemiological environment—causing peaks analogous to those associated with the Black Death, the Spanish influenza epidemic, and HIV/AIDS, but writ even larger.

Heavy losses of life could also be the result of major disruption of global trade flows and of wars waged with weapons of mass destruction. The lethality of modern weaponry, nuclear, chemical, radiological, or biological, may make wars between major countries less likely, as the results would be correctly perceived as mutually devastating. But technological changes tend to make such weapons potentially accessible to rogue states and even to small groups of terrorists, creating enormous risks. Research advances may render synthesizing viruses and creation of enhanced pathogens feasible relatively cheaply. Such work may soon be carried out by small groups of scientists or even a single curious or disgruntled researcher, amplifying the danger of accidental or malevolent release of extremely lethal substances, with incalculable consequences.

Spontaneous and unforeseen changes in the cultural-spiritual domain might also radically alter the long-term near-stationary character of the global population endorsed by prevailing expert opinion and depicted in the United Nations medium and low projections. If continuing scientific and technological advances create truly affluent societies in much of the world—surely a realistic long-term prospect if international peace can be preserved, terrorist dangers can be controlled, and the energy problem can be solved—the force of material incentives keeping fertility very low may weaken. Devoting 20 or 25 years in a leisure-rich, century-length average life span to the adventure of rearing children may become attractive, not because it is encouraged by governments shuffling money from one pocket to the other, but as an option freely chosen by individuals for its own expected nonmaterial rewards. A return to above-replacement fertility, now dismissed by most demographers as implausible in a high-income, postmodern society, but kept alive in the United Nations' high-fertility projection, perhaps more as a gesture toward symmetry than expected relevance to the real world, could then come into its own. That projection assumes convergence by 2300 to an average total fertility rate of 2.35 and to an annual population growth rate of 0.5 percent. Both these rates are low by twentieth-century standards, and presumably both rates could be supported, year after year, by a technologically advanced society that wished to shy away from crass interference with individual liberties. But those assumptions yield a global total of 36 billion souls in 2300. Welcome to the world of growth, preserving historical continuity. Good-bye to the brave new world of stasis and depopulation.

References

Hajnal, John (1955). The prospects for population forecasts. *Journal of the American Statistical Association,* 50 (June), pp. 309-322.

United Nations (2003). *World Population Prospects: The 2002 Revision,* vol. I: *Comprehensive Tables* (United Nations publications, Sales No. E.03.XIII.6).

United Nations (2004). World Population in 2300. Proceedings of the United Nations Expert Meeting on World Population in 2300, New York, 9 December 2003.

VII. WHY THE WORLD'S POPULATION WILL PROBABLY BE LESS THAN 9 BILLION IN 2300

*Tim Dyson**

The production by the United Nations Population Division of demographic projections for each country of the world to the year 2300 is certainly a bold and interesting exercise (see United Nations, 2003). It might be viewed as roughly comparable to someone back in 1703 – say Edmund Halley (1656-1742) – hazarding what would happen to the human population over the following three centuries. No one alive today can ever *know* what the size of the human population will be in 2300.[1] Clearly, the degree of uncertainty attaching to any such an *extremely* long look into the future is very great.

Yet perhaps the United Nations has some small advantages compared to our stargazer back around 1703. For example, we have a better idea of the starting point – i.e. the size, distribution and demographic characteristics of the world's population today. We know that the human population is currently increasing at about 1.2 per cent per year – a rate that is declining. There have been advances in methods and understanding (although I would not want to press this point too far). Nevertheless, aided by powerful computers, Edwin Cannan's presentation in 1895 of the cohort-component method of population projection underpins the present United Nations exercise; and Cannan was also one of the first to appreciate the crucial consideration that birth control, and falling birth rates, might one day sweep the world. That said, the accuracy of his own population projection for England and Wales was very poor – even over a time-horizon as short as 15 years (Langford, 2003).

In my view, the United Nations could certainly have done things differently when making these very long-run projections. For example, it might have undertaken a *regional* rather than a country-level approach. This would have been less demanding in terms of computing power. More importantly, however, a regional approach would have made it easier to develop and handle the demographic assumptions required for the projections. This point seems particularly valid in relation to *migration* – which will probably become increasingly important in the future. The current projections assume that international migration will be zero after 2050 – which is clearly unrealistic. Instead, it seems likely to me that demographic and economic differentials will continue to operate far beyond the year 2050 to promote, for example, migration *from* regions like West Asia and North Africa *to* regions like Europe and North America (see Demeny, 2003). Lastly on this point, political boundaries change. So there should be no real need to adopt current national boundaries when undertaking projections over the very long run. Thus – and with appropriate caveats – the results of a world regional projection exercise could easily be 'cut up' according to the current distribution of national populations within each region, should any clamor for country-level results require it.

Another criticism of these projections to 2300 is that the extension of the time-scale beyond 2050 (or to be generous, say beyond 2075) adds relatively little to our understanding of the future. To illustrate – and simplifying somewhat for reasons of space – one can summarize much of the draft report's main conclusions (see United Nations, 2003, pp. 1-7) as follows: (a) according to the 'medium' scenario the world's population will rise from 6.1 billion in 2000 to around 8.9 billion in 2050, and will be about 9.0 billion in 2300; (b) small but sustained deviations in total fertility result in big differences in eventual population size – e.g. in the low scenario, in which total fertility is essentially 0.25 of a birth lower than in the medium scenario, the world's population in 2300 is only 2.3 billion (compared to 9.0 billion); (c) most of the future increase in the world's population will occur in the less developed regions; (d) there will be major shifts in the regional composition of

* Development Studies Institute, London School of Economics, Houghton Street, London, United Kingdom.

the world's population – e.g. with Africa constituting a larger share, and Europe a smaller one; (e) the size of India's population will probably surpass that of China; (f) populations everywhere will grow older – importantly, the United Nations notes that in the medium scenario *almost all* of the projected world population increase of 3 billion between the years 2000 and 2100 *occurs at ages above 15 years* (United Nations, 2003, p. 18); (g) dependency ratios will increase; and (h), particularly if longevity continues to rise, ages of retirement (where they exist) will probably have to be raised. For the most part, these conclusions are known *already*, and they will unfold mostly in the period to 2050. Relatively little is added, I think, by the *very* long extension to 2300.

The figure below illustrates a similar point. Notice that in the United Nations' medium scenario the size of the world's population does not change much after 2050 – i.e. essentially things remain *flat* for the following 250 years (although, admittedly, there continue to be changes in fertility, mortality and age structure deriving from the projection assumptions). The cautious nature of the medium projection for the very long run – essentially hugging a figure of about 9.0 billion – is entirely understandable. And it is underscored by the similarity after 2150 of the medium scenario to the zero-growth scenario (which, by definition, holds the size of the population constant). If the United Nations Population Division's current educated view is that the world's population will reach about 8.9 billion in 2050 – when the average level of total fertility will be almost exactly 2 live births per woman, and the average population growth rate will be approaching zero – then it would be a brave projector indeed who in their central, 'medium' projection deviated much from that number over the very long run!

The exercise of making official population projections is inherently rather conservative. Almost by definition, such projections don't allow for *discontinuities* or *feedback*. To simplify, the trajectories of fertility and mortality incorporated in most projections – including those of the United Nations – are essentially the outcome of a mixture of extrapolation and assumption. Moreover, the trajectories are developed largely *independently* of each other. This is fine – provided one is concerned with the relatively short run (although even

World population according to the different United Nations scenarios, 2000-2300

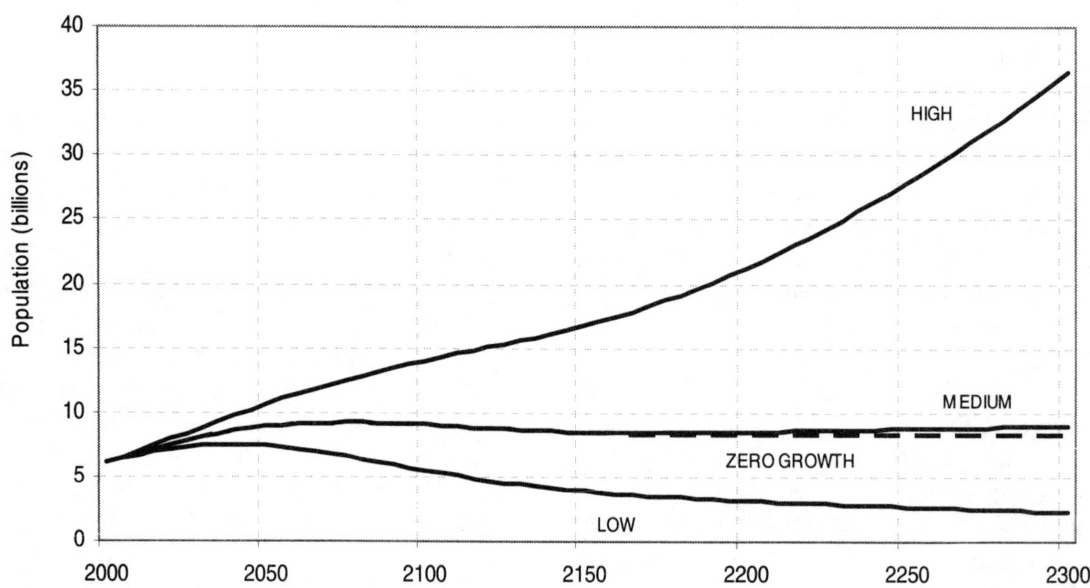

Source: United Nations, DESA, Population Division, World Population in 2300 (ESA/P/WP.187), 2003.

then such an approach can turn out to be mistaken). However, working on the basis of independence may be more questionable if one is considering the very long run. True, it is impossible to predict and incorporate discontinuities and feedback effects in quantitative terms in these projections. However, perhaps one could explore these issues a little more in the accompanying text.

Returning to the figure, at the *world* level one might consider the 'high' scenario to be possible for a few decades (although I concur that it is less likely than the medium scenario). Of course, in the high scenario fertility falls *slower* than is generally anticipated, and the global population reaches 10.6 billion in 2050 (compared to 8.9 billion in the medium scenario). In this context it is worth recalling that fertility declines seem to have slowed in some countries during the 1990s and 'are close to stalling in Bangladesh, Indonesia, Colombia, Dominican Republic, Peru and Turkey' (Bongaarts, 2002, pp. BP, 14-6). Also, for major populations like India, the United Nations' approach of projecting future fertility trends at the *national* level tends to bring about *faster* assumed falls in fertility than when assumptions regarding future fertility trends are developed at the sub-national level and then aggregated up (see Dyson, 2004, p. 76). Finally, it is worth recalling that even as recently as in its 1994 revision of world population prospects the United Nations' own *medium* variant projection put the global population in 2050 as high as 9.8 billion (United Nations 1995).

That said, certain aspects of the high scenario are highly questionable – even in relation to the next fifty years. Thus in this scenario between 2000 and 2050 Ethiopia's population rises from 65.6 to 197.9 million, Somalia's increases from 8.7 to 45.0 million, and Mali's rises from 11.9 to 52.6 million. Growth of this magnitude in these contexts seems unlikely.

Demographic trends do not unfold in a vacuum. After all, *a central concern of population theory since well before Malthus has been with the operation of feedback effects*. Populations must at least have minimal supplies of food, energy, water, etc. Thus in Ethiopia, for example, fertility will surely decline *faster* than is envisaged by the high scenario, and there may well be upward pressure on the death rate too during the coming decades.[2] Of course, increased out-migration from such countries is another very distinct possibility – but it is one which seems likely to *accelerate*, rather than to delay, the speed of fertility adjustment in the sending populations.[3]

The message of this essay so far has been that beyond 2050 the high scenario in the figure – which almost implies that the world's population will increase forever – is implausible, as apparently the United Nations itself agrees (United Nations, 2003, p. 12). In my view the human population will not remotely approach 36.4 billion in 2300 (although others have a different perspective).[4] The trajectory of world population growth *will* level out – probably before the end of the present century. Moreover, I think that at some stage there is a strong likelihood of *global population decline* – although population reductions will probably occur sooner in some world regions than in others. I now sketch two different rationales for why the world's population will probably be less than 9.0 billion in 2300, and then combine them in a third speculation about the future.

The first and most important rationale concerns fertility – and it leads me to see qualified merit in something *tending* in the direction of the United Nations' low scenario over the very long run (see figure). Of course, in recent decades the dominant trend in fertility everywhere has been *downwards*. And in all scenarios of these very long run United Nations projections fertility declines significantly between 2000-2005 and the middle of the present century (with varying degrees of (modest) recovery setting in during the second half of the century). Thus in the medium scenario the average level of total fertility per woman for the world as a whole falls from 2.69 births per woman in 2000-2005 to 2.02 births per woman in 2045-2050. Nowadays it is almost commonplace to observe that a majority of humanity *already* lives in countries with levels of fertility that are approaching, are around, or are below replacement. For example, for 2000-05 the United Nations Population Division puts average levels of fertility at 1.38 births in Europe (population in 2000 of 728 million), 1.78 births in Eastern Asia (population

1,481 million), 2.05 births in Northern America (population 316 million), and 1.75 births in Australia/New Zealand (population 23 million). Combined, these populations – all with a Total Fertility *below* the conventional rough and ready replacement figure of 2.1 children per woman– comprised 42 per cent of humanity in the year 2000.

The United Nations' medium scenario envisages that Total Fertility in the world's more developed regions will *rise* from an average level of 1.56 births per woman during 2000-2005 to 1.85 births per woman during 2045-2050 – before eventually settling at 2.06 births per woman for the remaining 250 years of the projection. Key issues, however, are whether there *will* be such a recovery in fertility and, still more, the extent to which recent European and East Asian fertility experience may actually presage the future behavior of an increasing fraction of people living elsewhere in the world. In this context it is remarkable that in the table which summarizes future fertility trends in the United Nations' medium scenario (see United Nations, 2003, table A.16) *none of the 21 world regions experiences an average level of Total Fertility below 1.85 births per woman during 2045-2050 or any subsequent time period* – this despite the fact that both Europe and Eastern Asia *already* have levels that are below 1.85 children per woman (well below in the case of Europe).

In my view, and for reasons elaborated elsewhere (Dyson, 2001 and 2002), national levels of fertility that are well below replacement may become common in the decades, even centuries which stretch ahead. The argument, in essence, is that fertility decline so liberates women from the domestic domain that in many ways the lives women lead become increasingly like those lived by men. And men don't have children, and they spend little time in childcare activities if their partners do. Consequently marriage, in the sense of a life-long commitment for the having and rearing of children, becomes increasingly unattractive – especially for women, who can lead lives that are quite independent of those of men. These developments are not only happening in places like Europe and Japan; spurred by declining fertility they are unfolding in many other regions of the world too – and usually far quicker than anyone expects. Thus in much of southern India levels of total fertility per woman are already either around or below 2.1 births per woman (Dyson, 2004). In countries like South Korea, Thailand and Malaysia, women are 'staying away from marriage in droves' (Jones, 1997, p. 74). A telling retort by an Indonesian woman reflects the huge increase in lifetime independence, and the likely implications for future levels of fertility: '*Why would I want to marry a child, in order to have a child?*'(Hull, 2002, p. 8). To some extent what we have here may be a self-sustaining process – in which over the long run fertility decline radically changes the lives of women and leads them to have still fewer numbers of children.

Of course, fertility will never fall to zero. And at some stage levels of fertility probably will be revived somewhat – despite such (welcome) changes in the circumstances of women in human society. But this will require the instigation of economic and social policies by governments – e.g. relating to taxation, maternity leave from employment, and the provision of nursery school education – on a scale that has rarely been entertained anywhere hitherto. More importantly, however, it will also require a fundamental *renegotiation of gender roles*. If the lives of women have become – and are increasingly becoming – more like those lived by men, in many societies the raising of fertility in the future will require that the lives *men* lead must become increasingly like those lived by women (or, at least, women of the past). In short, the goal of raising fertility will require that future reductions in gender differentiation are less one-sided than they generally have been during recent decades.

The relevance of these arguments to the United Nations projections for the very long run is that a population trajectory somewhere *between* the medium and the low scenarios may well apply (see figure). However I agree with the Population Division that at some stage pressures will arise for some degree of fertility *recovery* – at least from *very* low levels. That is, some degree of *circumscribed* homeostatic feedback may well come into play.

The most important *ultimate* source for such a feedback response may *not* lie in the narrowly economic 'problem' of 'supporting' a relatively large population of elderly people. Thus, when the United Nations raises the prospect of a future in which most old people might depend either directly or indirectly on younger generations for support (United Nations, 2003, pp. 18-19), it misses the point that in most societies most elderly people take care of themselves – *and* help their offspring – for most of their adult lives. Instead, the main source of a feedback response may lie in more fundamental 'social replacement' problems arising from (potentially rapid) population *decline*. Some of the feedback effects may be informed by the conscious decisions of national governments (which will also be even more concerned with regulating migration), but others will probably emerge from more subtle rationales that arise from within general populations themselves. That said, there is little reason to believe that any such recovery in fertility will necessarily stop – as opposed to *slow* – population decline. We know from history that feedback mechanisms often operate in ways that are *bounded* i.e. within overall contexts that are changing nevertheless.[5]

The second rationale for why there will probably be fewer than 9.0 billion people alive in the year 2300 relates to mortality. No person or organization likes to contemplate disaster. And, unsurprisingly, these United Nations population projections envisage that in virtually all world regions life expectancy will be appreciably higher in 2045-50 than in 1995-2000. Thus looking across the aforementioned 21 world regions, only one – Southern Africa – is projected to have a lower average level of life expectancy in the later period, and then only in the case of females. Overall the United Nations' assumptions relating to mortality envisage that female life expectancy in the more developed regions as a whole will increase from 79 to 85 years between 1995-2000 and 2045-50, with a corresponding increase for the less developed regions of from 64 to 75 years. The corresponding figures for males are 71 and 79 years, and 61 and 71 years. These average figures seem as reasonable as any to me.

However, if we are looking at the *next three hundred years*, then it seems likely that major mortality crises, killing significant fractions of some populations, will occur. Leaving aside the possibility of some self-inflicted disaster (e.g. a nuclear war, or a terrorist attack using chemical or biological weapons), perhaps the main threats here are the emergence of some new and deadly infection – of which both HIV/AIDS and SARS are possible recent portents – or, more importantly, some major climate change which could have either natural or anthropogenic causes (for present purposes, it matters little which).

Apropos climate change, we know that relatively small changes have contributed to the occurrence of famines in the past – for example, the major famines of the late 1890s which killed several million people around the world (Davis, 2001). Of course, we like to think that really devastating famines are things of the past. But an *abrupt and major* change in the global climate would surely sweep any complacency aside.[6] In this context the recent significant reduction in seawater salinity measured in the North Atlantic, caused by increased melt water from the Greenland ice sheet and raised discharges from the Siberian rivers, is very noteworthy. It could threaten the major ocean current known as the 'Atlantic Conveyer', and it has been mooted by scientists at the Woods Hole Oceanographic Institute that there may be a fifty per cent chance of this ocean current being 'switched off' during the next one hundred years (Palmer, 2003; Calvin, 1998). Were this to occur, it would produce more than just a 'big freeze' in Western Europe; almost certainly, it would cause a sudden change in the *world's* climate – one to which very populous, poor countries like Ethiopia, Somalia and Mali (with 2050 populations of 170.9, 39.7 and 46.0 million respectively, even on the United Nations' medium scenario) would be especially vulnerable.

In the twentieth century the world was generally a place of significant demographic *growth*. And a corollary of this was that the numerical effects of a major mortality crisis were usually soon 'made-up' i.e. populations recovered in size fairly speedily after a disaster. However, this has not been the case for most of human history, and this is *not* the future we expect. Beyond about 2075 (and putting the 'high' scenario on one side) the United Nations projections themselves envisage a world of either zero or negative demographic growth (see figure). Yet, to reiterate, looking out over a period as long as three centuries, a major mortality crisis seems almost inevitable.

Conclusion

Therefore my *third speculation* about the future is that levels of human fertility will generally be below the replacement level and that consequently there will eventually be population decline. In this world migration becomes increasingly important in determining population trends at the national level. In addition, some populations – perhaps even humanity as a whole – may experience downward '*steps*' in population size, in which reductions due to crises are either not made up, or are made up only slowly. Thus, because of a combination of below replacement fertility and occasional crises, the world's population will probably be less than 9 billion in 2300.

Despite my various reservations outlined above, the production by the United Nations Population Division of these very long run population projections strikes me as worthwhile. The matter of where humanity is going deserves greater attention than it usually receives. No doubt, these very long run projections will be refined in later attempts. The exercise provokes thought and debate, and serves as a useful backcloth for discussion. Even so, it should not be taken too seriously – a qualification that applies very much more to the contents of the present essay.

References

Bongaarts, J. (2002). The end of the fertility transition in the developing world. In *United Nations Expert Group Meeting on Completing the Fertility Transition*, New York, 11-14 March (ESA/P/WP.172).

Calvin, W. H. (1998). The great climate flip-flop. *The Atlantic Monthly* (January), pp. 47-64.

Davis, S. (2001). *Late Victorian Holocausts: El Niño Famines and the Making of the Third World*, London: Verso.

Demeny, P. (2003). Population policy in Europe at the dawn of the twenty-first century. *Population and Development Review*, vol. 29, No.1, pp. 1-28.

Dyson, T. (2001). A partial theory of world development: The neglected role of the demographic transition in the shaping of modern society. *International Journal of Population Geography*, vol. 7, No.2, pp. 67-90.

Dyson, T. (2002). On the future of human fertility in India. In *United Nations Expert Group Meeting on Completing the Fertility Transition*, New York, 11-14 March (ESA/P/WP.172).

Dyson, T. (2004). India's population – the future. In *Twenty-first Century India: Population, Economy, Human Development, and the Environment,* T. Dyson, R. Cassen and L. Visaria, eds. New Delhi: Oxford University Press.

Hull, T. (2002). The marriage revolution in Indonesia. Paper delivered at the Australian Population Association Conference, Sydney, October 1-4.

Jones, G. W. (1997). The demise of universal marriage in East and South-East Asia. In *The Continuing Demographic Transition,* G. W. Jones, R. M. Douglas, J. C. Caldwell and R. M. D'Souza, eds. New York: Oxford University Press.

Langford, C. (2003). Cannan, Edwin (1861-1935). In *Encyclopedia of Population,* P. Demeny and G. McNicoll, eds. New York: Macmillan Reference.

Palmer, P. (2003). Warming could bring colder UK winters. Available at: http://news.bbc.co.uk/2/hi/science/nature/3266833.stm (accessed December 2003).

Robinson, W. C. (2003). Demographic history and theory as guides to the future of world population growth. *Genus* vol. LIX, Nos. 3-4, pp. 11-41.

United Nations (1995). *World Population Prospects: The 1994 Revision* (United Nations publication, Sales No. E.95.XIII.16).

United Nations (2003). World Population in 2300. Proceedings of the United Nations Expert Meeting on World Population in 2300, New York (ESA/P/WP.187/Rev.1).

Wrigley, E. A. (1988). *Continuity, Chance and Change.* Cambridge: Cambridge University Press.

Notes

[1] Halley made contributions to the study of both mortality and nuptiality. He did not see the comet that carries his name, predicting its reappearance for around 1758.

[2] The high scenario puts the country's Total Fertility in 2045-50 as high as 3.05 births per woman, which I think is unlikely.

[3] The argument being that, at least over the longer run, out-migrants will transmit back new ideas about family and sexual behavior – and hence speed-up the pace of fertility decline. On this argument out-migration will not serve as a 'valve' that will operate to slow the fertility response.

[4] A recent paper by Warren Robinson takes a different view: '[i]f history is any guide, future technological growth should lead to future population growth as the global production function shifts upwards yet again … [t]he ultimate population of the Earth may well be many times the present stabilization goal of 8 to 10 billion – 20 or 30 billion perhaps …' (see Robinson, 2003, pp. 34 and 36).

[5] For example, in England between the middle of the sixteenth century and the end of the eighteenth, the so-called 'nuptiality valve' operated to check periods of relatively rapid population growth (see Wrigley (1988)). In brief, during periods of growth levels of living declined, marriages were delayed, and therefore with a lag the birth rate was reduced, helping to restore a measure of 'quasi-equilibrium'. However, overall the population could grow at 0.5 percent per year without reducing average levels of living.

[6] It should be noted that the tendency of ignoring the possibility of disaster characterizes exercises other than texts which accompany population projections. Thus the publication *Population, Environment and Development - World Population Monitoring Report 2001* (United Nations 2001) contains only a brief treatment of carbon emissions and climate change, and virtually no discussion of the possibility of *sudden* alterations in climate.

VIII. REFLECTIONS ON THE NEXT FEW CENTURIES*

*François Héran***

In presenting a set of scenarios for population changes over the next 300 years, the United Nations Population Division has taken a courageous step, for which it should be commended. Compared with previous projections, the study breaks new ground by working at the national, rather than the regional level. Most significantly, however, it makes three major parameter adjustments: the time horizon is extended from 2150 to 2300; life expectancy at birth is no longer limited at 85 years, exceeding 100 years in several countries; and it is assumed that fertility will remain below replacement level for almost 100 years before rising back to replacement.

According to this model, mankind plunges into the future like a diver, holding his breath for a long time before rising back to the surface. And yet, the story concludes with the same happy ending one has come to expect of United Nations demographers: our sights remain firmly set on the return to demographic equilibrium, as defined by the strict replacement of generations. Despite the concessions made to the "second demographic transition", the projections are still guided by the original demographic transition theory. Anyone wishing to interpret the work of the United Nations Population Division for the general public (and researchers at a national institute such as the *Institut national d'études démographiques*, INED) needs to make two points clear: first, that these are *targeted* projections, and second, explain the choice of the central target or medium scenario. Put more precisely, far from being the result of the projection, as the layperson might expect, the destination is determined in advance. One might conclude from this that the predictive power of the projection is, by definition, zero. It soon becomes clear, however, that the projection has considerable practical application and, moreover, that it is the only realistic choice—provided that one does not see it as the product of a natural state of things, but as a viable and liveable reality, rooted in the wider social and political context.

In order to discuss these points in more detail, I shall examine the various criticisms made of the United Nations projections. Some of those criticisms relate to the long-term projections to the time horizon of 2150, while others relate more specifically to the extended time horizon of 2300.

The pro-natalist school's criticisms of the United Nations projections are not new. The advocates of this school believe that the theory of the inexorable return to equilibrium can never be justified (Dupâquier 1999). They object to the notion of "demographic transition", because the premise of a spontaneous return to equilibrium would have the effect—perhaps even the goal—of deterring action by the public and by political decision-makers. They prefer the theory of "demographic revolution", which was described, and deplored, by Alfred Landry as far back as 1934. According to this theory, the rise of individualism and the increase in the cost of children will inevitably plunge wealthy societies below replacement level, resulting in depopulation. It is for refusing to face up to this "catastrophe foretold" that the United Nations demographers, too wary of Malthusian ideology, are criticized.

Another viewpoint, based on detailed analyses of the United Nations projections, has been put forward by Jacques Vallin and Graziella Caselli—co-authors, with Guillaume Wunsch, of the major eight-volume population treatise currently being published by INED (Vallin and Caselli, 2004). They begin by praising the Population Division for having succeeded, since 1958, in correctly forecasting the 2000 world population figure of 6

---

[*] The original French version of this essay may be accessed on the World Wide Web site of the Population Division at www.unpopulation.org.

[**] Institut National d'Études Démographiques, Paris, France.

billion, with a tighter and tighter range at each new projection. They cite several reasons for this remarkable success: the targeted projection method is better than mathematical extrapolation for setting a flexible range of scenarios whose varying degrees of plausibility may be evaluated at a later date; the components method minimizes errors by imposing measurable constraints; the projections made since 1958, using a time horizon of 2000, were short range; and, most importantly, it was possible to predict population changes for developing countries with reasonable accuracy by setting it within the demographic transition model.

With respect to developed countries, however, Vallin and Caselli note that the 11 projections published by the United Nations between 1958 and 1993 were wide of the mark: the total finally reached in 2000 (below 1.2 billion) was ultimately outside the ranges assumed *under the low variant*. Subsequently, in order to achieve an accurate determination of the effective evolution of developed countries, the initial assumptions had to be revised sharply downwards. If European population changes have defied projections for so long, it is because, as we now know, the sustained decline in European fertility below the replacement level invalidated the revered demographic transition model. It was this phenomenon that inspired the idea of the "second transition" of fertility, expounded by Van de Kaa and Lesthaeghe.

However, the United Nations was fortunate: Europe's population was not large enough for the overestimate to have an impact on the overall accuracy of the global projections. And yet, according to Vallin and Caselli, this will not be the case in the future. When the demographic transition has exhausted most of its effects (only sub-Saharan Africa is still at the beginning of the process), the uncertainty about the future will no longer be confined to developed countries. Instead, it will spread to the entire planet, especially if the projection assumes a longer time horizon. Instead of a return to equilibrium, we may discover completely new paths, full of unpredictable twists and turns. Who can tell, for example, whether or not India and China will settle permanently below the replacement level?

Added to this are other uncertainty factors which limit the predictive power of the projections. Just as events have sent us crashing through the fertility floor, they may also smash through the ceiling of life expectancy. How far will life expectancy rise? Without a theory for accurately defining the future evolution of fertility, we also lack an equivalent theory for mortality. The convergence-stabilization principle supposes that fertility will be maintained at around 2.1 children per woman, and that life expectancy will stabilize, at some undetermined level. If life expectancy continues to increase at the rate seen in recent decades, defying even the most optimistic projections (with the striking exception of countries affected by AIDS), it will tend to destabilize growth by raising population pyramids even further.

As for international migration, its flows and direction remain great unknowns, because it is such a volatile phenomenon. Over the last three centuries, the nature of migratory flows has changed considerably. The great migrations of people towards the New World—54 million between 1815 and 1930, according to Dudley Baines—are unparalleled today. These flows have also seen spectacular inversions (southern Europe became a net receiver of manpower, after long being a net supplier).

In three centuries, anything can happen in the area of migration, including (as incongruous as it may appear today) major migratory movements from North to South, the reverse of current flows, linked to new forms of development cooperation. If the South develops around a few countries or a few major population areas, it may well polarize an immigration originating from the North, bringing transfers of technology and training. This assumption is consistent with the fact that migration continues to be controlled by countries in a dominant position, regardless of the direction of the flow. As Vallin has pointed out, Europe shipped off its excess population overseas in past centuries, and had no qualms about using all the coercive force it could muster. Once its transition was complete, it tapped the excess manpower of the Third World, and then barely managed to slam the doors shut again before the crisis came. Is it so absurd to imagine that developed countries, while retaining their power to control migratory flows, will conclude that their interests would be best served by a policy of development cooperation that will lead to increased migration exchange with developing countries?[1]

Vallin and Caselli do not enter into this sort of speculation—that is our concern. However, their conclusion is clear: the future of the three components of population change—fertility, mortality, migration—is more uncertain than ever. We no longer know which theory to adhere to in order to predict how they may develop. Extended over three centuries, these uncertainties preclude us from according the projections any predictive or "predictionist" value.

Should we not therefore opt for the technique of probability-based projections, as proposed by demographers such as Wolfgang Lutz or Nico Keilman? The problem is that it becomes impossible, over a time horizon of 300 years, to make sense of the leap of faith that must be attached to each projection. There seems little advantage to knowing that there is a 95 per cent chance that within 300 years the world population will range from 2.5 to 36 billion (the range predicted by the United Nations for 2300). Would it not make more sense to acknowledge that when it comes to such a long period, we simply have no idea?

At the meeting of experts convened by the Population Division on 30 June 2003, Laurent Toulemon, INED demographer and formerly responsible for updating the population projections of the *Institut national de statistique* following the 1999 census, voiced his doubts about the value of extending the projections already published for 2150 out to 2300. He noted that the added value of 150 more years was diminished because the major changes occur in the previous century: according to the medium scenario, the population of developed and developing countries will have already reached the 2300 figures by 2100. This is also true, in relative terms, of the other scenarios. In the case of the high and low-fertility scenarios, for example, the exponential divergences already start to occur during the period 2000-2150, and widen further during the period 2150-2300.

The doubts about the value of the projections increase when we consider the upheavals and catastrophes of the twentieth century. Will we, in the future, be able to prevent conflict, war and genocide, with all their direct and indirect consequences (premature deaths, deferred child-bearing, displaced populations)? Will urban densification and increased trade between continents not encourage new global epidemics, like AIDS or Spanish flu? And what of technological catastrophes (nuclear accidents, for example), environmental catastrophes (such as the heat-wave of August 2003 in France) or cosmic catastrophes (asteroid falling to Earth)? Dramatic events such as these are unpredictable over the short and medium term, and are more so over the long term. It might be argued that they invalidate from the outset the assumption of a stabilization of behaviour over hundreds of years.

How much value should we attach to these criticisms and doubts?

To begin with, we must clear up one error. To align the medium scenario of the projections with the replacement level has no intrinsic normative value. It is first and foremost a reference model, which allows us to measure the discrepancies between it—the model—and reality. Moreover, the model is essential to the theory of "demographic revolution" itself. When, in the 1930s, Adolphe Landry proposed to combat depopulation, he advocated the goal of an "optimum population level" which could restore the replacement of generations. There is nothing to indicate that the catastrophe scenario of the "demographic revolution" or its recent adaptations would provide a more effective forecasting framework than the classic transition model. It would be paradoxical to laud its capacity to predict Europe's current declining fertility rate, since it failed to predict the baby boom of 1940-1960 (which was, after all, much closer in time).

It is not because the medium scenario of a targeted projection is predetermined by the forecaster that it would be a “foregone conclusion”. Far from presupposing the status quo, the maintenance of the medium scenario assumes major changes in behaviour associated with a solid collective capacity for action and reaction. The Population Division has indeed assumed the maintenance of the status quo, but in order to do so it has created another scenario, which consists of maintaining current fertility rates for three centuries. This constant-fertility scenario, which was prepared for illustrative purposes, is quite dramatic. It produces an exponential shift in the fertility rate which demonstrates, by contradiction, that it is impossible to impose a permanent freeze on the behaviour differences that currently separate the regions of the world. There is nothing new in this revelation: it is a fundamental truth that growth becomes exponential if the underlying rate is assumed to remain constant over a long period of time. But it is worthwhile illustrating this with a concrete example. Under the constant-fertility scenario, the population of mainland France would be scarcely 21 million in 2300, while its overseas departments and territories (Martinique, Guadeloupe, French Guyana, Réunion, New Caledonia and Mayotte) would have a grand total of 234 million! The numerical relationship between mainland France and its overseas departments and territories would quite simply be inverted. In more general terms, if the level of fertility were to remain fixed for 300 years, the countries that currently lie below the replacement level would see their populations reduced to one eighth of their current size, while those lying above the replacement level, even if only by one quarter of a child, would see their population increase exponentially, with dramatic results.

At the continental level, the discrepancies soar towards infinity if current fertility rates remain unchanged for 300 years: Africa would have a population of 115 trillion and account for 86 per cent of the world population, instead of 13 per cent today. Europe or Northern America, on the other hand, would be close to extinction: 90 million inhabitants instead of 730, or almost zero per cent of the world population. The moment we freeze the present, it becomes unreal and untenable, because each new historic climate imposes highly unequal and extremely rapid rates of change which, we have every reason to suppose, will not continue over time. What separates countries and continents at a given moment are chronological discrepancies in paths and rates of progress, not irreducible differences in nature, as we sometimes imagine.

But here is perhaps the most important point: the high fertility scenario envisaged by the United Nations demographers is no longer realistic, even though it merely adds a few decimal points of children to the fertility level of the medium scenario. It would give mainland France a total population of 248 million by 2300, with a fertility rate of between 2.15 and 2.35 children per woman, depending on the period. This is scarcely one half of a child more than the current level of 1.9. It is a well-known fact that a slight shift in a growth factor can lead to an exponential increase. The low-fertility scenario is also improbable. In the case of France, it would assume a stagnation of fertility for nearly a century, at around 1.35 children. This would produce a population loss of almost two thirds, which no government could accept. (Please forgive the constant references to France; experts in any other country would certainly react in a similar fashion.)

Thus, in this context, the slightest shift can produce quite dramatic results. Even if the high and low fertility scenarios diverge from the medium scenario by just a fraction of a child, either way, they will ultimately, over the decades, produce increasingly unrealistic discrepancies, which end up making the medium scenario the only viable projection. The scenario of the return to equilibrium is not realistic per se; it is realistic only in comparison with the alternative scenarios.

Does this mean that mankind is destined, assuming that no catastrophe occurs, to follow a predetermined path? The United Nations Population Division is really asking us to assume a kind of demographic determinism over the long term, except that it is a determinism that remains undetermined. We know for sure that mankind cannot allow itself to tolerate sustained growth surpluses or deficits, for fear of destabilization. And yet, it would be hard to say what detours and changes of pace will be required to avoid those surpluses and deficits, since mankind is comprised of many different countries. If one were to seek an appropriate image to describe the progress of populations, it would not so much be that of the cyclist or driver who maintains his trajectory only by correcting the steering. Rather, it would be that of the rollercoaster car that is attached to the track by a mobile bar to increase the thrill of the ride. The car may shift around its trajectory, and slow down or speed up in response to turbulence. Sometimes it may even seem to move backwards as it counteracts the swinging effect, but it will always be pulled back to the central axis, just the same, and somehow continue its trajectory in the right direction, without coming off the track. It is a model of viability, with all its various constraints, but of a viability that is turbulent, if not frankly chaotic.

Need we recall that the United Nations projections do not lend themselves at all to normative interpretation? A disciple of Malthus may be concerned to see certain fertility rates soaring up to the skies, while a pro-natalist demographer will be horrified to see other rates in steep decline. However, whether they like it or not, neither can do without the regulating idea of a balance to be maintained among the regions of the world and within each society. The pro-growth approach itself, in its concern to compensate for ageing, will find it hard to advocate a fertility level that permanently exceeds the replacement level. It is not enough merely to quote the formula of Alfred Sauvy, "grow or grow old", because we must still acknowledge the fact that eternally extended growth is quite untenable, even if it remains moderate. The man of good sense, who is neither pro-growth nor Malthusian, but simply a realist, will rigorously evaluate the unrealistic long-term consequences of the high or low variants of the demographic projections. If mankind is able to react in time to these shifts in search of a viable long-term solution (and, over a period of 300 years, mankind will have plenty of opportunities to react), it will stand every chance of ensuring that the world's population remains in close range to the medium scenario of the projections. Initially proposed as a simple illustrative example, the notion of the tendential equilibrium asserts its legitimacy in the long run by eliminating the other scenarios, thus gaining in value and ultimately establishing itself as the only reasonable reference goal.

What, then, really is the "predictive power" of the long-term projections of the United Nations, compared with that of projections by research economists or other international institutions? The conclusion reached by Vallin and Caselli is frankly positive: "All in all, this comparison tends to strengthen our belief in the idea that, until otherwise proven, the United Nations projections offer the most complete and solid framework for speculations about the future of the world's population" (Vallin and Caselli, 2004, p. 385). They go on to say that the projections "are based on a rather subtle mix of reasoning, pragmatism, intuition and guesswork". We might be tempted to use this judgement against the very long-term projections published by these two authors in 1996 and, more recently, in Volume 5 of their population treatise. For they were quite content to offer a range of scenarios—part demography; part fiction—for the world's population during the years 2150 to 2300: rapid transition to the single child; splitting of the modal fertility age, at around 25 and 55; delaying menopause until after age 55; increasing life expectancy to 150 years (even 180 or 240 in extreme instances, depending on whether the survivorship curve remains rectangular); and, lastly, a dramatic increase in the proportion of male births. The instructional value of these scenarios is undeniable (if we note, for example, that a single-child regime would cut the world's population to less than 200 million by 2250, or that a rapid transition to late maternity could lead to fluctuations in the fertility rate which would still not be cancelled out after 300 years).

And yet, it is hard to give the same degree of credit to each scenario. A rapid increase in life expectancy, which would raise the population pyramids, seems within reach, since it responds to an old and powerful demand for longevity.[2] On the other hand, there seems to be no compelling reason to have a fertility age centred on the age of 55, unless we want to give a minority of women the opportunity to catch up late in life. Rather than working on delaying menopause, it would be better to focus the efforts of science on improving reproductive health in the 10 years preceding menopause, in order to reduce the risks to women's fertility and fecundity (risks that increase with age). As for negative selection of girls at birth, it has no chance of developing over the next 300 years if we make a serious effort to ensure equal human rights between men and women. Demographers have a role to play here. If they perform their early-warning function by informing Governments and public opinion about the negative consequences of such selection, they will make it easier for policy makers to react, and we may say that the worst-case scenarios will function as prophecies that will never be realized.

Lastly, a word about the assumption that the single-child regime will spread across the whole planet. This is problematical, to say the least, judging by the resistance encountered in the largest countries. But what of Europe? Northern Spain and Italy are often cited as examples of regions where the single child is already a reality. It is true that the fertility rate of the city of Barcelona has stabilized at 1.1 children per woman, but can what is true of an urban environment that is constantly renewed by migration also be applied at the global level and be sustainable for hundreds of years? Could we imagine, to take another example, the continuation of the socio-economic trauma suffered by the former Soviet republics in the 1990s, as if the iron curtain were never to open fully and as if systems for state protection were permanently being dismantled?

Overall, it is hard to agree with Vallin and Caselli when they maintain, with a hint of provocation, that their worst-case scenarios are just as probable as the scenario of stabilization at the exact level of the replacement of generations. Southern and central Europe no doubt show how the population dynamics of a society, whether in terms of fertility or health, depends on a successful balance (even if it must take very diverse forms) between the exercise of personal responsibility (empowerment of women, personal preventive behaviour) and sustainable effective and fair institutional support. Ideally, the achievement of this balance would be a major factor of population forecasts. Automatic calculators allow us to give our imaginations free rein, of course, but they tell us nothing about the capacities for analysis and reaction that may be employed by a properly informed and governed society to identify and counteract a major population shift. The United Nations demographers have implicitly adopted an entirely different education tool: instead of presenting the worst-case scenario, their own reference scenarios appeal to the intelligence of nations.

The return to equilibrium is an admissible and legitimate idea if we make it quite clear that it has nothing to do with some natural mechanism that maintains a constant equilibrium. It is not a stabilizing force inherent in the biological nature of the species, but the socially constructed capacity of societies to evaluate the sum effect of individual behaviours and react accordingly. The idea of a final return to equilibrium has the value of a regulating idea, in the Kantian sense of the term: it is an issue that we must ourselves raise, if we wish to have solid reasons to act.

There remains one significant unknown: how and when will the world population recover equilibrium? We might wonder about how the United Nations demographers deal with the extension of the time horizon from 2150 to 2300. They essentially insert an interim period of almost a century (95 years), during which most countries are adrift in the purgatory of the "second demographic transition" before regaining the equilibrium level. Why would this plunge below the replacement level last the same amount of time in all countries? Because they are able to imitate existing models disseminated widely in the media and adopt technologies that are disseminated more and more widely (despite difficulties of all sorts), developing countries have, in the space of a few decades, adopted behaviours that developed countries have in some cases taken centuries to implement. It is reasonable to believe that they will continue to evolve faster than developed countries and will not have to wait 100 years to reach the point of equilibrium envisaged by the United Nations. How fast innovations are disseminated is certainly difficult to predict, because the process is so heterogeneous and contradictory. Today, in West Africa, you might see cyber-cafés along the side of the road even though, at a distance of five miles from the road, there are villages still lacking electricity. The same heterogeneity can be seen in customs: for example, polygamy may exist side-by-side with very western forms of urban life. These are more reasons to believe that the rate of change must be heterogeneous.

What, then, shall we say of the catastrophes and the upheavals that were so abundant in the last century? Should we factor into long-term population forecasts the harm caused by the folly of mankind and the wrath of nature? And yet, one cannot foresee a catastrophe without being among those who conspire to cause it! The extent to which catastrophes are foreseeable is in itself variable. Nobody predicted the outbreak of the First World War or imagined that it would be so long and devastating. The Second World War was expected, however, and largely pre-announced. It was its consequences that defied the projections. The demographers did not see the baby boom coming, nor did they imagine that it would last such a long time. Nor did they foresee how the baby boom would end, or the extent of the "second demographic transition" in Europe. Even less did they imagine declines in fertility as rapid as those that occurred in Latin America and the Caribbean, Asia or Northern Africa. The outbreak of the major epidemics was just as unforeseeable. It may seem fanciful, then, to imagine that better governed human societies will prove increasingly better able to provide for dramatic events, or at least attenuate their effects, through increasingly solid institutional mechanisms. However, it is the only path that offers room for progress. While it may be madness to count on the wisdom of mankind, we could wisely hope that people would use their power of reason.

Let us consider the example of Condorcet in this context. How can we fail to feel sadness in reading the wish he expressed 200 years ago to see the end of all wars, at a time when revolutionary France was at war with its neighbours and with itself? Aware that projects for perpetual peace conceived by certain philosophers had no chance of succeeding, Condorcet believed that the source of hatred among nations would dry up with the gradual erosion of economic inequalities between them, that peoples who had committed massacres would be so permanently chastened by their disgrace that they would not do so again, and that the "brotherhood of nations" might be sealed through "perpetual confederations" and "well-constructed" institutions. It was all premature, no doubt, and yet it was nobly conceived. Just as the second half of the twentieth century at least began to learn the lessons of the first half, we might believe that the twenty-first century will learn the lessons of the twentieth even more effectively. The United Nations, for which Condorcet had foreseen the necessity, exists and acts. In historical terms, it is a young organization, and therefore full of promise. More than ever, it will retain its *raison d'être*, as will the increasing number of peace-oriented intercontinental organizations. Despite various reversals and upheavals, history is tending to advance in the direction indicated by Condorcet—that is to say, towards more effective anticipation of crises and a greater capacity to react. One might even go as far as to state that this will be a powerful factor in reducing uncertainty about population changes over the next few hundred years.

We prefer to leave nothing to providence or chance: we want to believe that we shall have a say in our future. This leaves the choice between two educational approaches: either the apocalyptic prophesy of Cassandra or Jeremiah ("we are heading towards disaster, repent!"); or faith in the spread of knowledge, following the lead of Bacon and Condorcet ("guided by science, we can act with full knowledge of the facts"). If demographers have good reasons to believe that equilibrium is the only viable long-term solution for the development of world population, that does not mean that the achievement of this goal is written into the nature of things or guaranteed by some spontaneous and mysterious power of correction. It will depend upon the capacities for action and reaction developed by societies and their rulers. We sometimes think that the regulating idea of demographic equilibrium will tend to deter people from acting, while catastrophic thinking will have the opposite effect. As a good political strategy, however, good governance must aim to produce emancipated citizens. The worst is not certain. Nor is the happy ending. Let us not be content merely to postulate it or to await its coming as a natural consequence of population dynamics. We need to work to produce it and, in that sense, the long-term scenarios of the United Nations offer a powerful tool for reflection.

NOTES

[1] During the meetings of experts convened by the Population Division, it was proposed that the volume of international migration be estimated by considering that it would be proportionate to the populations of the countries involved and the inverse of the distance between them. This is a gravitational model first proposed back in 1885 by Ravenstein. Its main use is to fix the maximum range of migratory flows allowed by the size of the populations concerned. Beyond this role of arithmetical safeguard, however, we know that such models have no predictive power. If migration mechanically obeyed the laws of gravity (from "high-pressure" demographics towards "low pressure" demographics, or from poor regions towards wealthy regions), the vast majority of developing countries would have migrated long ago, and Mexican migration to the United States of America, to take just one example, would be far greater than it is. In fact, scarcely 3 per cent of the world's population currently live abroad. Migratory flows cannot be explained solely by demographic factors. War, conflict and persecution are responsible for most of it. The deregulated nature of the labour market (far more marked in the United States of America or southern Europe than in northern Europe, for example) is a powerful factor in the attraction of illegal migrants. Then there are the controls exercised at national or community borders, which are more effective than people think (requiring migrants to make three attempts to enter instead of one certainly has the effect of slowing down flows and reducing numbers).

[2] Four centuries ago, Francis Bacon ended his utopia on the city of the wise with a research project that emphasized the following objectives: "Prolong life. Give youth back to a certain degree. Delay the ageing process. Heal those thought to be incurably sick. Ease pain …" (*The New Atlantis*, 1627). One hundred and fifty years later, and 200 years before our own age, Condorcet stated that mankind was able to fight effectively against infectious diseases and extend the human lifespan for an "indefinite" and unknown period (*Tableau historique des progrès de l'esprit humain*, 1794, 10th and final period).

IX. THE FUTURE OF HUMAN LIFE EXPECTANCY

*S. Jay Olshansky**

1. Scope of review

The following review is based on an examination of two documents published by the United Nations Population Division: a set of long-range projections made during the summer of 2003 that focused primarily on forecasts of population growth to the year 2050, but which included a forecast to 2300 (United Nations, 2003b), and long-range projections of the global population from 2050 to 2300 made several months later (United Nations, 2003c). Both documents published by the United Nations contain summaries of the methods, assumptions, and results of their projections as well as preliminary views of how the forecasts should be made. Only in the latter document (United Nations, 2003c) concrete projection results were presented. Included among the numerous assumptions are those involving decisions made about the future course of fertility, mortality, and migration. Because my expertise is in the field of mortality and aging, my review will focus on the mortality assumptions, the methods used to forecast mortality, and the conclusions drawn from such forecasts.

2. Overall assessment of United Nations (2003b) forecast[1]

The underlying assumption of the mortality projection model is that incremental increases in life expectancy at birth are expected to diminish as higher levels of life expectancy are reached, with a limiting life table value of 92.5 years to the year 2050. This notion of diminishing returns in projected levels of life expectancy makes sense given that it has been demonstrated in the scientific literature that diminishing returns are likely to occur in the coming decades in low mortality populations (Olshansky, Carnes, and Cassel, 1990). The rationale for why this will occur is straightforward. The modern rise in life expectancy in the 20th century was initially caused by rapid declines in death rates among infants and children, but recent gains have been fueled by reductions in mortality at middle and older ages (Olshansky and Ault, 1986; Kannisto et al., 1994). If another quantum leap in life expectancy is going to occur, it will have to be a result of adding decades of life to people who have already lived for 70 years or more (Olshansky, Carnes, and Désesquelles, 2001). Thus, large gains in life expectancy can occur for low mortality populations in the future only under one condition – if the future course of mortality decline is fundamentally ***different*** from the past. This conclusion is at odds with recent forecasts made by mathematical demographers who suggest that future increases in life expectancy will continue throughout the 21st century on the long-term track they have followed for the past 150 years (Oeppen and Vaupel, 2002). It should be emphasized that adding decades of life to the elderly will be a daunting task given that it will require fundamental changes to the underlying biology of the species that influences duration of life (Olshansky et al., 2002). In other words, adding person-years-of-life back into the life table is far easier to accomplish when it involves saving infants and children from dying of infectious diseases than it would have to be in the future by adding a significant number of person-years as a consequence of saving people over the age of 70. Along these lines, my colleagues and I anticipate what we believe is both a realistic and optimistic scenario in the coming decades – reductions in death rates at all ages for both males and females (in low mortality populations) by one-half (Olshansky, Carnes, and Cassel, 1990; Olshansky, Carnes, and Désesquelles, 2001; Carnes, Olshansky, and Grahn, 2003). This projection scenario would yield life expectancies at birth that are in the range of what the United Nations has predicted for most developed nations by the year 2050 – perhaps somewhat lower.

* Professor, School of Public Health, University of Illinois at Chicago.

As such, the country-specific projected levels of life expectancy for the year 2050 are in large part quite reasonable in my view for the developed nations. The highest projected life expectancy at birth is for Japan at 88.1 years, which is certainly a reasonable estimate given that their underlying cause of death schedule cannot yield many more person-years from reductions in heart disease – the number one cause of death in most other developed nations and which is already at extremely low levels in Japan. The projected levels of life expectancy at birth for the year 2050 for most other developed nations, and some developing nations, is in the 80-88 years range. These projections are consistent with recent declines in mortality in these nations and certainly fall within the realm of biological plausibility given that such figures are already observed in some extremely favored low mortality populations.

At the lower end, it is hard to believe that the developing nations with a projected life expectancy at birth below 60 years will not experience dramatic improvements in early age mortality as a result of more frequent and more widely distributed immunizations, the development of new technologies for making clean water available, and anticipated improvements in overall living standards. Relatively small advances in public health will yield large gains in life expectancy at birth in these countries in the coming decades, so it is my view that there will not be a single country in the year 2050 that has a period life expectancy at birth (for males and females combined) of less than 70 years. Thus, it is my opinion that the United Nations has underestimated the projected life expectancy at birth of most nations where the anticipated life expectancy at birth is under 70 years.

Although the United Nations made longer-term forecasts to the year 2300 in this publication, the focus of discussion was on the projection time frame extending between 2000 and 2050. Since the subsequent United Nations document published later in 2003 focuses exclusively on the 2050 to 2300 time frame, my evaluation of the methods, assumptions, and conclusions associated with these longer-term forecasts will appear in the following sections.

3. Methods of projection (United Nations, 2003c)

The Lee and Carter (1992) method of modeling and forecasting mortality was the primary method used. Specific attention is paid to the anticipated impact of HIV/AIDS, and the excess mortality from this single infectious disease was superimposed on the projected life tables for a short time following 2050. Details of exactly how HIV/AIDS diminished with time are not provided. For extending life tables beyond the age range for which data currently exist for humans, a method developed by Coale and Kisker was used (references and details not provided).

4. Key assumptions

1. By the year 2050, HIV/AIDS is assumed to be largely controlled and little more than an endemic disease that responds favorably to treatment. AIDS is projected to diminish following 2050, but the rate at which this is projected to occur is not presented.

2. No limit was set on projected levels of life expectancy at birth. As such, the life table had to be closed and assumptions about distributions of death had to be made for age ranges not currently experienced by any population.

3. Countries with observed low life expectancies in 1995-2000 were initially observed to experience extremely rapid increases in projected levels of life expectancy at birth. This was considered unacceptable, so the rate of increase in life expectancy at birth was "adjusted." The nature of this adjustment is not specified.

4. The rate of increase in life expectancy at birth is projected to diminish over time. For example, for females an increase of 8 years is projected to occur between 2100-2200, but the increase is expected to be 5 years between 2200-2300.

5. Sex differences in life expectancy at birth are projected to decline markedly by 2300.

6. The relative nation-specific rankings of life expectancy at birth observed in 2000 are projected to remain the same during the entire projection time frame.

5. Overall assessment of United Nations (2003c) forecast

Before discussing the results of this forecast, it is appropriate to state clearly why the Lee and Carter (1992) forecasting methodology is the most appropriate to use in this instance. The authors of the United Nations report state clearly that forecasting mortality is an exceptionally risky effort, perhaps much more so than is the case with fertility and migration, because there are so many uncertainties and questions involved.

A) Will there be medical breakthroughs that dramatically extend the duration of life?

B) Will the detection and treatment of disease improve in the future as it has in the past, and can we expect the rate of advancement in such technologies to accelerate?

C) Will it ever become possible to develop technologies that lead to "engineered negligible senescence" in humans (i.e., will it become possible to slow the rate of aging)?

D) Even if such technologies are developed, will they be available to enough people to have a measurable impact on the life expectancy of entire populations?

E) Is it realistically possible to eliminate or dramatically reduce the risk of death from the top three killer diseases today – heart disease, cancer, and stroke?

F) Alternatively, will the observed global obesity pandemic continue to worsen, leading to significant increases in obesity-related diseases and disorders among future generations of middle-aged and older persons?

G) Will there be another global pandemic of influenza in the coming centuries as there has been like clockwork every 40 years or so during the past thousand years?

H) Will death rates from communicable diseases continue to rise throughout the nations of the developed and developing world as they have in recent decades, and can we expect to see even more disturbing trends in the evolution of antibiotic resistant microorganisms?

I) Will the observed stagnation in life expectancy at older ages during the past quarter century in some countries (such as the United States) continue?

Because of this great complexity and wide range of possible outcomes with regard to the future course of mortality, the best approach to take when making forecasts of life expectancy at birth is one based on parsimony. The greatest advantage of the Lee and Carter (1992) forecasting methodology is parsimony. However, the strength of this methodology, its simplicity, is also its greatest weakness, and the weakness is most evident in this latest long-term forecast of life expectancy made by the United Nations. The problem is not with the methodology, but rather the assumptions that underlie the forecast. As soon as a decision was made to continue to extend recently observed historical trends in life expectancy far into the future, with no cap on life expectancy at birth, presumptive answers to all of the questions in the previous paragraph were provided. The decision was made to assume that the answer to questions A - E is yes, and the answer to questions F - I is no. The resulting projection has led to what I view as an overestimate of the future course of human life expectancy over the long-term.

There are several reasons why I believe the long-range United Nations projections overestimate the future of human life expectancy. First, if the trend in life expectancy observed throughout the past 150 years is to continue in this century let alone the subsequent two centuries, two conditions are required. The underlying cause of the future rise in life expectancy will have to result from fundamentally different forces than those that resulted in gains in life expectancy at birth upon which the forecast is made. Dramatic gains such as those projected will require identifying and controlling the underlying biology of humans that affects duration of life (i.e., aging).

Although mathematical demographers have invoked the notion of engineered negligible senescence (ENS) as one plausible reason why life expectancy in the United States will rise dramatically in the coming decades, it is important to recognize that ENS has never been observed in any mammal, and when it does occur, it is only among species that reach a fixed size in adulthood. Since humans do not qualify under either of these conditions, there is reason to question whether ENS can ever realistically be achieved (Hayflick, 2004). Even if an intervention of this sort could be developed, it would have to be both broadly available and widely used in order to have a detectable effect on the life table of an entire population (Olshansky, Carnes and Hayflick, 2002). If the United Nations does not believe the technologies that save the lives of children, such as immunizations and other public health measures, will be widely available to today's developing nations by the year 2050 (which is one of the assumptions of the first set of projections of the United Nations (2003b)), then why would it be assumed that anti-aging interventions will become available globally between now and 2300? Which is more plausible – the global distribution and use of existing public health interventions that have been proven to work in reducing early age mortality, or the global distribution of technologies that do not currently exist, and which must solve one of the greatest puzzles in the biomedical sciences – ageing? If given the task of developing realistic forecasts of the future of human life expectancy, my choice would be the former.

The second problem involves what the data on health and longevity tell us today. Recent trends in obesity and communicable diseases have been changing at an alarming pace throughout the nations of the developed and developing world (Olshansky et al., 2004). There is definitive evidence that obesity has crept down the age structure in most of today's developed countries, and there is reason to believe similar trends will occur in developing nations if food supplies increase as a result of anticipated improvements in GDP. Obesity carries with it a broad range of elevated risks of fatal and non-fatal diseases expressed throughout the age structure. Although there is no question that obesity is a public health problem that can be solved based on knowledge that exists today, the observed trend in recent decades suggests that humans are not making use of this knowledge. Should forecasts of human life expectancy rely on the reversal of this trend, or should such trends be taken into account? Since the Lee and Carter (1992) methodology relies on trends in life expectancy only – essentially ignoring the potential future public health impact of current trends in obesity because their negative effects are delayed – the presumptive decision of the United Nations forecast is to assume the problem of obesity will be solved. The modern rise of obesity is a blind spot in the Lee and Carter (1992) methodology and the assumptions upon which the United Nations life expectancy forecasts are based.

The third problem with long-term forecasts of life expectancy made by the United Nations involves observed trends in communicable diseases. Although the United Nations projections did take into account the impact of HIV/AIDS, in the grand scheme of global trends in infectious disease mortality, this disease is a mere drop in the bucket. The fact is that most deaths from communicable diseases are not caused by HIV/AIDS, but rather, the long list of largely preventable diseases such as malaria, diphtheria, tuberculosis, influenza, and many others (Olshansky et al., 1997). There are also particularly disturbing trends associated with the emergence of antibiotic resistant organisms, the rise of truly new infectious diseases (e.g., SARS), an increased ability to spread communicable diseases more efficiently across the globe, and the dramatic rise in the absolute number and percentage of the human population that is immunocompromised (caused by AIDS, treatments for cancer and heart disease, and population aging). Also, observed trends in death rates from infectious diseases are on the rise in many developed nations (Olshansky et al., 2004), and there is a long historical precedent suggesting a global pandemic of influenza is on the horizon. Taken together, all of these events associated with communicable diseases represent a disturbing trend that, although preventable in theory, suggest that serious thought should be given to the likelihood that such causes of death may have a significant negative impact on the future of human longevity. The modern re-emergence of communicable diseases is a blind spot in the Lee and Carter (1992) methodology and the assumptions upon which the United Nations life expectancy projections are based. Again I would ask the question – which is more plausible – the near elimination of almost all communicable diseases as required under the United Nations mortality projection scenario, or the continued threat of a suite of microorganisms that have extremely short generation times and which have adapted themselves to their human and animal hosts and reservoirs over far longer time periods than the projection time frame for these forecasts?

Finally, there is the problem of an observed stagnation in mortality declines and gains in life expectancy in some developed nations. For example, in the United States life expectancy for females at age 65 has remained constant at about 19.0 years for the last quarter century (Olshansky et al., 2004). Since another quantum leap in life expectancy in low mortality populations requires large reductions in death rates at older ages (Olshansky, Carnes, and Désesquelles, 2001), it would seem that there is reason to be skeptical about the future course of declining old-age mortality. More recently observed trends demonstrating a stagnation in old-age mortality in some populations are a blind spot in the Lee and Carter (1992) methodology which is based on longer-terms trends in life expectancy that do not detect recent events of interest.

6. Recommendations

1. Alter the composition of the outside research team advising the United Nations on their mortality projection models. As currently composed, the assumptions of the projection models are heavily skewed in a direction favoring what I see as unrealistically high estimates of life expectancy at birth. Included should be biologists who are familiar with human aging who can then comment on the plausibility of anti-aging interventions; public health experts who can comment on recent trends in public health; and biodemographers who can comment on the biological plausibility of mathematical extrapolation models.

2. There is an entire body of scientific literature missing from both publications with regard to the future of human mortality and life expectancy. A number of researchers, me and my colleagues among them, suggest that the future of human life expectancy is likely to be far different from that presented in both United Nations publications. To ignore this literature is like pretending such a debate is not taking place. I would strongly encourage better scholarship.

3. I believe the best approach to take with regard to projections of life expectancy is to use the Lee and Carter (1992) methodology, but apply a different set of assumptions, as outlined below:

a. As far as the regular United Nations projections are concerned (United Nations, 2003a, as referred to in United Nations, 2003b), no population should have a projected life expectancy at birth that is below 70 in the year 2050. It is difficult to believe that the basic tools of public health will remain elusive to most of today's developing nations for the next fifty years. I recommend setting 70 as the target life expectancy for males and females combined, and either adjust the Lee and Carter methodology to accommodate such increases, or perform a linear interpolation between current levels and 70 years for each country for the next 50 years.

b. For the *2002 Revision* (United Nations, 2003a), I believe the projections of life expectancy for all nations where life expectancy at birth is expected to rise above 70 years are appropriate. No changes recommended.

c. In the United Nations (2003c) publication presenting the results of the long-range projections, forecasts of life expectancies should not be allowed to rise higher than the highest projected national life expectancy at birth anticipated for the year 2050 (i.e., Japan). Allow all nations to have their death rates drift lower in accord with the Lee and Carter methodology until the Japanese 2050 target life expectancy is reached, and then assume constant life expectancy for all subsequent years.

4. Eliminate the assumption that there is no cap on human life expectancy. This will not only avoid the problem that arises when assumptions have to be made about survival into age ranges into which no human has ever been documented to survive, but such an assumption is in accord with the present limiting value of biology on the duration of life. As they currently stand, the United Nations (2003c) forecast of life expectancy at birth is based on the assumption that dramatic events will take place over the next three hundred years that influence and dramatically extend the duration of life. My recommendation is to base forecasts on what can be observed today, not on speculation about the development of technologies that may or may not come to pass.

REFERENCES

Carnes, B. A., S. J. Olshansky and D. Grahn (2003). Biological Evidence for Limits to the Duration of Life. *Biogerontology,* vol. 4, No. 1, pp. 31-45.

Hayflick, L. (2004). Anti-aging is an oxymoron. *Journal of Gerontology: Biological Sciences* (in press).

Kannisto, V., J. Lauritsen, A. R. Thatcher and J. W. Vaupel (1994). Reductions in mortality at advanced ages: several decades of evidence from 27 countries. *Population and Development Review,* vol. 20, No. 4, pp. 793-810.

Lee, R. D., and R. Carter (1992). Modeling and forecasting U.S. Mortality. *Journal of the American Statistical Association,* vol. 87, No. 419, pp. 659-675.

Oeppen, J., and J. W. Vaupel (2002). Broken limits to life expectancy. *Science,* vol. 296, No. 10, pp. 1029-1031.

Olshansky, S. J., B. A. Carnes and C. Cassel (1990). In Search of Methuselah: Estimating the Upper Limits to Human Longevity. *Science,* vol. 250, pp. 634-640.

Olshansky, S. J., B. A. Carnes, R. A. Rogers and L. Smith (1997). Infectious Diseases: New and Ancient Threats to World Health. *Population Bulletin,* vol. 52, No. 2, pp. 1-58.

Olshansky, S. J., B. A. Carnes and A. Désesquelles (2001). Prospects for Human Longevity. *Science,* vol. 291, No. 5508, pp. 1491-1492.

Olshansky, S. J., and B. Ault (1986). The Fourth Stage of the Epidemiologic Transition: The Age of Delayed Degenerative Diseases. *The Milbank Quarterly,* vol. 64, No. 3, pp. 355-391.

Olshansky, S. J., L. Hayflick, B. A. Carnes and others (2002). Position Statement on Human Aging. *Journal of Gerontology: Biological Sciences,* vol. 57A, No. 8, pp. B1-B6.

Olshansky, S. J., D. Ludwig, R. Hershow, D. Passaro, J. Layden, B. A. Carnes, J. Brody, L. Hayflick and R. Butler (2004). Will Human Life Expectancy Decline in the 21st Century? (under review).

Tuljapurkar, S., Li Nan and Boe Carl (2000). A universal pattern of mortality decline in the G7 countries. *Nature,* No. 405, pp. 789-792.

Wilmoth, J. R., L. J. Deegan, H. Lundström and S. Horiuchi (2000). Increase of maximum life-span in Sweden, 1861-1999. *Science,* No. 289, pp. 2366-2368.

United Nations (2003a). *World Population Prospects: The 2002 Revision,* vol. I, *Comprehensive Tables* (United Nations publication, Sales No. E.03.XIII.6).

United Nations (2003b). Long-Range Population Projections. Proceedings of the United Nations Technical Working Group on Long-Range Population Projections, New York, 30 June 2003. Working Paper No. ESA/P/WP.186 (August).

United Nations (2003c). World Population in 2300. Proceedings of the United Nations Expert Meeting on World Population Projections, New York. Working Paper No. ESA/WP.187 (December).

NOTE

[1]The no-AIDS and constant mortality assumptions were developed for comparison purposes only and therefore neither was intended to be taken as a serious projection. The focus of this review is on what the authors of the report describe as the "normal" mortality projection scenario.

X. PROJECTING THE UNKNOWABLE: A PROFESSIONAL EFFORT SURE TO BE MISINTERPRETED

*Michael S. Teitelbaum**

The subtitle of this essay summarizes its two primary points. First, the report by the United Nations Population Division, *World Population in 2300* (United Nations, 2004), represents a serious and highly professional effort to gaze quantitatively into the long-term demographic future of the world, its regions, and constituent states. The Report deploys some of the most sophisticated tools available today, and its authors present the findings in a measured and sophisticated way. Finally, as anticipated by the Technical Working Group convened in 2003 by the United Nations Population Division, the challenges posed by this exercise have indeed proven to be "interesting" and the results to be "illuminating" (United Nations, 2003, p. 9).

Having said that, it must be noted that the core goals of the effort might be described as located somewhere on a continuum between the Implausible and the Impossible. The truth is that none of us has the ability to see very far into the future, with the meaning of "far" depending greatly upon the subject matter being addressed. For example, forward assessments of geological patterns such as the movement of tectonic plates or mountain erosion due to wind may safely go out tens or hundreds of years, while for comparably sophisticated forward assessments of local weather patterns a 10-day timescale is considered extreme. With respect to human phenomena, plausible projections about biological evolution may be stretched out over more years and decades than comparable projections about interest rates or electoral popularity.

Among human social, economic and political trends, projections of demographic change do offer some of the longest-term foresight available. This is not because demographers are more prescient than economists or political pundits, nor that the tools of demographic projection are more sophisticated than those addressing economic or political trends. Rather it is because demographic phenomena are generally slower-moving than the economic or political, and also because the rapidity of demographic change is moderated by the well-known phenomenon of demographic momentum. Indeed, it is perhaps because of this relative credibility of long-range projections about demographic change that there has been such interest among non-demographers in formally requesting that the United Nations Population Division undertake such Olympian forward assessments.

This leads to the second of the two primary points: that non-specialists almost certainly will misinterpret, misunderstand, or misconstrue the results of these long-term demographic projections--no matter how sophisticated the methods used or how measured the interpretation of the results. Perversely, non-demographers (including politicians, journalists, senior civil servants, policy advocates) may actually be more interested in very long-term demographic projections, however much skepticism should attach to them, than to more credible short-term demographic projections. The reason is a simple one: demographic changes over the short-term (say a few years or a decade) are likely to be small and hence of limited policy or journalistic interest. In most settings, it is only over much longer terms (e.g. multiple decades or a century or more) that one can see really major demographic shifts. Of course it is possible to credibly analyze long-term demographic changes over the past (hence there is an important sub-field of historical demography), but it is future changes over similarly long time periods that often pique the interest of non-demographers.

Moreover, while we may be confident that the outstanding professional talent of the United Nations Population Division will provide the readers of long-range projections with copious details on their many technical complexities and uncertain-

*Alfred P. Sloan Foundation, New York, NY.

ties, most of the non-technical discussions of the outputs of such projections are alas likely to exclude or minimize all the caveats or technical uncertainties of the original.

Finally, it is fair to note that both politicians and journalists are often attracted to controversial topics. Few demographic reports are likely to raise as much controversy as are demographic projections, by country, that stretch out over more than a century. Depending on the assumptions, of course, it is the outputs of such projections that are most likely to include politically explosive shifts in the sizes or compositions of national populations. The garbled press reports (some verging on the hysterical) on the United Nations Population Division's 2000 report *Replacement Migration* (United Nations, 2000) offer a sobering lesson as to what might be expected for the new projections to the year 2300.

Hypothetical scenarios, projections, forecasts

Any forward-looking calculations that address human society and organization 300 years into the future can be understood only as hypothetical scenarios, and not as forecasts. The word *scenario* (from the Latin *scaenarium,* a place for erecting stages) is defined as "a sequence of events especially when imagined; *especially* : an account or synopsis of a possible course of action or events"[1] In contrast, "forecast" has a far stronger assurance of plausibility, of predicting future events on the basis of credible information:

> **a:** to calculate or predict (some future event or condition) usually as a result of study and analysis of available pertinent data; *especially* : to predict (weather conditions) on the basis of correlated meteorological observations **b** : to indicate as likely to occur.

The English words "projections" and "to project" fall somewhere in between these notions, as "an estimate of future possibilities based on a current trend." Demographers' somewhat specialized usage of "projection" is sometimes at variance with common language usage. Occasionally demographers used "projection" as nearly synonymous with "scenario," as in one recent expert description that "Projection results are generally produced in one of three forms: as a single projection, as a set of scenarios, or as probability distributions" (O'Neill and Lutz, 2003, p. 809).

All demographers understand that projections can be either illustrative (often designed to illustrate the implications of a set of assumptions that are not considered plausible, such as extrapolation of a constant fertility rate for 50-100 years),[2] or as representing a range of future trends that are deemed plausible (as in the United Nations' own "high" and "low" variant assumptions). Unfortunately, such nuanced distinctions between illustrative and plausible projections are sometimes entirely lost on non-experts, who unwisely misconstrue quite implausible illustrative projections as realistic possibilities.

Moreover, what seems "plausible" at any given point in time may be very different from the reality that ensues. One might ask, for example, how "plausible" the powerful and long-lasting post-World War II baby boom in the United States might have seemed even to sophisticated demographers in 1945 or how plausible today's period total fertility rate of 1.0 in Hong Kong might have seemed to demographers in 1960.

The truth is that much about the future of demographic trends a century (or three centuries) from now is <u>unknowable</u>, and quite literally so. None of us has any way of detecting whether fertility rates over the coming century will be lower or higher than at present, nor whether erratic/unstable or fluctuate in some stable and predictable way. We cannot anticipate with any confidence whether efficient means to determine the sex of offspring will be developed, and if so whether such behavior will be socially and legally sanctioned and used sufficiently to affect the net reproduction rate. We cannot know what collective reactions might be embraced if fertility rates in a given country were to remain well below replacement for many decades. We cannot anticipate the size, rates, or even direction of international migrations. Nor can we predict if current national boundaries will be roughly comparable to those of today, very different from today's, or even totally absent. We cannot know whether new diseases or epidemics will emerge that can sharply affect the quantities and contours of the life tables we currently use for demographic projections.

It is salutary, and sobering, to address the following thought experiment: consider what range of "plausible" 300-year demographic projections a sophisticated statistician in 1700 might have developed for the year 2000. Some might decline to undertake such a hypothetical exercise on grounds that 300 years ago there were few if any reliable demographic rates or estimates available, much less credible projection techniques, but we can respond to this concern by asking a similar question for "only" a 100-year projection conducted. One can only wonder how likely the most sophisticated analyst of 1900 would have been to anticipate the influenza pandemic of 1918-1919,[3] the very low European fertility rates of the 1930s, the mass mortality surrounding the World Wars, the dramatic demographic increase of the developing world during the 1960s and 1970s, the sharp fertility declines in China over the past two decades, and the very low fertility that now characterizes much of the industrialized world. The challenges posed by such a 100-year projection from 1900 should give us due pause about the uses we and others make of 300-year projections from 2000.

MINIMIZING MISINTERPRETATIONS

As noted earlier, it may be impossible to prevent misinterpretation of 300-year projections by journalists, politicians, advocates, and others with insufficient understanding of the limits of demographic projections approaches. Yet there may be a few editorial rules that, if followed, could at least reduce confusion. In particular, I respectfully suggest the following modifications be considered for the final version of this United Nations report:

1. Avoid use of the indicative future tense, such as "will be" or "will increase to." Projections that depend heavily upon a set of assumptions need to be described always in the subjunctive mood, as in "would be" or "would increase to."
2. Official United Nations languages other than English may convey with greater clarity that such calculations addressing the long-term future are wholly conditional upon a specified set of assumptions that may or may not turn out to be correct. To the extent possible, such conditional formulations should be amply deployed in versions of the report in these languages.
3. Avoid use of the verb "to project", as in "We project that..." This formulation often is misunderstood by non-technical readers to mean the same as "We predict that..." The same might be said for usages such as "Our projection is that..." or "Life expectancy is projected to..."
4. Modify tables 1, 2, and 3 so that they no longer include the illustrative "constant" projection scenarios. Their inclusion may lead non-technical readers to imagine that such constant scenarios, like the other four scenarios, have some plausibility, yet presumably there is no intention to suggest that a world 2300 population of 133,592 billion people has any plausibility whatever.

Another unintended effect of including the "constant" scenario in the tables is to trivialize what would otherwise be very significant differences among the other scenario outcomes. (Note that the "constant" scenarios are not included in the related figures, perhaps for this same reason.)

The best way forward would seem to be a set of additional but separate tables that present the relevant data and trends under the "constant" scenario.

A FINAL WORD FROM THE POET

Non-demographers who request and use 300-year demographic projections may be interested to know that in the Inferno of Dante's Divine Comedy, there is a special place in the Eighth Circle of Hell reserved for those who presume to peer too far into the future. Their punishment, for all eternity, is to have their heads permanently pivoted 180 degrees to the rear:

> ARGUMENT.—The Poet relates the punishment of such as presumed, while living, to predict future events. It is to have their faces reversed and set the contrary way on their

limbs, so that, being deprived of the power to see before them, they are constrained ever to walk backward (Alighieri, 1909, Canto XX: Circle Eight, Bolgia 4).

REFERENCES

Alighieri, Dante (1909-14). *The Divine Comedy*, translated by Henry F. Cary, vol. XX. The Harvard Classics. New York: P.F. Collier & Son.

O'Neill, Brian, and Wolfgang Lutz (2003). Projections and Forecasts, Population. In *Encyclopedia of Population*, Paul Demeny and Geoffrey McNicoll, eds. New York: Macmillan Reference.

United Nations (2000). Replacement Migration: Is It a Solution to Declining and Ageing Populations? Population Division Working Paper No. ESA/P/WP.160, New York.

United Nations (2003). Long-range Population Projections: Proceedings of the United Nations Technical Working Group on Long-Range Population Projections. Population Division Working Paper No. ESA/P/WP.186, New York.

United Nations (2004). World Population in 2300. Proceedings of the United Nations Expert Meeting on World Population in 2300. Population Division Working Paper No. ESA/P/WP.187/Rev.1, New York.

NOTES

[1] Definitions from Merriam-Webster Dictionary.

[2] Another well-known example is Ansley Coale's illustrative projection that if population growth rates of the 1960s were to continue indefinitely, the earth would become a ball of human flesh expanding outward into space at the radial velocity of the speed of light…

[3] This "Spanish Influenza" pandemic between September 1918 and April 1919 affected 20-40 per cent of the worldwide population, and caused over 20 million people deaths. Moreover, mortality rates were (implausibly?) high for young healthy adults as well as the usual high-risk categories, with overall mortality rates highest for adults aged 20-50.

XI. THE IMPLICATIONS OF THE UNITED NATIONS LONG-RANGE POPULATION PROJECTIONS

Continuing Rapid Population Growth

*Charles F. Westoff**

Media attention to population issues is extremely limited. When journalists do write about population, which is not very often, the most likely article deals with low fertility in Europe and with issues surrounding the resulting aging of the population and its implications for pension systems. The "population explosion" has been replaced by the "birth dearth". Related pieces occasionally appear about whether immigration to these countries with impending negative growth will be acceptable. In contrast, the prospect of world population growing from six to nine billion in 50-100 years now falls in the "ho-hum" category. What we are in fact witnessing is an increasing polarization of the population landscape into problems of under-replacement and aging populations on the one hand, and one of still rapid growth and under-development on the other. In the middle are many still-growing developing countries going through the transition from high to low growth. The point of this essay is to try to restore some balance on population horizons by focusing on the many populations that are still in the rapid growth stage.

The concern with low fertility in Europe and Japan reflects the ethnocentric orientation of the Western press. Low fertility has been here before but is now largely forgotten. Fertility rates were declining rapidly in the early decades of the twentieth century, reaching very low levels by the start of World War II. Although the Depression may have accelerated the decline of fertility, the process had started decades earlier. The decline was interrupted abruptly with the post-war baby booms and attention became drawn elsewhere to the sudden rapid growth in the developing world as death rates fell sharply while birth rates remained high. The low fertility today in Europe and Japan, though exaggerated somewhat by the postponement of births, is certainly not inconsequential but neither is the continued high rates of growth in other parts of the world.

These contrasts have been dramatically highlighted in the recent long-range projections of the United Nations. Although these projections have been stretched out to the year 2300, it seems more fruitful to focus mainly on the next 100 years. (Some critical observations on these long-range projections are offered at the end of this essay). The long-range projections are primarily useful to illustrate various "what if" scenarios. At reasonable extremes of low and high fertility assumptions, Europe's population in 2300 is projected to fall between 200 million and 2.2 billion and the population of Japan between a low of 36 million and a high of 335 million. These are enormous ranges and serve mainly to demonstrate the numerical consequences of small differences in fertility over a long time period. At the opposite extreme is Africa, projected by 2300 to a range between 620 million and 8 billion. Both sets of calculations yield ranges in 2300 of roughly ten to one between high and low figures. It is obviously more realistic and potentially more useful to limit the horizon to the next 100 years where the range between high and low is only a factor of two (in Europe, a low of 362 million and a high of 790 million; in Africa, the range is between 3.2 billion and 1.5 billion). The focus is mainly on the countries in Africa that are facing extremely high growth prospects.

Growth prospects in Africa

What do we know about fertility trends in Africa? We know that Africa as a whole has the highest fertility in the world, with a total fertility rate (TFR) estimated at 4.9 births per woman in the 2000-2005 period. Despite the high prevalence of AIDS in parts of the continent, it has the high-

* Office of Population Research, Princeton University, New Jersey.

est rate of growth in the world (currently 2.2 per cent). We also know that fertility varies enormously by region, from a low TFR of 2.8 in Southern Africa to a high of 6.3 in Middle Africa. We know that fertility has declined rapidly in some countries, partly due to postponement of marriage but mainly due to the increasing use of contraception. Countries showing rapid declines in fertility are South Africa, Zimbabwe, Kenya and the countries of North Africa. Fertility will no doubt decline all over Africa eventually but how long it "eventually" takes underscores the point that time is everything in demographic calculations. We know from the United Nations "constant fertility" scenario that current rates are unsustainable in the long run (by 2300 in this scenario, Africa's population would reach 115 trillion and comprise 86 per cent of the world's total population).[1] It is clear from the United Nations projections that many countries in sub-Saharan Africa particularly are in store for a great additional increase in their populations. A few illustrations follow.

Some country illustrations

The total fertility rate (TFR) in Uganda currently is 7.1 and is projected (in the medium scenario) to fall precipitously to 2.9 children per woman by 2050 and to 1.85 children per woman by 2100. Evidently the AIDS situation has been controlled and the population is expected to grow from 23 million to 103 million in only 50 years and to reach 167 million by 2100 with further growth reaching a maximum of 170 million by 2115. This seven-fold increase in a century would result from an annual growth rate of 3 per cent in the 2000-2050 period and just under 1 per cent in the following 50 years.

There are other extreme cases of potential rapid growth (even with the medium scenario). The population of Niger is projected to increase from 11 million to 99 million over the course of this century; Somalia from 9 to 66 million; Liberia from 3 to 14 million; Mali from 12 to 70 million. And these numbers appear despite declining fertility rates that are assumed to drop to 1.85 by the last quarter of the century. (It is further assumed that AIDS will no longer be a factor after 2050 and that life expectancy will be continually improving).

Larger populations in Africa are also projected to increase significantly by 2100: Nigeria from 115 million to 302 million; Ethiopia from 66 to 222 million. Even Egypt, with a moderate current fertility rate of 3.3 children per woman can expect a near-doubling in only 50 years, expanding from 68 to 127 million with little growth thereafter.

The projections to 2100 (medium scenario) of the most rapidly growing populations in Africa are shown in the table below (limited to countries with populations in the year 2000 of at least 5 million). The current population of these countries totals 614 million; their projected numbers are 1.6 billion by 2050 and 2.0 billion by 2100, a tripling over this century. Many of the countries in this category show very dramatic increases, as noted above for Niger and Uganda.

These projections are all based on the medium scenario which for Africa as a whole assume fertility to decline from a current TFR of 5.0 children per woman to 2.4 children per woman by 2050 and 1.85 by 2100. Even the lowest fertility assumptions (the United Nations low scenario with the TFR dropping to 1.6 children per woman by 2100) yield expectations of rapid growth in which these same countries more than double in population size in 50 years from around 600 million to 1.3 billion. The United Nations high scenario shows a three-fold increase in 50 years and a four-fold increase over the century.

Rapid growth potential in Asia

Africa is not the only region with high growth prospects in the next 100 years. Although there are many more Asian than African countries that have entered the transition from high to low fertility, there are notable exceptions where population growth remains high and prospects for further growth are strong. Many of these countries are current hot spots of international tensions. They include Afghanistan, expected to increase (in the medium scenario) more than four-fold from 21 million to 90 million by 2100 and Iraq with 23 million projected to increase to 58 million by

TOTAL POPULATION OF AFRICAN COUNTRIES* WITH RAPID GROWTH, MEDIUM SCENARIO: 2000-2100

	Population (millions)			*Ratio*
	2000	*2050*	*2100*	*2100 / 2000*
Angola	12	43	63	5.3
Benin	6	16	19	3.2
Burkina Faso	12	42	65	5.4
Burundi	6	19	28	4.7
Cameroon	15	25	27	1.8
Chad	8	25	35	4.4
Cote d' Ivoire	16	28	30	1.9
Dom. Rep. Congo	49	152	203	4.1
Egypt	68	127	132	1.9
Ethiopia	66	171	222	3.4
Ghana	20	40	44	2.2
Guinea	8	20	24	3.0
Madagascar	16	46	62	3.9
Malawi	11	26	33	3.0
Mali	12	46	70	5.8
Mozambique	18	31	34	1.9
Niger	11	53	99	9.0
Nigeria	115	258	302	2.6
Rwanda	8	17	21	2.6
Senegal	9	22	25	2.8
Somalia	9	40	66	7.3
Sudan	31	60	65	2.1
Uganda	23	103	167	7.3
United Republic of Tanzania	35	69	77	2.2
Zambia	10	19	22	2.2
Total	614	1 554	2 006	3.3
All Africa	796	1 803	2 254	2.8

*Confined to countries with at least 5 million in 2000; smaller populations are included in the total figures.

2050 and to 68 million by 2100. Other countries in the region with rapid population growth prospects are Pakistan with 143 million projected to 409 million by 2100, Saudi Arabia from 22 to 61 million and Syria from 17 to 35 million. The case of Yemen is extreme: its population is projected to increase from 18 million in 2000 to 84 million by 2050 to 144 million in 2100. Nepal is another fast-growing population with the potential to increase from 24 million to 51 million in 2050 and 58 million by 2100.

The population of Israel, which includes an Arab minority, is projected to increase from 6 to 10 million in 50 years and then stop growing but the Occupied Palestinian Territory population could see an increase by a factor of five, from 3 million in 2000 to 11 million by 2050 and 15 million by the end of the century, a demographic factor very much in the political thinking in the area.

Although the rates of growth in the two giants of the region – China and India – have declined, population momentum will add substantially to the numbers in just the next 50 years. India's population is projected to increase by 50 per cent in the next 50 years to 1.5 billion and overtake China (1.4 billion). As a result, the population of the whole of Asia (3.7 billion) is projected in the medium scenario to increase by 42 per cent by 2050 and to peak at 5.3 billion by 2065.

Latin America and the Caribbean

The number of countries with further rapid growth potential in Latin America is now quite small. They include Bolivia, expected to double in size in 50 years from 8 to 16 million; Guatemala from 11 to 26 million in just 50 years; Nicaragua and Honduras which are projected to double in 50 years; and Paraguay from 5 to 12 million to 14 million by 2100. Fertility rates in the larger countries of the region – Brazil, Mexico, Colombia and Peru – have declined, in some instances quite sharply, but their populations will still be growing in 50 years and are projected to increase by over 40 per cent in 50 years from 339 million to 481 million before leveling off and beginning to decline. The population of Latin America and the Caribbean as a whole, now 520 million, is projected (medium scenario) to reach a maximum of 779 million by the year 2065.

Conclusions

The "population explosion" stage of the demographic transition is far from finished in many of the least developed countries of the world. The increasing focus on below-replacement fertility in most of the developed countries should not obscure the rapid growth in many other parts of the world and the continuing increase in world population by another 50 per cent to 9 billion by the end of this century. The inevitable eventual slowing and ultimate cessation of that growth has little significance for the complications of that growth for social and economic development in this century. How much the slowing of population growth would facilitate development is not entirely clear but it seems abundantly clear that such development will certainly not benefit from the rapid population growth on the horizon.

A few observations on the long-range projections

Extending population projections beyond 100 years is an intriguing though dubious exercise. Much of the "what if" rationale could be achieved by back-of-the-envelope calculations though these would not provide the age and geographic detail in the United Nations tables. Two criteria to evaluate this work are the plausibility of the assumptions, and clearly a lot of guesswork is involved, and the usefulness of the results.

One obvious problem is the assumption of zero international migration after 2050, but there seems no reasonable alternative. Modeling migration with a 210 country matrix is obviously impossible. Some assumptions for larger regions might be reasonable (we can guess plausibly that there will be more out-migration from Africa to Europe than vice versa) but this is about the extent of such knowledge. Although international migration may not significantly affect population growth in many developing countries, it is a very important issue in many developed countries and the prospects for such migration seem to be increasing. The demography of this issue has been well documented in the recent United Nations report *Replacement Migration* (United Nations, 2000). The assumption of zero international migration in the United Nations projections after 2050 seriously reduces their usefulness for developed countries. In the United States, for example, a recent Census Bureau projection highlights the significant population growth implications of immigration over the next 100 years. In their "medium" series the United States population grows from 275 million in 2000 to 571 million by 2100. With zero international migration, the population by 2100 reaches 377 million. In this exercise, net migration accounts for 65 per cent of the country's growth. The United Nations projections for Europe show only part of the story – what would happen (after 2050) with zero migration. Given the constraints, particularly of the fertility rates projected for the hundred years between 2200 and 2300, it is difficult to see how useful such calculations are for the Europeans.

The mortality assumptions of continuous improvement in life expectancy and the end of AIDS in 50 years seem reasonable. Other epidemic diseases or environmental catastrophes could obviously occur but incorporating their effects into the projections would be sheer guesswork.

The future course of fertility is more problematic. The assumption that fertility will decline seems completely reasonable in the light of recent demographic history. What does not seem reasonable is that all countries with below-replacement levels will return to replacement as if some magnetic force were present to guarantee the survival of every nation. All of the medium scenario projections feature replacement fertility for every country during the last 100 years up to 2300. The high scenario substitutes a uniform TFR of 2.35 and the low scenario a universal 1.85. But what other assumptions might be more defensible for this period? One might make a case for some sort of regional mixture, between 1.85 and 2.35 but a better alternative might be to truncate the exercise at 2200 or alternatively, to show such projections in the distant future by region only and not by individual country. Who knows what the political map of the world will be then? As one of the participants in the advisory committee noted at the outset, the ignorance of that map in 2300 might be put in perspective if one imagines trying to have projected national populations in 2000 from the vantage of 1700. That may be something of an exaggeration but perhaps not.

Reference

United Nations (2000). Replacement Migration: Is It a Solution to Declining and Ageing Populations? Population Division Working Paper No. ESA/P/WP/160, New York.

Note

[1] The most colorful image of this kind of absurdity was the one by Ansley Coale decades ago in his calculation that if the then 2 per cent annual rate of growth were to continue unchanged for the next 5000 years, our descendants would constitute a solid sphere of flesh the radius of which would be expanding at the speed of light. Somewhat gratuitously, he added that 35 years later there would be two such spheres.

XII. FORETELLING THE FUTURE

*John R. Wilmoth**

In late 2003, the United Nations Population Division projected the demographic profile of the world's population forward over a period of nearly 300 years. I have been asked to provide written comments on these long-range population projections. The task is not easy, not only because the forces that drive demographic trends are complex, but also because foretelling the future is a game of artful speculation, which must be approached with due modesty.

Before discussing specific aspects of the long-term projections, I will first address the issue of whether an exercise in population forecasting over a period of 3 centuries is a sensible approach. The correct answer surely depends on the purpose one has in mind. From a scientific point of view, I concur with Joel Cohen's assessment that the size and characteristics of populations 300 years into the future "cannot be known to any useful degree of credibility." Undoubtedly, there would be a broad consensus on this point amongst academic demographers – and amongst reasonable people from all walks of life. One may be tempted to conclude, therefore, that the purpose of this exercise was mainly political, motivated by a conviction that paying more attention to population trends is inherently valuable and justifies a certain suspension of disbelief concerning the limitations of demographic forecasting. But was this really the case?

The executive summary seems to be mute on the issue of why we need population projections until the year 2300. However, the introduction to the full report states (under point 6) that such projections are needed in order to explore the implications of long periods of below-replacement fertility. Shortly thereafter (point 7), the report acknowledges the vast uncertainty that surrounds future demographic trends and suggests that "the projection variants proposed in this document can best be thought of as illustrative scenarios and not as possible forecasts of the long-term evolution of national populations." Although this explanation seems perfectly reasonable to me, I wonder whether most consumers of this information will see these projections merely as "illustrative scenarios" of possible population futures. That depends, no doubt, on the wording and presentation of the original report (in particular, its executive summary) and on the tone of press releases and other communications with the media. I do not have time to offer a full assessment of whether these long-range projections have been presented to the public in a manner that is consistent with the goals and caveats mentioned in points 6 and 7 of the report's introduction. Nevertheless, I will make some general comments on this topic.

First, I must note that in my use of the terms, a population "projection" and a "forecast" are the same thing. I am aware that there are statements in the demographic literature attempting to distinguish between these two terms. However, as Ryder has noted, this distinction is baseless when one considers the entomology of the two terms – although one is of Latin origin and the other Germanic, both mean "to throw forward." For this reason, the subtlety inherent in the report's assertion that "projection variants" are not "possible forecasts" of future trends seems unlikely to have averted misunderstandings about this point. In my opinion, rather than trying to distinguish between projections and forecasts, it would be more useful to assert that neither term implies a "prediction" about future population trends.

Nevertheless, even with proper warnings, I think that both projections and forecasts are often interpreted as predictions of the future in the mind of the average listener. Furthermore, most people are unlikely to notice anything more than the "medium variant," which they see as a professional's "best guess" concerning future demographic trends. Although some may take note of

* Department of Demography, University of California, Berkeley.

the uncertainty implied by presenting multiple variants, I believe from experience that even the most sophisticated consumers of such information do not see demographic projections and forecasts as mere illustrations of possible future paths for the world's population – in other words, at best they view them as predictions with a degree of uncertainty. Perhaps this issue could have been addressed most effectively by choosing a different title for the report and then stating clearly the motivation behind this unusual exercise at several key juncture throughout the report, as well as in the executive summary.

In addition, it could be noted that long-range population forecasts may be useful for the purpose of improving the scientific credibility of short-range forecasts. I became quite convinced of this point last year when reviewing the projection model used for evaluating the financial well-being of the U.S. Social Security trust fund. Short-term projections are often based on assumptions that are convenient and plausible over a period of a few decades, but which often become implausible or even impossible if extended over centuries or millennia. For example, observed mortality trends can be extrapolated into the future, but after some number of years, a naïve extrapolation of the original death rates themselves can result in negative values, which are clearly impossible (in the absence of reincarnation).

For this reason, demographers routinely project trends in the logarithm of age-specific death rates – after computing the anti-log of extrapolated values, projected levels of the mortality rates themselves are necessarily above zero. Although this practice is well known and widely practiced already (including amongst demographers at the United Nations), I suspect that other improvements in methodology could result from a careful consideration of how to constrain the long-range forecasts (in terms of both functional form and assumptions) in order to avoid implausible or impossible results, accompanied by explicit efforts to reconcile the logic and assumptions of the United Nations' short- and long-range population projections. Beginning in 2003, the United States Social Security Administration adopted an approach known as the "infinite time horizon." At first, I thought it was a crazy idea, but later I changed my mind for the simple reason that this approach imposes a level of intellectual rigor on the projection process that tends to be lacking otherwise. I believe that this may be useful approach for the United Nations to consider as well.

Finally, I will offer a few comments about future trends in one of the main components of population forecasts, i.e., fertility. I should emphasize that these comments are highly speculative – they are limited by the inevitable narrowness of my knowledge and experiences, and they are based in some cases on very little empirical evidence. Of course, they are not being delivered entirely "off the cuff," and they do reflect some months and years of thinking about such topics in the present and other contexts. Nevertheless, they are no more than the careful speculations of an informed observer.

Regarding fertility trends, I believe that reproduction below the replacement level will not endure for more than a few decades in any individual large society. Although I have not conducted a throughout review of this topic, this belief does not seem to be contradicted by any existing evidence. In the case of the United States, the period of below-replacement fertility during the first half of the twentieth century was extremely brief (only 1933-1940, according to my calculations). In more recent decades, of course, this phenomenon has been much more robust – the total fertility rate for the United States population fell below replacement in 1972 and did not rise above this level for even one year until 2000. Nevertheless, from 1990 onward fertility amongst American women has been only slightly below or above the replacement level (averaging 2.05 children per woman during the 1990s, and slightly higher in more recent years). Thus, the period of United States fertility that was substantially below replacement levels was less than two decades.

I am not well informed about the duration of a similar period in other countries, nor do I know the record interval of below-replacement fertility for a national population (perhaps 3-4 decades? maybe held by Japan?). However, in those countries where fertility has been substantially below replacement level for more than a decade, there appears to be an increasing public outcry, accompanied by a significant degree of national soul-searching to uncover the causes of the situation. Not surprisingly, below-replacement fertility is generally viewed as pernicious, since it may lead eventually to population decline (for an entire nation if not countered by immigration, and in any case for the progeny of the current population of the country). Admittedly, the jury is still out on whether countries with the current lowest levels of fertility will have any success in raising them in the near future. Nevertheless, I would be cautious about assuming the continuation over many decades of a phenomenon that is only a few decades old.

ANNEX TABLES

TABLE A1. POPULATION OF THE WORLD BY DEVELOPMENT GROUP AND SCENARIO: 1950-2300

Year	World			More developed regions			Less developed regions		
	Medium	High	Low	Medium	High	Low	Medium	High	Low
	Population (millions)								
1950	2 519	—	—	813	—	—	1 706	—	—
1955	2 756	—	—	863	—	—	1 893	—	—
1960	3 021	—	—	915	—	—	2 106	—	—
1965	3 335	—	—	966	—	—	2 368	—	—
1970	3 692	—	—	1 007	—	—	2 685	—	—
1975	4 068	—	—	1 047	—	—	3 021	—	—
1980	4 435	—	—	1 083	—	—	3 352	—	—
1985	4 831	—	—	1 115	—	—	3 716	—	—
1990	5 264	—	—	1 149	—	—	4 115	—	—
1995	5 674	—	—	1 174	—	—	4 500	—	—
2000	6 071	6 071	6 071	1 194	1 194	1 194	4 877	4 877	4 877
2005	6 454	6 502	6 404	1 209	1 212	1 205	5 245	5 290	5 198
2010	6 830	6 966	6 689	1 221	1 231	1 210	5 609	5 736	5 478
2015	7 197	7 447	6 939	1 230	1 249	1 211	5 967	6 198	5 729
2020	7 540	7 913	7 159	1 237	1 267	1 207	6 303	6 646	5 952
2025	7 851	8 365	7 334	1 241	1 282	1 199	6 610	7 082	6 135
2030	8 130	8 818	7 454	1 242	1 298	1 187	6 888	7 520	6 268
2035	8 378	9 279	7 518	1 240	1 314	1 168	7 138	7 965	6 350
2040	8 594	9 741	7 529	1 235	1 331	1 144	7 358	8 409	6 385
2045	8 774	10 193	7 492	1 228	1 350	1 115	7 546	8 843	6 377
2050	8 919	10 633	7 409	1 220	1 370	1 084	7 699	9 263	6 325
2055	9 032	11 045	7 299	1 203	1 383	1 045	7 829	9 662	6 254
2060	9 114	11 426	7 160	1 188	1 398	1 008	7 926	10 027	6 152
2065	9 173	11 791	6 994	1 175	1 417	973	7 998	10 374	6 021
2070	9 208	12 145	6 806	1 163	1 440	939	8 045	10 705	5 868
2075	9 221	12 494	6 601	1 153	1 467	904	8 068	11 027	5 696
2080	9 216	12 830	6 379	1 144	1 498	871	8 071	11 332	5 508
2085	9 195	13 151	6 152	1 138	1 532	840	8 057	11 619	5 312
2090	9 162	13 455	5 926	1 134	1 569	813	8 028	11 886	5 113
2095	9 119	13 744	5 705	1 132	1 609	788	7 987	12 135	4 917
2100	9 064	14 018	5 491	1 131	1 651	766	7 933	12 367	4 726
2105	9 001	14 282	5 284	1 130	1 695	745	7 871	12 587	4 539
2110	8 933	14 538	5 084	1 130	1 740	725	7 802	12 798	4 359
2115	8 864	14 790	4 894	1 131	1 787	708	7 733	13 003	4 187
2120	8 797	15 042	4 718	1 134	1 835	692	7 664	13 207	4 026
2125	8 734	15 296	4 556	1 137	1 885	679	7 597	13 411	3 877
2130	8 673	15 553	4 408	1 141	1 936	668	7 532	13 617	3 740
2135	8 616	15 817	4 271	1 145	1 988	658	7 471	13 829	3 613
2140	8 567	16 096	4 145	1 150	2 041	649	7 416	14 055	3 496
2145	8 526	16 397	4 029	1 155	2 096	641	7 371	14 301	3 388
2150	8 494	16 722	3 921	1 161	2 152	633	7 333	14 571	3 288
2155	8 469	17 072	3 821	1 166	2 209	625	7 304	14 863	3 196
2160	8 452	17 445	3 727	1 171	2 268	617	7 281	15 176	3 111
2165	8 440	17 839	3 640	1 176	2 329	609	7 264	15 510	3 031
2170	8 434	18 256	3 558	1 180	2 391	600	7 254	15 865	2 957

TABLE A1 (*continued*)

Year	World			More developed regions			Less developed regions		
	Medium	*High*	*Low*	*Medium*	*High*	*Low*	*Medium*	*High*	*Low*
				Population (millions)					
2175	8 434	18 696	3 481	1 185	2 454	593	7 249	16 242	2 889
2180	8 439	19 158	3 410	1 190	2 519	585	7 249	16 640	2 825
2185	8 448	19 644	3 343	1 194	2 585	577	7 254	17 059	2 766
2190	8 462	20 153	3 281	1 199	2 653	569	7 263	17 500	2 711
2195	8 479	20 684	3 221	1 203	2 723	562	7 275	17 961	2 660
2200	8 499	21 236	3 165	1 207	2 795	554	7 291	18 441	2 612
2205	8 521	21 809	3 112	1 212	2 868	546	7 309	18 941	2 566
2210	8 545	22 403	3 061	1 216	2 943	539	7 329	19 460	2 523
2215	8 570	23 016	3 013	1 220	3 019	531	7 350	19 997	2 481
2220	8 596	23 649	2 965	1 224	3 098	524	7 372	20 550	2 441
2225	8 622	24 301	2 920	1 228	3 179	517	7 395	21 122	2 403
2230	8 649	24 972	2 875	1 231	3 261	510	7 418	21 711	2 366
2235	8 676	25 662	2 832	1 235	3 346	502	7 441	22 316	2 329
2240	8 702	26 370	2 789	1 239	3 432	495	7 463	22 938	2 293
2245	8 727	27 097	2 746	1 242	3 521	488	7 485	23 576	2 258
2250	8 752	27 842	2 704	1 246	3 612	482	7 506	24 230	2 223
2255	8 776	28 606	2 662	1 249	3 705	475	7 526	24 901	2 188
2260	8 799	29 391	2 621	1 253	3 800	468	7 547	25 591	2 153
2265	8 823	30 196	2 581	1 256	3 898	461	7 567	26 298	2 120
2270	8 845	31 021	2 541	1 260	3 998	455	7 586	27 024	2 086
2275	8 868	31 868	2 501	1 263	4 100	448	7 605	27 768	2 053
2280	8 889	32 737	2 462	1 266	4 205	442	7 623	28 532	2 020
2285	8 911	33 628	2 423	1 269	4 312	435	7 642	29 316	1 988
2290	8 932	34 543	2 385	1 272	4 422	429	7 659	30 121	1 956
2295	8 952	35 481	2 347	1 275	4 535	423	7 677	30 946	1 925
2300	8 972	36 444	2 310	1 278	4 650	416	7 694	31 793	1 894

TABLE A2. AVERAGE ANNUAL RATE OF CHANGE OF THE POPULATION OF THE WORLD BY DEVELOPMENT GROUP AND SCENARIO: 1950-2300

Period	*World*			*More developed regions*			*Less developed regions*		
	Medium	*High*	*Low*	*Medium*	*High*	*Low*	*Medium*	*High*	*Low*
	Average annual rate of change (per cent)								
1950-1955	1.800	—	—	1.204	—	—	2.078	—	—
1955-1960	1.841	—	—	1.172	—	—	2.138	—	—
1960-1965	1.974	—	—	1.089	—	—	2.347	—	—
1965-1970	2.037	—	—	0.831	—	—	2.510	—	—
1970-1975	1.938	—	—	0.779	—	—	2.356	—	—
1975-1980	1.726	—	—	0.667	—	—	2.080	—	—
1980-1985	1.712	—	—	0.586	—	—	2.063	—	—
1985-1990	1.715	—	—	0.596	—	—	2.039	—	—
1990-1995	1.503	—	—	0.432	—	—	1.792	—	—
1995-2000	1.350	—	—	0.336	—	—	1.606	—	—
2000-2005	1.224	1.372	1.068	0.249	0.301	0.192	1.455	1.626	1.277
2005-2010	1.134	1.381	0.871	0.198	0.306	0.083	1.344	1.620	1.049
2010-2015	1.047	1.333	0.737	0.157	0.299	0.007	1.235	1.548	0.894
2015-2020	0.931	1.214	0.623	0.112	0.277	-0.061	1.096	1.398	0.765
2020-2025	0.809	1.111	0.484	0.064	0.248	-0.129	0.952	1.272	0.605
2025-2030	0.698	1.054	0.325	0.015	0.238	-0.213	0.823	1.198	0.429
2030-2035	0.601	1.020	0.170	-0.033	0.248	-0.315	0.713	1.150	0.261
2035-2040	0.508	0.972	0.029	-0.078	0.263	-0.415	0.608	1.086	0.110
2040-2045	0.416	0.908	-0.099	-0.115	0.279	-0.507	0.504	1.006	-0.026
2045-2050	0.326	0.845	-0.224	-0.142	0.295	-0.581	0.401	0.928	-0.163
2050-2055	0.252	0.760	-0.297	-0.272	0.190	-0.724	0.334	0.843	-0.225
2055-2060	0.182	0.677	-0.385	-0.259	0.217	-0.716	0.248	0.742	-0.330
2060-2065	0.128	0.629	-0.468	-0.221	0.266	-0.704	0.180	0.679	-0.430
2065-2070	0.077	0.593	-0.545	-0.198	0.322	-0.722	0.117	0.629	-0.516
2070-2075	0.029	0.566	-0.614	-0.176	0.373	-0.749	0.058	0.591	-0.593
2075-2080	-0.012	0.532	-0.681	-0.147	0.415	-0.749	0.007	0.547	-0.671
2080-2085	-0.045	0.493	-0.726	-0.111	0.450	-0.717	-0.036	0.499	-0.727
2085-2090	-0.071	0.458	-0.749	-0.072	0.480	-0.665	-0.071	0.455	-0.763
2090-2095	-0.095	0.425	-0.758	-0.040	0.502	-0.615	-0.103	0.415	-0.781
2095-2100	-0.120	0.396	-0.764	-0.020	0.516	-0.582	-0.134	0.380	-0.794
2100-2105	-0.140	0.373	-0.771	-0.008	0.523	-0.558	-0.158	0.353	-0.805
2105-2110	-0.152	0.355	-0.772	0.003	0.526	-0.531	-0.174	0.332	-0.812
2110-2115	-0.155	0.345	-0.760	0.019	0.529	-0.491	-0.180	0.319	-0.805
2115-2120	-0.151	0.338	-0.733	0.038	0.532	-0.440	-0.179	0.311	-0.783
2120-2125	-0.144	0.335	-0.698	0.056	0.534	-0.385	-0.174	0.307	-0.752
2125-2130	-0.140	0.334	-0.662	0.070	0.534	-0.335	-0.172	0.305	-0.720
2130-2135	-0.132	0.337	-0.630	0.080	0.532	-0.295	-0.164	0.309	-0.691
2135-2140	-0.115	0.350	-0.599	0.086	0.530	-0.267	-0.147	0.324	-0.660
2140-2145	-0.095	0.370	-0.569	0.090	0.528	-0.252	-0.124	0.347	-0.628
2145-2150	-0.075	0.393	-0.541	0.091	0.527	-0.250	-0.101	0.374	-0.597
2150-2155	-0.058	0.414	-0.518	0.089	0.527	-0.257	-0.082	0.397	-0.568
2155-2160	-0.042	0.431	-0.497	0.085	0.527	-0.267	-0.063	0.417	-0.542
2160-2165	-0.027	0.447	-0.476	0.082	0.526	-0.271	-0.045	0.436	-0.517
2165-2170	-0.014	0.462	-0.455	0.080	0.525	-0.268	-0.029	0.453	-0.493

TABLE A2 (*continued*)

Period	World			More developed regions			Less developed regions		
	Medium	*High*	*Low*	*Medium*	*High*	*Low*	*Medium*	*High*	*Low*
	Average annual rate of change (per cent)								
2170-2175	0.000	0.476	-0.434	0.080	0.523	-0.264	-0.013	0.469	-0.469
2175-2180	0.012	0.489	-0.414	0.079	0.521	-0.262	0.001	0.484	-0.445
2180-2185	0.022	0.501	-0.395	0.077	0.520	-0.265	0.013	0.498	-0.422
2185-2190	0.032	0.511	-0.379	0.074	0.520	-0.271	0.025	0.510	-0.402
2190-2195	0.040	0.520	-0.364	0.072	0.519	-0.275	0.035	0.520	-0.383
2195-2200	0.047	0.527	-0.351	0.070	0.518	-0.276	0.043	0.528	-0.367
2200-2205	0.052	0.533	-0.339	0.069	0.517	-0.275	0.050	0.535	-0.352
2205-2210	0.056	0.537	-0.329	0.068	0.516	-0.275	0.054	0.540	-0.340
2210-2215	0.058	0.540	-0.321	0.066	0.515	-0.275	0.057	0.544	-0.331
2215-2220	0.060	0.542	-0.316	0.065	0.514	-0.277	0.059	0.547	-0.324
2220-2225	0.062	0.544	-0.311	0.063	0.514	-0.280	0.061	0.549	-0.318
2225-2230	0.062	0.545	-0.307	0.062	0.513	-0.282	0.062	0.550	-0.313
2230-2235	0.062	0.545	-0.306	0.061	0.512	-0.283	0.062	0.550	-0.310
2235-2240	0.060	0.545	-0.306	0.060	0.511	-0.284	0.060	0.550	-0.311
2240-2245	0.058	0.543	-0.307	0.058	0.510	-0.284	0.058	0.548	-0.312
2245-2250	0.056	0.542	-0.309	0.057	0.509	-0.285	0.056	0.547	-0.314
2250-2255	0.055	0.542	-0.310	0.056	0.509	-0.286	0.055	0.547	-0.315
2255-2260	0.054	0.541	-0.311	0.055	0.508	-0.287	0.054	0.546	-0.316
2260-2265	0.053	0.540	-0.312	0.054	0.507	-0.288	0.053	0.545	-0.317
2265-2270	0.051	0.540	-0.313	0.053	0.506	-0.290	0.051	0.544	-0.318
2270-2275	0.050	0.539	-0.314	0.052	0.506	-0.291	0.050	0.544	-0.320
2275-2280	0.049	0.538	-0.316	0.051	0.505	-0.291	0.049	0.543	-0.321
2280-2285	0.048	0.537	-0.316	0.050	0.505	-0.292	0.048	0.542	-0.322
2285-2290	0.047	0.537	-0.317	0.049	0.504	-0.292	0.047	0.541	-0.323
2290-2295	0.046	0.536	-0.318	0.048	0.503	-0.293	0.046	0.541	-0.324
2295-2300	0.045	0.535	-0.319	0.047	0.503	-0.295	0.045	0.540	-0.325

TABLE A3. TOTAL FERTILITY OF THE WORLD BY DEVELOPMENT GROUP AND SCENARIO: 1950-2300

	World			*More developed regions*			*Less developed regions*		
Period	*Medium*	*High*	*Low*	*Medium*	*High*	*Low*	*Medium*	*High*	*Low*
				Total fertility (children per woman)					
1950-1955...........	5.017	—	—	2.837	—	—	6.164	—	—
1955-1960...........	4.953	—	—	2.822	—	—	6.010	—	—
1960-1965...........	4.968	—	—	2.684	—	—	6.026	—	—
1965-1970...........	4.905	—	—	2.365	—	—	6.006	—	—
1970-1975...........	4.477	—	—	2.125	—	—	5.421	—	—
1975-1980...........	3.904	—	—	1.912	—	—	4.633	—	—
1980-1985...........	3.565	—	—	1.851	—	—	4.131	—	—
1985-1990...........	3.368	—	—	1.828	—	—	3.826	—	—
1990-1995...........	3.034	—	—	1.687	—	—	3.401	—	—
1995-2000...........	2.830	2.830	2.830	1.575	1.575	1.575	3.113	3.113	3.113
2000-2005...........	2.692	2.898	2.477	1.564	1.641	1.481	2.922	3.156	2.680
2005-2010...........	2.589	2.948	2.216	1.570	1.734	1.398	2.777	3.174	2.365
2010-2015...........	2.499	2.940	2.049	1.600	1.825	1.368	2.648	3.128	2.160
2015-2020...........	2.411	2.866	1.953	1.636	1.911	1.360	2.526	3.012	2.038
2020-2025...........	2.326	2.788	1.865	1.690	2.004	1.377	2.412	2.896	1.929
2025-2030...........	2.248	2.716	1.783	1.753	2.115	1.396	2.309	2.791	1.832
2030-2035...........	2.179	2.652	1.710	1.808	2.214	1.400	2.222	2.703	1.748
2035-2040...........	2.115	2.591	1.644	1.840	2.282	1.398	2.144	2.625	1.673
2040-2045...........	2.063	2.543	1.590	1.853	2.326	1.379	2.086	2.566	1.614
2045-2050...........	2.017	2.502	1.539	1.848	2.345	1.351	2.035	2.517	1.561
2050-2055...........	1.961	2.381	1.546	1.887	2.347	1.468	1.968	2.383	1.554
2055-2060...........	1.925	2.260	1.565	1.943	2.348	1.609	1.920	2.248	1.557
2060-2065...........	1.903	2.184	1.585	2.014	2.348	1.745	1.888	2.165	1.561
2065-2070...........	1.885	2.136	1.610	2.041	2.345	1.810	1.865	2.112	1.582
2070-2075...........	1.874	2.126	1.632	2.052	2.343	1.826	1.853	2.101	1.607
2075-2080...........	1.878	2.132	1.630	2.059	2.344	1.839	1.858	2.108	1.607
2080-2085...........	1.887	2.143	1.636	2.062	2.346	1.844	1.867	2.121	1.614
2085-2090...........	1.899	2.156	1.647	2.065	2.349	1.846	1.880	2.134	1.623
2090-2095...........	1.908	2.166	1.660	2.065	2.350	1.847	1.889	2.144	1.634
2095-2100...........	1.914	2.172	1.668	2.064	2.349	1.849	1.895	2.150	1.640
2100-2105...........	1.922	2.182	1.675	2.063	2.349	1.852	1.904	2.161	1.648
2105-2110...........	1.932	2.194	1.681	2.064	2.350	1.853	1.915	2.175	1.657
2110-2115...........	1.947	2.214	1.696	2.063	2.351	1.850	1.932	2.197	1.675
2115-2120...........	1.964	2.234	1.714	2.063	2.351	1.847	1.952	2.219	1.696
2120-2125...........	1.983	2.254	1.734	2.062	2.350	1.846	1.973	2.242	1.717
2125-2130...........	1.991	2.270	1.749	2.061	2.350	1.849	1.981	2.260	1.733
2130-2135...........	1.998	2.281	1.760	2.061	2.350	1.852	1.990	2.272	1.745
2135-2140...........	2.011	2.294	1.773	2.061	2.351	1.853	2.004	2.286	1.761
2140-2145...........	2.023	2.307	1.788	2.061	2.351	1.851	2.018	2.301	1.779
2145-2150...........	2.032	2.320	1.803	2.060	2.351	1.848	2.029	2.315	1.797
2150-2155...........	2.040	2.330	1.818	2.059	2.350	1.847	2.038	2.327	1.814
2155-2160...........	2.050	2.339	1.831	2.059	2.350	1.848	2.049	2.337	1.829
2160-2165...........	2.055	2.347	1.843	2.059	2.350	1.851	2.055	2.346	1.842
2165-2170...........	2.055	2.350	1.849	2.059	2.351	1.852	2.055	2.350	1.848
2170-2175...........	2.055	2.351	1.849	2.059	2.351	1.851	2.055	2.350	1.849

TABLE A3 (*continued*)

Period	World			More developed regions			Less developed regions		
	Medium	*High*	*Low*	*Medium*	*High*	*Low*	*Medium*	*High*	*Low*
				Total fertility (children per woman)					
2175-2180...........	2.054	2.350	1.849	2.058	2.351	1.849	2.054	2.350	1.850
2180-2185...........	2.054	2.350	1.849	2.058	2.350	1.848	2.053	2.350	1.849
2185-2190...........	2.054	2.350	1.849	2.058	2.350	1.848	2.053	2.350	1.849
2190-2195...........	2.054	2.350	1.850	2.058	2.350	1.850	2.053	2.350	1.850
2195-2200...........	2.053	2.350	1.850	2.058	2.351	1.851	2.053	2.350	1.850
2200-2205...........	2.053	2.350	1.850	2.058	2.351	1.851	2.052	2.350	1.850
2205-2210...........	2.053	2.350	1.849	2.057	2.351	1.850	2.052	2.350	1.850
2210-2215...........	2.052	2.350	1.849	2.057	2.350	1.849	2.052	2.350	1.849
2215-2220...........	2.052	2.350	1.849	2.057	2.350	1.849	2.052	2.350	1.850
2220-2225...........	2.052	2.350	1.849	2.057	2.350	1.849	2.052	2.350	1.850
2225-2230...........	2.052	2.350	1.850	2.057	2.351	1.850	2.051	2.350	1.850
2230-2235...........	2.052	2.350	1.850	2.057	2.351	1.850	2.051	2.350	1.850
2235-2240...........	2.052	2.350	1.850	2.057	2.350	1.850	2.051	2.350	1.850
2240-2245...........	2.052	2.350	1.849	2.057	2.350	1.850	2.051	2.350	1.850
2245-2250...........	2.052	2.350	1.849	2.057	2.350	1.849	2.051	2.350	1.850
2250-2255...........	2.052	2.350	1.849	2.057	2.350	1.849	2.051	2.350	1.850
2255-2260...........	2.051	2.350	1.850	2.057	2.350	1.850	2.051	2.350	1.850
2260-2265...........	2.051	2.350	1.850	2.056	2.351	1.850	2.051	2.350	1.850
2265-2270...........	2.051	2.350	1.850	2.056	2.350	1.850	2.051	2.350	1.850
2270-2275...........	2.051	2.350	1.849	2.056	2.350	1.850	2.051	2.350	1.850
2275-2280...........	2.051	2.350	1.849	2.056	2.350	1.850	2.050	2.350	1.850
2280-2285...........	2.051	2.350	1.849	2.056	2.350	1.850	2.050	2.350	1.850
2285-2290...........	2.051	2.350	1.849	2.056	2.350	1.850	2.050	2.350	1.850
2290-2295...........	2.051	2.350	1.850	2.056	2.350	1.850	2.050	2.350	1.850
2295-2300...........	2.051	2.350	1.850	2.056	2.350	1.850	2.050	2.350	1.850

Table A4. Life expectancy at birth of the world by development group and sex: 1950-2300

Period	World		More developed regions		Less developed regions	
	Male	Female	Male	Female	Male	Female
	Life expectancy at birth (years)					
1950-1955..................	45.17	47.93	63.53	68.54	40.24	41.88
1955-1960..................	48.19	51.04	65.55	70.98	43.58	45.24
1960-1965..................	51.03	53.75	66.65	72.53	47.03	48.40
1965-1970..................	54.61	57.52	67.30	73.83	51.56	53.01
1970-1975..................	56.53	59.51	67.83	74.78	54.00	55.45
1975-1980..................	58.05	61.50	68.58	75.90	55.81	57.74
1980-1985..................	59.42	63.15	69.23	76.49	57.34	59.75
1985-1990..................	60.94	64.79	70.22	77.41	59.05	61.64
1990-1995..................	61.72	65.94	70.17	77.73	60.07	63.12
1995-2000..................	62.47	66.86	71.07	78.53	60.91	64.26
2000-2005..................	63.33	67.63	72.13	79.40	61.74	65.09
2005-2010..................	64.25	68.41	73.01	80.09	62.69	65.96
2010-2015..................	65.10	69.39	73.84	80.69	63.57	67.08
2015-2020..................	65.89	70.36	74.66	81.36	64.38	68.18
2020-2025..................	66.84	71.39	75.43	82.01	65.40	69.33
2025-2030..................	67.88	72.51	76.09	82.59	66.53	70.59
2030-2035..................	68.99	73.64	76.73	83.10	67.74	71.88
2035-2040..................	70.06	74.73	77.35	83.59	68.91	73.13
2040-2045..................	71.05	75.74	77.99	84.08	69.97	74.28
2045-2050..................	71.98	76.66	78.64	84.57	70.97	75.32
2050-2055..................	73.04	77.51	79.43	85.25	72.12	76.31
2055-2060..................	74.10	78.43	80.17	85.88	73.23	77.29
2060-2065..................	75.09	79.28	80.88	86.49	74.28	78.20
2065-2070..................	76.02	80.06	81.58	87.08	75.25	79.04
2070-2075..................	76.89	80.79	82.25	87.67	76.15	79.82
2075-2080..................	77.71	81.49	82.89	88.24	77.01	80.55
2080-2085..................	78.49	82.16	83.51	88.79	77.82	81.25
2085-2090..................	79.23	82.79	84.09	89.31	78.59	81.91
2090-2095..................	79.93	83.39	84.66	89.80	79.31	82.54
2095-2100..................	80.60	83.96	85.20	90.28	79.99	83.13
2100-2105..................	81.23	84.50	85.73	90.74	80.64	83.69
2105-2110..................	81.84	85.02	86.25	91.19	81.26	84.23
2110-2115..................	82.42	85.53	86.75	91.62	81.86	84.75
2115-2120..................	82.99	86.03	87.24	92.05	82.43	85.25
2120-2125..................	83.53	86.51	87.72	92.46	82.98	85.74
2125-2130..................	84.06	86.98	88.19	92.87	83.51	86.21
2130-2135..................	84.57	87.44	88.65	93.27	84.02	86.67
2135-2140..................	85.07	87.89	89.10	93.66	84.52	87.11
2140-2145..................	85.55	88.32	89.54	94.04	85.00	87.54
2145-2150..................	86.01	88.74	89.96	94.40	85.46	87.95
2150-2155..................	86.46	89.15	90.38	94.76	85.90	88.35
2155-2160..................	86.90	89.54	90.79	95.11	86.33	88.74
2160-2165..................	87.32	89.92	91.19	95.46	86.75	89.12
2165-2170..................	87.73	90.29	91.59	95.79	87.16	89.48
2170-2175..................	88.14	90.66	91.97	96.12	87.56	89.85

TABLE A4 (*continued*)

Period	World		More developed regions		Less developed regions	
	Male	Female	Male	Female	Male	Female
	Life expectancy at birth (years)					
2175-2180	88.53	91.02	92.35	96.44	87.95	90.20
2180-2185	88.91	91.36	92.72	96.76	88.32	90.54
2185-2190	89.28	91.70	93.08	97.07	88.69	90.87
2190-2195	89.64	92.03	93.44	97.37	89.05	91.20
2195-2200	89.99	92.35	93.79	97.67	89.40	91.51
2200-2205	90.34	92.65	94.14	97.96	89.74	91.82
2205-2210	90.67	92.95	94.47	98.25	90.07	92.12
2210-2215	91.00	93.24	94.81	98.53	90.39	92.41
2215-2220	91.31	93.52	95.13	98.81	90.70	92.68
2220-2225	91.62	93.79	95.46	99.08	91.01	92.95
2225-2230	91.91	94.05	95.77	99.35	91.30	93.21
2230-2235	92.20	94.30	96.08	99.61	91.58	93.46
2235-2240	92.48	94.55	96.39	99.87	91.86	93.71
2240-2245	92.76	94.79	96.69	100.12	92.13	93.95
2245-2250	93.03	95.03	96.98	100.37	92.40	94.18
2250-2255	93.29	95.26	97.27	100.62	92.66	94.41
2255-2260	93.55	95.49	97.56	100.86	92.92	94.64
2260-2265	93.81	95.71	97.84	101.10	93.17	94.86
2265-2270	94.05	95.93	98.12	101.33	93.41	95.07
2270-2275	94.30	96.14	98.39	101.56	93.65	95.29
2275-2280	94.54	96.35	98.66	101.79	93.88	95.49
2280-2285	94.77	96.56	98.92	102.01	94.11	95.70
2285-2290	95.00	96.76	99.18	102.23	94.34	95.90
2290-2295	95.23	96.96	99.44	102.45	94.56	96.09
2295-2300	95.45	97.15	99.69	102.66	94.77	96.28

TABLE A5. TOTAL POPULATION BY MAJOR AREA, ESTIMATES AND MEDIUM SCENARIO: 1950-2300

Year	*Africa*	*Asia*	*Europe*	*Latin America and the Caribbean*	*Northern America*	*Oceania*
			Population (millions)			
1950..............	221.2	1 398.5	547.4	167.1	171.6	12.8
1955..............	246.7	1 541.9	575.2	190.8	186.9	14.3
1960..............	277.4	1 701.3	604.4	218.3	204.2	15.9
1965..............	313.7	1 899.4	634.0	250.5	219.6	17.7
1970..............	357.3	2 143.1	655.9	284.9	231.9	19.4
1975..............	408.2	2 397.5	675.5	321.9	243.4	21.6
1980..............	469.6	2 632.3	692.4	361.4	256.1	22.8
1985..............	541.8	2 887.6	706.0	401.5	269.5	24.7
1990..............	622.4	3 167.8	721.6	441.5	283.5	26.7
1995..............	707.5	3 430.1	727.4	481.1	299.4	28.9
2000..............	795.7	3 679.7	728.0	520.2	315.9	31.0
2005..............	888.0	3 917.5	724.7	558.3	332.2	33.0
2010..............	984.2	4 148.9	719.7	594.4	348.1	34.8
2015..............	1 084.5	4 370.5	713.4	628.3	364.0	36.6
2020..............	1 187.6	4 570.1	705.4	659.2	379.6	38.3
2025..............	1 292.1	4 742.2	696.0	686.9	394.3	39.9
2030..............	1 398.0	4 886.6	685.4	711.1	407.5	41.5
2035..............	1 504.2	5 006.7	673.6	731.6	419.3	42.8
2040..............	1 608.3	5 103.0	660.6	748.0	429.7	43.9
2045..............	1 708.4	5 175.3	646.6	760.0	439.2	44.9
2050..............	1 803.3	5 222.1	631.9	767.7	447.9	45.8
2055..............	1 889.4	5 255.2	615.5	774.7	451.0	46.2
2060..............	1 965.6	5 269.9	599.6	778.3	454.4	46.4
2065..............	2 032.6	5 270.8	585.4	778.8	458.3	46.6
2070..............	2 090.8	5 259.0	573.1	776.7	461.9	46.7
2075..............	2 140.4	5 234.5	562.6	772.3	464.7	46.7
2080..............	2 181.5	5 200.3	554.1	766.1	467.0	46.7
2085..............	2 213.0	5 160.1	547.5	758.6	469.0	46.6
2090..............	2 235.2	5 116.7	543.0	750.2	470.8	46.4
2095..............	2 248.7	5 069.9	540.1	741.4	472.3	46.2
2100..............	2 254.3	5 019.2	538.4	732.5	473.6	46.1
2105..............	2 252.8	4 966.3	537.5	724.0	474.5	45.9
2110..............	2 245.1	4 913.9	537.1	715.9	475.2	45.7
2115..............	2 231.7	4 865.0	537.4	708.3	476.1	45.5
2120..............	2 213.9	4 821.2	538.3	701.3	477.3	45.3
2125..............	2 192.8	4 782.7	539.7	695.0	478.9	45.1
2130..............	2 169.7	4 747.0	541.4	689.4	480.8	45.0
2135..............	2 145.7	4 714.7	543.4	684.7	483.0	44.8
2140..............	2 122.6	4 687.6	545.6	680.7	485.3	44.8
2145..............	2 101.5	4 666.7	547.9	677.5	487.7	44.8
2150..............	2 083.1	4 650.8	550.4	675.0	490.1	44.8
2155..............	2 067.2	4 639.1	552.9	673.1	492.3	44.8
2160..............	2 053.7	4 631.5	555.4	671.9	494.3	44.8
2165..............	2 041.9	4 627.9	557.8	671.3	496.2	44.9
2170..............	2 031.5	4 628.0	560.1	671.4	498.1	44.9

TABLE A5 (*continued*)

Year	Africa	Asia	Europe	Latin America and the Caribbean	Northern America	Oceania
			Population (millions)			
2175..............	2 023.1	4 631.4	562.5	672.0	500.1	45.0
2180..............	2 016.7	4 637.3	564.8	673.1	502.0	45.1
2185..............	2 012.2	4 645.4	567.1	674.6	503.8	45.1
2190..............	2 009.4	4 655.7	569.3	676.4	505.5	45.2
2195..............	2 008.1	4 668.0	571.5	678.5	507.1	45.4
2200..............	2 008.2	4 681.7	573.7	680.8	508.8	45.5
2205..............	2 009.8	4 696.1	575.8	683.1	510.4	45.6
2210..............	2 012.9	4 710.8	578.0	685.5	512.0	45.8
2215..............	2 017.2	4 725.3	580.0	687.9	513.5	45.9
2220..............	2 022.5	4 739.8	582.1	690.2	514.9	46.1
2225..............	2 028.5	4 754.4	584.1	692.6	516.4	46.2
2230..............	2 035.0	4 769.1	586.1	694.8	517.7	46.4
2235..............	2 041.6	4 783.5	588.1	697.0	519.1	46.5
2240..............	2 048.1	4 797.4	590.0	699.2	520.4	46.7
2245..............	2 054.4	4 810.8	591.9	701.3	521.7	46.8
2250..............	2 060.4	4 824.0	593.8	703.5	523.0	47.0
2255..............	2 066.1	4 837.1	595.7	705.5	524.2	47.1
2260..............	2 071.8	4 849.9	597.5	707.6	525.4	47.3
2265..............	2 077.4	4 862.4	599.3	709.6	526.6	47.4
2270..............	2 082.8	4 874.7	601.1	711.5	527.7	47.6
2275..............	2 088.1	4 886.6	602.8	713.5	528.9	47.7
2280..............	2 093.3	4 898.4	604.6	715.4	530.0	47.8
2285..............	2 098.3	4 909.9	606.3	717.3	531.0	48.0
2290..............	2 103.2	4 921.3	608.0	719.1	532.1	48.1
2295..............	2 108.0	4 932.4	609.6	720.9	533.1	48.2
2300..............	2 112.7	4 943.2	611.3	722.7	534.1	48.4

TABLE A6. AVERAGE ANNUAL RATE OF POPULATION CHANGE BY MAJOR AREA: 1950-2300

Period	*Africa*	*Asia*	*Europe*	*Latin America and the Caribbean*	*Northern America*	*Oceania*
	Average annual rate of change (per cent)					
1950-1955	2.185	1.953	0.990	2.653	1.705	2.149
1955-1960	2.342	1.967	0.991	2.693	1.767	2.155
1960-1965	2.462	2.203	0.957	2.748	1.456	2.112
1965-1970	2.599	2.414	0.677	2.574	1.096	1.926
1970-1975	2.663	2.243	0.591	2.446	0.967	2.071
1975-1980	2.805	1.869	0.494	2.315	1.013	1.139
1980-1985	2.860	1.851	0.388	2.103	1.019	1.559
1985-1990	2.775	1.853	0.436	1.902	1.020	1.565
1990-1995	2.561	1.591	0.161	1.717	1.090	1.610
1995-2000	2.350	1.405	0.016	1.564	1.071	1.414
2000-2005	2.195	1.252	-0.090	1.412	1.003	1.221
2005-2010	2.058	1.148	-0.139	1.255	0.940	1.076
2010-2015	1.941	1.041	-0.176	1.107	0.888	0.980
2015-2020	1.815	0.893	-0.225	0.963	0.841	0.912
2020-2025	1.687	0.739	-0.268	0.821	0.761	0.848
2025-2030	1.576	0.600	-0.307	0.693	0.660	0.755
2030-2035	1.464	0.485	-0.347	0.569	0.568	0.634
2035-2040	1.339	0.381	-0.390	0.442	0.492	0.523
2040-2045	1.207	0.281	-0.429	0.318	0.435	0.446
2045-2050	1.081	0.180	-0.460	0.202	0.395	0.391
2050-2055	0.933	0.126	-0.529	0.181	0.135	0.160
2055-2060	0.791	0.056	-0.522	0.093	0.152	0.107
2060-2065	0.670	0.004	-0.478	0.014	0.173	0.068
2065-2070	0.564	-0.045	-0.427	-0.055	0.155	0.039
2070-2075	0.470	-0.093	-0.369	-0.114	0.123	0.019
2075-2080	0.380	-0.131	-0.306	-0.161	0.098	-0.014
2080-2085	0.287	-0.155	-0.237	-0.196	0.084	-0.046
2085-2090	0.200	-0.169	-0.166	-0.223	0.076	-0.069
2090-2095	0.120	-0.184	-0.106	-0.236	0.066	-0.079
2095-2100	0.050	-0.201	-0.064	-0.240	0.052	-0.080
2100-2105	-0.013	-0.212	-0.035	-0.234	0.038	-0.079
2105-2110	-0.069	-0.212	-0.012	-0.227	0.032	-0.081
2110-2115	-0.119	-0.200	0.011	-0.213	0.037	-0.086
2115-2120	-0.160	-0.181	0.033	-0.198	0.050	-0.087
2120-2125	-0.192	-0.160	0.051	-0.182	0.066	-0.082
2125-2130	-0.212	-0.150	0.064	-0.161	0.080	-0.069
2130-2135	-0.222	-0.137	0.073	-0.137	0.090	-0.046
2135-2140	-0.216	-0.115	0.080	-0.115	0.097	-0.023
2140-2145	-0.200	-0.090	0.086	-0.094	0.099	-0.004
2145-2150	-0.176	-0.068	0.090	-0.075	0.096	0.001
2150-2155	-0.153	-0.050	0.091	-0.055	0.089	0.003
2155-2160	-0.132	-0.033	0.088	-0.036	0.082	0.009
2160-2165	-0.115	-0.015	0.086	-0.017	0.078	0.017
2165-2170	-0.102	0.001	0.084	0.001	0.077	0.026
2170-2175	-0.083	0.014	0.084	0.018	0.078	0.031

TABLE A6 (*continued*)

Period	*Africa*	*Asia*	*Europe*	*Latin America and the Caribbean*	*Northern America*	*Oceania*
	Average annual rate of change (per cent)					
2175-2180	-0.063	0.026	0.083	0.033	0.076	0.034
2180-2185	-0.044	0.035	0.081	0.045	0.072	0.038
2185-2190	-0.028	0.044	0.079	0.055	0.068	0.043
2190-2195	-0.013	0.053	0.077	0.062	0.065	0.050
2195-2200	0.001	0.059	0.075	0.066	0.064	0.057
2200-2205	0.016	0.062	0.075	0.068	0.063	0.061
2205-2210	0.030	0.062	0.074	0.069	0.062	0.063
2210-2215	0.043	0.062	0.072	0.069	0.059	0.065
2215-2220	0.052	0.061	0.071	0.069	0.057	0.067
2220-2225	0.059	0.061	0.069	0.067	0.055	0.069
2225-2230	0.064	0.062	0.068	0.065	0.054	0.069
2230-2235	0.065	0.060	0.067	0.063	0.053	0.066
2235-2240	0.064	0.058	0.066	0.062	0.051	0.063
2240-2245	0.061	0.056	0.065	0.061	0.050	0.061
2245-2250	0.058	0.055	0.064	0.060	0.048	0.061
2250-2255	0.056	0.054	0.062	0.059	0.047	0.062
2255-2260	0.055	0.053	0.061	0.058	0.046	0.061
2260-2265	0.054	0.052	0.060	0.056	0.045	0.060
2265-2270	0.053	0.050	0.059	0.055	0.044	0.058
2270-2275	0.051	0.049	0.058	0.054	0.043	0.057
2275-2280	0.049	0.048	0.057	0.053	0.041	0.057
2280-2285	0.048	0.047	0.056	0.052	0.040	0.056
2285-2290	0.047	0.046	0.056	0.051	0.039	0.056
2290-2295	0.046	0.045	0.055	0.050	0.038	0.055
2295-2300	0.045	0.044	0.054	0.049	0.038	0.054

TABLE A7. TOTAL FERTILITY BY MAJOR AREA, MEDIUM SCENARIO: 1950-2300

Period	Africa	Asia	Europe	Latin America and the Caribbean	Northern America	Oceania
	Total fertility (children per woman)					
1950-1955	6.736	5.885	2.662	5.889	3.469	3.898
1955-1960	6.802	5.633	2.660	5.934	3.723	4.115
1960-1965	6.860	5.632	2.578	5.971	3.341	4.006
1965-1970	6.802	5.680	2.359	5.553	2.542	3.590
1970-1975	6.708	5.063	2.163	5.032	2.011	3.249
1975-1980	6.586	4.174	1.973	4.484	1.783	2.818
1980-1985	6.426	3.659	1.882	3.899	1.806	2.624
1985-1990	6.082	3.402	1.829	3.386	1.893	2.560
1990-1995	5.632	2.975	1.575	3.007	2.019	2.547
1995-2000	5.221	2.718	1.419	2.720	2.006	2.451
2000-2005	4.906	2.547	1.380	2.527	2.050	2.337
2005-2010	4.567	2.418	1.372	2.357	2.045	2.229
2010-2015	4.193	2.303	1.401	2.229	2.026	2.160
2015-2020	3.840	2.208	1.438	2.125	2.015	2.119
2020-2025	3.521	2.129	1.520	2.040	1.990	2.084
2025-2030	3.233	2.059	1.627	1.981	1.957	2.044
2030-2035	2.977	2.000	1.724	1.944	1.936	2.003
2035-2040	2.750	1.951	1.788	1.908	1.911	1.969
2040-2045	2.556	1.928	1.825	1.881	1.886	1.943
2045-2050	2.397	1.911	1.842	1.863	1.851	1.918
2050-2055	2.209	1.884	1.876	1.851	1.901	1.889
2055-2060	2.063	1.872	1.924	1.849	1.970	1.857
2060-2065	1.961	1.866	1.986	1.850	2.050	1.881
2065-2070	1.896	1.860	2.018	1.850	2.069	1.918
2070-2075	1.863	1.854	2.035	1.851	2.067	1.961
2075-2080	1.856	1.864	2.047	1.853	2.067	1.973
2080-2085	1.850	1.881	2.057	1.853	2.066	1.977
2085-2090	1.850	1.902	2.067	1.853	2.065	1.978
2090-2095	1.850	1.915	2.069	1.868	2.063	1.976
2095-2100	1.851	1.921	2.067	1.889	2.062	1.975
2100-2105	1.853	1.931	2.065	1.922	2.061	1.976
2105-2110	1.856	1.943	2.065	1.947	2.060	1.980
2110-2115	1.860	1.963	2.066	1.977	2.060	1.984
2115-2120	1.864	1.990	2.067	2.000	2.059	1.986
2120-2125	1.869	2.018	2.066	2.016	2.058	1.987
2125-2130	1.875	2.027	2.064	2.033	2.058	1.990
2130-2135	1.882	2.034	2.064	2.049	2.057	2.006
2135-2140	1.902	2.045	2.064	2.056	2.057	2.029
2140-2145	1.928	2.054	2.064	2.059	2.056	2.053
2145-2150	1.961	2.054	2.064	2.058	2.056	2.056
2150-2155	1.992	2.056	2.063	2.057	2.056	2.057
2155-2160	2.022	2.059	2.062	2.055	2.055	2.058
2160-2165	2.038	2.062	2.062	2.055	2.055	2.060
2165-2170	2.038	2.062	2.062	2.055	2.055	2.061
2170-2175	2.041	2.061	2.062	2.055	2.054	2.059

TABLE A7 (*continued*)

Period	Africa	Asia	Europe	Latin America and the Caribbean	Northern America	Oceania
			Total fertility (children per woman)			
2175-2180	2.040	2.060	2.062	2.054	2.054	2.057
2180-2185	2.039	2.060	2.062	2.054	2.054	2.057
2185-2190	2.038	2.060	2.061	2.053	2.054	2.058
2190-2195	2.037	2.060	2.061	2.053	2.054	2.059
2195-2200	2.037	2.060	2.061	2.053	2.053	2.059
2200-2205	2.037	2.059	2.061	2.053	2.053	2.058
2205-2210	2.037	2.059	2.061	2.052	2.053	2.057
2210-2215	2.036	2.059	2.061	2.052	2.053	2.058
2215-2220	2.035	2.059	2.061	2.052	2.053	2.058
2220-2225	2.035	2.059	2.060	2.052	2.053	2.058
2225-2230	2.035	2.059	2.060	2.052	2.053	2.057
2230-2235	2.035	2.059	2.060	2.051	2.053	2.057
2235-2240	2.035	2.058	2.060	2.051	2.053	2.057
2240-2245	2.034	2.058	2.060	2.051	2.052	2.057
2245-2250	2.034	2.058	2.060	2.051	2.052	2.057
2250-2255	2.034	2.058	2.060	2.051	2.052	2.057
2255-2260	2.034	2.058	2.060	2.051	2.052	2.057
2260-2265	2.034	2.058	2.060	2.051	2.052	2.057
2265-2270	2.034	2.058	2.060	2.051	2.052	2.057
2270-2275	2.034	2.058	2.060	2.050	2.052	2.057
2275-2280	2.034	2.058	2.060	2.050	2.052	2.057
2280-2285	2.034	2.058	2.060	2.050	2.052	2.057
2285-2290	2.034	2.058	2.060	2.050	2.052	2.057
2290-2295	2.034	2.058	2.060	2.050	2.052	2.057
2295-2300	2.034	2.058	2.059	2.050	2.052	2.057

TABLE A8. LIFE EXPECTANCY AT BIRTH BY MAJOR AREA AND SEX: 1950-2300

	Africa		*Asia*		*Europe*		*Latin America and the Caribbean*		*Northern America*		*Oceania*	
Period	*Male*	*Female*	*Male*	*Female*	*Male*	*Female*	*Male*	*Female*	*Male*	*Female*	*Male*	*Female*
					Life expectancy at birth (years)							
1950-1955	36.49	39.12	40.70	42.12	62.95	67.95	49.74	53.10	66.10	71.92	58.03	62.90
1955-1960	38.60	41.23	44.19	45.59	65.32	70.64	52.49	56.19	66.71	72.97	59.83	64.88
1960-1965	40.67	43.33	47.94	48.95	66.55	72.28	54.87	58.84	66.89	73.58	61.09	66.45
1965-1970	42.79	45.54	53.21	54.27	67.23	73.66	56.74	60.94	66.98	74.22	61.82	67.36
1970-1975	44.82	47.65	55.87	56.83	67.39	74.36	58.59	63.30	67.90	75.55	63.05	68.67
1975-1980	46.80	49.69	57.71	59.20	67.57	75.17	60.51	65.67	69.57	77.27	64.64	70.39
1980-1985	48.30	51.33	59.38	61.36	67.87	75.71	61.90	68.03	70.81	77.48	66.51	72.14
1985-1990	49.81	52.97	61.21	63.40	68.98	76.65	63.49	69.84	71.24	77.97	67.83	73.23
1990-1995	49.45	52.77	62.69	65.40	68.47	76.72	64.73	71.39	71.92	78.47	69.22	74.68
1995-2000	48.48	51.58	64.14	67.32	69.10	77.43	65.99	72.87	73.50	79.32	70.75	75.81
2000-2005	47.89	49.99	65.52	69.02	70.14	78.20	67.07	73.90	74.52	80.13	71.76	76.64
2005-2010	48.66	49.86	66.68	70.39	71.06	78.79	68.24	74.94	75.17	80.78	72.70	77.49
2010-2015	50.49	51.55	67.41	71.52	72.01	79.28	69.33	75.95	75.65	81.37	73.61	78.36
2015-2020	52.41	53.51	68.00	72.52	73.09	79.89	70.33	76.94	75.91	81.95	74.48	79.19
2020-2025	54.34	55.42	68.86	73.59	74.08	80.60	71.28	77.88	76.27	82.32	75.31	80.00
2025-2030	56.45	57.66	69.81	74.68	74.89	81.26	72.17	78.77	76.71	82.60	76.12	80.88
2030-2035	58.54	59.96	70.83	75.75	75.62	81.83	73.02	79.63	77.26	82.90	76.76	81.67
2035-2040	60.46	62.12	71.83	76.78	76.26	82.39	73.81	80.42	77.91	83.27	77.33	82.32
2040-2045	62.21	64.09	72.73	77.70	76.89	82.95	74.54	81.16	78.59	83.71	77.90	82.89
2045-2050	63.85	65.92	73.58	78.51	77.52	83.50	75.22	81.84	79.29	84.22	78.39	83.45
2050-2055	65.61	67.69	74.63	79.37	78.36	84.27	76.15	82.69	79.93	84.80	78.96	84.00
2055-2060	67.25	69.33	75.58	80.17	79.08	84.88	76.86	83.24	80.68	85.52	79.56	84.53
2060-2065	68.78	70.81	76.46	80.90	79.78	85.47	77.55	83.78	81.42	86.21	80.14	85.05
2065-2070	70.17	72.16	77.30	81.59	80.47	86.06	78.21	84.29	82.12	86.88	80.72	85.55
2070-2075	71.45	73.39	78.08	82.22	81.13	86.65	78.86	84.79	82.80	87.52	81.29	86.04
2075-2080	72.64	74.52	78.82	82.83	81.76	87.21	79.49	85.28	83.46	88.13	81.84	86.51
2080-2085	73.74	75.58	79.53	83.41	82.36	87.75	80.10	85.76	84.09	88.72	82.39	86.99
2085-2090	74.77	76.56	80.20	83.97	82.94	88.26	80.69	86.22	84.70	89.29	82.92	87.45
2090-2095	75.72	77.47	80.84	84.51	83.50	88.75	81.27	86.67	85.29	89.83	83.45	87.92
2095-2100	76.61	78.31	81.45	85.02	84.05	89.22	81.84	87.11	85.86	90.36	83.96	88.37
2100-2105	77.45	79.10	82.03	85.51	84.58	89.68	82.39	87.54	86.41	90.86	84.47	88.81
2105-2110	78.23	79.85	82.60	85.99	85.10	90.13	82.93	87.96	86.94	91.35	84.96	89.24
2110-2115	78.97	80.55	83.14	86.45	85.61	90.56	83.45	88.38	87.45	91.82	85.45	89.66
2115-2120	79.68	81.22	83.66	86.90	86.10	90.98	83.96	88.78	87.95	92.27	85.92	90.08
2120-2125	80.34	81.86	84.16	87.34	86.58	91.39	84.46	89.17	88.43	92.70	86.39	90.50
2125-2130	80.97	82.46	84.65	87.76	87.06	91.79	84.95	89.55	88.89	93.12	86.86	90.92
2130-2135	81.57	83.03	85.12	88.17	87.53	92.19	85.43	89.93	89.34	93.53	87.31	91.33
2135-2140	82.14	83.58	85.58	88.57	87.99	92.59	85.90	90.30	89.78	93.92	87.76	91.73
2140-2145	82.68	84.10	86.03	88.96	88.44	92.97	86.35	90.66	90.20	94.30	88.19	92.13
2145-2150	83.19	84.59	86.47	89.34	88.89	93.35	86.80	91.01	90.62	94.67	88.62	92.51
2150-2155	83.68	85.06	86.89	89.71	89.32	93.71	87.24	91.36	91.01	95.02	89.05	92.90
2155-2160	84.15	85.51	87.31	90.07	89.75	94.08	87.67	91.70	91.40	95.37	89.46	93.28
2160-2165	84.60	85.93	87.71	90.42	90.18	94.44	88.09	92.03	91.78	95.70	89.87	93.65
2165-2170	85.03	86.34	88.11	90.78	90.59	94.79	88.51	92.36	92.14	96.03	90.27	94.01

TABLE A8 (*continued*)

Period	Africa		Asia		Europe		Latin America and the Caribbean		Northern America		Oceania	
	Male	Female	Male	Female	Male	Female	Male	Female	Male	Female	Male	Female
	Life expectancy at birth (years)											
2170-2175	85.44	86.73	88.49	91.12	91.00	95.14	88.91	92.68	92.50	96.34	90.67	94.37
2175-2180	85.84	87.11	88.87	91.46	91.40	95.48	89.31	92.99	92.84	96.65	91.05	94.71
2180-2185	86.22	87.48	89.24	91.79	91.80	95.81	89.70	93.30	93.18	96.94	91.44	95.06
2185-2190	86.59	87.83	89.60	92.10	92.19	96.14	90.08	93.60	93.51	97.23	91.82	95.40
2190-2195	86.95	88.17	89.94	92.41	92.57	96.47	90.45	93.90	93.83	97.51	92.19	95.74
2195-2200	87.30	88.50	90.29	92.71	92.95	96.79	90.82	94.19	94.14	97.78	92.56	96.07
2200-2205	87.64	88.83	90.62	93.00	93.33	97.11	91.18	94.48	94.44	98.05	92.92	96.40
2205-2210	87.96	89.14	90.94	93.28	93.69	97.42	91.54	94.76	94.73	98.31	93.28	96.72
2210-2215	88.28	89.44	91.25	93.56	94.05	97.72	91.88	95.03	95.02	98.56	93.63	97.03
2215-2220	88.58	89.73	91.56	93.83	94.41	98.03	92.22	95.30	95.30	98.80	93.97	97.33
2220-2225	88.88	90.01	91.86	94.09	94.77	98.33	92.56	95.57	95.58	99.04	94.31	97.62
2225-2230	89.16	90.28	92.16	94.34	95.11	98.62	92.89	95.83	95.84	99.27	94.64	97.91
2230-2235	89.44	90.54	92.44	94.59	95.46	98.91	93.21	96.08	96.10	99.50	94.96	98.19
2235-2240	89.71	90.79	92.72	94.83	95.79	99.20	93.52	96.34	96.36	99.72	95.29	98.47
2240-2245	89.97	91.03	92.99	95.07	96.13	99.48	93.84	96.58	96.61	99.94	95.61	98.76
2245-2250	90.23	91.27	93.26	95.30	96.46	99.76	94.14	96.83	96.85	100.15	95.93	99.04
2250-2255	90.47	91.51	93.52	95.53	96.78	100.03	94.44	97.07	97.09	100.35	96.24	99.31
2255-2260	90.72	91.74	93.78	95.75	97.10	100.31	94.74	97.30	97.32	100.55	96.54	99.57
2260-2265	90.95	91.96	94.03	95.97	97.42	100.57	95.03	97.54	97.55	100.75	96.85	99.84
2265-2270	91.19	92.18	94.27	96.18	97.73	100.84	95.31	97.77	97.77	100.94	97.15	100.10
2270-2275	91.41	92.39	94.51	96.39	98.03	101.10	95.59	97.99	97.99	101.13	97.45	100.36
2275-2280	91.63	92.60	94.75	96.60	98.34	101.35	95.87	98.21	98.21	101.31	97.74	100.62
2280-2285	91.85	92.80	94.98	96.80	98.63	101.61	96.14	98.43	98.41	101.49	98.04	100.88
2285-2290	92.06	93.00	95.21	97.00	98.93	101.86	96.40	98.65	98.62	101.66	98.32	101.13
2290-2295	92.27	93.20	95.43	97.20	99.22	102.11	96.66	98.86	98.82	101.83	98.61	101.37
2295-2300	92.47	93.39	95.65	97.39	99.51	102.35	96.92	99.07	99.02	102.00	98.89	101.62

TABLE A9. TOTAL FERTILITY OF THE WORLD BY DEVELOPMENT GROUP, MAJOR AREA AND REGION, MEDIUM SCENARIO: SELECTED PERIODS

Major area and region	*1950-1955*	*2000-2005*	*2050-2055*	*2100-2105*	*2150-2155*	*2200-2205*	*2250-2255*	*2295-2300*
	Total fertility (children per woman)							
World	5.017	2.692	1.961	1.922	2.040	2.053	2.052	2.051
More developed regions	2.837	1.564	1.886	2.063	2.059	2.058	2.057	2.056
Less developed regions	6.164	2.922	1.967	1.904	2.038	2.052	2.051	2.050
Africa	6.736	4.906	2.209	1.853	1.992	2.037	2.034	2.034
Southern Africa	6.461	2.793	1.853	1.892	2.043	2.033	2.030	2.030
Eastern Africa	6.969	5.610	2.262	1.849	1.980	2.032	2.030	2.029
Middle Africa	5.908	6.279	2.349	1.850	1.969	2.037	2.032	2.031
Western Africa	6.853	5.558	2.261	1.850	1.985	2.035	2.033	2.033
Northern Africa	6.824	3.211	1.862	1.865	2.056	2.052	2.052	2.052
Asia	5.885	2.547	1.884	1.931	2.056	2.059	2.058	2.058
Western Asia	6.459	3.448	2.105	1.880	2.005	2.051	2.051	2.051
South-central Asia	6.077	3.246	1.876	1.859	2.052	2.052	2.050	2.050
South-eastern Asia	5.951	2.548	1.856	1.933	2.055	2.052	2.051	2.051
Eastern Asia	5.683	1.775	1.850	2.090	2.081	2.079	2.078	2.077
Latin America and the Caribbean	5.889	2.527	1.849	1.922	2.057	2.053	2.051	2.050
South America	5.692	2.450	1.849	1.938	2.055	2.052	2.050	2.049
Caribbean	5.217	2.394	1.847	1.925	2.080	2.066	2.060	2.057
Central America	6.874	2.760	1.850	1.885	2.055	2.052	2.051	2.050
Oceania	3.898	2.337	1.864	1.976	2.057	2.058	2.057	2.057
Polynesia	6.887	3.163	1.874	1.909	2.054	2.055	2.054	2.054
Micronesia	6.412	3.404	1.874	1.960	2.060	2.059	2.057	2.057
Melanesia	6.287	3.909	1.864	1.850	2.063	2.062	2.061	2.061
Australia/New Zealand	3.273	1.747	1.850	2.061	2.058	2.056	2.055	2.055
Northern America	3.469	2.050	1.901	2.061	2.056	2.053	2.052	2.052
Europe	2.662	1.380	1.875	2.065	2.063	2.061	2.060	2.059
Eastern Europe	2.912	1.180	1.887	2.070	2.064	2.061	2.060	2.060
Southern Europe	2.651	1.315	1.848	2.071	2.073	2.071	2.070	2.069
Western Europe	2.390	1.581	1.884	2.062	2.059	2.058	2.057	2.056
Northern Europe	2.319	1.611	1.894	2.061	2.058	2.056	2.055	2.055

TABLE A10. LIFE EXPECTANCY AT BIRTH OF THE WORLD BY DEVELOPMENT GROUP, MAJOR AREA, REGION AND SEX: SELECTED PERIODS

Major area and region	*1950-1955*	*2000-2005*	*2050-2055*	*2100-2105*	*2150-2155*	*2200-2205*	*2250-2255*	*2295-2300*
			Male life expectancy at birth (years)					
World	45.17	63.33	73.04	81.23	86.46	90.34	93.29	95.45
More developed regions	63.53	72.13	79.43	85.73	90.38	94.14	97.27	99.69
Less developed regions	40.24	61.74	72.12	80.64	85.90	89.74	92.66	94.77
Africa	36.49	47.89	65.61	77.45	83.68	87.64	90.47	92.47
Southern Africa	43.44	43.93	57.93	75.73	84.30	89.18	92.46	94.70
Eastern Africa	34.88	42.36	63.96	77.31	83.86	87.85	90.63	92.56
Middle Africa	34.51	41.58	61.43	74.53	81.71	86.18	89.30	91.47
Western Africa	34.23	48.97	65.99	77.51	83.44	87.19	89.89	91.80
Northern Africa	40.74	64.46	75.12	81.66	86.10	89.57	92.40	94.54
Asia	40.70	65.52	74.63	82.03	86.89	90.62	93.52	95.65
Western Asia	43.64	67.11	76.51	82.25	86.16	89.38	91.96	93.82
South-central Asia	40.03	62.47	73.38	81.58	86.47	89.91	92.51	94.37
South-eastern Asia	39.91	64.36	75.26	82.30	86.90	90.40	93.15	95.18
Eastern Asia	41.36	69.73	75.68	82.61	87.99	92.29	95.84	98.55
Europe	62.95	70.14	78.36	84.58	89.32	93.33	96.78	99.51
Eastern Europe	60.56	64.03	74.47	81.78	86.73	90.50	93.52	95.78
Southern Europe	61.45	74.57	79.97	84.84	89.28	93.26	96.85	99.77
Western Europe	65.14	75.30	81.18	86.60	91.44	95.78	99.66	102.80
Northern Europe	66.83	74.92	80.88	86.04	90.48	94.36	97.76	100.45
Latin America and the Caribbean	49.74	67.07	76.15	82.39	87.24	91.18	94.44	96.92
South America	50.28	66.48	76.03	82.19	87.11	91.18	94.60	97.21
Caribbean	50.78	64.89	73.90	80.29	85.39	89.45	92.79	95.36
Central America	47.67	69.50	76.93	83.30	87.97	91.56	94.41	96.55
Northern America	66.10	74.52	79.93	86.41	91.01	94.44	97.09	99.02
Oceania	58.03	71.76	78.96	84.47	89.05	92.92	96.24	98.89
Polynesia	46.75	68.90	77.98	83.51	88.01	91.71	94.70	96.96
Micronesia	51.76	70.26	79.62	84.42	88.78	92.65	95.95	98.59
Melanesia	36.51	59.30	73.82	82.11	87.44	91.22	94.08	96.09
Australia/New Zealand	67.02	76.29	81.26	85.89	89.98	93.75	97.27	100.23
			Female life expectancy at birth (years)					
World	47.93	67.63	77.51	84.50	89.15	92.65	95.26	97.15
More developed regions	68.54	79.40	85.25	90.74	94.76	97.96	100.62	102.66
Less developed regions	41.88	65.09	76.31	83.69	88.35	91.82	94.41	96.28
Africa	39.12	49.99	67.69	79.10	85.06	88.83	91.51	93.39
Southern Africa	45.61	49.06	56.01	77.49	87.18	92.07	95.07	97.04
Eastern Africa	37.67	43.77	65.48	78.60	84.94	88.76	91.42	93.27
Middle Africa	37.76	43.77	63.41	76.12	82.98	87.22	90.20	92.27
Western Africa	36.85	50.27	67.37	78.78	84.49	88.05	90.63	92.46
Northern Africa	43.02	68.21	79.33	85.17	89.14	92.24	94.71	96.58
Asia	42.12	69.02	79.37	85.51	89.71	93.00	95.53	97.39
Western Asia	46.79	71.31	81.01	85.61	88.86	91.68	93.96	95.56
South-central Asia	38.87	63.93	77.12	84.23	88.45	91.43	93.69	95.34
South-eastern Asia	42.09	69.15	79.89	85.98	90.01	93.09	95.50	97.27
Eastern Asia	44.66	74.75	81.64	87.61	92.30	96.02	99.10	101.46

TABLE A10 (*continued*)

Major area and region	*1950-1955*	*2000-2005*	*2050-2055*	*2100-2105*	*2150-2155*	*2200-2205*	*2250-2255*	*2295-2300*
Europe	67.95	78.20	84.27	89.68	93.71	97.11	100.03	102.35
Eastern Europe	67.02	74.44	80.79	86.91	90.92	93.98	96.45	98.30
Southern Europe	65.15	80.95	85.89	90.08	93.92	97.35	100.42	102.92
Western Europe	69.89	81.72	87.14	91.86	96.05	99.80	103.15	105.86
Northern Europe	71.51	80.51	86.06	90.70	94.60	97.96	100.88	103.18
Latin America and the Caribbean	53.10	73.90	82.69	87.54	91.36	94.48	97.07	99.07
South America	53.85	73.93	83.02	87.67	91.43	94.58	97.24	99.31
Caribbean	53.54	68.97	78.02	83.75	88.44	92.12	95.06	97.32
Central America	50.77	75.39	82.94	88.05	91.80	94.73	97.06	98.83
Northern America	71.92	80.13	84.80	90.86	95.02	98.05	100.35	102.00
Oceania	62.90	76.64	84.00	88.81	92.90	96.40	99.31	101.62
Polynesia	50.89	73.44	82.97	87.93	91.84	95.06	97.62	99.56
Micronesia	55.33	73.98	84.39	88.61	92.50	95.92	98.77	101.05
Melanesia	38.60	61.66	77.32	85.22	89.98	93.30	95.79	97.56
Australia/New Zealand	72.29	81.81	86.78	90.88	94.53	97.87	100.95	103.53

TABLE A11. TOTAL POPULATION BY COUNTRY, MEDIUM SCENARIO: 1950-2300

Country or area	*1950*	*2000*	*2050*	*2100*	*2150*	*2200*	*2250*	*2300*
				Population (thousands)				
Afghanistan	8 151	21 391	69 517	90 255	76 818	70 442	71 681	73 410
Albania	1 215	3 113	3 670	3 252	2 983	3 042	3 153	3 259
Algeria	8 753	30 245	48 667	45 607	42 572	43 287	44 549	45 619
Angola	4 131	12 386	43 131	63 019	57 121	53 234	54 475	56 173
Argentina	17 150	37 074	52 805	51 002	47 108	47 650	49 409	50 983
Armenia	1 354	3 112	2 334	1 623	1 563	1 624	1 684	1 739
Australia	8 219	19 153	25 560	24 583	24 934	25 921	26 839	27 702
Austria	6 935	8 102	7 376	6 199	6 352	6 627	6 885	7 119
Azerbaijan	2 896	8 157	10 942	10 324	9 852	10 098	10 352	10 539
Bahamas	79	303	395	365	346	353	361	368
Bahrain	116	677	1 270	1 183	1 078	1 097	1 134	1 166
Bangladesh	41 783	137 952	254 599	259 946	234 356	232 414	238 173	242 696
Barbados	211	267	258	211	210	218	225	232
Belarus	7 745	10 034	7 539	5 745	5 839	6 077	6 269	6 428
Belgium	8 639	10 251	10 221	9 543	9 862	10 299	10 682	11 015
Belize	69	240	421	411	376	380	392	402
Benin	2 046	6 222	15 602	18 741	16 974	16 420	16 889	17 301
Bhutan	734	2 063	5 288	6 417	5 788	5 512	5 633	5 759
Bolivia	2 714	8 317	15 748	16 838	14 760	14 281	14 763	15 230
Bosnia and Herzegovina	2 661	3 977	3 564	2 737	2 737	2 846	2 933	3 004
Botswana	419	1 725	1 380	1 369	1 372	1 418	1 481	1 522
Brazil	53 975	171 796	233 140	212 450	202 206	208 831	216 338	222 609
Brunei Darussalam	48	334	685	699	651	668	693	716
Bulgaria	7 251	8 099	5 255	3 969	3 990	4 151	4 287	4 404
Burkina Faso	3 960	11 905	42 373	65 179	62 177	58 764	59 747	61 178
Burundi	2 456	6 267	19 459	27 614	25 958	24 781	25 396	26 066
Cambodia	4 346	13 147	29 567	34 409	31 078	29 727	30 360	30 932
Cameroon	4 466	15 117	24 948	27 045	24 868	24 518	25 382	26 028
Canada	13 737	30 769	39 085	36 234	37 143	38 539	39 781	40 876
Cape Verde	146	436	812	833	764	763	787	807
Central African Republic	1 314	3 715	6 563	7 517	6 922	6 777	7 021	7 215
Chad	2 658	7 861	25 359	34 609	31 352	29 739	30 461	31 274
Channel Islands	102	144	126	112	116	121	127	131
Chile	6 082	15 224	21 805	21 359	19 845	20 016	20 651	21 166
China	554 760	1 275 215	1 395 182	1 181 496	1 149 121	1 200 725	1 246 731	1 285 238
China, Hong Kong SAR	1 974	6 807	9 431	8 084	8 057	8 347	8 577	8 764
China, Macao SAR	190	450	578	487	489	507	523	537
Colombia	12 568	42 120	67 491	67 519	60 233	58 903	60 739	62 254
Comoros	173	705	1 816	2 195	1 987	1 895	1 934	1 972
Congo	808	3 447	10 643	14 561	13 470	12 916	13 183	13 435
Costa Rica	966	3 929	6 512	6 190	5 818	5 916	6 064	6 176
Côte d'Ivoire	2 775	15 827	27 572	30 123	27 275	26 491	27 317	28 017
Croatia	3 850	4 446	3 587	3 246	3 351	3 487	3 598	3 689
Cuba	5 850	11 202	10 074	8 165	8 141	8 481	8 787	9 068
Cyprus	494	783	892	787	753	777	801	822
Czech Republic	8 925	10 269	8 553	6 650	6 785	7 041	7 274	7 483

TABLE A11 (*continued*)

Country or area	*1950*	*2000*	*2050*	*2100*	*2150*	*2200*	*2250*	*2300*
				Population (thousands)				
Dem. People's Rep. of Korea	10 815	22 268	24 966	22 515	21 990	22 812	23 499	24 056
Dem. Rep. of the Congo	12 184	48 571	151 644	203 341	182 502	172 953	177 611	182 697
Dem. Rep. of Timor-Leste	433	702	1 433	1 460	1 305	1 274	1 307	1 334
Denmark	4 271	5 322	5 273	4 902	5 046	5 242	5 413	5 560
Djibouti	62	666	1 395	1 706	1 547	1 485	1 526	1 564
Dominican Republic	2 353	8 353	11 876	10 998	9 500	9 336	9 716	10 060
Ecuador	3 387	12 420	18 724	17 866	16 188	16 234	16 820	17 338
Egypt	21 834	67 784	127 407	131 819	118 772	117 851	121 595	124 715
El Salvador	1 951	6 209	9 793	9 705	8 695	8 600	8 872	9 104
Equatorial Guinea	226	456	1 177	1 461	1 315	1 270	1 307	1 340
Eritrea	1 140	3 712	10 539	12 910	11 681	11 262	11 584	11 876
Estonia	1 101	1 367	657	522	540	560	576	588
Ethiopia	18 434	65 590	170 987	222 214	204 944	196 592	201 427	206 512
Fiji	289	814	969	889	789	781	809	832
Finland	4 009	5 177	4 941	4 597	4 747	4 955	5 144	5 314
France	41 829	59 296	64 230	60 172	61 220	63 897	66 291	68 502
French Guiana	25	164	354	364	327	324	335	344
French Polynesia	61	233	355	339	318	324	334	343
Gabon	469	1 258	2 488	2 746	2 476	2 406	2 471	2 525
Gambia	294	1 312	2 905	3 322	2 990	2 876	2 950	3 017
Georgia	3 527	5 262	3 472	2 684	2 631	2 732	2 815	2 881
Germany	68 376	82 282	79 145	73 069	75 813	79 395	82 564	85 334
Ghana	4 900	19 593	39 548	43 899	40 173	39 192	40 261	41 147
Greece	7 566	10 903	9 814	7 519	7 524	7 818	8 075	8 303
Guadeloupe	210	428	467	408	404	417	429	439
Guam	60	155	248	249	221	218	227	234
Guatemala	2 969	11 423	26 166	29 358	26 051	25 460	26 263	26 954
Guinea	2 550	8 117	19 591	23 783	21 268	20 318	20 833	21 353
Guinea-Bissau	505	1 367	4 719	6 969	6 425	6 022	6 138	6 305
Guyana	423	759	507	360	333	340	351	360
Haiti	3 261	8 005	12 429	12 723	10 836	10 442	10 817	11 134
Honduras	1 380	6 457	12 630	13 263	11 702	11 431	11 801	12 117
Hungary	9 338	10 012	7 589	6 211	6 435	6 708	6 940	7 140
Iceland	143	282	330	300	291	301	311	321
India	357 561	1 016 938	1 531 438	1 458 360	1 308 190	1 304 534	1 342 329	1 371 709
Indonesia	79 538	211 559	293 797	272 807	257 207	263 036	270 296	276 190
Iran, Islamic Rep. of	16 913	66 443	105 485	98 223	92 550	94 900	98 035	100 715
Iraq	5 158	23 224	57 932	68 042	61 717	60 072	61 730	63 066
Ireland	2 969	3 819	4 996	4 521	4 452	4 637	4 809	4 962
Israel	1 258	6 042	9 989	9 833	8 873	8 817	9 111	9 370
Italy	47 104	57 536	44 875	33 806	34 090	35 442	36 669	37 801
Jamaica	1 403	2 580	3 669	3 458	3 187	3 223	3 317	3 396
Japan	83 625	127 034	109 722	89 886	91 068	94 547	97 660	100 562
Jordan	472	5 035	10 154	10 664	9 757	9 659	9 904	10 077
Kazakhstan	6 703	15 640	13 941	11 677	11 079	11 422	11 751	12 019
Kenya	6 265	30 549	43 984	45 814	44 012	44 178	45 782	46 887

TABLE A11 (*continued*)

Country or area	1950	2000	2050	2100	2150	2200	2250	2300
			Population (thousands)					
Kuwait	152	2 247	4 926	4 559	4 142	4 158	4 288	4 393
Kyrgyzstan	1 740	4 921	7 235	6 758	6 348	6 489	6 702	6 882
Lao People's Dem. Republic	1 755	5 279	11 448	12 782	11 453	11 155	11 477	11 737
Latvia	1 949	2 373	1 331	1 031	1 067	1 109	1 143	1 172
Lebanon	1 443	3 478	4 946	4 506	4 291	4 420	4 567	4 694
Lesotho	734	1 785	1 377	1 648	1 682	1 677	1 723	1 755
Liberia	824	2 943	9 821	13 523	12 157	11 514	11 791	12 076
Libyan Arab Jamahiriya	1 029	5 237	9 248	8 978	8 387	8 506	8 761	8 968
Lithuania	2 567	3 501	2 526	2 370	2 434	2 514	2 568	2 607
Luxembourg	296	435	716	711	732	766	795	822
Madagascar	4 230	15 970	46 292	61 608	57 041	54 770	56 051	57 367
Malawi	2 881	11 370	25 949	32 789	30 115	29 156	30 141	30 982
Malaysia	6 110	23 001	39 551	39 622	36 244	36 264	37 422	38 346
Maldives	82	291	819	1 011	927	900	923	944
Mali	3 520	11 904	45 998	70 488	64 834	60 785	61 697	62 986
Malta	312	389	402	376	389	407	423	437
Martinique	222	386	413	376	371	383	393	401
Mauritania	825	2 645	7 497	9 754	8 939	8 576	8 788	9 002
Mauritius	493	1 186	1 461	1 336	1 306	1 353	1 394	1 428
Mexico	27 737	98 933	140 228	128 093	118 947	120 600	124 072	126 875
Micronesia, Fed. States of	32	107	158	174	154	149	153	156
Mongolia	761	2 500	3 773	3 427	3 145	3 202	3 310	3 407
Morocco	8 953	29 108	47 064	46 505	42 894	43 184	44 616	45 781
Mozambique	6 442	17 861	31 275	34 432	31 024	30 291	31 502	32 474
Myanmar	17 832	47 544	64 493	60 016	55 693	56 611	58 368	59 710
Namibia	511	1 894	2 654	2 899	2 768	2 770	2 877	2 954
Nepal	8 643	23 518	50 810	58 289	51 928	49 738	50 839	51 789
Netherlands	10 114	15 898	16 954	15 945	16 383	17 042	17 640	18 172
Netherlands Antilles	112	215	249	227	218	226	234	241
New Caledonia	65	215	382	365	335	338	348	356
New Zealand	1 908	3 784	4 512	4 245	4 273	4 441	4 591	4 726
Nicaragua	1 134	5 073	10 868	12 052	10 625	10 241	10 551	10 850
Niger	2 500	10 742	53 037	98 599	98 589	90 775	91 289	93 820
Nigeria	29 790	114 746	258 478	302 459	276 720	268 436	276 210	282 809
Norway	3 265	4 473	4 895	4 498	4 577	4 772	4 941	5 088
Occupied Palestinian Territory	1 005	3 191	11 114	14 932	13 576	12 856	13 132	13 484
Oman	456	2 609	6 812	8 198	7 377	7 042	7 223	7 421
Pakistan	39 659	142 654	348 700	408 534	358 793	342 511	351 082	359 100
Panama	860	2 950	5 140	5 137	4 626	4 610	4 781	4 936
Papua New Guinea	1 798	5 334	11 110	12 429	11 202	10 792	11 078	11 329
Paraguay	1 488	5 470	12 111	13 558	11 943	11 556	11 927	12 286
Peru	7 632	25 952	41 105	39 787	35 966	35 928	37 031	37 913
Philippines	19 996	75 711	126 965	128 798	118 182	118 544	122 389	125 433
Poland	24 824	38 671	33 004	26 094	25 686	26 626	27 410	28 051
Portugal	8 405	10 016	9 027	7 335	7 401	7 729	8 028	8 302
Puerto Rico	2 218	3 816	3 723	3 073	3 001	3 084	3 155	3 210
Qatar	25	581	874	848	772	771	790	804

TABLE A11 (*continued*)

Country or area	1950	2000	2050	2100	2150	2200	2250	2300
			Population (thousands)					
Republic of Korea	18 859	46 835	46 418	37 250	37 411	39 070	40 422	41 491
Republic of Moldova	2 341	4 283	3 580	2 756	2 652	2 751	2 850	2 943
Réunion	248	723	1 014	977	947	971	996	1 015
Romania	16 311	22 480	18 063	14 769	15 269	15 881	16 378	16 784
Russian Federation	102 702	145 612	101 456	79 537	83 083	86 743	89 491	91 647
Rwanda	2 162	7 724	16 973	20 552	19 090	18 659	19 246	19 742
St. Lucia	79	146	163	150	139	142	146	149
St. Vincent and Grenadines	67	118	129	114	111	114	119	122
Samoa	82	173	254	295	265	254	260	267
Sao Tome and Principe	60	149	349	406	371	360	370	380
Saudi Arabia	3 201	22 147	54 738	61 331	54 968	53 716	55 382	56 880
Senegal	2 500	9 393	21 589	25 256	22 824	22 189	23 028	23 839
Serbia and Montenegro	7 131	10 555	9 371	7 804	7 624	7 933	8 208	8 437
Sierra Leone	1 944	4 415	10 339	11 027	8 663	7 994	8 316	8 647
Singapore	1 022	4 016	4 538	3 586	3 632	3 783	3 911	4 014
Slovakia	3 463	5 391	4 948	3 998	3 949	4 104	4 235	4 346
Slovenia	1 473	1 990	1 569	1 159	1 157	1 199	1 236	1 268
Solomon Islands	90	437	1 071	1 188	1 040	1 002	1 033	1 063
Somalia	2 264	8 720	39 669	66 074	63 676	59 823	60 751	62 273
South Africa	13 683	44 000	40 243	38 322	38 045	39 958	41 633	42 804
Spain	28 009	40 752	37 336	29 122	29 177	30 491	31 689	32 787
Sri Lanka	7 483	18 595	21 172	18 694	18 111	18 770	19 411	19 943
Sudan	9 190	31 437	60 133	65 157	58 250	56 372	57 969	59 292
Suriname	215	425	459	428	397	399	408	415
Swaziland	273	1 044	948	945	923	952	1 003	1 035
Sweden	7 014	8 856	8 700	8 112	8 346	8 709	9 046	9 355
Switzerland	4 694	7 173	5 810	4 827	4 942	5 136	5 323	5 499
Syrian Arab Republic	3 495	16 560	34 174	35 012	31 697	31 530	32 558	33 413
Tajikistan	1 532	6 089	9 552	8 941	8 077	8 099	8 282	8 427
TFYR Macedonia	1 230	2 024	2 156	1 912	1 852	1 919	1 979	2 032
Thailand	19 626	60 925	77 079	70 351	69 186	72 140	74 748	76 861
Togo	1 329	4 562	10 005	11 493	10 546	10 341	10 671	10 928
Tonga	47	101	122	123	109	106	109	112
Trinidad and Tobago	636	1 289	1 221	1 051	1 037	1 080	1 114	1 141
Tunisia	3 530	9 519	12 887	11 390	10 809	11 162	11 551	11 887
Turkey	21 484	68 281	97 759	90 323	85 548	87 452	89 796	91 583
Turkmenistan	1 211	4 643	7 541	7 185	6 606	6 680	6 885	7 051
Uganda	5 210	23 487	103 248	167 099	158 825	149 004	151 074	154 511
Ukraine	37 298	49 688	31 749	24 129	24 794	25 798	26 652	27 387
United Arab Emirates	70	2 820	4 112	3 652	3 318	3 339	3 449	3 547
United Kingdom	49 816	58 689	66 166	64 375	66 236	68 895	71 229	73 239
United Rep. of Tanzania	7 886	34 837	69 112	76 662	69 351	67 890	70 018	71 534
United States of America	157 813	285 003	408 695	437 155	452 753	470 045	483 033	493 038
United States Virgin Islands	27	109	133	123	116	119	123	127
Uruguay	2 239	3 342	4 128	3 926	3 590	3 596	3 700	3 782
Uzbekistan	6 314	24 913	37 818	34 369	31 921	32 552	33 450	34 146

TABLE A11 (*continued*)

Country or area	*1950*	*2000*	*2050*	*2100*	*2150*	*2200*	*2250*	*2300*
			Population (thousands)					
Vanuatu	48	197	435	481	423	404	415	425
Venezuela	5 094	24 277	41 733	40 752	36 943	37 146	38 483	39 733
Viet Nam	27 367	78 137	117 693	110 152	104 719	107 501	110 845	113 585
Western Sahara	14	285	641	708	646	633	650	663
Yemen	4 316	18 017	84 385	144 206	136 745	126 633	127 591	129 861
Zambia	2 440	10 419	18 528	22 106	20 630	20 123	20 827	21 421
Zimbabwe	2 744	12 650	12 658	12 562	12 034	12 437	13 178	13 662

TABLE A12. AVERAGE ANNUAL RATE OF POPULATION CHANGE BY COUNTRY, MEDIUM SCENARIO: 1950-2300

Country or areay	*1950-2000*	*2000-2050*	*2050-2100*	*2100-2150*	*2150-2200*	*2200-2250*	*2250-2300*
	Average annual rate of change (per cent)						
Afghanistan	1.93	2.36	0.52	-0.32	-0.17	0.03	0.05
Albania	1.88	0.33	-0.24	-0.17	0.04	0.07	0.07
Algeria	2.48	0.95	-0.13	-0.14	0.03	0.06	0.05
Angola	2.20	2.50	0.76	-0.20	-0.14	0.05	0.06
Argentina	1.54	0.71	-0.07	-0.16	0.02	0.07	0.06
Armenia	1.67	-0.58	-0.73	-0.08	0.08	0.07	0.06
Australia	1.69	0.58	-0.08	0.03	0.08	0.07	0.06
Austria	0.31	-0.19	-0.35	0.05	0.08	0.08	0.07
Azerbaijan	2.07	0.59	-0.12	-0.09	0.05	0.05	0.04
Bahamas	2.69	0.53	-0.16	-0.11	0.04	0.05	0.04
Bahrain	3.53	1.26	-0.14	-0.19	0.03	0.07	0.06
Bangladesh	2.39	1.23	0.04	-0.21	-0.02	0.05	0.04
Barbados	0.47	-0.07	-0.41	0.00	0.07	0.06	0.06
Belarus	0.52	-0.57	-0.54	0.03	0.08	0.06	0.05
Belgium	0.34	-0.01	-0.14	0.07	0.09	0.07	0.06
Belize	2.50	1.12	-0.05	-0.18	0.02	0.06	0.05
Benin	2.22	1.84	0.37	-0.20	-0.07	0.06	0.05
Bhutan	2.07	1.88	0.39	-0.21	-0.10	0.04	0.04
Bolivia	2.24	1.28	0.13	-0.26	-0.07	0.07	0.06
Bosnia and Herzegovina	0.80	-0.22	-0.53	0.00	0.08	0.06	0.05
Botswana	2.83	-0.45	-0.02	0.00	0.07	0.09	0.05
Brazil	2.32	0.61	-0.19	-0.10	0.06	0.07	0.06
Brunei Darussalam	3.88	1.44	0.04	-0.14	0.05	0.07	0.07
Bulgaria	0.22	-0.86	-0.56	0.01	0.08	0.06	0.05
Burkina Faso	2.20	2.54	0.86	-0.09	-0.11	0.03	0.05
Burundi	1.87	2.27	0.70	-0.12	-0.09	0.05	0.05
Cambodia	2.21	1.62	0.30	-0.20	-0.09	0.04	0.04
Cameroon	2.44	1.00	0.16	-0.17	-0.03	0.07	0.05
Canada	1.61	0.48	-0.15	0.05	0.07	0.06	0.05
Cape Verde	2.18	1.25	0.05	-0.17	0.00	0.06	0.05
Central African Republic	2.08	1.14	0.27	-0.16	-0.04	0.07	0.05
Chad	2.17	2.34	0.62	-0.20	-0.11	0.05	0.05
Channel Islands	0.69	-0.28	-0.22	0.07	0.09	0.08	0.07
Chile	1.84	0.72	-0.04	-0.15	0.02	0.06	0.05
China	1.66	0.18	-0.33	-0.06	0.09	0.08	0.06
China, Hong Kong SAR	2.48	0.65	-0.31	-0.01	0.07	0.05	0.04
China, Macao SAR	1.72	0.50	-0.34	0.01	0.07	0.06	0.05
Colombia	2.42	0.94	0.00	-0.23	-0.04	0.06	0.05
Comoros	2.81	1.89	0.38	-0.20	-0.09	0.04	0.04
Congo	2.90	2.25	0.63	-0.16	-0.08	0.04	0.04
Costa Rica	2.81	1.01	-0.10	-0.12	0.03	0.05	0.04
Côte d'Ivoire	3.48	1.11	0.18	-0.20	-0.06	0.06	0.05
Croatia	0.29	-0.43	-0.20	0.06	0.08	0.06	0.05
Cuba	1.30	-0.21	-0.42	-0.01	0.08	0.07	0.06
Cyprus	0.92	0.26	-0.25	-0.09	0.06	0.06	0.05
Czech Republic	0.28	-0.37	-0.50	0.04	0.07	0.07	0.06

TABLE A12 (*continued*)

Country or areay	*1950-2000*	*2000-2050*	*2050-2100*	*2100-2150*	*2150-2200*	*2200-2250*	*2250-2300*
	Average annual rate of change (per cent)						
Dem. People's Rep. of Korea	1.44	0.23	-0.21	-0.05	0.07	0.06	0.05
Dem. Rep. of the Congo	2.77	2.28	0.59	-0.22	-0.11	0.05	0.06
Dem. Rep. of Timor-Leste	0.96	1.43	0.04	-0.22	-0.05	0.05	0.04
Denmark	0.44	-0.02	-0.15	0.06	0.08	0.06	0.05
Djibouti	4.75	1.48	0.40	-0.19	-0.08	0.05	0.05
Dominican Republic	2.53	0.70	-0.15	-0.29	-0.03	0.08	0.07
Ecuador	2.60	0.82	-0.09	-0.20	0.01	0.07	0.06
Egypt	2.27	1.26	0.07	-0.21	-0.02	0.06	0.05
El Salvador	2.32	0.91	-0.02	-0.22	-0.02	0.06	0.05
Equatorial Guinea	1.41	1.90	0.43	-0.21	-0.07	0.06	0.05
Eritrea	2.36	2.09	0.41	-0.20	-0.07	0.06	0.05
Estonia	0.43	-1.46	-0.46	0.07	0.07	0.06	0.04
Ethiopia	2.54	1.92	0.52	-0.16	-0.08	0.05	0.05
Fiji	2.07	0.35	-0.17	-0.24	-0.02	0.07	0.06
Finland	0.51	-0.09	-0.14	0.06	0.09	0.07	0.06
France	0.70	0.16	-0.13	0.03	0.09	0.07	0.07
French Guiana	3.73	1.54	0.05	-0.21	-0.02	0.07	0.06
French Polynesia	2.69	0.84	-0.09	-0.13	0.04	0.06	0.05
Gabon	1.97	1.36	0.20	-0.21	-0.06	0.05	0.04
Gambia	2.99	1.59	0.27	-0.21	-0.08	0.05	0.05
Georgia	0.80	-0.83	-0.52	-0.04	0.08	0.06	0.05
Germany	0.37	-0.08	-0.16	0.07	0.09	0.08	0.07
Ghana	2.77	1.40	0.21	-0.18	-0.05	0.05	0.04
Greece	0.73	-0.21	-0.53	0.00	0.08	0.06	0.06
Guadeloupe	1.42	0.17	-0.27	-0.02	0.06	0.05	0.04
Guam	1.91	0.93	0.01	-0.24	-0.02	0.07	0.07
Guatemala	2.69	1.66	0.23	-0.24	-0.05	0.06	0.05
Guinea	2.32	1.76	0.39	-0.22	-0.09	0.05	0.05
Guinea-Bissau	1.99	2.48	0.78	-0.16	-0.13	0.04	0.05
Guyana	1.17	-0.81	-0.69	-0.15	0.05	0.06	0.05
Haiti	1.80	0.88	0.05	-0.32	-0.07	0.07	0.06
Honduras	3.09	1.34	0.10	-0.25	-0.05	0.06	0.05
Hungary	0.14	-0.55	-0.40	0.07	0.08	0.07	0.06
Iceland	1.36	0.31	-0.19	-0.06	0.07	0.07	0.06
India	2.09	0.82	-0.10	-0.22	-0.01	0.06	0.04
Indonesia	1.96	0.66	-0.15	-0.12	0.04	0.05	0.04
Iran, Islamic Rep. of	2.74	0.92	-0.14	-0.12	0.05	0.07	0.05
Iraq	3.01	1.83	0.32	-0.20	-0.05	0.05	0.04
Ireland	0.50	0.54	-0.20	-0.03	0.08	0.07	0.06
Israel	3.14	1.01	-0.03	-0.21	-0.01	0.07	0.06
Italy	0.40	-0.50	-0.57	0.02	0.08	0.07	0.06
Jamaica	1.22	0.70	-0.12	-0.16	0.02	0.06	0.05
Japan	0.84	-0.29	-0.40	0.03	0.07	0.06	0.06
Jordan	4.73	1.40	0.10	-0.18	-0.02	0.05	0.03
Kazakhstan	1.69	-0.23	-0.35	-0.10	0.06	0.06	0.05
Kenya	3.17	0.73	0.08	-0.08	0.01	0.07	0.05
Kuwait	5.38	1.57	-0.15	-0.19	0.01	0.06	0.05

TABLE A12 (*continued*)

Country or areay	*1950-2000*	*2000-2050*	*2050-2100*	*2100-2150*	*2150-2200*	*2200-2250*	*2250-2300*
	Average annual rate of change (per cent)						
Kyrgyzstan	2.08	0.77	-0.14	-0.12	0.04	0.06	0.05
Lao People's Dem. Republic	2.20	1.55	0.22	-0.22	-0.05	0.06	0.04
Latvia	0.39	-1.16	-0.51	0.07	0.08	0.06	0.05
Lebanon	1.76	0.70	-0.19	-0.10	0.06	0.07	0.05
Lesotho	1.78	-0.52	0.36	0.04	-0.01	0.05	0.04
Liberia	2.55	2.41	0.64	-0.21	-0.11	0.05	0.05
Libyan Arab Jamahiriya	3.25	1.14	-0.06	-0.14	0.03	0.06	0.05
Lithuania	0.62	-0.65	-0.13	0.05	0.06	0.04	0.03
Luxembourg	0.77	0.99	-0.01	0.06	0.09	0.08	0.07
Madagascar	2.66	2.13	0.57	-0.15	-0.08	0.05	0.05
Malawi	2.75	1.65	0.47	-0.17	-0.06	0.07	0.06
Malaysia	2.65	1.08	0.00	-0.18	0.00	0.06	0.05
Maldives	2.53	2.07	0.42	-0.17	-0.06	0.05	0.04
Mali	2.44	2.70	0.85	-0.17	-0.13	0.03	0.04
Malta	0.44	0.07	-0.14	0.07	0.09	0.08	0.06
Martinique	1.10	0.14	-0.19	-0.02	0.07	0.05	0.04
Mauritania	2.33	2.08	0.53	-0.17	-0.08	0.05	0.05
Mauritius	1.75	0.42	-0.18	-0.05	0.07	0.06	0.05
Mexico	2.54	0.70	-0.18	-0.15	0.03	0.06	0.04
Micronesia, Fed. States of	2.41	0.78	0.18	-0.24	-0.07	0.05	0.05
Mongolia	2.38	0.82	-0.19	-0.17	0.04	0.07	0.06
Morocco	2.36	0.96	-0.02	-0.16	0.01	0.07	0.05
Mozambique	2.04	1.12	0.19	-0.21	-0.05	0.08	0.06
Myanmar	1.96	0.61	-0.14	-0.15	0.03	0.06	0.05
Namibia	2.62	0.68	0.18	-0.09	0.00	0.08	0.05
Nepal	2.00	1.54	0.27	-0.23	-0.09	0.04	0.04
Netherlands	0.90	0.13	-0.12	0.05	0.08	0.07	0.06
Netherlands Antilles	1.31	0.29	-0.19	-0.07	0.07	0.07	0.06
New Caledonia	2.40	1.15	-0.09	-0.17	0.02	0.06	0.05
New Zealand	1.37	0.35	-0.12	0.01	0.08	0.07	0.06
Nicaragua	3.00	1.52	0.21	-0.25	-0.07	0.06	0.06
Niger	2.92	3.19	1.24	0.00	-0.17	0.01	0.05
Nigeria	2.70	1.62	0.31	-0.18	-0.06	0.06	0.05
Norway	0.63	0.18	-0.17	0.03	0.08	0.07	0.06
Occupied Palestinian Territory	2.31	2.50	0.59	-0.19	-0.11	0.04	0.05
Oman	3.49	1.92	0.37	-0.21	-0.09	0.05	0.05
Pakistan	2.56	1.79	0.32	-0.26	-0.09	0.05	0.05
Panama	2.47	1.11	0.00	-0.21	-0.01	0.07	0.06
Papua New Guinea	2.17	1.47	0.22	-0.21	-0.07	0.05	0.04
Paraguay	2.60	1.59	0.23	-0.25	-0.07	0.06	0.06
Peru	2.45	0.92	-0.07	-0.20	0.00	0.06	0.05
Philippines	2.66	1.03	0.03	-0.17	0.01	0.06	0.05
Poland	0.89	-0.32	-0.47	-0.03	0.07	0.06	0.05
Portugal	0.35	-0.21	-0.41	0.02	0.09	0.08	0.07
Puerto Rico	1.09	-0.05	-0.38	-0.05	0.05	0.05	0.03
Qatar	6.29	0.81	-0.06	-0.19	0.00	0.05	0.03

TABLE A12 (*continued*)

Country or areay	*1950-2000*	*2000-2050*	*2050-2100*	*2100-2150*	*2150-2200*	*2200-2250*	*2250-2300*
	Average annual rate of change (per cent)						
Republic of Korea	1.82	-0.02	-0.44	0.01	0.09	0.07	0.05
Republic of Moldova	1.21	-0.36	-0.52	-0.08	0.07	0.07	0.06
Réunion	2.14	0.68	-0.07	-0.06	0.05	0.05	0.04
Romania	0.64	-0.44	-0.40	0.07	0.08	0.06	0.05
Russian Federation	0.70	-0.72	-0.49	0.09	0.09	0.06	0.05
Rwanda	2.55	1.57	0.38	-0.15	-0.05	0.06	0.05
St. Lucia	1.22	0.22	-0.16	-0.15	0.03	0.05	0.04
St. Vincent and Grenadines	1.13	0.18	-0.23	-0.07	0.07	0.07	0.06
Samoa	1.49	0.77	0.30	-0.22	-0.08	0.05	0.05
Sao Tome and Principe	1.81	1.70	0.30	-0.18	-0.06	0.05	0.05
Saudi Arabia	3.87	1.81	0.23	-0.22	-0.05	0.06	0.05
Senegal	2.65	1.66	0.31	-0.20	-0.06	0.07	0.07
Serbia and Montenegro	0.78	-0.24	-0.37	-0.05	0.08	0.07	0.06
Sierra Leone	1.64	1.70	0.13	-0.48	-0.16	0.08	0.08
Singapore	2.74	0.24	-0.47	0.03	0.08	0.07	0.05
Slovakia	0.88	-0.17	-0.43	-0.02	0.08	0.06	0.05
Slovenia	0.60	-0.48	-0.61	0.00	0.07	0.06	0.05
Solomon Islands	3.16	1.79	0.21	-0.27	-0.07	0.06	0.06
Somalia	2.70	3.03	1.02	-0.07	-0.12	0.03	0.05
South Africa	2.34	-0.18	-0.10	-0.01	0.10	0.08	0.06
Spain	0.75	-0.18	-0.50	0.00	0.09	0.08	0.07
Sri Lanka	1.82	0.26	-0.25	-0.06	0.07	0.07	0.05
Sudan	2.46	1.30	0.16	-0.22	-0.07	0.06	0.05
Suriname	1.36	0.15	-0.14	-0.15	0.01	0.05	0.03
Swaziland	2.68	-0.19	-0.01	-0.05	0.06	0.10	0.06
Sweden	0.47	-0.04	-0.14	0.06	0.09	0.08	0.07
Switzerland	0.85	-0.42	-0.37	0.05	0.08	0.07	0.07
Syrian Arab Republic	3.11	1.45	0.05	-0.20	-0.01	0.06	0.05
Tajikistan	2.76	0.90	-0.13	-0.20	0.01	0.04	0.03
TFYR Macedonia	1.00	0.13	-0.24	-0.06	0.07	0.06	0.05
Thailand	2.27	0.47	-0.18	-0.03	0.08	0.07	0.06
Togo	2.47	1.57	0.28	-0.17	-0.04	0.06	0.05
Tonga	1.52	0.39	0.01	-0.23	-0.05	0.06	0.05
Trinidad and Tobago	1.41	-0.11	-0.30	-0.03	0.08	0.06	0.05
Tunisia	1.98	0.61	-0.25	-0.10	0.06	0.07	0.06
Turkey	2.31	0.72	-0.16	-0.11	0.04	0.05	0.04
Turkmenistan	2.69	0.97	-0.10	-0.17	0.02	0.06	0.05
Uganda	3.01	2.96	0.96	-0.10	-0.13	0.03	0.04
Ukraine	0.57	-0.90	-0.55	0.05	0.08	0.07	0.05
United Arab Emirates	7.40	0.75	-0.24	-0.19	0.01	0.06	0.06
United Kingdom	0.33	0.24	-0.05	0.06	0.08	0.07	0.06
United Rep. of Tanzania	2.97	1.37	0.21	-0.20	-0.04	0.06	0.04
United States of America	1.18	0.72	0.13	0.07	0.07	0.05	0.04
United States Virgin Islands	2.80	0.40	-0.16	-0.11	0.06	0.07	0.06
Uruguay	0.80	0.42	-0.10	-0.18	0.00	0.06	0.04
Uzbekistan	2.75	0.83	-0.19	-0.15	0.04	0.05	0.04
Vanuatu	2.83	1.59	0.20	-0.26	-0.09	0.05	0.05

TABLE A12 (*continued*)

Country or areay	*1950-2000*	*2000-2050*	*2050-2100*	*2100-2150*	*2150-2200*	*2200-2250*	*2250-2300*
	Average annual rate of change (per cent)						
Venezuela..	3.12	1.08	-0.05	-0.20	0.01	0.07	0.06
Viet Nam...	2.10	0.82	-0.13	-0.10	0.05	0.06	0.05
Western Sahara	6.06	1.62	0.20	-0.18	-0.04	0.05	0.04
Yemen...	2.86	3.09	1.07	-0.11	-0.15	0.02	0.04
Zambia	2.90	1.15	0.35	-0.14	-0.05	0.07	0.06
Zimbabwe	3.06	0.00	-0.02	-0.09	0.07	0.12	0.07

TABLE A13. TOTAL FERTILITY BY COUNTRY, MEDIUM SCENARIO: SELECTED PERIODS

Country or area	1950-1955	2000-2005	2050-2055	2100-2105	2150-2155	2200-2205	2250-2255	2295-2300
	Total fertility (children per woman)							
Afghanistan	7.70	6.800	2.487	1.850	1.970	2.072	2.065	2.062
Albania	5.60	2.282	1.850	1.970	2.075	2.072	2.071	2.071
Algeria	7.28	2.797	1.850	1.900	2.051	2.050	2.050	2.050
Angola	6.39	7.200	2.678	1.850	1.900	2.041	2.034	2.032
Argentina	3.15	2.444	1.850	1.850	2.045	2.042	2.041	2.041
Armenia	4.49	1.150	1.850	2.066	2.060	2.057	2.055	2.054
Australia	3.18	1.696	1.850	2.060	2.057	2.055	2.054	2.054
Austria	2.09	1.276	1.930	2.063	2.061	2.059	2.058	2.058
Azerbaijan	5.49	2.100	1.850	2.050	2.068	2.066	2.065	2.065
Bahamas	4.05	2.291	1.850	1.970	2.049	2.045	2.044	2.044
Bahrain	6.97	2.657	1.850	1.900	2.055	2.053	2.051	2.051
Bangladesh	6.70	3.458	1.850	1.850	2.047	2.046	2.046	2.046
Barbados	4.67	1.500	1.850	2.047	2.043	2.040	2.038	2.038
Belarus	2.61	1.200	1.850	2.074	2.070	2.067	2.066	2.066
Belgium	2.33	1.660	1.900	2.059	2.056	2.055	2.054	2.053
Belize	6.65	3.152	1.850	1.850	2.039	2.034	2.032	2.031
Benin	6.80	5.655	1.974	1.850	2.039	2.032	2.031	2.030
Bhutan	5.90	5.024	1.984	1.850	2.052	2.050	2.050	2.050
Bolivia	6.75	3.820	1.850	1.850	2.070	2.061	2.056	2.054
Bosnia and Herzegovina	4.82	1.300	1.850	2.080	2.075	2.073	2.072	2.072
Botswana	6.70	3.704	1.850	1.850	2.042	2.032	2.030	2.030
Brazil	6.15	2.213	1.850	2.050	2.055	2.052	2.051	2.051
Brunei Darussalam	7.00	2.482	1.850	1.970	2.063	2.061	2.059	2.058
Bulgaria	2.48	1.100	1.850	2.059	2.054	2.052	2.051	2.050
Burkina Faso	6.33	6.683	2.617	1.850	1.900	2.033	2.031	2.030
Burundi	6.80	6.800	2.465	1.850	1.970	2.034	2.031	2.030
Cambodia	6.29	4.765	1.952	1.850	2.051	2.050	2.050	2.050
Cameroon	5.68	4.605	1.925	1.850	2.044	2.034	2.031	2.030
Canada	3.73	1.477	1.900	2.064	2.061	2.059	2.058	2.057
Cape Verde	6.60	3.302	1.850	1.850	2.032	2.030	2.030	2.030
Central African Republic	5.52	4.920	2.044	1.850	2.048	2.035	2.032	2.031
Chad	5.77	6.650	2.315	1.850	1.970	2.035	2.031	2.031
Channel Islands	2.07	1.540	1.900	2.067	2.064	2.062	2.061	2.060
Chile	4.95	2.353	1.850	1.850	2.042	2.041	2.040	2.040
China	6.22	1.825	1.850	2.095	2.085	2.082	2.081	2.080
China, Hong Kong SAR	4.44	1.000	1.850	2.075	2.073	2.071	2.070	2.070
China, Macao SAR	5.03	1.100	1.850	2.059	2.055	2.053	2.052	2.051
Colombia	6.76	2.623	1.850	1.850	2.060	2.055	2.053	2.052
Comoros	6.33	4.899	1.963	1.850	2.050	2.050	2.050	2.050
Congo	5.68	6.290	2.171	1.850	2.050	2.030	2.030	2.030
Costa Rica	6.72	2.280	1.850	1.970	2.051	2.050	2.050	2.050
Côte d'Ivoire	7.00	4.726	1.931	1.850	2.042	2.033	2.031	2.030
Croatia	2.76	1.650	1.900	2.070	2.066	2.063	2.062	2.061
Cuba	4.10	1.550	1.850	2.063	2.059	2.058	2.057	2.057
Cyprus	3.71	1.903	1.850	2.080	2.076	2.074	2.073	2.072

TABLE A13 (*continued*)

Country or area	*1950-1955*	*2000-2005*	*2050-2055*	*2100-2105*	*2150-2155*	*2200-2205*	*2250-2255*	*2295-2300*
	Total fertility (children per woman)							
Czech Republic	2.69	1.160	1.900	2.063	2.061	2.060	2.059	2.058
Dem. People's Rep. of Korea	3.35	2.021	1.850	2.065	2.055	2.052	2.051	2.050
Dem. Rep. of the Congo	6.00	6.700	2.357	1.850	1.970	2.038	2.033	2.031
Dem. Rep. of Timor-Leste	6.44	3.847	1.850	1.850	2.052	2.050	2.050	2.050
Denmark	2.54	1.770	1.900	2.070	2.067	2.065	2.064	2.063
Djibouti	7.80	5.695	2.165	1.850	2.050	2.042	2.040	2.039
Dominican Republic	7.40	2.710	1.850	1.850	2.078	2.068	2.062	2.058
Ecuador	6.70	2.764	1.850	1.850	2.059	2.054	2.052	2.051
Egypt	6.56	3.290	1.850	1.850	2.052	2.051	2.050	2.050
El Salvador	6.46	2.883	1.850	1.850	2.057	2.054	2.052	2.051
Equatorial Guinea	5.50	5.890	1.982	1.850	2.040	2.033	2.031	2.030
Eritrea	6.97	5.432	2.040	1.850	2.039	2.033	2.031	2.030
Estonia	2.06	1.220	1.900	2.062	2.058	2.057	2.056	2.056
Ethiopia	7.15	6.140	2.307	1.850	1.970	2.034	2.031	2.030
Fiji	6.63	2.877	1.850	1.850	2.065	2.063	2.061	2.061
Finland	2.97	1.730	1.900	2.056	2.053	2.052	2.051	2.051
France	2.73	1.890	1.850	2.061	2.058	2.056	2.055	2.055
French Guiana	5.00	3.327	1.850	1.850	2.053	2.052	2.051	2.050
French Polynesia	6.00	2.437	1.850	1.900	2.055	2.053	2.052	2.051
Gabon	4.00	3.987	1.851	1.850	2.036	2.032	2.030	2.030
Gambia	6.09	4.704	1.937	1.850	2.036	2.032	2.030	2.030
Georgia	3.00	1.400	1.850	2.071	2.064	2.061	2.060	2.059
Germany	2.16	1.350	1.900	2.064	2.061	2.059	2.058	2.058
Ghana	6.90	4.108	1.862	1.850	2.034	2.031	2.030	2.030
Greece	2.29	1.270	1.850	2.078	2.075	2.073	2.072	2.071
Guadeloupe	5.61	2.100	1.850	2.046	2.043	2.041	2.041	2.040
Guam	5.53	2.877	1.850	1.850	2.064	2.062	2.060	2.060
Guatemala	7.09	4.412	1.850	1.850	2.063	2.056	2.053	2.052
Guinea	7.00	5.823	2.121	1.850	2.050	2.033	2.031	2.030
Guinea-Bissau	5.58	7.100	2.566	1.850	1.900	2.035	2.032	2.031
Guyana	6.68	2.314	1.850	1.900	2.062	2.054	2.052	2.051
Haiti	6.30	3.983	1.862	1.850	2.118	2.090	2.074	2.065
Honduras	7.50	3.723	1.850	1.850	2.063	2.055	2.052	2.051
Hungary	2.73	1.200	1.900	2.060	2.056	2.055	2.054	2.053
Iceland	3.70	1.952	1.850	2.069	2.066	2.065	2.064	2.064
India	5.97	3.013	1.850	1.850	2.055	2.051	2.050	2.050
Indonesia	5.49	2.352	1.850	1.970	2.051	2.050	2.050	2.050
Iran, Islamic Rep. of	7.00	2.333	1.850	1.970	2.052	2.051	2.050	2.050
Iraq	7.18	4.770	1.850	1.850	2.050	2.050	2.050	2.050
Ireland	3.38	1.900	1.850	2.079	2.076	2.074	2.072	2.072
Israel	4.16	2.701	1.850	1.850	2.066	2.063	2.062	2.061
Italy	2.32	1.230	1.850	2.073	2.070	2.068	2.066	2.066
Jamaica	4.22	2.356	1.850	1.900	2.052	2.051	2.050	2.050
Japan	2.75	1.320	1.900	2.061	2.060	2.059	2.058	2.058
Jordan	7.38	3.566	1.850	1.850	2.051	2.050	2.050	2.050

TABLE A13 (*continued*)

Country or area	1950-1955	2000-2005	2050-2055	2100-2105	2150-2155	2200-2205	2250-2255	2295-2300
				Total fertility (children per woman)				
Kazakhstan	4.41	1.950	1.850	2.070	2.062	2.060	2.059	2.059
Kenya	7.51	4.000	1.850	1.850	2.038	2.032	2.030	2.030
Kuwait	7.21	2.662	1.850	1.850	2.035	2.033	2.032	2.031
Kyrgyzstan	4.51	2.644	1.850	1.900	2.038	2.034	2.032	2.032
Lao People's Dem. Republic	6.15	4.776	1.850	1.850	2.053	2.051	2.050	2.050
Latvia	2.00	1.100	1.900	2.065	2.060	2.058	2.058	2.057
Lebanon	5.74	2.179	1.850	2.050	2.055	2.052	2.051	2.050
Lesotho	5.84	3.835	1.850	1.850	2.031	2.030	2.030	2.030
Liberia	6.45	6.800	2.497	1.850	1.970	2.035	2.031	2.030
Libyan Arab Jamahiriya	6.87	3.015	1.850	1.850	2.053	2.051	2.050	2.050
Lithuania	2.71	1.250	1.850	2.061	2.059	2.058	2.058	2.058
Luxembourg	1.98	1.730	1.900	2.069	2.066	2.065	2.064	2.064
Madagascar	6.90	5.695	2.165	1.850	2.050	2.017	2.016	2.016
Malawi	6.78	6.096	2.290	1.850	2.050	2.037	2.033	2.031
Malaysia	6.83	2.896	1.850	1.850	2.063	2.061	2.061	2.060
Maldives	7.00	5.331	1.906	1.850	2.036	2.035	2.035	2.035
Mali	7.11	7.000	2.595	1.850	1.900	2.032	2.030	2.030
Malta	4.14	1.766	1.900	2.068	2.064	2.062	2.061	2.061
Martinique	5.71	1.900	1.850	2.047	2.043	2.041	2.041	2.040
Mauritania	6.30	5.791	2.219	1.850	2.050	2.032	2.031	2.030
Mauritius	6.27	1.947	1.850	2.049	2.044	2.043	2.042	2.042
Mexico	6.87	2.500	1.850	1.900	2.053	2.051	2.050	2.050
Micronesia, Fed. States of	7.20	3.798	1.850	1.850	2.071	2.070	2.070	2.070
Mongolia	6.00	2.418	1.850	1.900	2.058	2.053	2.051	2.051
Morocco	7.18	2.745	1.850	1.850	2.051	2.050	2.050	2.050
Mozambique	6.50	5.629	2.092	1.850	2.057	2.038	2.033	2.031
Myanmar	6.00	2.856	1.850	1.850	2.058	2.052	2.051	2.050
Namibia	6.00	4.563	1.910	1.850	2.039	2.028	2.026	2.025
Nepal	5.75	4.264	1.887	1.850	2.050	2.050	2.050	2.050
Netherlands	3.06	1.720	1.900	2.062	2.059	2.057	2.055	2.055
Netherlands Antilles	5.65	2.051	1.850	2.059	2.054	2.052	2.051	2.050
New Caledonia	5.00	2.453	1.850	1.850	2.056	2.054	2.052	2.052
New Zealand	3.69	2.010	1.850	2.068	2.064	2.063	2.062	2.061
Nicaragua	7.33	3.745	1.850	1.850	2.059	2.054	2.052	2.051
Niger	7.70	8.000	3.351	1.850	1.850	2.034	2.031	2.030
Nigeria	6.90	5.420	2.047	1.850	2.045	2.038	2.036	2.035
Norway	2.60	1.795	1.850	2.063	2.061	2.059	2.058	2.058
Occupied Palestinian Territory	7.38	5.571	2.133	1.850	2.050	2.051	2.051	2.050
Oman	7.20	4.964	2.005	1.850	2.054	2.051	2.051	2.050
Pakistan	6.28	5.080	1.888	1.850	2.057	2.052	2.051	2.050
Panama	5.68	2.700	1.850	1.850	2.053	2.051	2.050	2.050
Papua New Guinea	6.24	4.086	1.866	1.850	2.062	2.060	2.060	2.060
Paraguay	6.50	3.840	1.850	1.850	2.061	2.056	2.053	2.052
Peru	6.85	2.864	1.850	1.850	2.060	2.055	2.052	2.051
Philippines	7.29	3.176	1.850	1.850	2.061	2.060	2.060	2.060
Poland	3.62	1.260	1.850	2.066	2.061	2.060	2.059	2.058

TABLE A13 (*continued*)

Country or area	*1950-1955*	*2000-2005*	*2050-2055*	*2100-2105*	*2150-2155*	*2200-2205*	*2250-2255*	*2295-2300*
				Total fertility (children per woman)				
Portugal	3.04	1.450	1.850	2.069	2.065	2.063	2.062	2.062
Puerto Rico	4.97	1.892	1.850	2.054	2.053	2.053	2.053	2.053
Qatar	6.97	3.221	1.850	1.850	2.051	2.050	2.050	2.050
Republic of Korea	5.40	1.410	1.850	2.058	2.056	2.054	2.053	2.053
Republic of Moldova	3.50	1.400	1.850	2.077	2.071	2.068	2.065	2.064
Réunion	5.65	2.300	1.850	1.970	2.018	2.017	2.016	2.016
Romania	2.87	1.320	1.900	2.066	2.061	2.059	2.059	2.059
Russian Federation	2.85	1.140	1.900	2.074	2.065	2.062	2.061	2.060
Rwanda	7.80	5.741	1.988	1.850	2.030	2.024	2.022	2.022
St. Lucia	6.00	2.272	1.850	1.970	2.071	2.070	2.070	2.070
St. Vincent and Grenadines	7.33	2.232	1.850	2.050	2.034	2.031	2.031	2.030
Samoa	7.30	4.118	1.886	1.850	2.063	2.061	2.060	2.060
Sao Tome and Principe	5.68	3.987	1.851	1.850	2.033	2.031	2.030	2.030
Saudi Arabia	7.18	4.530	1.850	1.850	2.054	2.052	2.051	2.050
Senegal	6.70	4.974	1.976	1.850	2.042	2.035	2.032	2.031
Serbia and Montenegro	3.22	1.650	1.850	2.088	2.083	2.081	2.081	2.080
Sierra Leone	6.09	6.500	2.226	1.850	2.050	2.077	2.053	2.042
Singapore	6.40	1.358	1.850	2.085	2.085	2.086	2.087	2.089
Slovakia	3.52	1.280	1.850	2.056	2.052	2.050	2.049	2.049
Slovenia	2.80	1.140	1.850	2.064	2.060	2.059	2.057	2.056
Solomon Islands	6.40	4.421	1.850	1.850	2.076	2.073	2.071	2.071
Somalia	7.25	7.250	2.716	1.850	1.900	2.032	2.030	2.030
South Africa	6.50	2.613	1.850	1.900	2.043	2.033	2.031	2.030
Spain	2.57	1.150	1.850	2.079	2.077	2.075	2.074	2.073
Sri Lanka	5.94	2.008	1.850	2.056	2.052	2.051	2.050	2.050
Sudan	6.67	4.388	1.911	1.850	2.061	2.056	2.055	2.054
Suriname	6.56	2.453	1.850	1.850	2.052	2.050	2.050	2.050
Swaziland	6.90	4.540	1.850	1.850	2.055	2.037	2.032	2.031
Sweden	2.21	1.635	1.900	2.066	2.063	2.062	2.061	2.061
Switzerland	2.28	1.409	1.900	2.062	2.059	2.057	2.056	2.055
Syrian Arab Republic	7.20	3.318	1.850	1.850	2.053	2.051	2.050	2.050
Tajikistan	6.00	3.057	1.850	1.850	2.055	2.050	2.047	2.047
TFYR Macedonia	5.32	1.900	1.850	2.091	2.085	2.082	2.081	2.081
Thailand	6.40	1.925	1.850	2.048	2.042	2.041	2.040	2.040
Togo	7.10	5.328	1.906	1.850	2.040	2.033	2.031	2.030
Tonga	7.30	3.706	1.850	1.850	2.051	2.050	2.050	2.050
Trinidad and Tobago	5.30	1.550	1.850	2.063	2.048	2.042	2.040	2.039
Tunisia	6.93	2.006	1.850	2.079	2.073	2.071	2.071	2.070
Turkey	6.90	2.433	1.850	1.970	2.050	2.050	2.050	2.050
Turkmenistan	6.00	2.700	1.850	1.850	2.052	2.048	2.047	2.046
Uganda	6.90	7.100	2.599	1.850	1.900	2.032	2.030	2.030
Ukraine	2.81	1.150	1.900	2.073	2.068	2.065	2.064	2.064
United Arab Emirates	6.97	2.815	1.850	1.850	2.056	2.053	2.052	2.051
United Kingdom	2.18	1.600	1.900	2.058	2.055	2.053	2.053	2.052
United Rep. of Tanzania	6.74	5.108	1.862	1.850	2.043	2.034	2.031	2.030

TABLE A13 (*continued*)

Country or area	*1950-1955*	*2000-2005*	*2050-2055*	*2100-2105*	*2150-2155*	*2200-2205*	*2250-2255*	*2295-2300*
	Total fertility (children per woman)							
United States of America	3.45	2.110	1.900	2.061	2.055	2.053	2.052	2.051
United States Virgin Islands	4.76	2.145	1.850	2.050	2.064	2.062	2.061	2.061
Uruguay	2.73	2.303	1.850	1.850	2.052	2.051	2.050	2.050
Uzbekistan	5.97	2.436	1.850	1.970	2.054	2.050	2.049	2.049
Vanuatu	7.60	4.125	1.868	1.850	2.074	2.071	2.070	2.070
Venezuela	6.46	2.721	1.850	1.850	2.056	2.053	2.051	2.051
Viet Nam	5.75	2.303	1.850	1.970	2.052	2.051	2.050	2.050
Western Sahara	6.53	3.892	1.850	1.850	2.041	2.040	2.040	2.040
Yemen	8.20	7.005	2.822	1.850	1.900	2.050	2.050	2.050
Zambia	6.59	5.638	2.151	1.850	2.050	2.035	2.031	2.030
Zimbabwe	6.70	3.904	1.850	1.850	2.053	2.030	2.023	2.021

TABLE A14. MALE LIFE EXPECTANCY AT BIRTH BY COUNTRY: SELECTED PERIODS

Country or area	*1950-1955*	*2000-2005*	*2050-2055*	*2100-2105*	*2150-2155*	*2200-2205*	*2250-2255*	*2295-2300*
	Life expectancy at birth (years)							
Afghanistan	32.0	43.0	62.7	74.5	81.1	85.2	88.1	90.1
Albania	54.4	70.9	77.9	82.0	85.8	89.4	93.0	96.1
Algeria	42.1	68.1	77.0	82.6	86.5	89.7	92.4	94.4
Angola	28.6	38.8	58.8	72.6	80.5	85.5	89.0	91.4
Argentina	60.4	70.6	77.7	83.0	87.7	91.9	95.6	98.6
Armenia	61.8	69.0	76.0	80.9	85.3	89.3	92.8	95.7
Australia	66.9	76.4	81.4	86.0	90.1	93.9	97.4	100.5
Austria	63.2	75.4	81.5	86.6	91.3	95.5	99.5	102.7
Azerbaijan	57.4	68.7	75.8	83.2	88.0	91.2	93.5	95.1
Bahamas	58.3	63.9	72.9	82.2	86.9	89.8	92.0	93.5
Bahrain	49.6	72.5	78.7	83.4	87.5	91.1	94.3	96.8
Bangladesh	38.3	61.0	74.5	81.0	84.7	87.4	89.5	91.0
Barbados	55.0	74.5	79.5	83.6	87.4	90.9	94.0	96.6
Belarus	61.1	64.9	75.9	82.0	86.7	90.4	93.4	95.7
Belgium	65.0	75.7	81.7	87.3	92.1	96.4	100.2	103.2
Belize	57.1	69.9	75.5	81.3	85.4	88.7	91.4	93.5
Benin	32.5	48.4	67.2	78.4	84.2	87.9	90.5	92.4
Bhutan	34.5	62.0	75.1	82.5	87.0	90.2	92.7	94.6
Bolivia	38.5	61.8	75.3	80.7	85.4	89.4	92.9	95.8
Bosnia and Herzegovina	52.6	71.3	77.0	82.7	87.1	90.6	93.5	95.6
Botswana	44.7	38.9	48.6	72.1	82.4	87.5	90.6	92.7
Brazil	49.3	64.0	74.8	81.5	86.8	91.1	94.6	97.3
Brunei Darussalam	59.6	74.2	79.3	83.6	87.9	91.8	95.5	98.5
Bulgaria	62.2	67.4	76.7	82.0	86.4	90.0	93.2	95.6
Burkina Faso	30.5	45.2	66.0	78.1	84.2	88.0	90.7	92.5
Burundi	37.5	40.4	62.2	76.1	83.2	87.4	90.4	92.4
Cambodia	38.1	55.2	69.4	79.0	83.4	86.2	88.2	89.7
Cameroon	34.5	45.1	61.4	76.0	83.2	87.4	90.2	92.1
Canada	66.8	76.7	81.3	85.9	90.0	93.5	96.7	99.2
Cape Verde	47.0	67.0	76.7	82.5	86.9	90.4	93.3	95.5
Central African Republic	33.0	38.5	58.7	74.3	82.3	86.9	90.0	92.1
Chad	31.1	43.7	64.2	76.4	83.0	87.1	90.1	92.2
Channel Islands	67.4	75.7	80.3	85.2	89.9	94.5	98.6	102.0
Chile	52.9	73.0	78.1	83.9	88.6	92.3	95.4	97.7
China	39.3	68.9	74.9	82.1	87.5	91.8	95.4	98.1
China, Hong Kong SAR	57.2	77.3	82.7	87.8	92.1	95.6	98.5	100.5
China, Macao SAR	51.5	76.5	82.3	86.4	90.3	93.8	97.0	99.6
Colombia	49.0	69.2	76.9	83.0	87.9	91.8	95.0	97.2
Comoros	39.5	59.4	75.6	82.6	86.7	89.7	91.9	93.6
Congo	39.8	46.6	65.3	77.2	82.2	85.1	87.1	88.6
Costa Rica	56.0	75.8	80.0	86.5	91.1	94.4	96.8	98.5
Côte d'Ivoire	34.5	40.8	64.1	77.2	83.8	87.8	90.6	92.6
Croatia	59.0	70.3	77.3	83.1	87.7	91.4	94.5	96.8
Cuba	57.8	74.8	79.1	84.2	88.5	92.3	95.8	98.7
Cyprus	65.1	76.0	80.4	84.9	88.9	92.4	95.4	97.8
Czech Republic	64.5	72.1	79.2	83.6	87.7	91.3	94.6	97.3

TABLE A14 (*continued*)

Country or area	1950-1955	2000-2005	2050-2055	2100-2105	2150-2155	2200-2205	2250-2255	2295-2300
	Life expectancy at birth (years)							
Dem. People's Rep. of Korea	48.0	60.5	73.5	80.1	84.7	88.2	91.0	93.0
Dem. Rep. of the Congo	37.5	40.8	61.4	74.4	81.6	86.1	89.3	91.5
Dem. Rep. of Timor-Leste	29.6	48.7	69.6	78.4	82.7	85.6	87.8	89.4
Denmark	69.6	74.2	79.6	84.5	88.6	92.2	95.4	97.9
Djibouti	31.5	44.7	65.2	77.5	83.9	87.8	90.6	92.5
Dominican Republic	44.7	64.4	72.4	78.1	83.0	87.5	91.4	94.5
Ecuador	47.1	68.3	76.3	81.7	86.1	89.9	93.3	96.0
Egypt	41.2	66.7	76.7	82.0	86.2	89.7	92.6	94.9
El Salvador	44.1	67.7	76.4	81.9	86.2	89.7	92.8	95.1
Equatorial Guinea	33.0	47.8	67.5	78.3	84.1	87.8	90.6	92.5
Eritrea	34.5	51.2	68.7	77.5	82.9	86.8	89.6	91.7
Estonia	61.7	66.5	76.6	83.4	87.9	91.3	93.9	95.9
Ethiopia	31.4	44.6	64.3	77.0	83.6	87.6	90.4	92.4
Fiji	50.8	68.1	76.5	82.1	86.8	90.7	94.0	96.5
Finland	63.2	74.4	80.5	85.7	90.4	94.6	98.5	101.7
France	63.7	75.2	81.3	86.6	91.3	95.6	99.4	102.6
French Guiana	50.3	72.5	78.8	83.9	88.3	92.1	95.4	98.0
French Polynesia	48.0	70.7	77.9	83.5	88.0	91.6	94.7	96.9
Gabon	35.5	55.8	71.5	79.8	84.4	87.5	89.9	91.6
Gambia	28.6	52.7	70.1	79.4	84.4	87.7	90.2	92.0
Georgia	57.5	69.5	76.0	82.4	87.0	90.6	93.4	95.5
Germany	65.3	75.2	81.3	87.0	92.2	96.8	100.8	104.0
Ghana	40.5	56.5	71.5	80.8	85.6	88.8	91.2	93.0
Greece	64.3	75.7	80.2	84.8	89.0	92.6	95.9	98.5
Guadeloupe	55.0	74.8	80.7	85.6	89.5	92.7	95.3	97.4
Guam	55.4	72.4	78.6	82.8	86.8	90.6	94.3	97.5
Guatemala	41.8	63.0	75.7	81.8	86.5	90.3	93.4	95.8
Guinea	30.5	48.8	68.2	78.5	84.1	87.8	90.5	92.5
Guinea-Bissau	31.1	43.8	63.6	75.8	82.5	86.8	89.8	91.9
Guyana	50.8	60.1	71.1	79.5	84.8	88.5	91.4	93.5
Haiti	36.3	49.0	69.5	76.6	82.1	86.4	89.7	92.1
Honduras	40.5	66.5	74.4	81.2	86.1	89.8	92.9	95.2
Hungary	61.5	67.7	76.9	83.5	88.3	92.2	95.6	98.2
Iceland	70.0	77.6	81.8	85.8	89.5	93.0	96.4	99.3
India	39.4	63.2	73.1	81.8	86.9	90.4	93.0	94.9
Indonesia	36.9	64.8	75.8	81.9	85.9	89.1	91.5	93.4
Iran, Islamic Rep. of	44.9	68.9	77.4	82.8	87.2	90.9	94.1	96.6
Iraq	43.1	59.2	75.3	82.8	87.5	91.0	93.6	95.5
Ireland	65.7	74.4	79.5	84.3	88.7	92.7	96.4	99.3
Israel	64.4	77.1	82.0	86.2	90.2	93.7	97.0	99.6
Italy	64.3	75.5	80.0	84.5	88.6	92.4	95.8	98.7
Jamaica	56.9	73.7	79.2	84.7	88.8	92.1	94.8	96.9
Japan	61.6	77.9	84.5	89.3	93.7	97.7	101.4	104.5
Jordan	42.2	69.7	77.6	84.7	89.2	92.4	94.6	96.2
Kazakhstan	51.7	60.9	73.7	80.6	85.2	88.6	91.2	93.2
Kenya	39.0	43.5	57.3	76.8	85.0	89.2	92.0	93.9

TABLE A14 (continued)

Country or area	1950-1955	2000-2005	2050-2055	2100-2105	2150-2155	2200-2205	2250-2255	2295-2300
	Life expectancy at birth (years)							
Kuwait	54.1	74.9	79.9	84.7	88.9	92.4	95.3	97.4
Kyrgyzstan	51.3	64.8	74.6	81.3	86.2	90.1	93.2	95.5
Lao People's Dem. Republic	36.5	53.3	71.7	81.0	86.0	89.3	91.9	93.7
Latvia	62.5	65.6	76.3	82.5	87.0	90.6	93.6	95.9
Lebanon	54.3	71.9	77.7	82.5	86.6	90.2	93.3	95.8
Lesotho	40.0	32.3	48.9	77.3	84.7	88.1	90.3	91.8
Liberia	37.1	40.7	60.4	72.6	78.8	82.5	85.1	86.9
Libyan Arab Jamahiriya	41.9	70.8	77.9	83.8	88.4	91.9	94.8	96.9
Lithuania	61.5	67.5	76.8	85.2	89.8	92.8	95.0	96.4
Luxembourg	63.1	75.1	81.5	87.0	91.9	96.3	100.2	103.4
Madagascar	36.4	52.5	70.7	80.2	85.3	88.8	91.4	93.2
Malawi	35.8	37.3	58.9	73.2	80.7	85.1	88.0	90.0
Malaysia	47.0	70.8	77.9	83.9	88.6	92.3	95.3	97.5
Maldives	40.1	67.8	77.0	83.3	87.5	90.7	93.2	95.1
Mali	32.2	48.0	66.0	75.6	80.3	83.3	85.6	87.2
Malta	64.2	75.9	82.0	87.7	92.8	97.4	101.3	104.4
Martinique	55.0	75.8	80.4	86.3	90.7	93.9	96.4	98.2
Mauritania	34.0	50.9	69.9	79.5	84.7	88.3	90.9	92.9
Mauritius	49.7	68.4	76.6	82.5	86.9	90.4	93.3	95.5
Mexico	48.9	70.4	77.3	83.9	88.6	92.1	94.8	96.8
Micronesia, Fed. States of	54.1	68.0	76.3	82.2	86.2	89.4	92.0	93.9
Mongolia	41.0	61.9	75.1	81.1	85.6	89.3	92.4	94.9
Morocco	41.9	66.8	76.5	82.6	87.1	90.7	93.8	96.1
Mozambique	30.1	36.6	56.5	72.6	81.3	86.4	89.7	92.0
Myanmar	35.6	54.6	68.1	79.9	86.1	89.9	92.6	94.5
Namibia	38.0	42.9	57.6	75.6	83.9	88.6	91.6	93.6
Nepal	36.8	60.1	74.5	81.2	85.0	87.6	89.7	91.2
Netherlands	70.9	75.6	80.1	84.7	88.9	92.8	96.2	99.0
Netherlands Antilles	59.1	73.3	78.8	83.9	88.3	92.2	95.6	98.2
New Caledonia	50.0	72.5	78.8	84.1	88.3	91.8	94.5	96.6
New Zealand	67.5	75.8	80.3	85.2	89.3	92.9	96.2	98.9
Nicaragua	40.9	67.2	77.0	82.5	87.0	90.7	93.9	96.4
Niger	31.9	45.9	65.6	77.2	83.5	87.7	90.7	92.9
Nigeria	35.0	51.1	65.7	78.0	84.1	87.7	90.3	92.1
Norway	70.9	76.0	81.4	86.8	91.5	95.6	99.3	102.1
Occupied Palestinian Territory	42.2	70.8	77.5	82.7	86.9	90.5	93.5	95.9
Oman	36.9	71.0	77.4	82.5	86.7	90.2	93.3	95.7
Pakistan	42.3	61.2	74.6	82.5	87.4	90.9	93.6	95.5
Panama	54.4	72.3	78.2	83.6	88.0	92.0	95.6	98.5
Papua New Guinea	33.8	56.8	73.0	82.1	87.6	91.4	94.2	96.1
Paraguay	60.7	68.6	76.9	82.0	86.4	90.2	93.6	96.3
Peru	42.9	67.3	76.3	82.6	87.3	91.0	93.9	96.0
Philippines	46.0	68.0	76.9	83.3	87.9	91.6	94.6	96.8
Poland	58.6	69.8	77.7	83.6	88.1	91.6	94.4	96.6
Portugal	56.9	72.6	78.6	83.7	88.2	92.3	96.1	99.3
Puerto Rico	62.7	71.2	77.4	85.9	90.1	93.0	95.2	96.8

TABLE A14 (*continued*)

Country or area	1950-1955	2000-2005	2050-2055	2100-2105	2150-2155	2200-2205	2250-2255	2295-2300
	Life expectancy at birth (years)							
Qatar	46.7	70.5	77.8	84.9	89.4	92.6	94.9	96.5
Republic of Korea	46.0	71.8	80.0	86.8	92.2	96.5	100.0	102.5
Republic of Moldova	55.0	65.5	76.0	80.8	84.9	88.6	92.0	94.9
Réunion	49.7	71.2	77.4	84.0	88.6	91.9	94.5	96.3
Romania	59.4	67.0	75.2	81.7	86.3	89.8	92.7	94.9
Russian Federation	60.5	60.8	72.1	80.9	86.4	90.3	93.3	95.4
Rwanda	38.5	38.8	63.8	77.8	84.6	88.7	91.6	93.5
St. Lucia	52.7	70.8	77.5	84.1	88.2	91.2	93.7	95.5
St. Vincent and Grenadines	49.8	72.6	78.1	83.6	88.3	92.2	95.6	98.2
Samoa	43.0	66.9	76.6	82.5	87.0	90.5	93.4	95.5
Sao Tome and Principe	44.0	67.0	76.8	83.0	87.5	91.0	93.9	96.0
Saudi Arabia	39.1	71.1	78.3	83.3	87.4	91.0	94.0	96.4
Senegal	35.5	50.8	70.0	77.4	83.0	87.6	91.5	94.4
Serbia and Montenegro	57.1	70.9	77.3	83.2	87.9	91.9	95.2	97.7
Sierra Leone	28.6	33.1	53.1	65.6	74.3	80.5	85.0	88.1
Singapore	58.8	75.9	81.4	86.8	91.4	95.3	98.5	100.8
Slovakia	62.4	69.8	77.3	83.3	88.0	91.8	95.0	97.4
Slovenia	63.0	72.6	79.4	83.9	87.8	91.3	94.4	96.9
Solomon Islands	44.9	67.9	77.2	82.1	86.3	90.0	93.3	95.8
Somalia	31.5	46.4	68.1	79.2	85.1	89.0	91.8	93.8
South Africa	44.0	45.1	59.1	76.0	84.5	89.4	92.7	95.0
Spain	61.6	75.9	81.7	87.0	91.8	96.2	100.3	103.6
Sri Lanka	56.2	69.9	77.5	83.5	88.1	92.0	95.3	97.7
Sudan	36.3	54.1	69.1	79.1	84.4	87.7	90.2	92.0
Suriname	54.4	68.5	77.0	82.8	86.8	89.6	91.7	93.1
Swaziland	38.7	33.3	47.8	69.1	80.2	86.1	89.6	91.8
Sweden	70.4	77.6	82.7	87.6	92.1	96.4	100.3	103.6
Switzerland	67.0	75.9	80.4	84.8	88.8	92.6	96.2	99.3
Syrian Arab Republic	44.8	70.6	77.8	83.0	87.2	90.8	93.8	96.1
Tajikistan	53.3	66.2	74.9	80.7	84.6	87.4	89.5	91.0
TFYR Macedonia	55.0	71.4	77.8	82.5	86.6	90.0	93.0	95.4
Thailand	49.8	65.3	76.2	83.3	88.6	92.7	96.1	98.6
Togo	34.5	48.2	64.7	77.3	83.6	87.4	90.0	91.9
Tonga	54.1	68.0	76.3	82.2	86.3	89.4	92.0	93.9
Trinidad and Tobago	58.2	68.4	75.3	82.4	87.5	91.2	94.1	96.1
Tunisia	44.1	70.8	78.1	83.1	87.4	91.2	94.5	97.1
Turkey	42.0	68.0	76.8	83.5	87.9	91.3	93.8	95.6
Turkmenistan	49.7	63.9	74.7	81.8	86.7	90.3	93.2	95.2
Uganda	38.5	45.4	69.5	79.4	84.6	88.0	90.6	92.4
Ukraine	61.3	64.7	75.7	81.6	86.2	89.9	93.1	95.6
United Arab Emirates	46.7	73.3	79.2	83.6	87.5	91.0	94.2	96.7
United Kingdom	66.7	75.7	81.1	86.2	90.6	94.4	97.8	100.4
United Rep. of Tanzania	35.5	42.5	64.1	77.1	84.0	88.1	90.7	92.4
United States of America	66.1	74.3	79.8	86.4	91.1	94.5	97.1	99.0
United States Virgin Islands	58.9	74.2	79.3	84.1	88.4	92.3	95.7	98.4
Uruguay	63.3	71.6	78.9	85.0	89.7	93.4	96.2	98.2

TABLE A14 (*continued*)

Country or area	*1950-1955*	*2000-2005*	*2050-2055*	*2100-2105*	*2150-2155*	*2200-2205*	*2250-2255*	*2295-2300*
	Life expectancy at birth (years)							
Uzbekistan	53.2	66.8	74.9	82.1	86.9	90.3	92.8	94.6
Vanuatu	40.6	67.5	75.3	81.3	85.8	89.3	92.1	94.3
Venezuela	53.8	70.9	77.8	82.6	86.8	90.6	94.2	97.2
Viet Nam	39.1	66.9	76.7	83.4	88.1	91.7	94.6	96.7
Western Sahara	34.0	62.3	75.3	81.9	86.0	89.1	91.5	93.3
Yemen	32.4	58.9	73.1	79.6	83.1	85.6	87.6	89.0
Zambia	36.3	32.7	55.5	73.3	82.2	87.2	90.3	92.4
Zimbabwe	45.9	33.7	49.7	68.5	79.4	85.7	89.7	92.2

TABLE A15. FEMALE LIFE EXPECTANCY AT BIRTH BY COUNTRY: SELECTED PERIODS

Country or area	1950-1955	2000-2005	2050-2055	2100-2105	2150-2155	2200-2205	2250-2255	2295-2300
	Life expectancy at birth (years)							
Afghanistan	31.7	43.3	65.7	76.7	82.7	86.5	89.2	91.0
Albania	56.1	76.7	83.5	87.3	90.8	94.1	97.2	99.8
Algeria	44.2	71.3	81.4	86.7	90.4	93.3	95.7	97.5
Angola	31.5	41.5	61.1	74.3	81.8	86.6	89.9	92.2
Argentina	65.1	77.7	84.9	89.0	92.6	95.8	98.6	101.0
Armenia	67.9	75.6	81.3	85.5	89.2	92.5	95.5	98.0
Australia	72.4	82.0	87.1	91.1	94.7	98.1	101.2	103.8
Austria	68.4	81.5	87.3	91.6	95.6	99.3	102.7	105.5
Azerbaijan	65.0	75.5	81.1	88.0	92.1	94.8	96.7	98.0
Bahamas	61.2	70.3	77.1	86.4	90.6	93.0	94.7	96.0
Bahrain	52.5	75.9	83.1	87.2	90.8	94.0	96.8	99.0
Bangladesh	36.7	61.8	77.7	83.4	86.7	89.1	91.0	92.4
Barbados	59.5	79.5	84.5	88.2	91.6	94.7	97.4	99.6
Belarus	70.0	75.3	82.5	87.4	91.1	94.1	96.6	98.5
Belgium	70.2	81.9	87.3	92.1	96.3	100.0	103.2	105.8
Belize	58.3	73.0	79.2	84.7	88.6	91.7	94.2	96.2
Benin	35.6	53.0	69.2	79.8	85.2	88.7	91.2	93.0
Bhutan	36.0	64.5	79.1	85.2	89.1	92.0	94.2	95.9
Bolivia	42.5	66.0	80.2	84.7	88.5	91.9	94.8	97.2
Bosnia and Herzegovina	54.8	76.7	82.1	87.2	91.1	94.2	96.6	98.4
Botswana	47.2	40.5	44.2	72.2	84.7	90.1	93.1	95.0
Brazil	52.7	72.6	82.7	87.6	91.4	94.6	97.3	99.3
Brunei Darussalam	61.1	78.9	84.3	88.6	92.6	96.3	99.6	102.2
Bulgaria	66.1	74.6	82.5	87.0	90.7	93.8	96.4	98.5
Burkina Faso	33.4	46.2	67.5	79.3	85.1	88.7	91.3	93.1
Burundi	40.6	41.4	63.8	77.4	84.3	88.4	91.2	93.1
Cambodia	40.8	59.5	73.4	81.7	85.4	87.8	89.6	91.0
Cameroon	37.5	47.4	61.1	76.6	84.0	88.1	90.8	92.7
Canada	71.6	81.9	86.3	90.3	93.9	97.0	99.8	102.0
Cape Verde	50.0	72.8	82.0	87.0	90.8	93.8	96.2	98.1
Central African Republic	38.0	40.6	60.0	75.6	83.5	88.0	90.9	92.8
Chad	34.0	45.7	66.4	77.9	84.1	88.1	90.9	92.9
Channel Islands	73.7	80.7	85.3	89.9	94.3	98.3	101.9	104.8
Chile	56.8	79.0	84.7	89.4	93.2	96.2	98.6	100.4
China	42.3	73.3	80.7	86.9	91.7	95.5	98.6	101.0
China, Hong Kong SAR	64.9	82.8	87.9	92.1	95.6	98.4	100.7	102.3
China, Macao SAR	56.5	81.2	87.0	90.7	94.0	97.1	99.8	102.0
Colombia	52.3	75.3	83.2	88.0	91.8	94.9	97.4	99.2
Comoros	42.0	62.2	79.1	85.4	89.1	91.7	93.7	95.2
Congo	44.6	49.7	67.0	79.1	83.7	86.3	88.2	89.5
Costa Rica	58.6	80.6	85.3	91.1	95.0	97.7	99.7	101.0
Côte d'Ivoire	37.5	41.2	65.2	78.2	84.7	88.6	91.3	93.2
Croatia	63.2	78.1	83.3	88.1	92.0	95.1	97.6	99.5
Cuba	61.3	78.7	84.2	88.6	92.3	95.6	98.7	101.2
Cyprus	69.0	80.5	85.0	88.9	92.4	95.4	98.0	100.0
Czech Republic	70.3	78.7	85.2	88.8	92.0	95.0	97.6	99.8

TABLE A15 (*continued*)

Country or area	1950-1955	2000-2005	2050-2055	2100-2105	2150-2155	2200-2205	2250-2255	2295-2300
	Life expectancy at birth (years)							
Dem. People's Rep. of Korea	50.0	66.0	78.1	84.0	88.0	91.0	93.3	95.0
Dem. Rep. of the Congo	40.6	42.8	63.6	76.0	82.9	87.1	90.2	92.3
Dem. Rep. of Timor-Leste	30.4	50.4	73.0	80.5	84.3	86.8	88.8	90.3
Denmark	72.4	79.1	84.6	88.9	92.6	95.8	98.5	100.7
Djibouti	34.5	46.8	66.6	78.7	84.8	88.6	91.3	93.2
Dominican Republic	47.3	69.2	77.4	82.2	86.4	90.1	93.4	96.0
Ecuador	49.6	73.5	81.8	86.6	90.4	93.7	96.6	98.9
Egypt	43.6	71.0	81.5	86.1	89.7	92.6	95.1	97.0
El Salvador	46.5	73.7	82.9	87.1	90.4	93.2	95.6	97.5
Equatorial Guinea	36.0	50.5	69.5	79.7	85.2	88.7	91.3	93.2
Eritrea	37.4	54.2	71.3	80.1	85.2	88.7	91.2	93.0
Estonia	68.3	76.8	83.4	88.9	92.5	95.3	97.4	99.0
Ethiopia	34.4	46.3	65.8	78.3	84.6	88.5	91.1	93.0
Fiji	55.0	71.5	81.0	86.1	90.2	93.6	96.4	98.6
Finland	69.6	81.5	86.8	91.3	95.3	98.9	102.2	104.8
France	69.5	82.8	87.9	92.4	96.4	100.0	103.3	106.1
French Guiana	56.9	78.3	84.2	88.8	92.7	96.0	98.8	101.0
French Polynesia	50.0	75.8	82.9	87.9	91.9	95.1	97.7	99.6
Gabon	38.6	57.5	74.0	81.7	85.9	88.8	91.0	92.6
Gambia	31.5	55.5	72.9	81.1	85.6	88.6	91.0	92.7
Georgia	65.4	77.6	81.8	87.2	91.1	94.2	96.5	98.3
Germany	69.6	81.2	86.9	92.0	96.5	100.5	104.0	106.8
Ghana	43.6	59.3	74.1	82.6	87.1	90.1	92.3	94.0
Greece	67.5	80.9	85.3	89.3	92.9	96.1	98.8	101.0
Guadeloupe	58.1	81.7	86.5	90.6	93.9	96.5	98.8	100.5
Guam	59.7	77.0	83.6	87.2	90.7	93.9	97.1	99.8
Guatemala	42.3	68.9	81.7	86.3	89.9	92.9	95.4	97.3
Guinea	31.5	49.5	69.3	79.5	84.9	88.5	91.1	93.0
Guinea-Bissau	34.0	46.9	66.4	77.7	83.9	87.8	90.7	92.7
Guyana	53.9	66.3	75.1	83.0	87.8	91.1	93.6	95.5
Haiti	38.9	50.0	71.3	78.1	83.4	87.5	90.7	93.0
Honduras	43.2	71.4	78.8	84.9	89.2	92.4	95.0	97.0
Hungary	65.8	76.0	83.3	88.8	92.9	96.3	99.1	101.4
Iceland	74.1	81.9	86.2	89.9	93.3	96.5	99.5	102.1
India	38.0	64.6	76.9	84.6	88.8	91.8	94.1	95.7
Indonesia	38.1	68.8	79.8	85.3	89.0	91.7	93.9	95.5
Iran, Islamic Rep. of	44.9	71.9	82.7	87.3	91.0	94.1	96.8	98.8
Iraq	44.9	62.3	79.7	86.2	90.2	93.1	95.4	97.0
Ireland	68.2	79.6	84.6	89.0	93.0	96.5	99.7	102.2
Israel	66.4	81.0	86.2	90.1	93.6	96.8	99.7	102.0
Italy	67.8	81.9	86.2	90.0	93.5	96.8	99.7	102.2
Jamaica	60.2	77.8	83.7	88.6	92.2	95.2	97.6	99.4
Japan	65.5	85.1	93.2	96.7	100.0	102.9	105.7	108.0
Jordan	44.3	72.5	81.8	88.2	92.1	94.8	96.7	98.0
Kazakhstan	61.9	71.9	79.9	85.8	89.5	92.3	94.4	96.1
Kenya	43.0	45.6	56.0	77.7	86.4	90.6	93.2	95.0

TABLE A15 (*continued*)

Country or area	1950-1955	2000-2005	2050-2055	2100-2105	2150-2155	2200-2205	2250-2255	2295-2300
	Life expectancy at birth (years)							
Kuwait	57.5	79.0	84.4	89.0	92.9	96.1	98.7	100.6
Kyrgyzstan	59.8	72.3	80.2	85.8	89.9	93.1	95.7	97.8
Lao People's Dem. Republic	39.2	55.8	75.5	83.0	87.3	90.3	92.7	94.4
Latvia	69.0	76.2	83.4	88.3	91.9	94.8	97.2	99.0
Lebanon	57.7	75.1	82.1	86.5	90.2	93.4	96.2	98.3
Lesotho	43.3	37.7	46.2	78.8	86.2	89.3	91.3	92.7
Liberia	40.0	42.2	61.6	74.1	80.2	83.7	86.1	87.8
Libyan Arab Jamahiriya	43.9	75.4	82.8	88.1	92.0	95.1	97.5	99.3
Lithuania	67.8	77.6	83.6	90.7	94.2	96.4	98.0	99.0
Luxembourg	68.9	81.4	87.2	92.3	96.8	100.8	104.2	107.0
Madagascar	37.0	54.8	74.3	82.2	86.6	89.8	92.2	94.0
Malawi	36.7	37.7	58.3	73.2	81.1	85.7	88.7	90.6
Malaysia	50.0	75.7	82.8	88.1	92.1	95.3	97.8	99.7
Maldives	37.6	67.0	79.9	85.9	89.8	92.7	95.0	96.6
Mali	33.3	49.1	67.9	77.3	81.7	84.5	86.6	88.0
Malta	67.7	80.7	86.8	92.1	96.8	100.9	104.3	107.0
Martinique	58.1	82.3	86.5	91.6	95.2	97.8	99.8	101.2
Mauritania	37.1	54.1	72.4	81.0	85.8	89.1	91.7	93.5
Mauritius	52.3	75.8	82.5	87.7	91.4	94.3	96.7	98.5
Mexico	52.5	76.4	83.5	88.9	92.6	95.4	97.6	99.3
Micronesia, Fed. States of	55.2	69.1	79.8	85.3	89.0	91.9	94.2	95.9
Mongolia	43.5	65.9	79.1	84.5	88.5	91.9	94.7	97.0
Morocco	43.9	70.5	81.2	86.8	90.8	94.1	96.7	98.7
Mozambique	32.5	39.6	56.2	73.0	82.0	87.1	90.5	92.7
Myanmar	38.2	60.2	74.0	83.4	88.4	91.7	94.1	95.9
Namibia	40.5	45.6	55.8	76.1	85.4	90.2	93.1	95.0
Nepal	35.8	59.6	77.5	83.4	86.8	89.2	91.1	92.4
Netherlands	73.4	81.0	85.5	89.6	93.2	96.5	99.5	101.9
Netherlands Antilles	61.6	79.2	84.3	88.9	92.9	96.3	99.3	101.5
New Caledonia	53.0	77.7	83.6	88.3	92.0	95.0	97.4	99.2
New Zealand	71.8	80.7	85.2	89.7	93.4	96.7	99.6	102.0
Nicaragua	43.7	71.9	82.2	86.7	90.3	93.4	96.1	98.2
Niger	32.5	46.5	68.6	79.0	84.8	88.7	91.6	93.6
Nigeria	38.0	51.8	66.1	78.7	84.8	88.4	90.9	92.6
Norway	74.5	81.9	87.3	92.1	96.1	99.6	102.6	105.0
Occupied Palestinian Territory	44.3	74.0	82.1	86.7	90.4	93.6	96.2	98.3
Oman	38.3	74.4	82.0	86.6	90.3	93.5	96.1	98.2
Pakistan	39.8	60.9	77.2	84.3	88.7	91.8	94.2	96.0
Panama	56.2	77.4	84.3	88.6	92.3	95.7	98.7	101.2
Papua New Guinea	35.7	58.7	76.2	85.0	90.0	93.3	95.7	97.4
Paraguay	64.7	73.1	81.9	86.1	89.7	92.9	95.7	98.0
Peru	45.0	72.4	82.0	87.1	90.9	93.9	96.2	98.0
Philippines	49.6	72.0	81.6	87.4	91.5	94.8	97.3	99.2
Poland	64.2	78.0	84.0	88.8	92.5	95.3	97.6	99.4
Portugal	61.9	79.6	84.7	89.2	93.3	96.9	100.2	103.0
Puerto Rico	66.0	80.1	84.0	91.6	95.3	97.8	99.7	101.0

Table A15 (*continued*)

Country or area	1950-1955	2000-2005	2050-2055	2100-2105	2150-2155	2200-2205	2250-2255	2295-2300
	Life expectancy at birth (years)							
Qatar	49.3	75.4	83.0	89.4	93.3	95.9	97.7	99.0
Republic of Korea	49.0	79.3	85.9	91.6	96.1	99.7	102.5	104.6
Republic of Moldova	63.0	72.2	81.5	85.5	89.1	92.3	95.4	98.0
Réunion	55.6	79.3	83.9	89.7	93.5	96.1	98.1	99.5
Romania	62.8	74.2	80.8	86.6	90.6	93.7	96.2	98.0
Russian Federation	67.3	73.1	78.5	86.0	90.4	93.4	95.8	97.6
Rwanda	41.6	39.7	65.8	79.2	85.7	89.5	92.2	94.1
St. Lucia	55.3	74.1	81.9	88.0	91.7	94.4	96.6	98.2
St. Vincent and Grenadines	52.3	75.6	82.2	87.4	91.7	95.3	98.4	100.7
Samoa	49.6	73.4	82.1	87.3	91.1	94.1	96.4	98.2
Sao Tome and Principe	49.2	72.8	81.9	86.9	90.7	93.7	96.2	98.1
Saudi Arabia	40.7	73.7	82.3	86.8	90.5	93.7	96.3	98.4
Senegal	37.5	55.1	74.8	80.5	85.1	89.0	92.3	95.0
Serbia and Montenegro	58.8	75.6	82.3	87.4	91.4	94.8	97.6	99.7
Sierra Leone	31.5	35.5	55.2	67.3	75.7	81.6	86.0	89.0
Singapore	62.1	80.3	85.8	90.5	94.5	97.8	100.4	102.4
Slovakia	66.2	77.6	83.4	88.3	92.1	95.2	97.8	99.7
Slovenia	68.1	79.8	85.9	89.5	92.7	95.5	98.0	100.0
Solomon Islands	46.4	70.7	81.5	85.9	89.7	93.0	95.8	98.0
Somalia	34.5	49.5	71.9	81.3	86.5	90.0	92.7	94.6
South Africa	46.0	50.7	57.3	78.0	87.6	92.5	95.6	97.5
Spain	66.3	82.8	87.9	92.5	96.6	100.4	103.9	106.8
Sri Lanka	54.7	75.9	83.0	88.3	92.5	95.8	98.6	100.7
Sudan	39.1	57.1	71.1	80.5	85.4	88.5	90.9	92.6
Suriname	57.7	73.7	81.7	86.7	89.9	92.2	93.9	95.1
Swaziland	41.5	35.4	44.8	67.9	80.6	87.0	90.6	92.7
Sweden	73.3	82.6	87.7	92.3	96.4	100.2	103.6	106.5
Switzerland	71.6	82.3	86.5	90.2	93.7	97.0	100.2	102.9
Syrian Arab Republic	47.2	73.1	82.0	86.7	90.4	93.6	96.2	98.2
Tajikistan	58.4	71.4	79.7	84.7	88.0	90.3	92.0	93.3
TFYR Macedonia	55.0	75.8	82.6	86.8	90.4	93.4	96.0	98.0
Thailand	54.3	73.5	81.7	88.0	92.6	96.3	99.2	101.4
Togo	37.5	51.1	66.1	78.6	84.7	88.3	90.8	92.6
Tonga	55.2	69.1	79.8	85.3	89.0	91.9	94.2	95.9
Trinidad and Tobago	59.9	74.4	79.5	86.4	91.1	94.5	97.0	98.8
Tunisia	45.1	74.9	82.9	87.3	91.0	94.2	97.1	99.3
Turkey	45.2	73.2	81.8	87.9	91.7	94.5	96.6	98.0
Turkmenistan	56.6	70.4	79.6	85.7	89.9	93.0	95.5	97.3
Uganda	41.6	46.9	72.0	80.9	85.7	88.9	91.3	93.0
Ukraine	69.7	74.7	82.3	87.0	90.7	93.7	96.3	98.4
United Arab Emirates	49.3	77.4	83.9	87.7	91.2	94.3	97.0	99.2
United Kingdom	71.8	80.7	86.1	90.7	94.6	97.9	100.8	103.0
United Rep. of Tanzania	38.6	44.1	66.0	78.4	84.9	88.7	91.2	92.7
United States of America	72.0	79.9	84.7	90.9	95.1	98.1	100.4	102.0
United States Virgin Islands	71.5	82.0	86.3	90.6	94.3	97.6	100.4	102.6
Uruguay	69.4	78.9	85.5	90.2	93.7	96.5	98.6	100.2

TABLE A15 (*continued*)

Country or area	*1950-1955*	*2000-2005*	*2050-2055*	*2100-2105*	*2150-2155*	*2200-2205*	*2250-2255*	*2295-2300*
	Life expectancy at birth (years)							
Uzbekistan	59.9	72.5	80.1	86.4	90.5	93.3	95.5	97.0
Vanuatu	43.5	70.5	79.3	85.2	89.3	92.4	94.9	96.8
Venezuela	56.6	76.7	83.9	87.7	91.0	94.1	97.0	99.5
Viet Nam	41.8	71.6	81.5	87.1	91.1	94.3	96.8	98.7
Western Sahara	37.1	65.6	79.5	85.3	88.9	91.6	93.7	95.2
Yemen	32.7	61.1	75.9	81.5	84.6	86.8	88.5	89.8
Zambia	39.4	32.1	54.2	73.2	82.8	87.8	91.0	93.0
Zimbabwe	49.1	32.6	46.7	67.4	80.0	87.1	91.2	93.7

TABLE A16. POPULATION DENSITY BY COUNTRY, MEDIUM SCENARIO: SELECTED YEARS

Country or area	1950	2000	2050	2100	Maximum up to 2150	Year of maximum	2300
	Persons per square kilometer						
Afghanistan	13	33	107	138	139	(2095)	113
Albania	44	114	134	119	136	(2040)	119
Algeria	4	13	20	19	21	(2060)	19
Angola	3	10	35	51	51	(2105)	45
Argentina	6	14	19	19	20	(2065)	19
Armenia	48	110	83	58	126	(1990)	62
Australia	1	2	3	3	3	(2050)	4
Austria	84	98	89	75	98	(2005)	86
Azerbaijan	33	94	126	119	127	(2055)	122
Bahamas	8	30	39	36	39	(2050)	37
Bahrain	168	981	1 841	1 714	1 869	(2065)	1 690
Bangladesh	321	1 060	1 956	1 997	2 075	(2075)	1 864
Barbados	491	622	600	490	658	(2025)	539
Belarus	37	48	36	28	49	(1990)	31
Belgium	286	339	338	316	348	(2025)	364
Belize	3	11	18	18	19	(2070)	18
Benin	18	56	141	169	170	(2095)	156
Bhutan	16	44	113	137	137	(2095)	123
Bolivia	3	8	15	16	16	(2080)	14
Bosnia and Herzegovina	52	78	70	54	84	(1990)	59
Botswana	1	3	2	2	3	(2005)	3
Brazil	6	20	28	25	28	(2055)	26
Brunei Darussalam	9	63	130	133	139	(2075)	136
Bulgaria	66	73	48	36	81	(1985)	40
Burkina Faso	14	44	155	238	242	(2115)	224
Burundi	96	244	758	1 075	1 084	(2110)	1 015
Cambodia	25	74	168	195	195	(2090)	175
Cameroon	10	32	54	58	58	(2085)	56
Canada	1	3	4	4	4	(2050)	4
Cape Verde	36	108	202	207	214	(2075)	200
Central African Republic	2	6	11	12	12	(2095)	12
Chad	2	6	20	27	27	(2105)	25
Channel Islands	524	741	644	576	744	(2005)	672
Chile	8	20	29	29	30	(2070)	28
China	59	137	150	127	156	(2030)	138
China, Hong Kong SAR	1 889	6 514	9 025	7 736	9 025	(2050)	8 386
China, Macao SAR	10 581	24 990	32 114	27 061	32 114	(2050)	29 848
Colombia	12	41	65	65	67	(2070)	60
Comoros	77	316	814	984	986	(2095)	884
Congo	2	10	31	43	43	(2105)	39
Costa Rica	19	77	128	121	129	(2065)	121
Côte d'Ivoire	9	50	87	95	96	(2085)	88
Croatia	69	80	64	58	87	(1990)	66
Cuba	53	102	92	74	105	(2020)	83

TABLE A16 (*continued*)

Country or area	1950	2000	2050	2100	Maximum up to 2150	Year of maximum	2300
	Persons per square kilometer						
Cyprus	53	85	97	85	97	(2035)	89
Czech Republic	115	133	111	86	134	(1995)	97
Dem. People's Rep. of Korea	90	185	207	187	209	(2040)	200
Dem. Rep. of the Congo	5	21	67	90	90	(2100)	81
Dem. Rep. of Timor-Leste	29	47	96	98	101	(2080)	90
Denmark	101	125	124	116	129	(2025)	131
Djibouti	3	29	60	74	74	(2095)	67
Dominican Republic	49	173	245	227	248	(2060)	208
Ecuador	12	45	68	65	69	(2065)	63
Egypt	22	68	128	132	137	(2075)	125
El Salvador	94	300	473	468	491	(2070)	439
Equatorial Guinea	8	16	42	52	52	(2095)	48
Eritrea	11	37	104	128	128	(2095)	118
Estonia	26	32	16	12	37	(1990)	14
Ethiopia	18	66	171	222	222	(2105)	207
Fiji	16	45	53	49	54	(2040)	46
Finland	13	17	16	15	17	(2020)	17
France	76	108	117	109	118	(2040)	125
French Guiana	0	2	4	4	4	(2075)	4
French Polynesia	17	64	97	93	98	(2065)	94
Gabon	2	5	10	11	11	(2085)	10
Gambia	29	131	290	332	334	(2090)	302
Georgia	51	75	50	39	78	(1990)	41
Germany	196	236	227	209	236	(2010)	244
Ghana	22	86	174	193	194	(2090)	181
Greece	59	85	76	58	85	(2010)	64
Guadeloupe	124	253	276	241	289	(2035)	259
Guam	108	283	451	452	472	(2075)	426
Guatemala	27	105	241	271	276	(2085)	249
Guinea	10	33	80	97	97	(2095)	87
Guinea-Bissau	18	49	168	248	249	(2110)	224
Guyana	2	4	3	2	4	(2010)	2
Haiti	118	290	451	462	481	(2075)	404
Honduras	12	58	113	119	122	(2080)	108
Hungary	101	108	82	67	116	(1980)	77
Iceland	1	3	3	3	3	(2040)	3
India	120	342	515	491	524	(2065)	461
Indonesia	44	117	162	151	163	(2055)	152
Iran, Islamic Rep. of	10	41	65	61	66	(2060)	62
Iraq	12	53	132	156	156	(2090)	144
Ireland	43	55	73	66	73	(2050)	72
Israel	61	293	484	477	499	(2070)	454
Italy	160	196	153	115	196	(2000)	129
Jamaica	130	238	339	319	343	(2060)	314
Japan	222	337	291	239	340	(2010)	267

TABLE A16 (*continued*)

Country or area	1950	2000	2050	2100	Maximum up to 2150	Year of maximum	2300
	Persons per square kilometer						
Jordan	5	57	114	120	123	(2080)	113
Kazakhstan	3	6	5	4	6	(1990)	5
Kenya	11	54	77	80	80	(2095)	82
Kuwait	9	126	276	256	277	(2055)	247
Kyrgyzstan	9	26	38	35	38	(2060)	36
Lao People's Dem. Republic	8	23	50	55	56	(2085)	51
Latvia	31	38	21	17	44	(1990)	19
Lebanon	141	340	483	440	484	(2055)	459
Lesotho	24	59	45	54	59	(2005)	58
Liberia	9	31	102	140	140	(2100)	125
Libyan Arab Jamahiriya	1	3	5	5	5	(2065)	5
Lithuania	40	54	39	37	58	(1990)	40
Luxembourg	114	168	277	275	283	(2150)	318
Madagascar	7	27	80	106	106	(2105)	99
Malawi	31	121	276	349	349	(2100)	329
Malaysia	19	70	120	121	125	(2070)	117
Maldives	273	970	2 731	3 369	3 373	(2095)	3 146
Mali	3	10	38	58	58	(2110)	52
Malta	975	1 216	1 257	1 174	1 307	(2025)	1 364
Martinique	209	364	389	354	403	(2030)	378
Mauritania	1	3	7	10	10	(2100)	9
Mauritius	243	584	720	658	722	(2045)	703
Mexico	15	52	73	67	74	(2055)	66
Micronesia, Fed. States of	46	152	226	247	251	(2085)	223
Mongolia	0	2	2	2	2	(2055)	2
Morocco	20	65	105	104	108	(2070)	103
Mozambique	8	23	40	44	44	(2090)	41
Myanmar	27	72	98	91	98	(2055)	91
Namibia	1	2	3	4	4	(2100)	4
Nepal	60	164	355	408	411	(2090)	362
Netherlands	298	469	500	470	509	(2035)	536
Netherlands Antilles	140	269	311	283	317	(2035)	301
New Caledonia	4	12	21	20	21	(2065)	19
New Zealand	7	14	17	16	17	(2040)	18
Nicaragua	9	42	90	99	101	(2085)	89
Niger	2	8	42	78	82	(2120)	74
Nigeria	33	126	284	332	333	(2095)	311
Norway	11	15	16	15	16	(2035)	17
Occupied Palestinian Territory	162	514	1 789	2 403	2 403	(2105)	2 170
Oman	2	12	32	39	39	(2095)	35
Pakistan	51	185	452	530	534	(2090)	466
Panama	12	40	69	69	72	(2075)	66
Papua New Guinea	4	12	25	27	28	(2085)	25
Paraguay	4	14	30	34	35	(2085)	31

TABLE A16 (*continued*)

Country or area	*1950*	*2000*	*2050*	*2100*	*Maximum up to 2150*	*Year of maximum*	*2300*
		Persons per square kilometer					
Peru	6	20	32	31	33	(2065)	30
Philippines	67	254	426	432	448	(2075)	421
Poland	82	127	108	86	127	(2000)	92
Portugal	92	109	99	80	110	(2010)	91
Puerto Rico	250	430	420	347	459	(2025)	362
Qatar	2	53	79	77	81	(2075)	73
Republic of Korea	191	474	470	377	508	(2025)	420
Republic of Moldova	71	130	109	84	132	(1990)	89
Réunion	99	289	406	391	407	(2060)	406
Romania	71	98	78	64	101	(1990)	73
Russian Federation	6	9	6	5	9	(1990)	5
Rwanda	88	313	688	833	833	(2100)	800
St. Lucia	130	239	266	246	276	(2035)	244
St. Vincent and Grenadines	172	302	330	293	339	(2035)	313
Samoa	29	61	90	104	105	(2095)	94
Sao Tome and Principe	63	155	363	423	424	(2090)	396
Saudi Arabia	1	10	25	29	29	(2085)	26
Senegal	13	49	112	131	132	(2090)	124
Serbia and Montenegro	70	103	92	77	103	(2000)	83
Sierra Leone	27	62	144	154	161	(2080)	121
Singapore	1 676	6 584	7 440	5 880	8 088	(2030)	6 580
Slovakia	72	112	103	83	113	(2015)	90
Slovenia	73	99	78	58	99	(1995)	63
Solomon Islands	3	16	38	42	43	(2085)	38
Somalia	4	14	63	105	108	(2115)	99
South Africa	11	36	33	31	37	(2005)	35
Spain	56	82	75	58	83	(2010)	66
Sri Lanka	116	288	328	289	336	(2035)	309
Sudan	4	13	25	27	28	(2085)	25
Suriname	1	3	3	3	3	(2030)	3
Swaziland	16	61	55	55	63	(2005)	60
Sweden	17	22	21	20	22	(2025)	23
Switzerland	119	181	147	122	181	(2000)	139
Syrian Arab Republic	19	90	186	191	198	(2075)	182
Tajikistan	11	43	68	64	69	(2065)	60
TFYR Macedonia	48	80	85	75	87	(2035)	80
Thailand	38	119	151	138	151	(2045)	150
Togo	24	84	184	211	212	(2095)	201
Tonga	66	140	170	170	177	(2070)	156
Trinidad and Tobago	124	251	238	205	262	(2020)	222
Tunisia	23	61	83	73	83	(2050)	77
Turkey	28	89	127	117	127	(2055)	119
Turkmenistan	3	10	16	15	16	(2065)	15
Uganda	26	118	517	837	852	(2115)	774
Ukraine	64	86	55	42	90	(1990)	47

TABLE A16 (*continued*)

Country or area	*1950*	*2000*	*2050*	*2100*	*Maximum up to 2150*	*Year of maximum*	*2300*
	Persons per square kilometer						
United Arab Emirates	1	34	49	44	50	(2040)	42
United Kingdom	206	243	274	266	274	(2150)	303
United Rep. of Tanzania	9	39	78	87	88	(2085)	81
United States of America	17	31	45	48	49	(2150)	54
United States Virgin Islands	79	320	390	361	391	(2055)	374
Uruguay	13	19	24	22	24	(2060)	22
Uzbekistan	15	60	91	83	92	(2060)	82
Vanuatu	4	16	36	39	40	(2085)	35
Venezuela	6	28	47	46	49	(2070)	45
Viet Nam	84	240	362	338	364	(2060)	349
Western Sahara	0	1	2	3	3	(2085)	2
Yemen	8	34	160	273	279	(2115)	246
Zambia	3	14	25	30	30	(2105)	29
Zimbabwe	7	33	33	32	34	(2015)	35

TABLE A17. MEDIAN AGE BY COUNTRY, MEDIUM SCENARIO: 1950-2300

Country or area	1950	2000	2050	2100	2150	2200	2250	2300
	Median age of population (years)							
Afghanistan	18.6	18.1	26.1	42.1	45.2	43.4	44.2	45.2
Albania	20.6	26.7	41.9	46.3	44.6	45.5	47.1	48.7
Algeria	19.9	21.7	40.0	45.4	44.6	45.4	46.7	47.8
Angola	19.4	16.3	22.0	39.2	44.2	43.4	44.4	45.7
Argentina	25.7	27.9	40.0	46.3	46.0	46.5	48.2	49.7
Armenia	22.4	30.7	51.5	44.7	43.5	45.1	46.7	48.2
Australia	30.4	35.2	43.7	45.3	45.7	47.6	49.3	50.9
Austria	35.8	38.3	50.3	45.1	46.3	48.3	50.2	51.9
Azerbaijan	22.8	25.6	40.2	45.9	45.1	46.1	47.3	48.2
Bahamas	20.7	26.1	39.6	45.2	44.5	45.4	46.5	47.3
Bahrain	18.9	26.9	39.4	46.9	45.0	45.9	47.4	48.8
Bangladesh	21.6	20.0	35.7	43.9	44.4	43.8	44.9	45.8
Barbados	24.6	32.6	48.6	44.7	44.4	46.1	47.6	48.9
Belarus	27.2	36.5	50.0	43.5	44.1	45.7	47.2	48.4
Belgium	35.6	39.1	46.3	45.1	46.7	48.7	50.6	52.1
Belize	20.8	19.8	37.8	45.2	44.3	44.8	46.1	47.3
Benin	23.7	16.6	28.5	42.2	44.8	44.0	45.2	46.2
Bhutan	20.1	18.3	31.1	44.2	46.9	45.6	46.5	47.5
Bolivia	19.2	20.1	34.5	45.1	46.5	45.1	46.6	48.1
Bosnia and Herzegovina	20.0	35.1	49.4	44.3	44.1	45.8	47.2	48.4
Botswana	16.8	19.1	25.6	37.1	42.5	43.6	45.5	46.8
Brazil	19.2	25.4	41.2	45.6	44.6	46.0	47.6	49.0
Brunei Darussalam	22.4	25.0	37.4	47.0	45.4	46.7	48.4	50.0
Bulgaria	27.3	39.1	50.6	43.8	43.8	45.6	47.1	48.4
Burkina Faso	18.5	15.5	22.7	39.8	45.1	44.4	45.2	46.3
Burundi	19.5	15.8	23.4	39.7	44.7	44.0	45.1	46.3
Cambodia	18.7	17.5	30.4	42.2	44.7	43.4	44.2	45.1
Cameroon	20.3	18.1	28.7	40.7	43.9	43.4	44.9	46.1
Canada	27.7	36.9	45.8	44.5	45.6	47.3	48.8	50.2
Cape Verde	21.4	18.5	37.3	45.1	45.9	45.6	47.1	48.3
Central African Republic	22.6	18.3	26.8	40.0	43.8	43.4	44.9	46.1
Chad	21.5	16.7	24.5	41.1	44.8	43.9	44.9	46.1
Channel Islands	35.7	38.6	47.4	43.8	45.8	47.7	49.8	51.5
Chile	22.2	28.3	39.7	46.3	46.3	46.7	48.2	49.4
China	23.9	30.0	43.8	45.3	44.3	46.3	48.1	49.6
China, Hong Kong SAR	23.7	36.1	48.5	47.0	46.5	48.3	49.6	50.6
China, Macao SAR	25.3	33.5	49.2	45.9	45.7	47.4	48.9	50.2
Colombia	18.7	24.0	38.4	46.3	47.5	46.4	47.8	49.0
Comoros	18.2	18.0	31.4	44.0	46.6	45.3	46.2	47.1
Congo	20.0	16.7	24.6	40.4	43.8	42.8	43.6	44.4
Costa Rica	21.6	24.5	41.6	47.8	46.8	47.7	48.9	49.8
Côte d'Ivoire	18.3	18.1	30.0	41.7	44.6	43.9	45.2	46.3
Croatia	27.9	38.9	44.9	43.0	44.6	46.3	47.8	49.0
Cuba	23.3	33.0	48.8	45.1	44.7	46.5	48.2	49.7

TABLE A17 (*continued*)

Country or area	*1950*	*2000*	*2050*	*2100*	*2150*	*2200*	*2250*	*2300*
	Median age of population (years)							
Cyprus	23.7	33.4	44.1	46.7	45.3	46.6	48.1	49.3
Czech Republic	32.7	37.6	51.7	43.7	44.7	46.3	47.8	49.2
Dem. People's Rep. of Korea	19.5	29.4	40.7	43.6	42.8	44.5	45.8	46.9
Dem. Rep. of the Congo	18.1	16.5	24.1	40.6	44.4	43.4	44.5	45.8
Dem. Rep. of Timor-Leste	19.6	17.4	34.1	42.4	43.9	42.8	43.9	44.8
Denmark	31.8	38.7	45.3	43.4	45.1	46.6	48.2	49.5
Djibouti	16.5	18.3	27.5	41.6	44.9	44.1	45.2	46.3
Dominican Republic	17.7	23.1	37.9	45.0	45.3	44.3	46.0	47.6
Ecuador	20.6	22.7	39.4	45.6	45.5	45.5	47.1	48.5
Egypt	20.0	21.3	36.5	45.1	45.7	45.2	46.6	47.8
El Salvador	18.3	21.8	38.2	45.7	46.1	45.4	46.8	48.0
Equatorial Guinea	23.8	18.2	27.6	42.3	44.9	44.0	45.2	46.3
Eritrea	17.3	16.9	28.3	41.8	44.6	43.7	44.9	46.0
Estonia	29.9	37.9	52.3	43.1	44.8	46.3	47.6	48.6
Ethiopia	17.9	16.9	25.8	41.0	44.7	44.0	45.1	46.2
Fiji	16.6	23.1	40.2	45.7	46.3	45.7	47.3	48.6
Finland	27.7	39.4	45.8	44.4	46.0	48.0	49.8	51.5
France	34.5	37.6	45.1	45.9	46.4	48.5	50.3	52.0
French Guiana	26.6	23.7	37.6	46.6	47.2	46.6	48.2	49.6
French Polynesia	17.8	25.1	40.0	46.0	45.4	46.3	47.8	49.0
Gabon	28.4	18.9	32.3	43.0	44.8	43.8	45.0	46.0
Gambia	19.5	19.4	31.0	42.7	45.0	44.0	45.0	46.1
Georgia	27.3	34.8	48.4	45.0	44.2	45.9	47.2	48.3
Germany	35.4	39.9	46.8	44.9	46.7	48.9	50.9	52.6
Ghana	17.4	18.8	32.6	43.1	45.3	44.5	45.7	46.6
Greece	26.0	39.1	51.3	45.2	45.0	46.8	48.3	49.7
Guadeloupe	20.9	31.8	46.9	45.8	45.5	47.0	48.3	49.3
Guam	22.8	27.4	37.8	46.0	46.5	45.8	47.5	49.1
Guatemala	17.7	17.8	33.5	45.6	46.6	45.5	46.9	48.1
Guinea	18.8	17.6	28.5	42.4	45.2	44.1	45.1	46.2
Guinea-Bissau	21.7	16.6	23.1	40.2	44.8	43.9	44.8	46.0
Guyana	19.8	24.1	47.8	44.5	43.5	44.5	45.9	47.1
Haiti	22.4	18.9	32.6	43.9	45.1	43.5	45.0	46.2
Honduras	17.2	18.7	34.9	45.4	46.4	45.2	46.7	47.9
Hungary	29.9	38.1	49.6	43.2	44.8	46.7	48.3	49.7
Iceland	26.5	32.9	44.5	46.4	45.6	47.0	48.7	50.2
India	20.4	23.4	37.9	45.4	45.5	45.2	46.5	47.5
Indonesia	20.0	24.6	39.9	44.8	43.8	44.9	46.1	47.1
Iran, Islamic Rep. of	21.1	20.6	40.2	45.8	44.7	45.9	47.4	48.7
Iraq	17.0	18.7	32.2	44.6	46.8	45.7	47.0	48.0
Ireland	29.6	31.9	43.3	45.8	45.0	46.9	48.6	50.2
Israel	25.5	27.9	40.4	47.6	47.7	47.3	48.8	50.2
Italy	29.0	40.2	52.4	44.9	45.2	46.9	48.6	50.1
Jamaica	22.2	24.1	40.8	46.9	45.9	46.5	47.8	48.9

TABLE A17 (*continued*)

Country or area	1950	2000	2050	2100	2150	2200	2250	2300
	Median age of population (years)							
Japan	22.3	41.3	53.2	47.4	48.0	49.8	51.5	53.0
Jordan	17.2	20.1	36.9	46.0	47.1	46.4	47.6	48.5
Kazakhstan	23.2	27.9	42.9	44.8	43.5	44.8	46.1	47.2
Kenya	20.0	17.7	28.8	40.2	44.3	44.4	46.0	47.1
Kuwait	21.5	28.6	41.2	47.2	46.7	46.8	48.2	49.4
Kyrgyzstan	25.3	23.2	39.9	45.0	44.4	45.4	46.9	48.2
Lao People's Dem. Republic	18.9	18.5	32.4	43.8	45.7	44.6	45.9	46.9
Latvia	30.5	37.8	53.0	42.7	44.3	46.0	47.4	48.6
Lebanon	23.2	25.2	41.5	45.3	44.3	45.5	47.1	48.4
Lesotho	19.8	18.8	24.1	38.1	44.1	44.0	45.2	46.1
Liberia	19.2	16.6	23.3	39.1	42.6	41.6	42.5	43.6
Libyan Arab Jamahiriya	19.0	21.8	39.4	46.2	45.7	46.4	47.8	48.9
Lithuania	27.8	36.0	44.4	44.5	45.6	47.0	48.1	48.8
Luxembourg	35.0	37.0	43.0	45.4	46.6	48.8	50.7	52.4
Madagascar	19.0	17.5	27.6	42.2	45.6	44.7	45.6	46.7
Malawi	17.1	17.1	23.8	38.8	43.1	42.5	43.8	45.0
Malaysia	19.8	23.6	38.3	46.1	46.6	46.5	48.0	49.2
Maldives	24.7	17.7	31.0	44.4	46.6	45.7	46.8	47.8
Mali	17.2	15.4	22.6	39.4	43.2	42.1	42.8	43.7
Malta	23.7	36.5	46.0	45.3	46.9	49.1	51.0	52.7
Martinique	21.9	33.8	45.1	46.6	46.1	47.6	48.8	49.8
Mauritania	18.0	18.2	27.7	42.2	45.3	44.4	45.4	46.5
Mauritius	17.3	28.9	42.1	44.9	44.3	45.8	47.2	48.4
Mexico	19.1	22.9	42.1	46.7	45.8	46.5	47.8	48.9
Micronesia, Fed. States of	19.8	19.0	34.2	44.7	46.4	45.0	46.3	47.3
Mongolia	19.0	21.8	39.8	45.2	44.1	44.9	46.5	47.8
Morocco	17.7	23.0	38.3	45.2	45.6	45.8	47.3	48.6
Mozambique	19.1	17.8	26.5	39.8	43.5	43.1	44.7	46.0
Myanmar	21.8	23.4	37.9	44.4	44.3	45.1	46.4	47.5
Namibia	19.5	18.4	27.1	39.7	44.0	44.1	45.8	47.0
Nepal	21.1	19.5	32.1	43.6	45.5	44.0	45.0	45.8
Netherlands	28.0	37.6	44.9	43.8	45.3	47.0	48.7	50.1
Netherlands Antilles	23.3	32.0	42.8	46.1	45.2	46.7	48.4	49.8
New Caledonia	22.5	26.9	40.2	46.5	46.0	46.4	47.7	48.8
New Zealand	29.4	34.5	43.7	45.0	45.3	47.1	48.6	50.1
Nicaragua	17.6	18.1	34.1	45.7	47.3	45.8	47.1	48.5
Niger	17.9	15.1	20.0	37.7	45.3	45.1	45.3	46.5
Nigeria	19.1	17.3	28.4	41.6	44.6	43.8	45.0	46.1
Norway	32.7	37.2	46.1	45.7	46.4	48.4	50.1	51.6
Occupied Palestinian Territory	17.2	16.8	28.6	44.2	47.4	46.2	47.1	48.4
Oman	18.8	21.2	31.9	44.6	47.1	45.9	47.0	48.3
Pakistan	21.2	18.8	31.6	45.1	47.1	45.6	46.7	47.8
Panama	20.2	24.8	38.4	46.6	46.8	46.5	48.1	49.7
Papua New Guinea	20.3	19.1	32.8	44.4	47.1	46.0	47.2	48.3
Paraguay	20.9	19.7	33.6	45.5	46.9	45.6	47.0	48.4

TABLE A17 (*continued*)

Country or area	*1950*	*2000*	*2050*	*2100*	*2150*	*2200*	*2250*	*2300*
	Median age of population (years)							
Peru	19.1	22.7	39.2	46.2	46.1	45.9	47.2	48.4
Philippines	18.2	20.9	37.5	45.7	46.2	46.2	47.7	48.9
Poland	25.8	35.2	48.9	45.4	44.7	46.4	47.7	48.9
Portugal	26.2	37.0	48.5	44.7	44.9	46.9	48.7	50.4
Puerto Rico	18.4	31.8	48.1	46.6	46.2	47.4	48.5	49.4
Qatar	18.9	31.0	39.2	47.0	47.0	46.8	47.9	48.8
Republic of Korea	19.2	31.8	50.2	46.5	46.6	48.7	50.4	51.7
Republic of Moldova	26.6	31.7	47.3	44.7	43.4	44.9	46.5	48.1
Réunion	20.3	28.3	40.8	45.9	45.5	46.7	47.9	48.9
Romania	26.1	34.7	47.4	42.2	43.8	45.5	46.9	48.1
Russian Federation	25.0	36.8	48.6	41.7	43.7	45.5	47.0	48.1
Rwanda	16.7	17.0	27.5	41.4	44.8	44.3	45.6	46.8
St. Lucia	20.7	23.8	40.8	46.5	45.3	46.1	47.3	48.3
St. Vincent and Grenadines	15.4	22.7	43.2	45.4	45.0	46.5	48.1	49.5
Samoa	16.6	19.1	32.6	44.9	47.4	46.0	47.1	48.3
Sao Tome and Principe	24.6	18.4	33.2	44.7	46.9	46.0	47.2	48.4
Saudi Arabia	19.0	20.6	34.1	45.6	46.8	45.8	47.3	48.5
Senegal	19.2	17.6	30.4	42.1	44.6	44.0	45.6	47.2
Serbia and Montenegro	25.6	35.4	45.4	45.2	44.4	46.3	47.8	49.2
Sierra Leone	20.4	17.9	25.6	40.8	43.1	41.1	42.6	44.2
Singapore	20.0	34.5	52.0	45.5	46.2	48.1	49.7	51.0
Slovakia	27.3	34.0	47.6	45.1	44.6	46.4	47.9	49.1
Slovenia	27.7	38.1	53.1	45.1	44.8	46.4	47.8	49.1
Solomon Islands	18.3	18.0	33.7	45.3	46.9	45.5	46.9	48.3
Somalia	19.5	16.0	22.1	40.0	45.8	45.1	45.8	47.0
South Africa	20.9	22.6	31.8	40.9	42.7	44.8	46.7	48.0
Spain	27.7	37.4	51.9	46.8	46.6	48.7	50.6	52.4
Sri Lanka	20.3	28.1	43.6	45.6	45.0	46.5	48.1	49.4
Sudan	18.1	19.7	31.9	42.8	44.9	43.8	45.0	46.0
Suriname	20.1	23.5	41.0	45.1	44.9	45.2	46.2	47.0
Swaziland	18.4	17.4	24.5	35.8	41.2	42.3	44.6	45.9
Sweden	34.3	39.6	46.3	45.3	46.7	48.7	50.6	52.3
Switzerland	33.3	40.2	50.6	44.1	45.4	47.1	48.8	50.4
Syrian Arab Republic	19.2	19.0	37.1	45.6	46.1	45.7	47.2	48.4
Tajikistan	22.3	19.9	38.9	45.3	44.1	44.2	45.2	46.0
TFYR Macedonia	22.3	32.3	42.8	45.1	43.9	45.5	46.9	48.2
Thailand	18.6	27.5	42.2	45.2	44.9	46.8	48.5	49.9
Togo	19.4	17.7	28.8	41.4	44.2	43.6	44.9	46.0
Tonga	15.5	20.3	37.2	44.8	46.1	45.0	46.3	47.3
Trinidad and Tobago	20.7	27.6	44.1	44.6	44.3	46.0	47.5	48.6
Tunisia	20.9	24.4	42.6	45.9	44.6	45.9	47.5	48.9
Turkey	19.4	24.2	41.3	45.8	45.0	46.1	47.4	48.3
Turkmenistan	23.5	21.6	38.6	45.6	45.0	45.5	46.9	48.0
Uganda	17.7	15.1	22.5	40.3	45.4	44.5	45.2	46.2

TABLE A17 (*continued*)

Country or area	*1950*	*2000*	*2050*	*2100*	*2150*	*2200*	*2250*	*2300*
	Median age of population (years)							
Ukraine	27.6	37.3	50.7	42.6	43.8	45.5	47.0	48.3
United Arab Emirates	18.9	29.6	42.5	46.6	45.7	46.0	47.5	48.8
United Kingdom	34.6	37.7	43.8	44.5	45.9	47.7	49.3	50.7
United Rep. of Tanzania	16.9	16.8	29.7	42.0	44.6	43.9	45.2	46.2
United States of America	30.0	35.2	39.7	44.5	46.1	47.8	49.1	50.1
United States Virgin Islands	22.0	33.4	42.0	47.2	45.9	47.1	48.7	50.0
Uruguay	27.8	31.4	41.0	47.2	47.1	47.1	48.4	49.5
Uzbekistan	24.1	21.5	40.5	45.9	44.7	45.6	46.8	47.8
Vanuatu	16.8	18.6	33.4	44.6	46.7	45.3	46.4	47.6
Venezuela	18.3	23.1	38.8	46.3	45.6	45.8	47.4	49.0
Viet Nam	24.6	23.1	40.4	45.8	44.9	46.1	47.6	48.7
Western Sahara	18.7	22.1	34.1	44.1	45.7	44.8	46.1	47.0
Yemen	18.9	15.4	22.3	39.7	44.8	43.4	43.9	44.6
Zambia	17.5	16.7	24.1	38.7	43.8	43.5	44.9	46.2
Zimbabwe	19.0	17.5	24.7	36.0	41.1	42.2	44.7	46.2

TABLE A18. PROPORTION OF BROAD AGE GROUPS OF THE WORLD BY DEVELOPMENT GROUP, MAJOR AREA AND REGION, MEDIUM SCENARIO: 1950-2300

Major area and region	*1950*	*2000*	*2050*	*2100*	*2150*	*2200*	*2250*	*2300*
			0-14 years (percentage)					
World	34.3	30.1	20.1	16.4	16.5	16.5	16.0	15.6
More developed regions	27.4	18.3	15.7	16.9	16.4	15.7	15.3	14.9
Less developed regions	37.6	33.0	20.8	16.4	16.5	16.6	16.1	15.7
Africa	42.0	42.7	27.8	17.4	16.4	17.0	16.6	16.2
Southern Africa	39.0	35.0	23.3	17.7	17.6	16.8	16.1	15.7
Eastern Africa	43.4	45.6	29.8	17.7	16.2	17.0	16.6	16.2
Middle Africa	41.1	46.0	31.3	17.7	16.3	17.3	16.8	16.4
Western Africa	42.1	45.1	28.7	17.6	16.4	17.1	16.7	16.3
Northern Africa	41.2	35.8	19.8	15.9	16.5	16.6	16.1	15.7
Asia	36.5	30.4	18.6	16.0	16.6	16.5	16.0	15.6
Western Asia	39.2	36.0	22.9	16.4	16.1	16.6	16.2	15.9
India	38.9	34.1	18.6	15.5	16.5	16.6	16.1	15.8
Other South-central Asia	37.8	38.6	21.7	15.9	16.3	16.7	16.3	16.0
South-eastern Asia	38.9	32.4	18.4	15.9	16.8	16.5	16.0	15.6
China	33.5	24.8	16.1	16.6	17.0	16.2	15.6	15.1
Other Eastern Asia	36.9	17.7	13.9	16.1	16.0	15.5	15.0	14.6
Latin America and the Caribbean	40.0	31.9	18.1	15.5	16.5	16.3	15.8	15.4
Brazil	41.6	29.3	17.3	15.9	16.9	16.3	15.8	15.3
Other South America	37.5	32.2	18.6	15.3	16.2	16.3	15.8	15.3
Caribbean	38.5	29.5	18.4	16.1	16.7	16.7	16.1	15.6
Central America	42.3	35.3	18.2	15.2	16.3	16.2	15.8	15.4
Oceania	29.9	25.8	18.1	16.3	16.3	16.0	15.5	15.0
Polynesia	46.6	35.5	19.9	15.9	16.3	16.2	15.7	15.3
Micronesia	35.8	36.3	20.3	16.3	16.3	16.1	15.5	15.1
Melanesia	40.4	40.4	21.7	15.8	15.9	16.3	15.9	15.5
Australia/New Zealand	27.0	20.9	16.3	16.5	16.5	15.8	15.3	14.8
Northern America	27.2	21.6	17.7	16.9	16.3	15.7	15.3	15.0
Europe	26.2	17.5	14.8	17.0	16.5	15.9	15.4	14.9
Eastern Europe	28.1	18.1	14.3	17.6	17.1	16.4	15.9	15.5
Southern Europe	27.6	15.7	13.8	16.4	16.6	15.9	15.3	14.9
Western Europe	23.3	17.1	15.4	16.6	16.2	15.5	14.9	14.4
Northern Europe	23.7	19.1	15.9	16.9	16.3	15.7	15.2	14.8
				15-64 years(percentage)				
World	60.5	63.0	64.0	59.2	56.0	54.7	53.3	52.0
More developed regions	64.8	67.4	58.4	55.5	54.4	52.4	50.8	49.5
Less developed regions	58.5	61.9	64.9	59.7	56.2	55.1	53.7	52.4
Africa	54.8	54.1	65.4	63.1	57.7	56.3	55.2	53.9
Southern Africa	57.3	61.3	67.9	61.6	56.9	55.5	53.6	52.3
Eastern Africa	53.6	51.6	65.2	63.6	57.8	56.1	55.1	53.9
Middle Africa	55.1	51.1	64.4	64.5	58.8	56.8	55.9	54.5
Western Africa	54.8	52.0	65.4	63.6	58.0	56.7	55.6	54.4
Northern Africa	55.3	60.0	66.3	59.1	55.8	55.3	53.7	52.5

TABLE A18 (*continued*)

Major area and region	*1950*	*2000*	*2050*	*2100*	*2150*	*2200*	*2250*	*2300*
Asia	59.4	63.7	64.5	58.5	55.7	54.7	53.2	51.9
Western Asia	56.4	59.6	64.9	60.5	56.2	55.2	54.0	52.9
India	57.7	60.9	67.0	58.6	55.4	55.2	53.7	52.6
Other South-central Asia	57.6	57.5	67.3	60.0	56.2	55.6	54.3	53.2
South-eastern Asia	57.3	62.9	65.2	58.6	55.8	54.8	53.3	52.1
China	62.0	68.3	61.0	56.6	55.9	53.7	51.9	50.4
Other Eastern Asia	58.7	69.0	54.2	54.1	53.3	51.4	49.8	48.5
Latin America and the Caribbean	56.3	62.6	63.7	57.0	54.4	53.9	52.4	51.1
Brazil	55.5	65.5	62.9	57.0	55.2	54.0	52.3	51.0
Other South America	58.6	61.7	64.4	56.9	54.0	53.9	52.3	51.0
Caribbean	57.0	63.5	62.2	57.5	55.0	54.5	53.0	51.7
Central America	53.7	60.1	64.1	56.9	54.1	53.9	52.4	51.3
Oceania	62.8	64.4	62.8	56.9	54.6	53.2	51.5	50.0
Polynesia	51.1	59.9	65.4	58.1	54.6	53.8	52.3	51.0
Micronesia	62.0	59.0	66.1	57.5	54.6	53.3	51.7	50.2
Melanesia	55.7	57.0	68.5	59.8	54.9	54.5	53.0	51.7
Australia/New Zealand	64.7	66.9	60.0	55.3	54.4	52.6	50.8	49.3
Northern America	64.6	66.1	61.8	55.3	54.1	52.2	50.9	49.8
Europe	65.6	67.8	57.3	56.1	55.0	52.8	51.1	49.7
Eastern Europe	65.4	69.0	57.9	58.1	56.7	54.5	52.9	51.7
Southern Europe	64.7	67.9	54.0	55.5	54.7	52.8	51.0	49.5
Western Europe	66.5	67.0	57.4	54.9	53.7	51.5	49.6	48.1
Northern Europe	66.0	65.4	59.8	55.5	54.4	52.3	50.6	49.3
				65+ years (percentage)				
World	5.2	6.9	15.9	24.4	27.5	28.8	30.7	32.3
More developed regions	7.9	14.3	25.9	27.7	29.3	31.9	33.9	35.6
Less developed regions	3.9	5.1	14.3	23.9	27.2	28.2	30.1	31.8
Africa	3.2	3.2	6.8	19.5	25.9	26.7	28.2	29.9
Southern Africa	3.6	3.7	8.8	20.7	25.5	27.6	30.2	32.0
Eastern Africa	2.9	2.8	5.0	18.7	26.0	26.8	28.3	29.9
Middle Africa	3.8	3.0	4.2	17.8	25.0	25.9	27.3	29.1
Western Africa	3.0	2.9	5.9	18.8	25.5	26.2	27.7	29.3
Northern Africa	3.5	4.2	13.8	25.0	27.6	28.1	30.1	31.8
Asia	4.1	5.9	16.8	25.5	27.7	28.8	30.9	32.5
Western Asia	4.3	4.4	12.1	23.1	27.7	28.2	29.7	31.2
India	3.3	4.9	14.4	25.9	28.0	28.2	30.2	31.6
Other South-central Asia	4.7	3.9	11.0	24.1	27.5	27.6	29.4	30.9
South-eastern Asia	3.8	4.7	16.4	25.5	27.5	28.7	30.7	32.3
China	4.5	6.8	22.9	26.8	27.1	30.0	32.5	34.5
Other Eastern Asia	4.4	13.3	31.9	29.8	30.6	33.2	35.2	37.0
Latin America and the Caribbean	3.7	5.5	18.2	27.5	29.1	29.7	31.8	33.5
Brazil	3.0	5.2	19.8	27.1	27.9	29.7	31.9	33.7
Other South America	3.9	6.1	17.0	27.8	29.8	29.8	31.9	33.7
Caribbean	4.5	7.1	19.4	26.5	28.3	28.8	30.9	32.7
Central America	4.1	4.6	17.7	27.9	29.6	29.9	31.8	33.3

TABLE A18 (*continued*)

Major area and region	*1950*	*2000*	*2050*	*2100*	*2150*	*2200*	*2250*	*2300*
Oceania	7.3	9.8	19.1	26.8	29.1	30.9	33.1	35.0
Polynesia	2.3	4.6	14.7	26.0	29.1	30.0	32.0	33.7
Micronesia	2.2	4.6	13.5	26.2	29.1	30.6	32.8	34.7
Melanesia	3.8	2.6	9.7	24.4	29.2	29.2	31.1	32.7
Australia/New Zealand	8.3	12.2	23.7	28.2	29.1	31.7	34.0	36.0
Northern America	8.2	12.3	20.5	27.7	29.6	32.1	33.9	35.2
Europe	8.2	14.7	27.9	26.9	28.5	31.3	33.5	35.4
Eastern Europe	6.5	12.9	27.7	24.3	26.3	29.1	31.2	32.8
Southern Europe	7.6	16.4	32.3	28.0	28.7	31.4	33.7	35.7
Western Europe	10.2	15.9	27.3	28.5	30.2	33.1	35.5	37.5
Northern Europe	10.3	15.6	24.3	27.6	29.2	31.9	34.1	36.0

TABLE A19. START AND END OF THE DEMOGRAPHIC WINDOW PHASE AND CORRESPONDING DEPENDENCY RATIO, BY COUNTRY, MEDIUM SCENARIO

	Demographic window			*Dependency ratio*		
Country or area	*Start*[a]	*End*	*Length (years)*[a]	*Start*	*Minimum*	*End*
Afghanistan	2050	2085	35	52.6	43.2	47.0
Albania	2000	2030	30	54.9	44.8	49.3
Algeria	2010	2045	35	49.3	42.8	49.5
Angola	2060	2095	35	51.9	43.3	49.0
Argentina	1995	2035	40	62.1	52.2	52.2
Armenia	1995	2020	25	56.0	31.8	35.8
Australia	1965	2010	45	61.6	46.7	46.7
Austria	1950	1990	40	49.6	47.9	47.9
Azerbaijan	2005	2035	30	52.1	41.6	50.7
Bahamas	2000	2035	35	53.8	48.0	53.4
Bahrain	2000	2040	40	47.6	37.3	48.5
Bangladesh	2020	2060	40	52.0	44.4	49.9
Barbados	1980	2020	40	67.1	37.7	42.1
Belarus	1970	2015	45	61.3	38.9	39.7
Belgium	1950	1990	40	46.9	46.9	49.4
Belize	2020	2050	30	51.5	45.0	50.6
Benin	2045	2075	30	50.2	45.2	49.1
Bhutan	2035	2065	30	53.4	49.0	49.3
Bolivia	2025	2055	30	55.2	49.9	50.9
Bosnia and Herzegovina	1980	2015	35	50.0	36.7	38.3
Botswana	2045	2090	45	48.8	45.4	53.0
Brazil	2000	2035	35	52.7	45.7	49.9
Brunei Darussalam	2005	2050	45	48.9	40.7	48.2
Bulgaria	1950	1995	45	50.4	48.0	49.2
Burkina Faso	2060	2090	30	52.3	45.4	49.4
Burundi	2060	2090	30	51.4	45.0	50.1
Cambodia	2035	2075	40	52.8	46.8	51.1
Cameroon	2040	2075	35	51.8	46.8	51.5
Canada	1975	2010	35	53.0	42.8	42.8
Cape Verde	2025	2050	25	48.9	45.1	48.9
Central African Republic	2045	2085	40	52.2	45.9	52.5
Chad	2055	2085	30	50.7	43.8	48.4
Channel Islands	1950	2000	50	50.6	44.9	47.0
Chile	1995	2030	35	56.4	50.3	56.5
China	1990	2025	35	49.8	39.6	46.1
China, Hong Kong SAR	1980	2015	35	47.0	33.6	36.0
China, Macao SAR	1975	2020	45	54.2	29.0	39.9
Colombia	2010	2040	30	52.5	50.0	54.9
Comoros	2035	2070	35	51.5	47.1	50.7
Congo	2055	2090	35	49.5	43.4	50.2
Costa Rica	2005	2035	30	51.9	45.4	51.5
Côte d'Ivoire	2035	2075	40	51.4	47.0	51.8
Croatia	1950	1995	45	53.0	45.8	47.1

TABLE A19 (*continued*)

Country or area	Demographic window			Dependency ratio		
	Start[a]	End	Length (years)[a]	Start	Minimum	End
Cuba	1985	2015	30	53.3	42.5	44.5
Cyprus	1975	2015	40	55.7	48.3	51.1
Czech Rep.	1950	2005	55	47.8	40.5	40.5
Dem. People's Rep. of Korea	1985	2035	50	52.3	40.9	49.6
Dem. Rep. of the Congo	2055	2090	35	51.4	43.6	49.9
Dem. Rep. of Timor-Leste	2025	2075	50	53.7	42.4	50.1
Denmark	1950	2000	50	54.9	48.4	49.9
Djibouti	2045	2080	35	52.8	46.0	50.6
Dominican Republic	2010	2045	35	54.3	51.4	53.7
Ecuador	2010	2040	30	54.3	48.8	50.5
Egypt	2020	2050	30	56.2	46.7	48.9
El Salvador	2015	2045	30	56.1	49.1	53.3
Equatorial Guinea	2045	2080	35	52.2	43.3	50.1
Eritrea	2045	2080	35	49.6	44.1	49.8
Estonia	1950	1995	45	56.7	49.7	52.2
Ethiopia	2050	2085	35	52.9	45.5	51.0
Fiji	2010	2045	35	52.8	47.8	49.1
Finland	1965	2000	35	53.8	46.8	49.4
France	1950	1990	40	51.7	51.7	52.1
French Guiana	2015	2050	35	51.5	48.8	49.5
French Polynesia	2005	2040	35	49.2	47.2	50.9
Gabon	2030	2065	35	54.0	47.6	50.5
Gambia	2035	2070	35	54.1	47.1	50.2
Georgia	1975	2015	40	58.4	43.1	43.1
Germany	1950	1990	40	49.0	44.0	45.0
Ghana	2030	2065	35	52.4	48.5	50.7
Greece	1950	1990	40	54.9	49.1	49.1
Guadeloupe	1985	2020	35	59.9	50.0	50.7
Guam	2010	2035	25	53.0	51.5	57.6
Guatemala	2030	2060	30	53.3	47.3	50.0
Guinea	2045	2075	30	51.7	45.2	48.6
Guinea-Bissau	2060	2090	30	51.0	44.3	48.8
Guyana	2005	2030	25	52.3	45.1	47.7
Haiti	2030	2060	30	53.5	48.2	51.8
Honduras	2025	2055	30	53.8	48.9	51.5
Hungary	1950	2000	50	48.0	46.2	46.2
Iceland	1980	2015	35	59.7	48.4	49.2
India	2010	2050	40	54.8	47.4	49.4
Indonesia	2005	2040	35	51.8	44.2	47.9
Iran, Islamic Rep. of	2005	2045	40	51.8	40.4	47.1
Iraq	2035	2065	30	51.3	46.8	48.6
Ireland	1985	2020	35	67.3	46.6	52.7
Israel	1995	2030	35	64.2	55.8	55.8
Italy	1950	1985	35	52.8	47.8	47.8

TABLE A19 (*continued*)

Country or area	Demographic window			Dependency ratio		
	Start[a]	End	Length (years)[a]	Start	Minimum	End
Jamaica	2005	2035	30	58.0	48.0	49.4
Japan	1965	1995	30	47.5	43.7	43.9
Jordan	2020	2050	30	50.1	45.6	49.5
Kazakhstan	1995	2030	35	57.7	42.4	48.6
Kenya	2035	2075	40	52.6	48.9	53.1
Kuwait	1995	2030	35	44.0	35.4	44.0
Kyrgyzstan	2010	2045	35	51.0	45.1	48.6
Lao People's Dem. Republic	2030	2065	35	54.0	46.0	48.7
Latvia	1950	1995	45	57.5	48.0	52.7
Lebanon	2005	2035	30	51.6	42.6	47.9
Lesotho	2055	2095	40	51.1	45.8	49.3
Liberia	2060	2095	35	48.9	42.3	48.3
Libyan Arab Jamahiriya	2005	2045	40	51.8	41.6	49.7
Lithuania	1950	2000	50	58.1	49.9	51.6
Luxembourg	1950	2015	65	42.3	42.3	46.8
Madagascar	2045	2080	35	54.4	46.7	51.0
Malawi	2055	2090	35	52.1	45.7	51.6
Malaysia	2010	2045	35	52.9	49.0	50.3
Maldives	2035	2070	35	53.2	46.9	50.2
Mali	2060	2095	35	50.0	42.7	48.4
Malta	1970	2010	40	58.0	46.4	47.3
Martinique	1985	2015	30	56.9	48.9	49.1
Mauritania	2045	2080	35	54.9	46.0	50.6
Mauritius	1990	2030	40	53.9	41.2	50.7
Mexico	2010	2035	25	53.0	47.0	48.2
Micronesia, Fed. States of	2025	2060	35	55.4	50.0	50.5
Mongolia	2010	2045	35	46.8	41.7	47.7
Morocco	2010	2045	35	50.8	46.2	50.5
Mozambique	2050	2085	35	50.2	45.3	51.4
Myanmar	2010	2050	40	51.3	46.3	50.8
Namibia	2045	2080	35	50.1	46.4	53.3
Nepal	2030	2065	35	53.6	46.9	48.6
Netherlands	1950	2005	55	58.9	45.1	47.7
Netherlands Antilles	1980	2020	40	57.8	45.8	51.9
New Caledonia	2000	2035	35	54.4	47.1	50.7
New Zealand	1975	2015	40	63.1	49.8	51.2
Nicaragua	2030	2055	25	52.8	49.3	50.9
Niger	2070	2100	30	51.7	44.9	49.5
Nigeria	2040	2075	35	53.5	46.6	50.5
Norway	1950	1980	30	51.8	51.8	58.5
Occupied Palestinian Territory	2045	2070	25	53.6	47.8	48.9
Oman	2030	2065	35	54.7	49.7	49.7
Pakistan	2035	2065	30	53.2	46.2	47.4
Panama	2010	2040	30	55.7	51.7	55.0

TABLE A19 (*continued*)

Country or area	Demographic window			Dependency ratio		
	Start[a]	End	Length (years)[a]	Start	Minimum	End
Papua New Guinea	2030	2065	35	50.7	45.1	49.2
Paraguay	2030	2060	30	56.4	49.0	51.6
Peru	2010	2045	35	55.0	48.3	51.6
Philippines	2015	2050	35	53.2	46.5	49.3
Poland	1970	2015	45	54.3	38.6	41.6
Portugal	1950	1995	45	57.4	47.8	47.8
Puerto Rico	1985	2010	25	61.9	51.9	51.9
Qatar	1985	2025	40	40.0	35.4	48.2
Republic of Korea	1985	2020	35	52.1	37.8	39.8
Republic of Moldova	1975	2020	45	55.5	36.9	41.3
Réunion	1995	2030	35	55.4	46.5	52.2
Romania	1950	2015	65	50.9	42.3	43.3
Russian Federation	1950	2015	65	54.1	36.6	38.9
Rwanda	2045	2080	35	51.5	44.8	51.5
Saint Lucia	2005	2040	35	54.1	43.2	48.3
Saint Vincent and the Grenadines	2005	2035	30	56.1	44.9	48.9
Samoa	2030	2060	30	54.6	49.6	51.0
Sao Tome and Principe	2030	2060	30	51.7	49.2	50.8
Saudi Arabia	2025	2060	35	52.3	46.9	48.7
Senegal	2035	2075	40	52.1	46.4	50.8
Serbia and Montenegro	1950	2015	65	56.7	45.9	46.8
Sierra Leone	2050	2090	40	50.0	41.7	49.0
Singapore	1980	2015	35	46.6	34.2	35.1
Slovakia	1970	2015	45	57.3	38.5	40.9
Slovenia	1950	2000	50	52.7	42.5	42.5
Solomon Islands	2030	2060	30	51.2	46.2	48.6
Somalia	2065	2095	30	50.1	44.9	50.8
South Africa	2015	2065	50	54.2	46.8	52.0
Spain	1950	1990	40	52.4	49.7	49.7
Sri Lanka	1995	2025	30	54.9	43.7	47.4
Sudan	2030	2065	35	53.9	47.6	49.3
Suriname	2010	2035	25	54.1	44.1	50.2
Swaziland	2050	2095	45	48.5	46.4	55.1
Sweden	1950	1970	20	50.8	50.6	52.7
Switzerland	1950	1995	45	49.6	45.4	47.2
Syrian Arab Republic	2020	2050	30	51.9	44.1	49.6
Tajikistan	2015	2050	35	49.4	43.2	49.1
TFYR Macedonia	1980	2020	40	55.1	46.6	49.5
Thailand	1995	2030	35	50.0	43.1	48.4
Togo	2040	2075	35	52.8	46.2	50.6
Tonga	2020	2050	30	56.0	48.4	51.3
Trinidad and Tobago	2000	2025	25	46.5	39.1	49.4
Tunisia	2005	2035	30	47.6	41.4	46.6
Turkey	2005	2040	35	53.7	43.6	49.5

TABLE A19 (*continued*)

Country or area	*Demographic window*			*Dependency ratio*		
	Start[a]	*End*	*Length (years)*[a]	*Start*	*Minimum*	*End*
Turkmenistan	2010	2045	35	48.9	44.7	47.0
Uganda	2060	2090	30	52.3	44.8	49.2
Ukraine	1950	2000	50	53.5	46.3	46.3
United Arab Emirates	1975	2025	50	43.3	32.2	45.0
United Kingdom	1950	1975	25	49.4	49.4	59.5
United Rep. of Tanzania	2040	2075	35	48.4	43.8	50.0
United States of America	1970	2015	45	61.8	49.9	52.6
United States Virgin Islands	1990	2010	20	53.6	50.6	50.7
Uruguay	1950	2020	70	56.5	55.6	55.9
Uzbekistan	2010	2045	35	49.3	43.1	47.6
Vanuatu	2030	2060	30	52.2	46.9	48.8
Venezuela	2010	2040	30	53.8	49.9	50.3
Viet Nam	2005	2040	35	53.3	44.5	48.3
Western Sahara	2020	2060	40	56.1	47.6	50.3
Yemen	2060	2095	35	54.1	44.7	49.7
Zambia	2055	2090	35	49.9	45.0	51.7
Zimbabwe	2050	2090	40	48.8	46.4	54.8

[a] 1950 is shown for countries that had already entered the demographic window by that date. In these cases, the period may be longer than indicated.

United Nations publications may be obtained from bookstores and distributors throughout the world. Consult your bookstore or write to: United Nations, Sales Section, New York or Geneva.

COMMENT SE PROCURER LES PUBLICATIONS DES NATIONS UNIES

Les publications des Nations Unies sont en vente dans les librairies et les agences dépositaires du monde entier. Informez-vous auprès de votre libraire ou adressez-vous à : Nations Unies, Section des ventes, New York ou Genève.

КАК ПОЛУЧИТЬ ИЗДАНИЯ ОРГАНИЗАЦИИ ОБЪЕДИНЕННЫХ НАЦИЙ

Издания Организации Объединенных Наций можно купить в книжных магазинах и агентствах во всех районах мира. Наводите справки об изданиях в вашем книжном магазине или пишите по адресу: Организация Объединенных Наций, Секция по продаже изданий, Нью-Йорк или Женева.

COMO CONSEGUIR PUBLICACIONES DE LAS NACIONES UNIDAS

Las publicaciones de las Naciones Unidas están en venta en librerías y casas distribuidoras en todas partes del mundo. Consulte a su librero o diríjase a: Naciones Unidas, Sección de Ventas, Nueva York o Ginebra.

Litho in United Nations, New York
46752—October 2004—6,535
ISBN 92-1-151401-0

United Nations publication
Sales No. E.04.XIII.11
ST/ESA/SER.A/236